NEW EVANGELIZATION:
STARTING ANEW FROM CHRIST

CHARLES ANANG

Cover art: *The Sermon on the Mount*

Fra Angelico (1387-1455)

Museo di San Marco, Florence

@ Art Resource, New York

Cover design by Deepthi Krovi

To the Holy Spirit, His spouse Mary,
St. Catherine of Siena, St. Thérèse of Lisieux,
Pope John Paul II, and Pope Benedict XVI

Nihil Obstat   Rev. Charles Nahm

                            Censor Deputatus

                            16 October 2019

Imprimatur   Thomas Cardinal Collins

                            Archbishop of Toronto

                            10 October 2019

CONTENTS

PREFACE

This book was written because of the wishes of my spiritual director and seminary rector. It addresses all the laity in the Church, but also those who have a special role in forming and leading the faithful, namely, priests, religious, and consecrated members of societies and lay movements. God's providence has provided background for this work on the new evangelization from twenty years of seminary formation and from giving parish recollections as well as retreats to priests and religious sisters, and from being spiritual director to seminarians, priests, religious, and lay people. This experience has provided a more in-depth insight into the difficulties and joys of our times. The discernment gained recalls the intuition of Dom Chautard in *The Soul of the Apostolate* that his times were wrapped in what he called the "heresy of good works" and that the Church in France needed a renewal.

Our era too manifests many signs of the need for its own renewal within the Church, such as an overall loss of the sense of the sacred and of sin, the increasing estrangement from the practice of the faith in the West, and the large number of divorces and family breakups. To renew the Church today, it is necessary to diagnose the specific causes of the present crisis. Pope Emeritus Benedict XVI's article, "The Church and the Scandal of Sexual Abuse," identified the specific cause as loss of God: "Why did pedophilia reach such proportions? Ultimately the reason is the absence of God."[1] But much earlier, he had already offered this incisive diagnosis: the crisis after Vatican II was one of faith, in which pastoral ministry was treated as an end to itself, with self and experience dominating, and detached from spirituality and theology (see Dutch Catechism). Fr. Vincent Twomey described Ratzinger's insight thus: "Belief had been reduced exclusively to praxis, orthodoxy was exchanged for orthopraxis— now understood as becoming 'artisans of the future,' 'making a better world.' Theology and politics had become interchangeable." For Pope Benedict XVI, the Church's central digression was to turn inwards on herself and forget God, losing the

---

[1] Emeritus Pope Benedict XVI, "The Church and the Scandal of Sexual Abuse," *Inside the Vatican*, April 2019, Special Supplement Document, VI. When referring to the sexual revolution of 1968, that "sought to fight for … this all-out sexual freedom, one which no longer conceded any norms," he noted that, "At the same time, Catholic moral theology suffered a collapse that rendered the Church defenceless against these changes in society," Ibid., II-III.

dimensions of adoration and mystery. His close friend, Fr. Luigi Giussani, founder of Communion and Liberation, pointed more specifically to Christ: that our faith had become institutionalized and that people lacked a personal encounter with Christ.

Here we propose a wider thesis for understanding crises within the Church's history: that these crises are ultimately due to a lack of holiness (a loss of God, specifically neglecting Christ and the Holy Spirit). We can shed more light by looking at the customary way of addressing issues in the Church of implementing immediate corrective measures and programs.

Here are three recent examples. First, the Church has just published a new document on seminary formation, "The Gift of the Priestly Vocation" (*Ratio Fundamentalis Institutionis Sacerdotalis*). Though a necessary blessing for the Church, experience shows that programs do not ultimately sanctify— it is the example, and not the words, of saintly seminary faculty priests and laity that will ultimately form saintly priests. As St. Alberto Hurtado once said,

> being an apostle… is not about speaking about the truth but living it [here, applied to the new document or to the faculty], embodying it, being transformed in Christ. Being an apostle does not mean… possessing the light, but being that light…[2]

A second example is the present clergy sexual abuse scandals, which is likely a consequence of the compromising of holiness, often beginning with little capitulations that ultimately end up in leading double-lives. While the immediate protocols with transparency, accountability, and protective measures are necessary— this is the immediate and preliminary step— these are still addressing only the symptoms and not the roots or causes. A third example is Pope Francis' apostolic exhortation on "The Call to Holiness in Today's World" (*Gaudete et Exultate*), a very fine and needed document. Here too, it is not documents but lived holiness primarily that converts. The solution to these malaises is ultimately holiness.

---

[2] Saint Alberto Hurtado, "Ustedes son la luz del mundo," Address in Cerro San Cristóbal, Chile, 1940. Accessed on June 12, 2019, padrealbertohurtado.cl/escritos-2/, quoted in Pope Francis, *Christus vivit*, 53.

Let us turn to three historical examples to support our thesis. First, when St. Francis of Assisi went to Pope Innocent III for approval of his new Order, the pope had reservations, until God gave him a dream in which he saw Francis holding up the Lateran Basilica. By this dream, he understood that Francis had received a call to reform the universal Church. Herein we find a fundamental truth: it is not structures, like the Magisterium, but saints who convert. Second, if we look also to the decadent state of the Church that was a fertile ground for the upheaval of the Reformation, while God provided the all-necessary Council of Trent, it was primarily the plethora of saints He sent that brought about renewal and the Catholic Reformation. These saints included St. Ignatius of Loyola with his universal mission (e.g., he sent St. Peter Faber to reform Germany and St. Francis Xavier to set the East on fire), St. Philip Neri to evangelize Rome (the heart of the Church), and one historian held that St. Teresa of Jesus in Spain had more impact on the Church than St. Ignatius of Loyola and King Philip of Spain combined. The third and ultimate example of the power of holiness is that of the early Church which, without influence, wealth, or education, was able to evangelize the then-known world with the Holy Spirit and their faith alone.

Applying this thesis to today, Vatican II's *Lumen gentium* reminds lay persons of their call to transform society, and they do so through the "universal call to holiness"; but we are barely struggling to maintain our faith. The Church is in great need of a renewal so as to once again be "the salt of the earth and light of the world." She is no longer contagious; a patching-up of the externals is not the solution. This is the motivation for writing this book, the title of which calls for a "New Evangelization: Starting Anew from Christ." The subtitle was taken from *Novo millennio ineunte*, to emphasize that all evangelization has its goal and path in Christ— the slight modification from John Paul II's "starting afresh" to "starting anew" is to emphasize the "newness" of today's "new" evangelization: with newness of needs, spirituality, and method.

To address the specific issues noted earlier (e.g., by Ratzinger, Giussani), we look to: enable an encounter with Christ; renew the various constitutive pillars of evangelization (e.g., culture, anthropology, faith and science, lay mission, liturgy, preaching); and reconnect theology to mysticism and spirituality ("theology" is the study of God, an ineffable mystery, and must be carried out as a "kneeling theology"). But all this is to restore Christ to the heart of the Church, or as St. Oscar Romero taught, Christianity is a Person who has claimed our love: "Christianity is not a collection of truths to be believed, rules to be followed, or prohibitions. Seen that way, it puts us off. Christianity is a person who loved me immensely, who demands and claims my love. Christianity is Christ."[3] The crisis of holiness is ultimately a crisis of neglecting Christ, and, more directly, the intended Fruit of His pasch, the Holy Spirit.

Sources

Thus, above all, the key to renewal in the Church in the crisis of our times and in any troubled age is to look to Christ's Spirit, who, as the Acts of the Apostles describe, guided the nascent Church. How do we look to the Holy Spirit— by looking to saintly prophets of our contemporary period whom He has provided and through whom He speaks powerfully. As a consequence, **this book is not meant to be original in its primary thrust; it simply seeks to discern resonances of the voice of the Holy Spirit** (e.g., Newman, John Paul II, founders of the lay movements).

For the new evangelization in the third millennium, *this book draws heavily from Joseph Ratzinger, Hans Urs von Balthasar, and Henri de Lubac. Other scholars examined in this book include*: Yves Congar, Jean Daniélou, Karl Rahner, Karol Wojtyla, Henry Newman, Teilhard de Chardin, Reginald Garrigou-Lagrange, Thomas Aquinas, Charles Journet, Étienne Gilson, Jacques Maritain, Odo Casel, as well as spiritual lights such as St. Catherine of Siena, St. Teresa of Jesus, St. John of the Cross, St. Thérèse of Lisieux, St. Josemaría Escrivá, Luigi Giussani, Adrienne von Speyr, and Dom Jean-Baptiste Chautard.

Some sections will be syntheses and commentaries on the insights of other contemporary sources: Jean Mouroux, Georges Chevrot, Charles Arminjon, Jean d'Elbée, Tracey Rowland, Stratford Caldecott, David Schindler, Nicholas Healy, Stephen Barr, Peter Cameron, Sr. Madeleine of St. Joseph, José Luis Illanes, Walter Kasper, Christoph Schönborn, and the International Theological Commission.

---

[3] St. Oscar Romero, Homily (6 November 1977), in *Su Pensamiento*, I-II (San Salvador, 2000), 312.

The reason for enumerating these authors individually is simply *to acknowledge that the profound insights found in this book are theirs and not the author's, and to recommend that the reader look to the primary sources for the full texts.* A second reason for listing these authors is to point out that the summaries of their works cited *may at times be very close to their original wording, as they were originally made only for the author's own use.* Please note too that this book more fully develops themes previously introduced in the two earlier books written by this author.

Acknowledgments

I wish, above all, to express my gratitude to all of the authors whose works I have attempted to synthesize. I am indebted to many friends, especially Maria and Therese De Manche, Fr. Scott Birchall, and Fr. James Fleming, all of whom have followed this process with their loving prayers and support. Within this group, Linda Beairsto has opened my eyes to a vast new readership audience I had not considered and was instrumental in self-publishing, introducing me to John O. Burdett and especially Karla Congson, who undertook to introduce me to key people and supervise the whole publishing process. I would like to draw attention in particular to three persons or groups. First, my spiritual director was the one who encouraged me to write this manuscript in the first place and assisted in the progress towards publication. Second, I am indebted to the archdiocese of Toronto for its imprimatur (Thomas Cardinal Collins and Fr. Ivan Camilleri) and to its theological censor, Fr. Charles Nahm, for his kind work. Finally, I also wish to thank Katheryn Trainor for her very competent and arduous work of editing this manuscript. She has also provided helpful suggestions regarding the readership of this work. I also wish to indicate a debt I cannot repay to my two theses directors, Karl Cardinal Becker, S.J., and Fr. Gilles Pelland, S.J..

OUTLINE

This book's title, "New Evangelization: Starting Anew from Christ," points to the goal in the new evangelization to return to Christ to re-present Christ to the world. It is comprised of two Parts: Preparation (Renewal for Evangelization) and Evangelization (Presenting Christ Anew).[4]

Part 1: Preparation: Renewal for Evangelization

Part 1 presupposes that a renewal in key sectors is the necessary matrix for evangelization. Like the earth that requires removing weeds and tilling and fertilizing, the Church and the world needs preparation to receive the Gospel. It presents a renewal in the groundwork for the new evangelization in three contexts (culture, theological anthropology, evolution) and two foundations (theological reading, and personal sanctification). The Father has created the universe through Christ and created and redeemed man in Christ, so that the renewal must reflect the template and path of Christ.

Specific Chapters

This renewal in Christ entails specifically reconnecting many elements that have seen neglect within the Church: the cult of the saints and other elements (e.g., beauty, filial obedience, Tradition) to renew a wounded culture (Ch. 1); restoring man's identity of being created in the image of Christ to construct a new christocentric anthropology (including the Theology of the Body, Ch. 2); and restoring the harmony between faith and science in evolution, perhaps with Teilhard de Chardin's Christian synthesis (Ch. 3); with exhorting the new Christs to find a theological mentor to renew his teaching and preaching (Patristic, Medieval, or Contemporary era), especially by returning to the fonts of Scripture and the Church Fathers (Ch. 4); and, finally, restoring the primacy of sanctification before ministry, as the foremost problem is a lack of contemplation and sanctity within ministry (Ch. 5).

---

[4] It should be noted that two key areas for evangelization have not been developed in this book: unity (dialogue, ecumenism, interfaith dialogue, and spirituality of communion); and justice and peace. These two areas are briefly covered in an appendix to Chapter 6, "Love of the Church and her Mission" (under "dialogical axis" and "diaconal axis" respectively).

Part 2: Evangelization: Presenting Christ Anew

Part 2 is dedicated to encouraging a renewal in evangelization by returning to the model of Christ and the apostles: two requirements (love of the Church and understanding of lay mission), evangelization itself, and sacrament and word.

Specific Chapters

The evangelization to present Christ anew has several dimensions: beginning with a tender love of Christ in His Church and mission, to be truly a son or daughter of the Church (Ch. 6); understanding that it is principally the laity who are called to evangelize, to imbue through holiness all sectors of society with Christ's spirit and presence (Ch. 7); a renewed approach to evangelization that begins with an encounter with Christ (not doctrine or moral precepts), universality of breadth, and vicarious identification (priest and victim) (Ch. 8); a renewed patristic cosmic vision of the liturgy, that all salvation history is a cosmic liturgy that leads to adoration of God (Ch. 9); and the pressing need, as the Church and homiletic experts point out, for a renewal in preaching that truly inspires and feeds Christ's flock (Ch. 10).

This book that presents a vision of the call to renewal in Christ finds its apex in Pope John Paul II's understanding that the new evangelization is carried out under the leadership of Mary, "Morning Star of the New Evangelization" (Chapter 11).

BACKGROUND

John Paul II's Vision for the New Evangelization

Let us turn now to the vision of Pope John Paul II, since it was he who brought this project to the forefront in the Church and since he himself was given to understand that he had a special mission in the new evangelization. The Holy Father produced several documents that, when analyzed, give us an overview of his vision. The most pertinent documents are *Tertio millennio adveniente* and *Novo millennio ineunte*. What follows is the author's summary, drawn from a first reading of these texts.

Background: Personal Call to Lead the Church to a New Advent of Christ

To give background for the vision of John Paul II on the new evangelization, it is helpful to think of the *chairos* (a "favorable or sacred time") of God's first visitation in the cosmic plan of the Father sending His Son in the fullness of time, releasing the Holy Spirit to establish the Church through the apostles throughout the world. Now, as a renewal of that first *chairos*, Christ comes again at the critical juncture of the new millennium, with a new outpouring of the Holy Spirit and a new sending forth of new apostles, with John Paul II having a critical role in leading the Church into the third millennium. This was confirmed by Pope Benedict XVI in his homily at the beatification of Pope John Paul II:

> In his Testament, the new Blessed wrote: "When, on 16 October 1978, the Conclave of Cardinals chose John Paul II, the Primate of Poland, Cardinal Stefan Wyszynski, said to me: 'The task of the new Pope will be to lead the Church into the Third Millennium.'" And the Pope added: "I would like once again to express my gratitude to the Holy Spirit for the great gift of the Second Vatican Council, to which, together with the whole Church— and especially with the whole episcopate— I feel indebted. I am convinced that it will long be granted to the new generations to draw from the treasures that this Council of the twentieth century has lavished upon us. As a Bishop who took part in the Council from the first to the last day, I desire to entrust this great patrimony to all who are and will be called in the future to put it into practice…"

... This was his message: man is the way of the Church, and Christ is the way of man. With this message, which is the great legacy of the Second Vatican Council and of its "helmsman," the Servant of God Pope Paul VI, John Paul II led the People of God across the threshold of the Third Millennium, which thanks to Christ he was able to call "the threshold of hope." Throughout the long journey of preparation for the great Jubilee he directed Christianity once again to the future, the future of God, which transcends history while nonetheless directly affecting it.... He restored to Christianity its true face as a religion of hope, to be lived in history in an "Advent" spirit, in a personal and communitarian existence directed to Christ, the fullness of humanity and the fulfillment of all our longings for justice and peace.[5]

Already in the very first document of his pontificate, *Redemptor hominis*, Pope John Paul II made reference to this advent: "we also are in a certain way in a season of a new advent, a season of expectation."[6] He made a link between the new advent and his election as successor of Peter,[7] and posed the question about its preparation: "What should we do, in order that this new advent of the Church connected with the approaching end of the second millennium may bring us closer to Him...?"[8] Let us examine two documents to bring to light the vision of Pope John Paul II.

A. *Tertio Millennio Adveniente* Points to a Renewal of the Christ Event

This vision of a new advent is corroborated by the document celebrating the Jubilee Year 2000, as preparation for the third millennium, *Tertio millennio adveniente* ("As the Third Millennium Begins").

(i) Here, he sees this Jubilee of 2000 preparing for the third millennium:

> In the Church's history every jubilee is prepared for by Divine Providence. This is true also of the Great Jubilee of the Year 2000. (n. 24)

---

[5] Pope Benedict XVI, Papal Mass on the Occasion of the beatification of the Servant of God John Paul II, St. Peter's Square, Divine Mercy Sunday, 1 May 2011 (find in Vatican.va site, under homilies of Pope Benedict XVI).

[6] Pope John Paul II, *Redemptor hominis*, Ch. I, n. 1.

[7] Ibid., Ch. I, n. 2.

[8] Ibid., Ch. II, n. 7.

ii) Vatican II itself was a preparation for the third millennium:

> … we can affirm that the Second Vatican Council was a providential event, whereby the Church began the more immediate preparation for the Jubilee of the Second Millennium. (n. 24)

(iii) This preparation was a "hermeneutical key" for Pope John Paul II's pontificate:

> In fact, preparing for the Year 2000 has become as it were a hermeneutical key for my Pontificate. It is certainly not a matter of indulging in a new millennarism, as occurred in some quarters at the end of the first millennium. Rather, it is aimed at an increased sensitivity to all that the Spirit is saying to the Church and to the churches (Rev 2:7ff), as well as to individuals through charisms meant to serve the whole community. (n. 29)

(iv) All Christian history is viewed as a "single river":

> … the whole of Christian history appears to us as a single river, into which many tributaries flow. (n. 32)

For John Paul II, there are not two histories, the religious and the secular.[9] This unified vision is one of the great accomplishments of the documents of Vatican II. For example, *Gaudium et spes* looks at the yearnings of man and sees that he finds his happiness and fulfillment only in God.

Thus John Paul II seeks to reinterpret evangelization for us. First, evangelization entails involvement in the world, but not at the level of politics, economy, sociology, etc., which is one level of history. There is a second and deeper level of history: *God's concern is primarily the moments of conversion, when we become free for God, and this, of course, influences politics, economy,* etc.[10]

Having spent a lifetime working at evangelization, especially with totalitarian, atheistic regimes, John Paul II came to respond to the ultimate cause of human misery. If we are to find happiness, that is, God, then it will have to

---

[9] George Weigel supports this insight in his book *Witness to Hope*, Ch. 19 ("Only One World").
[10] Ibid.

be a work of God. The key is Christological— a renewal, as it were, of the first Incarnation: we have to set course for the Blessed Trinity through Christ, and we meet Christ through prayer, sacraments, etc.

John Paul II's Vision: A New Coming of Christ in the Third Millennium

In the vision of John Paul II, it appears that he was pointing to a renewal of the Christ event: a second coming of Christ, so to speak; and a renewal of the apostolic mission with a second wave of the first evangelization of the early Church, accompanied by a second outpouring of the Holy Spirit. This is apparent in *Tertio millennio adveniente*. He has stressed the journey of the Church during this century as representing "*the preparation of that new springtime of Christian life* which will be revealed by the Great Jubilee, if Christians are docile to the action of the Holy Spirit."[11] He sees this project for a new evangelization for the third millennium as prepared by the Holy Spirit Himself; he sees, in fact, that the entire twentieth-century has been the providential work of the Holy Spirit Himself, with the momentousness indicated by words like, "As the Third Millennium Draws Near."

He sees the entire twentieth-century as a leading up towards a new Pentecost, a new outpouring of the Holy Spirit at the dawn of the third millennium, and that the primary objective of the Jubilee "is the renewal of the faith and the witness of Christians."[12]

Like the early Church, it is a "New time of grace and of mission" (*Incarnationis mysterium*).[13] He uses the language of "New Advent" and refers to texts like Gal 4:4: "When the fullness of time had come, God sent forth his Son, born of woman" (n. 1). The very title of the first section, "Christ yesterday, today, and forever," indicates the new advent's continuity with the first advent of Jesus. In short, John Paul II sees a renewal of the first coming of Christ in cosmic dimensions.[14]

---

[11] *Tertio millennio adveniente* n. 18.

[12] Ibid., n. 42.

[13] *Incarnationis mysterium*, n. 3. This is another document in preparation for the Jubilee for the Third Millennium.

[14] This vision presented of Pope John Paul II's preparation for the third millennium through the Second Vatican Council and the Lord preparing the Church for a "new Pentecost" and "new springtime" is the personal interpretation of the author, based upon examination of texts

B. *Novo Millennio Ineunte* (NMI) Sets a Blueprint for a New Evangelization for the Third Millennium

Since *Novo millennio ineunte* is designated as the programmatic blueprint for the new evangelization in the third millennium, let us mine it for insights into the vision of John Paul II. It reproduces the same basic horizon in *Tertio millennio adveniente*, but goes further. At the heart of NMI, we find that John Paul II perceived a confluence of events through which God is preparing a new evangelization for the Church; within which plan he describes the evangelization of the different nations and continents and the history of the world.

Pope John Paul II discerned that the primary preparation for the new evangelization was the Second Vatican Council[15] and employed the motto, *Duc in Altum*, "Cast out into the deep" (Lk 5:4), the words to the apostles. It is, as it were, a second or new evangelization, following upon the first evangelization after Pentecost in the early Church— which means that we are called to be the new apostles in a new evangelization. As Pope John Paul II viewed his pontificate as more immediately intent on implementing the teachings of the Second Vatican Council, he saw that the goal of the Council itself was a new evangelization in the third millennium— *it made the new evangelization the hermeneutical key of his pontificate.*

Let us take note of a few highlights of *Novo millennio ineunte*. First, we notice the great joy John Paul II took in seeing what grace has been given us this Jubilee.

Second, we take note of its Christocentricity, especially in the first three sections: "Meeting Christ"; "To contemplate His face"; and "Starting afresh from Christ," so that we become "Witnesses to Love." This is actually the same program followed by the apostles themselves: they met Christ, then in reminiscence contemplated His example, and then moved forward with

---

mentioned. Readers may wish to look to George Weigel's authoritative work, *Witness to Hope*, for example, pp. 742-744, 746.

[15] George Weigel, *Witness to Hope: The Biography of Pope John Paul II* (New York: Cliffstreet Books, 1999), 742. Pope John Paul II himself personally asked George Weigel to write this biography and Weigel was given untrammelled access to the Pope and sources. Many regard Weigel's work as the uncontested standard of Pope John Paul II's life.

Christ. In fact, the chapters of *Novo millennio ineunte* essentially follow the outline of the program of Christ's first coming: (i) Advent, Incarnation (as analogous to a Jubilee year); (ii) post-Resurrection; (iii) ministry and preaching of the apostles; and (iv) love ("See how they love one another"). That is, we see a parallel between the first coming of Christ in the early Church with the Jubilee year that inaugurates the third millennium. The five steps of the early Church (Advent, Incarnation and life, post-Resurrection, the Acts of the Apostles, and community of love) roughly parallel the four chapters in *Novo millennio ineunte*:

(i)   Meeting Christ— a second "incarnation" in this Jubilee: a new or second outpouring of graces for this new evangelization;

(ii)   Post-Resurrection: today's new apostles recalling or contemplating Christ in Scripture, with faith, focusing on the sorrowful face of Jesus and on His two natures;

(iii)   Missionary work of new apostles— starting from Christ: with focus first on the interior life (holiness, prayer, Eucharist, Confession, primacy of grace, and preaching the word); and

(iv)   Witness of love of the new community: each age has its own emphasis or spirituality. Pope John Paul II identifies cultivating the "spirituality of communion" as the charism of the third millennium.

Third, we take note of the priority of the pastoral program comprehensively outlined by Pope John Paul II: holiness, prayer, Eucharist, Confession, primacy of grace, listening to the Word, and proclaiming the Word. This is essentially the program for the new evangelization, and it can be summarized as "holiness"— all other elements serve this union with God.

Thus, for John Paul II, there is a revolution by God at work, with two presuppositions. First, it builds upon the Christocentricity of his inaugural encyclical, *Redemptor hominis*: not only do we preach Christ, we are effective only in and with the only Mediator the Father has sent ("Christ yesterday, today, and forever"). Second, since it is a *divine revolution and thus is God's work, we can only collaborate*. The first apostles went out because they were sent forth by Jesus and did so in the power of the Holy Spirit; the new apostles, you and I, can only be sent by Christ, follow His footsteps, and act in the power of the Holy Spirit. Synthesizing all this, here are four dispositions for the new apostle engaged in the new evangelization.

C. Four Dispositions for Going Forward in the New Evangelization

(1) *Our New Evangelization Parallels the Acts of the Apostles.* Let us look to the Acts of the Apostles to understand the ramifications of this vision. First, it means that the Holy Spirit has a plan that embraces the entire Church and universe for the third millennium, just as He did for the early Church (Acts of the Apostles) and for the first millennium. And just as the first apostles would be led step-by-step in this first evangelization by the Holy Spirit, so the "new apostles" of the new evangelization are called to walk in lockstep with the Holy Spirit as our general and guide. This means that we need to go beyond mechanically plodding forward in our everyday ministry to see a universal engagement of God with the world in a plan specific to our needs and era, and see ourselves taking part within our own sphere in this universal "offensive." But this does not mean freelancing or doing our own thing in our ministry— our task is simply to be taken up and used as "instruments" or "apostles" (one who is sent), as Jesus Himself was sent ("As the Father has sent me, so I send you").

(2) *The Fullness of Time is the "Today" of Christian Time.* Second, the new apostles are called to be like the first apostles— to sense the momentousness of this new era, a special time of grace in which the Church has prayed for a new Pentecost and a "new springtime." The new apostles are called to "throw out into the deep" (*duc in altum*), to understand that what they do now at the beginning of the millennium would constitute a foundation for the entire millennium in a way similar to what the apostles and first disciples did for the foundation of the Church in the first millennium. It is a propitious time— a *chairos*. Perhaps we can hear Pope John Paul II's momentous words in *Novo millennio ineunte* as echoing Jesus' prophetic words on His first return visit to Nazareth:

> And he stood up to read… "The Spirit of the Lord is upon me, because he has anointed me to preach good news to the poor. He has sent me to proclaim release to the captives and recovering of sight to the blind, to set at liberty those who are oppressed, to proclaim the acceptable year of the Lord." "Today this scripture has been fulfilled in your hearing."[16]

---

[16] Lk 4:16-21.

It is as if John Paul II was saying to us, "Today this scripture has been fulfilled in your hearing"; and that "The Spirit of the Lord is upon me, because he has anointed me to preach good news to the poor."

The hermeneutical key for the document is the first section of *Tertio millennio adveniente*: "Jesus Christ is the Same Yesterday and Today and Forever" (Heb 13:8). He speaks of the "today" of Christian time: "In Christianity, time has a fundamental importance" (n. 10). In the light of the sacredness of time, let us now listen again to the words of Christ as addressed to us *today* (Luke 4:18-21): "Today this scripture has been fulfilled in your hearing." In other words, because all is *now* in Christ, we have to be alive to His call; as alive as St. Francis of Assisi was alive to nature and the presence of God.

Yet, this attention to time and God's call are not about recalling past events, but making present again the salvific events of Christ. The "now" of Christ's visitation is a principle of liturgy that is fundamental to our entire faith. The Christian calendar does not measure history from the beginning of time at creation, but from the center of history— Christ's Incarnation. It is the historical event of the Incarnation that constructs the center of history. This is the Christian conception of time; secular history and salvation form one history.

What we are celebrating is not man's seeking God, but God coming down to seek man; this is the essential difference between Christianity and all other religions. Universal history now ceases to be profane and becomes sacred history. This has tremendous spiritual consequences: each of us is called for a mission in this era. It means that time is in God's hands— in fact, everything is in His hands— and that our path is already marked out for us.

We have to go back and recapture something of the spirit of Christ's coming. In a Ignatian meditation spirit (entering the Gospel scenes), we seek to live anew the spirit of the events of the Incarnation through the Gospels. We recall vividly the language of the Gospel of Luke as he described those days of expectancy of the Messiah, the momentousness of those times. Let us meditate again on these times especially with Mary's heart: the preparation of Elizabeth (Lk 1:5); the annunciation (Lk 1:26-27); Mary's visitation of Elizabeth (Lk 1:39); the birth of John the Baptist (Lk 1:5-25); and the birth of Jesus and the visit of shepherds (Luke 2:1-14). Then, in the very first appearance of Christ in Nazareth during His ministry, Christ identifies His coming with the Old Testament promises of God. John Paul II thus links Christ's first coming to the Jubilee for the Third Millennium. The Holy Father, pointing to the fact that this Jubilee was inspired by the "promptings of the Holy Spirit," and employing his papal authority, he called for a Holy Year, a Jubilee, a year of God's favour, that will be an impetus for Christian evangelization and for renewal of faith and witness for the third millennium.

(3) *Evangelization is Primarily the Work of the Laity in the World.* In *Lumen gentium*, the Second Vatican Council emphasized that the missionary work, so necessary in our secularized society, is principally accomplished through the laity by virtue of their Baptism. For the laity are called to sanctify every part of society: the offices, factories, schools, homes, studios, and everywhere they go. They are called to be the leaven in society:

> You are the salt of the earth; but if salt has lost its taste, how shall its saltiness be restored? It is no longer good for anything except to be thrown out and trodden under foot by men. You are the light of the world. A city set on a hill cannot be hid. Nor do men light a lamp and put it under a bushel, but on a stand, and it gives light to all in the house. Let your light so shine before men, that they may see your good works and give glory to your Father who is in heaven.[17]

Bishops and priests, therefore, are called to help prepare these apostles for the work of evangelizing society. Christians are not just here merely to maintain the Church; but rather to bring the entire world to Christ, imitating Pope St. Pius X, whose motto was "to renew all things in Christ."

(4) *Urgency of the New Evangelization:* John Paul II emphasizes the urgency. Analogous to that of the early Church, our present day situation is marked by religious indifference and even opposition. The Pope pleads for action in the path of the early Church:

> How can we remain silent before the religious indifference which causes many people today to live as if God did not exist, or to be content with a vague religiosity, incapable of coming to grips with the question of truth

---

[17] Mt 5:13-16.

and the necessity of consistency? To this must also be added the widespread loss of the transcendent sense of human life, and confusion in the ethical sphere, even about the fundamental values of respect for life and the family. The sons and daughters of the Church too need to examine themselves in this regard. To what extent have they been shaped by the climate of secularism and ethical relativism? And what responsibility do they bear, in view of the increasing lack of religion, for not having shown the true face of God, by having "failed in their religious, moral, or social life?"

It cannot be denied that for many Christians, the spiritual life is passing through a time of uncertainty which affects not only the moral life, but also the life of prayer and the theological correctness of faith. (TMA n. 36)

George Weigel, who has had the privileged position to be Pope John Paul II's biographer by invitation, has presented his understanding of a trajectory that has reached its zenith. The vision is that John Paul II and Benedict XVI have brought to full bloom the Leonine social doctrine, to an "Evangelical Catholicism": one that separates itself from the State and its coercion; and one that is built upon the three pillars of Western civilization (Hebrew religion, Greek reason, and Roman law) that does not degenerate into relativism. Thus rooted, one can speak to the underlying problems of today: such as the questions about the incursion of militant Islam, or the human ecology that protects the rights of the human embryo and marriage, and thus can lead to the new evangelization, if there are a critical mass of disciples who are willing to act.[18]

The late French journalist André Frossard was a convert to Catholicism from the fashionable atheism of his class, an atheism that was once a Parisian intellectual fad but that has now taken on a much harder, Christophobic edge across the 21st-century Western world. When Frossard saw John Paul II at the Mass marking the beginning of the Pope's public ministry on October 22, 1978, he wired back to his Paris newspaper, "This is not a pope from Poland; this is a pope from Galilee." It was a brilliant metaphor, and it still speaks to us today.[19]

---

[18] George Weigel, "Benedict XVI and the Future of the West," *Standpoint* (July/August 2011).
[19] Ibid.

PART I: PREPARATION

RENEWAL FOR EVANGELIZATION

"It is no longer I who live, but Christ who lives in me"
(Gal 2:20)

CHAPTER 1

CULTURE AND THE CULT OF THE SAINTS

... Pope John Paul II continued to sharpen one of the distinctive themes of his pontificate— that culture is the driving force of history. It was a lesson he had first been taught by his father and by his early reading of the classics of Polish Romanticism. Seven decades of intellectual reflection and personal experience had refined and deepened an analysis that cut straight against the grain of modern delusions that politics and economics are the motors of historical change. The collapse of European communism in 1989-1991 had vindicated the claim that culture drives history. Now in the late 1990s, John Paul vigorously applied his "culture-first" view of historical change to the reevangelization of Western Europe...[1] (George Weigel)

Background

God created the universe and man in Christ (Col 1), the result of which is that all material reality is Christic and man himself as creation's summit is made in the image of Christ (*imago Christi*). This means that culture, anthropology, science, and faith life all find their origin and goal in Christ. Ephesians 1 affirm that every aspect of man, the Church, and the world has to be recapitulated in Christ. Regarding man specifically, this means that the universal call to holiness by Baptism entails simply being more and more assimilated to Christ to become "Christ himself" (a new Christ). This goal of assimilation to Christ is the focus this book for the task of the new Christ in the work of the new evangelization, a recapitulation. For a deeper look at Pope John Paul II's vision of the new evangelization, see the "Background" (front matter of this book) for a brief summary.

I. The Crisis of a Wounded Culture

The new apostle of Christ, engaged in the new evangelization, must "read the signs of the times," be acutely aware of the woundedness of society and of the Church. Athanasius points out the vital need that societies have of Christianity and its culture, pointing to the Barbarians' culture:

---

[1] George Weigel, *Witness to Hope: The Biography of Pope John Paul II* (New York: HarperCollins Publs. 2005), 792; see also 847-848.

> For as long as the barbarians... offered sacrifice to their gods, they became enraged with one another and could not pass one hour without their swords. Yet when they accepted the teaching of Christ, they left off war straightaway and turned to cultivation... they lifted their hands in prayer... they arm themselves against the devil and against the demons and are victorious through their moderation and the virtues of their soul.[2]

While the importance of culture is already known to many scholars, it may not as familiar to the laity and priests and consecrated souls. This chapter largely follows the analysis of Joseph Ratzinger, but among others also draws from John Paul II (through George Weigel), Tracey Rowland, Robert Sarah, St. Josemaría Escrivá, and Vincent Twomey.

A. The Battle for Culture

1. The Importance of Culture

The opening quotation reveals that John Paul II has long understood the central role of culture: "Culture is the driving force of history." In his biography of John Paul II, George Weigel notes that, in his great far-seeing vision, the Pope was not concerned about choosing between the "left" and the "right," but about following Christ and allowing Him to shape culture. Already as a young man, he had fought the more fundamental battle against the Nazis of preserving the rich Polish culture, the deeper battleground. He understood even then that winning the war but losing their culture would eventually bring the risk that the Polish people, without a moral or spiritual compass, would eventually turn out like their persecutors.

Robert Cardinal Sarah recounts his own experience of the Marxist dictatorship that attempted to spread its errors among the Catholic faithful in Guinea, but was unsuccessful due to the strong example and culture built by heroic Spiritan religious: "Despite the political sufferings that accompanied Sékou Touré's Marxist dictatorship, the Church in Guinea stood fast, for she was founded on the rock, on the sacrifices of missionaries,

---

[2] Athanasius of Alexandria, *De incarnatione verbi* 51:4, in *Sources Chrétiennes*, vol. 1999 (Paris, 1973), 450, quoted in Joseph Ratzinger, *Truth and Tolerance* (San Francisco: Ignatius Press, 2004), 218-219.

and on the joy of the Gospel…. The humility of the Spiritans' faith was the strongest defense against the egalitarian aberrations of the revolutionary Marxist ideology of the State Party in Guinea."[3] The fundamental issue was not fighting the political and military battles, but a more fundamental battle for culture, that preserved the uniqueness and dignity of man and also man's call to Christ. This was the power of the "Spiritans' faith" to preserve culture.

What is culture? Culture can be loosely defined as the sum of all the influences of our environment: physical, emotional, intellectual, spiritual, technological, artistic, etc.:

> The word "culture" in its general sense indicates all those factors by which man refines and unfolds his manifold spiritual and bodily qualities. It means his effort to bring the world itself under his control by his knowledge and his labor. It includes the fact that by improving customs and institutions he renders social life more human both within the family and in the civic community. Finally, it is a feature of culture that throughout the course of time man expresses, communicates, and conserves in his works great spiritual experiences and desires, so that these may be of advantage to the progress of many, even of the whole human family. (GS n. 53)

Its importance lies in the fact that good culture can form ("cultivate") and bad culture can deform.[4] A horrific example of the tragic consequence of bad culture was the genocide of almost two million Cambodians ("killing fields") carried out by the Khmer Rouge regime under the leadership of Pol Pot, who absorbed Marxist ideology during his studies, especially in Paris.

2. The Church's Wounds from Secular Culture

Since the Church exists in the world, a crisis in secular culture will not leave the Church unaffected. The current secular crisis of indifference to the existence of God, relativism, materialism, etc., was multivalent in its origins. Much of the present troubles in the Western world may derive from the turmoil of the 1960s. Fr. Twomey lists key pathology symptoms: an increasing critique among youth of liberal capitalism, a spirit marked by the embrace of existentialism, the rise of modern feminism, the Death-of-God

---

[3] Robert Cardinal Sarah, *God or Nothing*, 37.
[4] For a discussion on culture, see Joseph Ratzinger, *Truth and Tolerance*, especially 59-79.

theology, and above all the emergence of neo-Marxism, not to mention the sexual revolution that has a hostility to the existing order and all authority. The student revolts in 1968, especially in Paris, that were a catalyst for worldwide demonstrations at universities, were fuelled by the imperative to change, influenced by the desire for a Marxism with a human face.[5]

Fr. Twomey observes that Joseph Ratzinger identified clearly the pathology of the new culture as a desire to plan and forge man's destiny on his own (without God), and Twomey adds that "Theology could not but be affected by such dominant cultural assumptions" (p. 39). Those who have lived through this period and perceived the temptation of those within the Church to get involved with politics and to be exclusively concerned with social justice will likely be able to relate to the diagnosis below:

> Belief had been reduced exclusively to *praxis*, orthodoxy was exchanged for orthopraxis— now understood as becoming "artisans of the future," "making a better world." Theology and politics had become interchangeable…. This changed in 1968. The student revolts that year and subsequently… involved an instrumentalization of theology. As a result, Ratzinger said, "Precisely anyone who wished to defend the intrinsic claims of religion and theology was now also compelled to defend the essential profanity and the reasonableness of politics in opposition to a religion that had degenerated into ideology."[6]

And what is the fallout of this new culture today? Robert Cardinal Sarah, in a chapter titled "Issues in the Postmodern World" in *God or Nothing*, diagnoses with keen insight that the wealthy Western world, through its individualism (Enlightenment) and materialism, does not so much explicitly reject God as *ignore Him*, with its devastating fallout:

> Today, in the rich and powerful countries, the eclipse of God leads man toward practical materialism, disorderly or abusive consumption, and the creation of false moral norms. Material well-being and immediate satisfaction become the only reason for living. At the end of this process, it is no longer even about fighting God; Christ and the Father are ignored.

---

[5] D. Vincent Twomey, "The Spirit of 1968: The Paris Student Revolts in May 1968 Proved to be a Turning Point for Western Civilization," *Inside the Vatican* (June-July 2018): 38-39.
[6] Ibid., 39-40.

The reason for this is obvious: God no longer interests anyone. He is dead, and his departure leaves us indifferent.... For the Church and for Christians, the danger therefore becomes still more menacing. Western man seems to have made up his mind; he has liberated himself from God; he lives without God. The new rule is to forget heaven so that man might be fully free and autonomous. But the death of God results in the burial of good, beauty, love, and truth; if the source no longer flows, if even that water is transformed by the mud of indifference, man collapses.... Whether it is militant or still in the larval state, atheism always leads to the same consequences. Man is treated as an object, cut off from his spiritual roots and blinded by the artificial lights of material goods or achievements. Finally, all atheism seeks to change the very nature of man.[7]

Cardinal Sarah pinpoints the great issue of our time— subjectivism: "one of the most significant traits of our time. Feelings and personal desires are the only norm."[8]

B. The Church's Postconciliar "Crisis of God"

1. The Confusion after the Second Vatican Council

The crisis in society impacted the Church, as we find that the crisis in the Church coincided with the 1960s revolution and the postconciliar period. On the one hand, one cannot deny that the Council was the work of the Holy Spirit and has become the primary point of reference for the Church and her theology. Yet the Church herself is beginning to emerge from a period of confusion and turmoil following the Second Vatican Council, a crisis of culture within the Church.

Augustine Cardinal Mayer, from his vast experience as secretary of Commissions that helped draft the Council Decree for the Training of Priests and the Declaration on Christian Education, and later prefect of the Congregation for Liturgy and the Sacraments, in an interview, was able to describe in detail a number of concrete deviations that followed the Council: confused interpretations and deformations of the liturgy, focus in the liturgy on "speaking, singing, and gestures, whereas it consists above all in the loving

[7] Robert Cardinal Sarah, *God or Nothing*, 170-171.
[8] Ibid., 172-174.

and adoring inner attention to what Christ is giving us in the holy Mass" (with silence), indiscriminate use of General Absolution, indiscriminate removal of statues and holy paintings from churches, the exodus of thousands of nuns released from their holy vows, "too much emphasis on pastoral methods and not the priestly life as model of and witness to holiness," and some seminaries becoming little more than residence halls and in seminaries in some countries a "concealed homosexual subculture."[9] Priests who were formed during these postconciliar times will likely be able to immediately recognize this state.

How could such confusion follow the work of a holy Council? Cardinal Sarah's chapter, "In the Search of the Church," identified a key cause for the confusion that followed the Council: the media and certain elites circulating confusing reports about Vatican II. Others have corroborated this diagnosis. He points out that the original goal of the Council was contrary to their liberal agenda (of fashioning a very horizontal Church focused on man and not on God), to help the world that had lost its way to find God again: "During his various missions as apostolic nuncio, John XXIII had come to understand how distant contemporary societies were from God."[10]

> From the start of Vatican II, although concerned about *aggiornamento*, the renewal of the Church, and the reunion of Christians, the pope had strongly emphasized that the Council's chief task was to reveal God to the world, to defend and promote doctrine. That is why the Church, while rejoicing in the admirable inventions of human genius and in the progress of science, had to remind mankind that beyond the visible aspect of things the primordial duty remains to turn to God. For John XXIII, the Council was first of all an encounter with God in prayer, with Mary, like the apostles in the upper room on the eve of Pentecost.[11]

We find that Cardinal Sarah's overall assessment coincides with Cardinal Ratzinger's diagnosis: there was within the Church a "crisis of God," which can be synthesized thus: "Religion yes, God no."

---

[9] Crista Kramer von Reisswitz, "Vatican II: Was Reform of the Liturgy too Extreme," *Inside the Vatican*, (November 2002): 28.

[10] Robert Cardinal Sarah, *God or Nothing*, 106.

[11] Ibid., 102-103.

We can get some sense of the depth of the woundedness of the Church by the reaction of saintly souls, such as the horror and anguish that St. Josemaría Escrivá experienced after the Second Vatican Council. He once expressed his concern thus: "I am suffering desperately, my sons. We are living in a time of madness. Millions are confused."[12]

Seeing the loss of faith, St. Escrivá spoke of protecting the flock: the need of true shepherds who would set the dogs loose on wolves, drive the flock where there are not poisonous plants, and speak out. He asked for prayers for the Church and Pope: "I beg you to pray much for the Church, for the present Pope and for the next one, who will be a martyr from the start. Pray for the Christian people to have some defense against all these heresies and errors."[13] He saw traitors within the Church causing distress, such that "It's as if our mother [Church] were at the point of death."

St. Escrivá took upon himself the task of reparation and praying for the Church and mobilized his spiritual children to do the same: "Often he cried out, 'I'm suffering over souls.'" Deviating from his custom of quietly addressing only small groups, he did three marathon international tours in poor health to catechize (1972-1975), while also giving interviews, that would conclude with his death.[14]

> Why did he do all this [catechesis tours]? Because the teachings of the Second Vatican Council had been badly explained and poorly assimilated. There were too many closed mouths, too many geniuses who lost their brilliance, too many imposters in the pulpits, too many disused confessionals, too many catechisms growing moldy in attics, too many empty seminaries, too many divided parishes, too many of the faithful losing their way. Monsignor Escrivá decided to jump defenseless into the arena and take on the bulls.[15]

---

12 Pilar Urbano, *The Man of Villa Tevere: St. Josemaría Escrivá: His Years in Rome* (New York: Scepter Publishers, 2011), 343.
13 Ibid., 342.
14 Ibid., 342-345.
15 Ibid., 118.

2. Cardinal Ratzinger's Diagnosis of the Crisis of God

For Cardinal Ratzinger, the underlying cause of the postconciliar crisis in the Church went beyond a battle between left and right— it was a crisis of God, a flawed "hermeneutics of discontinuity." The principle of continuity is, as the Church has always understood, that her doctrine grew organically, the way a human embryo remains his identity, and is simply more developed as an adult. St. Vincent of Lerins teaches the fundamental truth:

> Is there to be no development of religion in the Church of Christ? Certainly, there is to be development and on the largest scale.... The religion of souls should follow the law of development of bodies. Though bodies develop and unfold their component parts with the passing of the years, they always remain what they were. There is a great difference between the flower of childhood and the maturity of age, but those who become old are the very same people who were once young. Though the condition and appearance of one and the same individual may change, it is one and the same nature, one and the same person.... If, however, the human form were to turn into some shape that did not belong to its own nature, or ever if something were added to the sum of its members or subtracted from it, the whole body would necessarily perish or become grotesque or at least be enfeebled. In the same way, the doctrine of the Christian religion should properly follow these laws of development, that is, by becoming firmer over the years, more ample in the course of time, more exalted as it advances in age.[16]

Those espousing the principle of discontinuity rejected the Tradition and followed personal agendas, deriving especially from a misreading of *Gaudium et spes* as accommodation to modernity's spirit.

> However, other forces were working with increasing strength, particularly journalists, who interpreted many things in a continually different way.... The liturgy began to crumble, and slip into personal preferences. In this respect one could soon see that what was originally desired was being driven in a different direction.[17]

---

[16] St. Vincent of Lerins, OOR of Friday of Week 27 of Ordinary Time.

[17] "However, other forces were working with increasing strength, particularly journalists, who interpreted many things in a continually different way.... The liturgy began to crumble, and slip into personal preferences. In this respect one could soon see that what was originally

Those espousing the principle of discontinuity rejected the Tradition and followed personal agendas,[18] deriving especially from a misreading of *Gaudium et spes* as accommodation to modernity's spirit. In an address in Rome in 2000, he treated of "partial interpretations" of the ecclesiology of *Lumen gentium*, arising from a "crisis of God." For him, to make the Second Vatican Council about the stereotypical battle of left versus right would be a case of "misdirection"— it did not respond to the problem.[19]

Cardinal Ratzinger finds the key source of the crisis already identified in an address by a senior and venerable German bishop, Bishop Buchberger, to the German bishops preparing for Vatican II: "Dear brothers, at the Council you should first of all speak about God. This is the most important theme." He was found to be prescient and his concern borne out by the fallout after the Council.

The fundamental error in all the various deviations was a certain *horizontalism*, in which the Church and other aspects of the Church were discussed but "God" was left out of the process: "The crisis has become a crisis of God. To sum up, one could say 'religion yes', 'God no'"; "The Second Vatican Council clearly wanted to speak of the Church within the discourse on God, to subordinate the discourse on the Church to the discourse on God and to offer an ecclesiology that would be theological (about God) in a true sense." This context is all-important because it is a return to our faith as *"mystery,"* and a return to *adoration*, to correct the "partial interpretations" of the Council's teachings.[20]

---

desired was being driven in a different direction." Benedict XVI, *Last Testament: In his own Words*, ed. Peter Seewald (New York: Bloomsbury Continuum, 2016), 141.

[18] "However, other forces were working with increasing strength, particularly journalists, who interpreted many things in a continually different way…. The liturgy began to crumble, and slip into personal preferences. In this respect one could soon see that what was originally desired was being driven in a different direction." Benedict XVI, *Last Testament: In his own Words*, ed. Peter Seewald (New York: Bloomsbury Continuum, 2016), 141.

[19] "The Ecclesiology of the Constitution on the Church, Vatican II, *'Lumen gentium'*", *L'Osservatore Romano*, Weekly Edition in English, September 19, 2001, 5. Cardinal Ratzinger made the presentation in Rome in November 2000 at a symposium on the reception of the Council.

[20] Ibid.

C. The Problem was a Hermeneutic of Discontinuity and Rupture

Tracey Rowland, dean of the Pope John Paul II Institute in Melbourne, goes more deeply into this issue. The hermeneutic of "discontinuity," that denies any continuity with past Councils, is fundamentally flawed, since the Church is a living organism. It has given rise to certain disastrous consequences, for it "risks ending in a split between the pre-conciliar Church and the post-conciliar Church." The elites sowing a principle of discontinuity believed that the Council texts do not truly express the teachings and the spirit of the Council that are yet to be attained, dangerously claiming that we must go beyond the texts themselves to some vague "spirit" of the Council. The position argues that it is necessary to go courageously beyond the texts and make room for the newness in which the Council's deepest intention would be expressed, even if it were still vague. Everything preceding the Council was to be jettisoned for the bright future ahead. Thus, two contrary hermeneutics— discontinuity (rupture) and continuity (reform)— arose and quarrelled with each other: "One caused confusion, the other, silently but more and more visibly, bore and is bearing fruit."[21]

1. Specific Cause: Reading Gaudium et Spes as Accommodating Modernity

In an interview with *Zenit* that summarizes much of her thoughts found in her book, *Culture and the Thomist Tradition: After Vatican II*, Tracey Rowland concludes that Cardinal Ratzinger diagnosed that many of the problems arising after the Council sprang specifically from a misreading of *Gaudium et spes.*[22] Dr. Rowland points out that *Gaudium et spes* was the key document that shaped the life of the Church in the years following Vatican II. While the document sought to recognize the positive aspects of the world and the need to go out to meet the world, it recognized a fundamental woundedness in the world and the need for purifying and supernaturalizing the world's culture.

---

[21] Ibid.

[22] Tracey Rowland, "*Gaudium et spes* and the Importance of Christ," in *Ratzinger's Faith: The Theology of Pope Benedict XVI* (Oxford: Oxford University Press, 2008), 30-47. Tracey Rowland is dean and permanent fellow of the John Paul II Institute for Marriage and Family in Melbourne and contributing author of *Culture and the Thomist Tradition: After Vatican II* (New York: Routledge, 2003).

Many instead, with an overly-optimistic view of the world's culture, have taken *Gaudium et spes* to mean that "modernity is OK" and that the Church is to accommodate herself to modernity's spirit since her task is to speak to the world in each age. This meant buying into the pop culture of the 1960s and 1970s, suppressing the Church's cultural heritage, like substituting age old hymns for banal and sentimental ones. She frames Cardinal Ratzinger's criticism thus: "Against this, Ratzinger has been critical of what he calls 'claptrap and pastoral infantilism' — 'the degradation of liturgy to the level of a parish tea party and the intelligibility of the popular newspaper.'"

John Paul II, a key author of *Gaudium et spes*, understood its great importance for the Church but himself read it in the context of GS 22: it is Christ, the Author and Source of all created life, who explains man.[23] In agreement with John Paul II, Cardinal Ratzinger saw clearly that ideas have consequences, and ideas that draw from a distorted culture can lead to a culture of death, as is evident with Marxism and Nazism. The implication of GS 22 is that, without Christ, the Origin and Goal of all reality, there can be no true culture:

> I think that there will be continuity in the sense that Benedict would no doubt agree that a de Lubacian-type [Henri de Lubac] reading of 'Gaudium et Spes' is desirable -- that *culture is not theologically neutral,* that we have a choice between a civilization of love and a culture of death, and *that Christ and a Christian anthropology are needed to rescue us from a web of cultural and moral practices which destroy human integrity and foster nihilism.*[24] (emphasis added)

Dr. Rowland sees that a reinterpretation of *Gaudium et spes* is a part of the major theological work of Ratzinger. Some scholars believe that the market has taken the place of the Eucharist as the object of adoration: "By making the test that of the place and nature of liturgy within a culture Benedict is also taking a very Augustinian position. Augustine would say that what we adore is a sign of what we love, and what we love is a declaration of our membership card of one of the two cities -- the city of God or… of Man."[25]

---

[23] John Paul II's view of the GS 22 text is described in George Weigel, *Witness to Hope*, 846.
[24] "Benedict XVI, Vatican II and Modernity (Part 1): Tracey Rowland on the Pope's Interpretation of the Council," Zenit.org, accessed July 22, 2018, *https://zenit.org/articles/benedict-xvi-vatican-ii-and-modernity-part-1/*.
[25] Ibid.

2. Two Papacies Engaging the Battle for Culture

Tracey Rowland concludes that, in light of this, the new Christ must be aware that he cannot evangelize in a vacuum, as if there was a one-size fits all program. Cardinal Ratzinger, reading the "signs of the times," sees that we are clearly in the middle of a battle against relativism— a battle of culture. It was a battle begun by John Paul II and continued by Pope Benedict XVI in their own particular contexts. Tracey Rowland describes the goals and contexts of the two papacies thus, seeing the wounds left over a few centuries:

> Comparing the two papacies there is a kind of historical eloquence in that Wojtyla, the Pole, is elected to see off the Marxists and focus on the promotion of an alternative Christian anthropology, while the German Ratzinger is elected to contend with problems created by, among others, Luther and Nietzsche. This papacy may well be focused on healing the wounds of the Reformation that began in Germany, and fighting what Benedict calls the "dictatorship of relativism" whose intellectual lineage is also strongly Germanic.[26]

But how do we address the wounds from a secular culture ignoring God and within the Church a crisis of God? We propose that we ultimately battle a culture without God with the culture of God in His saints.

II. Evangelizing Culture through the Cult of the Saints

A. The Priority of the Cult of the Saints

For Benedict XVI, the liturgy (the restoration of adoration or primacy of God) is a key to renewal.[27] But all the gifts of the Holy Spirit in the Church have one goal: holiness. Von Balthasar affirms this truth: "The ultimate reason for her whole institutional and objective side is the obligatory vocation to subjective and personal sanctity…. Christ has no other motive in

---

[26] Ibid.

[27] Ibid. Rowland also notes the following difference in methodology between the two Popes. Where Pope John Paul II draws from ethics and anthropology, the central themes of *Gaudium et spes*, "it is possible that Benedict will take a more ecclesiological focus, concentrating on themes in Lumen gentium and the [Vatican II] decree on ecumenism as well as dealing with the whole territory of liturgy."

sanctifying Himself than 'that they also might be sanctified through the truth' (John 17: 19)."[28] John Paul II, in *Novo millennio ineunte* (n. 30), the blueprint for the third millennium, wrote: "First of all, I have no hesitation in saying that all pastoral [parish] initiatives must be set in relation to holiness"— this is an incisive program for the third millennium. While the healing of culture and the crisis in the Church needs a multi-pronged surgery, the example of the early persecuted, saintly Church that evangelized the entire world points to the core: faith and the Holy Spirit, that finds its apex in martyrdom. The fundamental thesis here is that saints form saints and form religious culture. John Paul II points the way by the incredible output of canonizations,[29] having canonized over 480 saints and beatified 1300.

The Powerful Example of the Saints from "New France" (Quebec in Canada)

Let us turn to a striking example of the power of a culture that has been sanctified by faith— the early years of New France, the province of Quebec in Canada. Since its beginnings in the late sixteenth century, the vast majority of the servants of God, venerables, blesseds, and saints in Canada have come from Quebec or France, a list that is staggering:

> The Canadian Martyrs: Saint Isaac Jogues, Saint Jean de Brébeuf, Saint Charles Garnier, Saint Antoine Daniel, Saint Gabriel Lalemant, Saint Noel Chabanel, Saint René Goupil, Saint Jean de la Lande (these eight Canadian Martyrs lived in Canada from 1625 to 1649 and were canonized on June 29, 1930).

> Other Canadian Saints: Saint Marguerite Bourgeoys, Saint Marguerite d'Youville, Saint Marie de l'Incarnation, Saint François de Laval, Saint André Bessette, Saint Kateri Tekakwitha.

> The Canadian Blesseds: Blessed André Grasset, Blessed Marie-Rose Durocher, Blessed Marie-Léonie Paradis, Blessed Louis-Zéphirin Moreau, Blessed Frédéric Janssoone (Franciscan), Blessed Catherine de Saint-

---

[28] Hans Urs von Balthasar, *Two Sisters in the Spirit: Thérèse of Lisieux, Elizabeth of the Trinity* (San Francisco: Ignatius Press, 1992), Introduction.

[29] Philip Zaleski, "The Saints of John Paul II," *First Things* 161 (March 2006): 28-32. A biography of saints of interest here is a compilation of those raised to the altar by Pope John Paul II: Matthew and Margaret Bunson, *John Paul II's Book of Saints* (Huntington, IN: Our Sunday Visitor, 1999). P

Augustin, Blessed Dina Bélanger, Blessed Marie-Anne Blondin, Blessed Émilie Tavernier-Gamelin, Blessed Bishop Vasyl Velychkovsky, C.Ss.R., Bishop and Martyr (Ukrainian), Blessed Bishop Nykyta Budka (Greek-Ukrainian).

The Canadian Venerables: Venerable Vital Grandin, Venerable Alfred Pampalon (Redemptorist), Venerable Élisabeth Bergeron, Venerable Délia Tétreault.

Causes Introduced to the Vatican for Elevation to Sainthood: Jérôme Le Royer de la Dauversière, Jeanne Mance (layperson), Pierre-Joseph-Marie Chaumonot (Jesuit), Didace Pelletier (religious brother), Jeanne LeBer (layperson in seclusion), Rosalie Cadron-Jetté, Marcelle Mallet, Élisabeth Bruyère, Élisabeth Turgeon, Marie Fitzbach, Éléonore Potvin, Catherine-Aurélie Caouette, Alexis-Louis Mangin (priest), Théophanius-Léo (Adolphe Chatillon), Gérard Raymond, Ovide Charlebois, Marie-Clément Staub (Assumptionist), Eugène Prévost, Antoine Kowalczyk, Louis Émond (layperson), Victor Lelièvre, Catherine de Hueck Doherty, Pauline Archer-Vanier and Georges Vanier, Carmelina Tarantino.[30]

In this list, all but a few have Quebec or French origin or formation, and the few exceptions came from places with faith, like Ukraine (Bishop Vasyl Velychkovsky, Blessed Bishop Nykyta Budka), Russia (Catherine Doherty), and Italy (Sr. Carmelina Tarantino). This is an impressive display of the power of a culture that has been formed by the Catholic faith. Yet, we would argue that, not only does a Christian culture produce saints, but saints also help produce a sacred culture— we shall demonstrate this truth in the rest of the chapter. Yet, many priests are not aware of the centrality of the cult of the saints and fail to mention them on their feast days in their daily Masses, and certainly not offering a short synopsis at Mass for edification or in the homily.

Saints' Mediation and Witness

Pope Benedict told the 700,000 young people at World Youth Day in Cologne in 2005 that definitive change and revolution in the world only

---

[30] This list was taken in August 2016 from the website www.catholicdoors.com/misc/canada.htm. One can also find a list at the CCCB (Canadian Conference of Catholic Bishops) website.

comes from God, and astonishingly pointed to "the saints." He told them to contemplate the saints, from whom "we learn what it means 'to adore' and what it means to live according to the measure of the child of Bethlehem, by the measure of Jesus Christ and of God himself." He affirmed that saints are our models, but more decisively and remarkably, the "true reformers" in the Church's history:

> They [saints] show us the way to attain happiness, they show us how to be truly human. Through all the ups and downs of history, they were the true reformers who constantly rescued it from plunging into the valley of darkness; it was they who constantly shed upon it the light that was needed to make sense– even in the midst of suffering- of God's words… "It is very good." One need only think of such figures as St. Benedict, St. Francis of Assisi, St. Teresa of Avila, St. Ignatius of Loyola, St. Charles Borromeo, the founders of 19-century religious orders who inspired and guided the social movement, or the saints of our own day — Maximilian Kolbe, Edith Stein, Mother Teresa, Padre Pio.[31]

The thesis of this vital role of the saints is based upon the keys principle of mediation in the Church (e.g., of Christ, the Church, the angels, and our Lady). We see this principle of mediation among saints themselves, where we find that many saints also have saints as their models and intercessors: St. Teresa of Calcutta, St. Maximilian Kolbe, and Cardinal van Thuan all look to St. Thérèse of Lisieux, and Blessed Dina Bélanger revealed that St. Thérèse was given to her as a spiritual guide; Blessed Catherine of St. Augustine was given St. Jean de Brébeuf as spiritual director after his death, and St. Catherine of Siena was given St. Mary Magdalene as a spiritual mother.

Cardinal Sarah, when asked about the future of the priesthood, surprisingly emphasized holiness over numerous vocations (quality over quantity), for only twelve saintly apostles: "turned the world upside down":

> At the risk of startling you, I think that the number of priests is not such a fundamental problem. Besides, Saint Gregory the Great says the same

---

[31] Pope Benedict XVI, Address at World Youth Day, Cologne, August 20, 2005, accessed August 18, 2018,
http://www.vatican.va/holy_father/benedict_xvi/speeches/2005/august/documents/hf_b cn-xvi_spc_20050820_vigil wyd_en.html.

thing…. What matters most is the quality of a priest's heart, the strength of his faith, and the substance of his interior life…. When Christ inaugurated the priesthood, he had twelve apostles around him; they turned the whole world upside down.[32]

St. Philip Neri affirmed a similar truth, "Only give me ten persons truly detached from worldly things and I will not despair of converting the world with them."[33] Consecrating the world to God requires souls consecrated wholly to God— these are the saints. In addition to the saints' intercession, the Church and many saintly people have long affirmed the need for their witness of holiness. Bishop Fulton Sheen observed: "The world has heard all the arguments why it should turn to Christ. The world is waiting for the ultimate argument: holiness."

B. Five Ways in which the Saints Extend the Action of Christ

1. Saints have become fully what all baptized are to be, **"new Christs"** through a **"mystical incarnation."** Analogous to the Holy Spirit's descent on Jesus at the Incarnation and at His Baptism, there is a parallel descent of the Holy Spirit at Baptism, such that the baptized becomes a new Christ and a prolongation of Christ in the world. All the means of sanctification at our disposal, such as the Liturgy, prayer, and mortification, have as their goal a quasi-incarnation of "new Christs," of Christ living in the world in His other selves— only then will the world believe. Venerable Concepción Cabrera de Armida, the Mexican foundress, calls this a "mystical incarnation." St. Escrivá frames this very succinctly when he teaches that the baptized are to be "*alter Christus, ipse Christus,*" to be "Christ himself" (*Christ is Passing By*, n. 183). Thus beyond the objective grace of holiness given at Baptism, the baptized is like the mustard seed that must grow into a large tree that shelters many birds.

2. As Jesus consecrates (uniting earth to heaven), Philip Zaleski writes of saints as **"reconsecrating" the world**: "To canonize is to renew the bond between heaven and earth; every canonization, in a sense, reconsecrates the

---

[32] Robert Cardinal Sarah, *God or Nothing*, 128-129.
[33] See Pietro Giacomo Bacci, *The Life of St. Philip Neri: Apostle of Rome and Founder of the Congregation of the Oratory (1902)*, (Kessinger Publishing, LLC, 2010).

world."[34] This is a reversal of the "stripping of the altars." Pope John Paul II speaks of fighting the current secularism and relativism by promoting a new springtime and a new evangelization. In *Crossing the Threshold of Hope*, John Paul II writes that "saints have become the foundation of a new world, a new Europe, and a new civilization." This sense of the new has arisen already in the Church itself, through the fresh wind of John Paul's pontificate that initiated or encouraged original forms of ecclesial activity and that gave us his canonization cannon.

History bears witness to a pattern, which we see in three critical periods when God sent an army of saints to reconsecrate the world: the Early Church, when she was persecuted and most vulnerable at her inception (e.g., martyrs, desert fathers, Church Fathers); the schism of the Western Church in the Reformation (e.g., Ignatius of Loyola, Philip Neri, Teresa of Jesus and John of the Cross); and the period before Vatican II as the Church prepared to enter the Third Millennium (the new lay movements as one example of this explosion of holiness).

3. Christ continues His call for all to be perfect as the heavenly Father is perfect through the saints, who remind us of our fundamental vocation, **the universal call to holiness**. Prior to the Council, there was a common perception that only priests and religious were capable of becoming saints. *Lumen gentium*, Vatican II's principal document, refuted that mindset, reminding us that the heart of Christian discipleship through Baptism is "the Universal Call to Holiness," which Pope John Paul II later confirmed in *Ecclesia de Eucharistia*. Many saints have revealed their lifelong inner passion to become saints: e.g., St. John Bosco observed that St. Dominic Savio's heart was on fire to become a saint; St. Thérèse's desire, "I wish to fulfill your will perfectly…. I desire to be a saint" (Notebook).

4. As Christ's saintly humanity touched deeply those he met, a key insight of von Balthasar is that **it is saints, not institutions (e.g., Magisterium), that convert people**. In the period of decadence in the Church of the twelfth century, God sent, not the hierarchy or an institution, but a poor mendicant, St. Francis of Assisi, who was told, "Go, repair [rebuild] my Church," and

---

[34] Philip Zaleski, *The Saints of John Paul II*, 32.

Pope Innocent III had a dream of him holding up the Lateran basilica (symbolizing the universal Church). Yes, saints as new Christs are saints for all times, but they are also saints for our own age. Saints are theology and the Gospel put into action, new revelations of the Gospel for us in each age (von Balthasar). And they serve to guide, inspire, and intercede for us. St. Ambrose had a dictum: "The life of the saints is the norm of life for all others"; St. Bernard of Clairvaux wrote that "when I think of them, I feel myself inflamed by a tremendous yearning"; St. Ignatius of Loyola and Edith Stein were converted by reading the lives of the saints; St. Philip Neri said that his favourite books had authors with names starting with "S" ("St.").

5. **As Christ chooses to give all graces through our Lady, so He rejoices to enlist the saints as stewards to distribute His graces.** St. Faustina reveals in her *Diary* that Jesus told her that, if she became a saint, she would have power over Him to help Poland and indeed all the world.

III. Re-Evangelizing Culture

To "consecrate" the world to the Divine again, we suggest renewing four foundational pillars of the Christian faith that the Holy Spirit generates: A. *Sacrament* (liturgy); B. *Word* (catechesis, preaching); C. *Apostles* (representing here religious orders); and a need for D. *Reform* (*Ecclesia semper reformanda est*). These re-integrating elements anticipate diverse chapters in this book.

A. <u>Sacrament</u>: Restoring a "Cosmic Liturgy"— Adoration [Ch. 9]

Evangelization has to begin with the liturgy. Some scholars view the Book of Revelation as portraying a heavenly liturgy (of which the Mass is a participation). One Scripture scholar perceived in this Book the history of the world unfolding within this recapitulating liturgy. John Paul II perceived in Rev 5 the Church's liturgy participating in the heavenly liturgy (CCC nos. 1136, 1139), with myriads of angels expressing praise of the Lord in the Paschal mystery:

> The hymn of the Book of Revelation that we meditate today concludes with a final acclamation cried out by "myriads of myriads" of angels (see Rev 5:11).... It is the moment of pure contemplation, of joyful praise, of the song of love to Christ in his paschal mystery. This luminous image of the

heavenly glory is anticipated in the Liturgy of the Church. In fact, as the Catechism of the Catholic Church reminds us, the Liturgy is an "action" of the whole Christ (Christus totus). Those who celebrate it here, live already in some way, beyond the signs, in the heavenly liturgy, where the celebration is totally communion and feast. It is in this eternal liturgy that the Spirit and the Church make us participate, when we celebrate the mystery of salvation in the sacraments. (General Audience, Nov. 3, 2004).

For Pope Benedict XVI, a consecrated world can only take place if all the activities become part of a cosmic liturgy, of *adoration*. In the same trajectory, Sandro Magister, in *Pope Benedict XVI: Preacher of the Holy Mysteries*, quotes a beautiful insight of Benedict XVI, that the liturgy is the apex and core of all salvation history: "He has identified his mission as successor to the apostles precisely in being the celebrant of a 'cosmic liturgy,' because 'when the world in all its parts has become a liturgy of God, when in its reality, it has become adoration, then it will have reached its goal and will be safe and sound.'"[35] He argues that this Pope is above all a "Preaching Pope," what sets his homilies apart is that "they are part of a liturgical action."

Chapter 9 will present the Pope's vision of three phases of salvation history: the sacrifice of Calvary being drawn into eternity, the sacrifice descending in each Mass, and the sacrifice drawing us into eternity. The new Christ must realize that it is not preaching but the liturgy that is the "source and summit" of Christian life and which is also the *principal means of evangelization*.

> It is a dizzying vision. But Pope Benedict has this unshakable certainty: when he celebrates Mass, he knows that the entire action of God is contained in it, woven together with the ultimate destiny of man and of the world. For him, the Mass is not a mere rite officiated by the Church. It is the Church herself, with the triune God dwelling within her.[36]

---

[35] Sandro Magister, "The Preaching Pope," *Inside the Vatican: 2005/2010 Anniversary*, April 2010, 38.

[36] Sandro Magister, "Homilies. The Liturgical Year Narrated by Joseph Ratzinger, Pope," *Chiesa*, accessed August 27, 2018,
http://chiesa.espresso.repubblica.it/articolo/209107bdc4.html?eng=y.

B. <u>Word</u>: Integral Catechesis with the Faith's Mystical Beauty [Ch. 4]

Spiritual writers have long noted that the greatest harm in the Church is caused by ignorance of the faith. We see that Communist dictators understand this principle as they seek first to eliminate the intelligentsia, seeking to remove the educated elite that guides and critiques culture and politics. Romano Guardini wrote powerfully on the need for truth:

> The Church forgives everything more readily than an attack on truth. She knows that if a man falls, but leaves truth unimpaired, he will find his way back again. But if he attacks the vital principle, then the sacred order of life is demolished. Moreover, the Church has constantly viewed with the deepest distrust every ethical conception of truth and dogma. Any attempt to base the truth of a dogma merely on its practical value is essentially uncatholic. The Church represents truth— dogma— as an absolute fact, based upon itself, independent of all confirmation from the moral or even from the practical sphere. Truth is truth because it is truth....
>
> The will has to admit that it is blind and needs the light, the leadership and the organising formative power of truth. It must admit as a fundamental principle the primacy of knowledge over the will, of the Logos over the Ethos.[37]

Pope Benedict XVI himself, addressing a group of prelates from the Conference of the Mexican Episcopate, made a call for accompanying the young that includes strong catechesis to form them so that they would transform society:

> They [youth] find themselves in a society marked by growing religious and cultural pluralism. Moreover they face, at times alone and disoriented, currents of thought according to which man achieves fullness through technological, political and economic power, with no need of God or even against God. For this reason it is necessary to accompany young people, to invite them enthusiastically so that, integrated again into the ecclesial community, they take up the commitment of transforming society as a fundamental requirement of following Christ.[38] In the same way, families

---

[37] Romano Guardini, *The Spirit of the Liturgy* (New York: Aeterna Press, 2015), 54.

[38] Pope Benedict XVI, "Integral Formation in all Ecclesial Fields" (Address to Mexican Episcopate for ad Limina visit at Castel Gandolfo on September 8, 2005).

need adequate accompaniment in order to discover and experience their dimension as "domestic church." The father and mother need to receive formation to help them become the "first evangelizers" of their children.[39]

Pope John Paul II argued for re-evangelization through the restoration of cultural memory, especially through the saints: "It is when night envelops that we must think of the breaking dawn, that we must believe that the Church is reborn each morning through her saints."[40] There is an additional problem involving our present theological path. Von Balthasar has lamented the divorce between theology and spirituality or mysticism since the Middle Ages that has impoverished theology, and thereby the faith of the Church. Tracey Rowland prescribes a structured program of study, comprising the great teachings of Pope John Paul II, including especially his "Theology of the Body":

> If, however, it is read more through the lens of de Lubac's "The Drama of Atheistic Humanism," then I think that the project of reaching out to so-called modern man and helping him to find himself by promoting John Paul II's theology of the body, the Trinitarian anthropology of the encyclicals "Redemptor Hominis," "Dives in Misericordia" and "Dominum et Vivificantem," and the values of the Gospel of Life in "Evangelium Vitae" and "Veritatis Splendor" -- that project has really only just begun and has a long way to go before it starts to bear fruit.[41]

C. <u>Apostles</u>: Renewing Original Charisms of Religious Communities [Ch. 7]

While the mission of evangelization of society belongs to the laity, if the world is to be "consecrated," then it will be primarily the consecrated souls that will lead the laity and the world to God. Adrienne von Speyr offers tremendous insight into the privileged role of consecrated souls. She describes the role of religious, with Mary and John as the first "religious," as an overflowing gift from the cross that precedes redemption and overflows into the world:

---

[39] Ibid.
[40] George Weigel, *Witness to Hope*, 795.
[41] Tracey Rowland, "Benedict XVI, Vatican II and Modernity (Part 1)."

> If the religious state thus receives the breath of life at the foot of the Cross, it is like a first-fruit of the Passion, even before the great and universal fruit of redemption and confession is plucked on Easter. The first-fruit consists in this: that Mary and John, at the foot of the Cross, share in the Son's suffering and are thus initiated into a new form of community.[42]

Thus religious life flows from and remains at the cross to proclaim redemption to the world. The Lord's cross is continued among religious as long as there is sin in the world. While there can be suffering in marriage, it is not its essence as it is for religious life:

> … every new arrival [candidate] is taken from the beginning into the school of the Rule. And therefore, too, suffering at once becomes essential. The private and the personal is immediately renounced; the renunciation is not, as in marriage, the result of a long schooling by destiny but the prerequisite for the beginning of the new life. It draws its substance from suffering. If the counsel to sell all and follow the Lord is really to lead to the Cross and not into a private adventure, then it must draw its strength from an experience of suffering…. Every person who wishes to become perfect in imitation of the Lord already stands in the shadow of the Cross and the coming suffering.[43]

The consecrated soul receives what John the beloved friend received, the most beautiful thing that Christ possesses: "Love, fruitfulness and the three forms of surrender that are expressed in the vows became bound here, at the foot of the Cross, into an indissoluble unity."[44] Because of this power, religious life is a source of grace for married life: "Married women must let their married life be given more Christian fruitfulness through the prayer, sacrifice, counsel, care, love and deportment of nuns…. if the latter [religious] did not exist, there would be really no Christian marriages."[45]

Pope Benedict XVI made a call for renewal in religious orders. He called them to a return to the original charism of their founders and foundresses: "Yes! Institutes of Consecrated Life also must ceaselessly 'start afresh from

---

[42] Adrienne von Speyr, *Handmaid of the Lord* (San Francisco: Ignatius Press, 1985), 130.
[43] Ibid., 129-130.
[44] Ibid., 131.
[45] Ibid., 175.

Christ' if they mean to preserve or rediscover their vitality and apostolic effectiveness. He is the firm rock on which you must build your communities and every project of community and apostolic renewal."[46]

The Holy Spirit is active today and is giving birth to new forms of communities: "The power of the Holy Spirit's breath is being felt in the Church, inspiring a new commitment to fidelity in the historical Institutes as well as in new forms of religious consecration in tune with the needs of the times."[47]

He is concerned about the crises of vocations and the impending disappearance of some religious communities, and notes that the orders that are austere and faithful to their charisms still receive many vocations:

> And it is interesting to note that those same Institutes that have preserved or chosen a tenor of life that is often very austere and which in any case are faithful to the Gospel lived *"sine glossa"* abound in vocations. I am thinking of the many faithful communities and new experiences of Consecrated Life that you know well. I am thinking of the missionary work of many groups and ecclesial movements in which numerous priestly and religious vocations are born. I am thinking of the young men and women who give up everything to enter cloistered monasteries and convents. It is also true today — and we can say so joyfully — that the Lord is continuing to send workers into his vineyard and to enrich his people with many holy vocations.[48]

D. <u>Reform</u>: Restoring Elements that have been Cast-off [Chs. 2-6, 8]

The fundamental dynamic within the Church is *"Ecclesia semper reformanda est,"* the Church is always to be reformed. The crises witnessed in the Church have been a result specifically of a number of "divorces" or casting off the higher

---

[46] Pope Benedict XVI, "Address of his Holiness Benedict XVI to Members of the Council for Relations between the Congregation for Institutes of Consecrated Life and Societies of Apostolic Life and the Men's and Women's International Unions Of Superiors General" (Consistory Hall, Monday, 18 February 2008). Vatican.va, accessed August 18, 2018, https://w2.vatican.va/content/benedict-xvi/en/speeches/2008/february/documents/hf_ben-xvi_spe_20080218_usg-uisg.html.
[47] Ibid.
[48] Ibid.

of two dimensions [transcendence] that reflects a certain schizophrenia, and that needs to be healed by reintegration. The casting off of the transcendent aspect undermines Christianity and saps the energy from its renewal.

1. Restoring Christ to the Centre of Christianity: [See christocentric anthropology in Ch. 2, Logos in evolution in Ch. 3]

Paul's failure at the Areopagus in Athens (Acts 17:15-34) led him to the firm resolution to preach but "Christ crucified" (1 Cor 1:23; 2:1-2). Yet our post-Vatican II period witnessed a denial of the centrality of Christ that necessitated the issuing of *Dominus Jesus* to re-establish the uniqueness, unicity, and newness of Christ, our only Mediator. John Paul II's pontificate, beginning with his inaugural *Redemptor hominis* ("The Redeemer of Man"), has helped to restore christocentricity to the faith through his teaching and documents.

Addressing seminarians at World Youth Day in Cologne, Germany, Benedict XVI spoke of his favourite theme of Christ: "The secret of holiness is friendship with Christ and faithful obedience to his will." He cited different saints who had stated that Christ was first and foremost in their lives: "May Christ be everything for you." In the same speech, he emphasized the importance of Mary, and urged the seminarians to turn to Mary often with confidence to help them learn about Jesus: "Mary teaches the seminarian to contemplate Jesus with the eyes of the heart and to make Jesus his very life."

2. Restoring Christ in Beauty and Culture [Luigi Giussani, Ch. 8]

Within the theological ambit, Hans Urs von Balthasar has written a "Theological Aesthetics" (*Glory of the Lord*), contemplating beauty, the third of the three transcendentals (along with the good and the true). Within faith life, Msgr. Luigi Giussani has long understood the power of beauty (e.g., art, music, nature) to reach hearts and facilitate the encounter with Christ, an insight he has imparted to the Communion and Liberation charism. Pope Benedict XVI, in a previously mentioned message, "The Feeling of Things, the Contemplation of Beauty," encouraged us *to restore our encounter with the saints, who were wounded by contact with the Beautiful [Bridegroom], to a central place.*

I have often affirmed my conviction that the true apology of Christian faith, the most convincing demonstration of its truth against every denial, are the saints, and the beauty that the faith has generated. Today, for faith to grow, we must lead ourselves and the persons we meet to encounter the saints and to enter into contact with the Beautiful. Drawing from seminal insights of the Byzantine theologian Nicholas Cabasilas, Benedict XVI describes the deepest beauty of this "contact with the Beautiful" as the wounding of the heart by the Bridegroom in saints: "it is the Bridegroom who has smitten them with this longing. It is he who has sent a ray of his beauty into their eyes. The greatness of the wound already shows the arrow which has struck home, the longing indicates who has inflicted the wound."[49]

In general, it is helpful to foster ("cultivate") culture within our lives, which overcomes a separation between that which is noble and the mundane. Cardinal Ratzinger believes that a person in a position of authority who does not like cultural aspects, like music, nature, good books, is a dangerous person. It is important that we incorporate activities that will uplift us, such as the beauty of nature (hiking, camping), the beauty of art (e.g., French Impressionists) and music (e.g., opera, symphonies, plays), the uplifting by fine poetry or reading, the writings of the saints, interest in ancient cultures (e.g., Roman, Greek, Aztec) and modern science (e.g., space travel, genome mapping), acquiring languages, or something as simple as gardening.

3. *Recovering Christ in Tradition and the Magisterium alongside Scripture* [Scholarship, Ch. 4]

We see an example of the power of Tradition in the influence of the Church Fathers on the conversion of Henry Newman. Of deep concern regarding "discontinuity" are the jettisoning of Tradition and the limited or erroneous interpretations of Scripture. For some, as noted by Tracey Rowland, Tradition has been taken to mean a certain constriction of one's freedom for a flight to "pure rationality."

In this context, Ratzinger's concern that Tradition has been outflanked by technical rationality is in part derived from the principle found in A.

---

[49] Nicholas Cabasilas, *The Life in Christ*, the Second Book, § 15, quoted in Joseph Ratzinger, "The Feeling of Things, the Contemplation of Beauty."

Rüstow's essay... that the quality of humanity which is lacking in animals is *not* intellect, which is in some sense shared by humans and animals, but Tradition, the possibility of handing on to others the product of the intellect and thus augmenting and enriching it as it is preserved from generation to generation. Ratzinger concludes that "tradition is the precondition for our humanity, and whoever destroys tradition destroys *humanitas* [humanity]— he is like a traveler in space who himself destroys the possibility of ground control, of contact with earth".... He further describes as "absurd" the projects of those who "seek to destroy the bearer of tradition as such, to undertake an ecclesiastical spaceflight with no ground station, to attempt to produce a new and purer Christianity in the test tube of the mere intellect."[50]

The result of this jettisoning Tradition would be disastrous, concluding that it would be "a Church which is nothing but a manager is nothing at all; she is no longer tradition, and, as an intellect that knows no tradition, she becomes pure nothingness, a monster of meaninglessness."[51]

Cardinal Ratzinger identifies Scriptural exegesis in particular as a source of discontinuity, that the historical (critical) method requires a "self-critique"[52] as well as being guided by faith: "in short, we need a synthesis between an exegesis that operates with historical reason and an exegesis that is guided by faith. We have to bring the two things into a proper relationship to each other. That is also a requirement of the basic relationship between faith and reason." [53]

4. Recovering a Supernatural Outlook for a Unity of Life [St. Escrivá in Ch. 7]

It was noted in the preconciliar period that there was a schizophrenia between our everyday life and faith life (Luigi Giussani). St. Escrivá teaches the importance of having a "supernatural outlook": "If you lose the

---

[50] Tracey Rowland, *Ratzinger's Faith*, 54-55.
[51] Joseph Ratzinger, *Principles of Catholic Theology* (San Francisco: Ignatius Press, 1987), 101.
[52] Richard J. Neuhaus, ed., *Biblical Interpretation in Crisis: The Ratzinger Conference on Bible and Church (Encounter Series)*, (Grand Rapids, MI: W. B. Eerdmans, 1989), 1-2
[53] Benedict XVI, *Light of the World: The Pope, The Church and The Signs Of The Times* (San Francisco: Ignatius Press, 2010), 172.

supernatural meaning of your life, your charity will be philanthropy; your purity, decency; your mortification, stupidity; your discipline, a whip; and all your works, fruitless" (*The Way*, no. 291). The supernatural outlook enables one to have a "unity of life": "Our heads should indeed be touching heaven, but our feet should be firmly on the ground" (*Friends of God*, 75). This also applies to how we view the elements of our faith, like the Eucharist. St. Faustina relates Jesus' lamenting our treating Him in the host as a "dead object" or religious receiving Him "out of habit"(*Diary* 1288).

5. Restoring Christ's Filial Obedience in the Church ["Church-man" in Ch. 6]

The foundation of Christ's life lies here: "My food is to do the will of him who sent me and to finish his work" (Jn 4:34). Jesus himself gave St. Faustina explicit instructions about obedience to her superiors as given to Himself, reminding her of His own obedience as man: "I have come to do my Father's will. I obeyed my parents, I obeyed my tormentors and now I obey the priests" (*Diary* 535, Jesus' words)[54]; "My daughter, know that you give Me greater glory by a single act of obedience than by long prayers and mortifications. Oh, how good it is to live under obedience, to live conscious of the fact that everything I do is pleasing to God!" (*Diary* 894).

The saints live especially the filial obedience owed to the Holy Father. St. Escrivá, after a long sea voyage to Rome, spent his first night facing the Vatican apartments in vigil praying for the Holy Father. He taught his spiritual children to love the Holy Father, whoever he may be, in advance: "God is not present where the Pope is absent. This is why I wanted the Work to be in Rome. Love the Holy Father much. Pray a lot for the Pope. Have a lot of affection for him… because he is the sweet Christ on earth."[55]

---

[54] St. Maria Faustina Kowalska, *Diary: Divine Mercy in My Soul* (Stockbridge, MA: Marians of the Immaculate Conception, 2003).
[55] Pilar Urbano, *The Man of Villa Tevere*, 13, 332.

CHAPTER 2

TOWARDS A NEW CHRISTOCENTRIC ANTHROPOLOGY

> For Ratzinger, the whole point of *Gaudium et spes*, correctly interpreted, is that **a "daring new" Christocentric theological anthropology** is the medicine that the world needs, and that it is the responsibility of the Church to administer it.[1] (Tracey Rowland, emphasis added)

Historical Background: *Today's Context of a Confused Anthropology*

Cardinal Ratzinger saw with clarity that "the whole point of *Gaudium et spes*... is that a 'daring new' Christocentric theological anthropology is the medicine that the world needs" (quotation above). The new Christ by Baptism today can find himself or herself confused and discouraged by a host of moral aberrations: the young engaging in promiscuity; many "couples" living together outside of marriage; legislation civilly ratifying same-sex gender ideology and euthanasia; transgender issues. There is also the growing specific problem of the "millennials" (first generation to come of age in the new millennium), as characterized by surveys, having a tendency to be absorbed in themselves.

What the new Christ may not realize is that all of these issues actually arise from a distorted anthropology, misconceptions of who the human being is. A "'daring new' Christocentric theological anthropology" would reset the parameters and structure for the lofty and ultimate meaning of man, his journey and destiny.

For a renewed Christocentric anthropology, with Christ as the center, we will take three steps. (I) We can establish a Christocentric foundation for all theology in Paul, and can take a contemporary point of departure from GS 22 to recover specifically the profound truth unknown to most Catholics that man is created in Christ's image. (II) As a first step towards formulating a Christocentric anthropology, we can begin with Pope John Paul II's anthropology, his *Theology of the Body*, as it identifies into man's core nature as self-gift, which is at the heart of the Trinity. (III) But one also must be able to protect such an anthropology, by being able to pinpoint the specific

---

[1] Tracey Rowland, *Ratzinger's Faith*, 46.

stratagems that today undermine the human person and the man-woman relationship, turning to Luigi Giussani and Alice von Hildebrand.

I. *"Image of Christ" as Point Of Departure for Anthropology*

While Christian theology's customary point of departure for anthropology was based upon man being made in the image and likeness of God (Gen 1), the New Testament revelation from Paul and John find man's image in Christ. That man is not just created in the image of God but specifically in the image of Christ has untold ramifications for theological anthropology. To arrive at Christ as point of departure for understanding man, let us take three steps. (A) Begin with Paul's christocentric vision that influenced the patristic theology of the Church Fathers. (B) We look to GS 22 as a renewed point of departure for contemporary theology. (C) The International Theological Commission's (ITC) document, *Communion and Stewardship: Human Persons Created in the Image of God*, confirms the insight of man as created in *imago Christi*.

A. Paul's Christocentric Vision that Formed Patristic Tradition

It is fitting to begin with Paul, who had a radically christocentric vision that formed the Church Fathers' vision. Paul had set Christ as first in the mind of God: "For in him all things were created... all things have been created through him and for him" (Col 1:16). Peter Chrysologus wrote that the human race also took its origin from Christ (not only from Adam) and that "The second Adam stamped his image on the first Adam when he created him" (CCC n. 359). He clearly identifies Christ as Creator and as creating Adam in His image, and making man "in his own image":

> St. Paul tells us that the human race takes its origin from two men: Adam and Christ.... The first Adam was made by the last Adam, from whom he also received his soul, to give him life. . . The second Adam stamped his image on the first Adam when he created him. That is why he took on himself the role and the name of the first Adam, in order that he might not lose what he had made in his own image.[2]

---

[2] St. Peter Chrysologus, *Sermo* 117: PL 52, 520-521.

Peter C. Bouteneff, in his work, *Beginnings: Ancient Christian Readings of the Biblical Creation Narratives*, sees that Paul reverses the point of departure from Adam to Christ. He correctly identifies and highlights in Paul the derivative place of Adam and creation.[3] Paul in fact lays the burden on Adam of being the agent of death's initiation into humanity.

Peter Bouteneff noted that some discerning commentators in recent decades have deduced that Paul did not start with and then enshrine a chronological scheme of creation, the Fall, and redemption. Bouteneff quotes James Barr's insight, that "Paul was not interpreting the story in and for itself; he was really *interpreting Christ* through the use of images from the story."[4]

Peter Bouteneff concludes that Paul has made Adam and the paradise story something different from what it ever was before. Paul not only transformed thinking about sin, he was the first to make the paradise story the primordial account of the fall of humanity. Paul's starting point and focus are not finally sin, but rather that which is new: Jesus Christ, Lord and Saviour. More specifically, Christ is "image of God and the model for Adam" and "to whose image humanity must conform":

> Paul does nothing less than define the direction and the sequence, as it were, of Christian reflection on Christ…. It is a sequence that begins with Christ himself: rather than Adam being a model or image for humanity or even the first real human being, it is Christ who is both. Christ is the first true human being, and Christ is the image of God and the model for Adam.
>
> Indeed, there is no mention in Paul of the person of Adam as created in God's image…. Paul's Adam is not so much the first human being as he is the first human to sin…. For him (and for the author of Hebrews), it is Christ who is the image of God (Col. 1:15; Heb. 1:3) and to whose image humanity must conform (Rom. 8:29). As Karl Barth puts it memorably, "Adam's humanity is a provisional copy of the real humanity that is in Christ."[5]

---

[3] Peter Bouteneff, *Beginnings: Ancient Christian Readings of the Biblical Creation Narratives* (Grand Rapids, MI: Baker Academic, 2008).

[4] James Barr, *Garden of Eden and the Hope of Immortality* (Minneapolis, MN: Fortress Press, 1993), 4.

[5] Peter Bouteneff, *Beginnings*, 45-46.

Dr. Bouteneff sees Paul's approach as ground-breaking and becoming the guiding rubric under which the Christian Fathers read Scripture: Christ is the starting point and everything points to Christ. Bouteneff highlights the subsequent patristic method of prefiguring Christ already ascribed to the Old Testament, as we find in Luke's portrayal of Emmaus (Lk 24), and other texts like John 5:46 ("If you believed Moses, you would believe me, for he wrote of me") and Matthew 12:39-40 ("For as Jonah was three days and three nights in the belly of the whale, so will the Son of man be three days and three nights in the heart of the earth"), in which parts of the Old Testament are shown to be referring to Christ. He adds that "We will see how in the patristic and liturgical legacy Paul's Adam-Christ typology became elaborated to the point where few scriptural verses were left unexplored for their relationship to Christ, Mary, or the Church."[6]

What Paul sees is essentially what God the Father sees. We tend to see salvation history linearly, i.e., beginning with creation and Adam's sin leading up to redemption. In stark contrast, the Father sees the deepest reality— through the prism of Christ— creating us in the image of Christ for union with His Son, through a gradual conformation by the Holy Spirit to the fullness of the "likeness" of Christ. It opens up a vast panorama in which Christ is the form of all creation and the template of man and angels. All things find their meaning in Him, including all morality, culture, truth, beauty, etc., an insight that Hans Urs von Balthasar has developed in his theology.

B. *Gaudium et Spes* 22 as a Renewed Point of Departure

We turn to the key landmark of the Church in our times, the Second Vatican Council, that takes up the Pauline orientation. The Council Fathers themselves urged that, for *Gaudium et spes* (GS), "the starting point should be Christ, the second Adam, from whom alone the Christian picture of man can be properly developed"; for the Old Testament image of God "only receives its full meaning from the fact that in the New Testament the Adam-figure and the doctrine of man as the image of God are transferred to Christ as the

---

[6] Ibid., 46.

definitive Adam."[7] This was synthesized in GS 22, which is regarded as Pope John Paul II's favourite conciliar text. Let us then take up GS 22 as the hermeneutical key for a contemporary understanding of man, a Christian anthropology that is a christocentric anthropology.

> The truth is that only in the mystery of the incarnate Word does the mystery of man take on light. For Adam, the first man, was a figure [copy] of Him Who was to come, namely Christ the Lord. *Christ, the final Adam, by the revelation of the mystery of the Father and his love, fully reveals man to man himself and makes his supreme calling clear.* It is not surprising, then, that in Him all the aforementioned truths find their root and attain their crown. (emphasis added)

It reveals a truth that may be startling for contemporary ears— the mystery of man finds his meaning in Christ: "The truth is that only in the mystery of the incarnate Word does the mystery of man take on light. For Adam, the first man, was a figure of Him Who was to come, namely Christ the Lord." If Christ is the "final Adam" and also "fully reveals man to man himself and makes his supreme calling clear," then its conclusion is logical: "It is not surprising, then, that in Him all the aforementioned truths find their root and attain their crown." But to go even more deeply, man is not just a product of chance (pure randomness), not only loved into creation, but the Father has given us the greatest possible gift: to be created in the image of His greatest possession, His beloved Son, for the destiny of being united to Him in a nuptial union and to ultimately become sons and daughters of the Father.

C. ITC's Commentary on GS 22 Confirms Man as Created in "*Imago Christi*"

GS 22's new insight is profound, but needs further elaboration to unfold its full significance. The International Theological Commission's (ITC) *Communion and Stewardship: Human Persons Created in the Image of God*, in the section, "*Imago Dei and imago Christi*," provides an authoritative commentary on the key text of GS 22. Two texts support our findings. The first states:

---

[7] Joseph Ratzinger, "The Dignity of the Human Person," in Herbert Vorgrimler, ed., *Commentary on the Documents of Vatican II*, vol. V, "Pastoral Constitution on the Church in the Modern World" (Montreal: Palm Publishers, 1969), 120-121.

> While it is true that man is created *ex nihilo* [theology derived from Genesis], it can also be said that he is created from the fullness (*ex plenitudine*) of Christ himself who is at once the creator, the mediator and the end of man [theology derived from Paul]. The Father destined us to be his sons and daughters, and "to be conformed to the image of his Son, who is the firstborn of many brothers" (Rom. 8:29). Thus, what it means to be created in the *imago Dei* is only fully revealed to us in the *imago Christi*.

The last statement is most significant for us: "Thus, what it means to be created in the *imago Dei* is only fully revealed to us in the *imago Christi*." It implies that Adam and Eve being created in the "image of God" as depicted in the Book of Genesis is in fact a preliminary revelation to a fuller revelation in the New Testament of creation in Christ and a step to full configuration in Jesus Christ. A second statement sheds more light:

> Just as man's beginnings are to be found in Christ, so is his finality. Human beings are oriented to the kingdom of Christ as to an absolute future, the consummation of human existence. Since "all things have been created through him and for him" (Col 1:16), they find their direction and destiny in him. The will of God that Christ should be the fullness of man is to find an eschatological realization. While the Holy Spirit will accomplish the ultimate configuration of human persons to Christ in the resurrection of the dead, *human beings already participate in this eschatological likeness to Christ here below*, in the midst of time and history. Through the Incarnation, Resurrection and Pentecost, the eschaton is already here; they inaugurate it and introduce it into the world of men, and anticipate its final realization.

To say that "man's beginnings are to be found in Christ" is implying that man was already created in the image of Christ, and not just in God. This is confirmed by a later sentence: "human beings already participate in this eschatological likeness to Christ here below, in the midst of time and history." What the text then adds to man's beginnings is that man's finality is also found in Christ. So, already created in the image and likeness of Christ at creation, but, through the advent of sin, we have lost not the "image" (basic structure) but the "likeness" of grace, as the Church Fathers teach. The text implies that, while the likeness (grace) is restored at Baptism, it is also a journey of growth in conformation to Christ during our lifetime.

Both of these elements point to the fact that Christ is everything for us: "at once the creator, the mediator and the end of man" (see Col 1: 16). The profound implication of this is that the goal of the spiritual life is conformation to Christ, or as St. Josemaría Escrivá teaches, the baptized is to become "another Christ, Christ Himself" (*ipse Christus*). So we are made in the image of Christ, to be so possessed by Christ, so as to become *ipse Christus*: "It is no longer I who live, but Christ who lives in me" (Gal 2:20). Christ is truly the beginning, the in-between, and the end for man. Such a christocentric vision turns theological anthropology on its head.

The contemporary christocentric focus on anthropology is captured succinctly in Karl Rahner's famous phrase: "Christology may be studied as self-transcending anthropology, anthropology is deficient Christology."[8] He explains that it means that "Christology is the end and beginning of anthropology. And this anthropology, when most thoroughly realised in Christology, is eternally theology."[9] A commentator gives further elaboration: "Theological anthropology can thus be developed from Christology... Christ is the archetype of humanity":

> Theological anthropology can thus be developed from Christology, after this has been revealed to us. Christ is the archetype of humanity. The previously mentioned Scotist tendency is again apparent: *the world, creation, etc. exist only with a view to the incarnation, the hypostatic union, and Jesus Christ.* Scholastic theology would say that Christ is the "final cause" of creation. In more biblical language we could say that the covenant is the goal of creation.
>
> Rahner tries in this way to translate the more formal, ontological categories of dogma into ontological, existential terms. On the one hand, he is concerned with the true humanity of Jesus; on the other hand, he sees in anthropology the possibility of leading people to Christ, or rather of illuminating their already existing relationship to Christ.[10] (emphasis added)

---

[8] Karl Rahner, "Current Problems in Christology," in *Theological Investigations* (New York: Crossroad Publ. Co., 1981), I:164, footnote 1.

[9] Karl Rahner, "On the Theology of the Incarnation," in *Theological Investigations* (London: Darton, Longman & Todd, 1966), IV: 117.

[10] Roman A. Siebenrock, "Christology," in *The Cambridge Companion to Karl Rahner*, eds. Declan Marmion, Mary E. Hines (Cambridge: Cambridge University Press, 2005), 117.

Rahner clearly sees creation as accomplished with a view to Christ's coming ("the incarnation, the hypostatic union, and Jesus Christ"), and since Christ is also the "final cause" of creation, man was created in view to a relationship with Christ (creation for the sake of the covenant). Rahner synthesizes what we have seen in Paul and GS 22.

The New Testament texts confirm our thesis from GS 22. Col 1:15-20 teaches that Christ is the author of both creation and redemption, and more specifically, it explains that Christ is "the first-born of all creation" and "in him all things were created, in heaven and on earth, visible and invisible." It implies that, with Christ as "the image of the invisible God," Christ is *the* image of the Father, and man is *an* image of Christ, *the* Image. Thus, Col 1 goes beyond the teaching of Gen 1 that man is made in the image of God to Christ as the template for the creation of man and also the universe. Man is ultimately created in the image of Christ Himself.

GS 22 recovers Paul's christocentric vision: Christ is first in the mind of the Father, creation only exists for His coming: so that all creation is christic, and man is the image of Christ. This christocentric theological anthropology has immense implications for man: meaning and structure of life, value, gender and marriage, path to holiness, destiny, and even evolution.

II. John Paul II's Theology of the Body

Historical Utilitarian Turns that Degrade the Body
Many commentators have pointed out how prophetic Pope Paul VI's *Humanae vitae* was, that we are now witnessing precisely the fallout that he predicted.[11] But as Michael Waldstein points out, the heart of the recent drama with artificial contraception is not about the freedom to do what one wants with one's body or about sexual relations as such. At the heart is a change in *vision* that degrades the human body, which in turn creates a dualism between the order of person and nature.

---

[11] See, for example, Marie Meaney, "The Prophetic Voice of Pope Paul VI," *Inside the Vatican* (June-July 2018): 42.

There were historical origins to this. It began with the *Mechanist view* of the universe (universe as a machine), inspired by philosophers like Francis Bacon and René Descartes, the goal of which is to have *power over nature*; for that which is not utilitarian is but abstract and useless. Michael Waldstein concludes that John Paul II's *Theology of the Body* is thus a defence of the body ("Redemption of the Body"). It is a theological response to the "Cartesian-Kantian-Schelerian form of subjectivity" that creates a dualism between person and body, and treats the body as subrational and akin to nature.

This dualism found concrete expression in some of the hostile reactions to *Humanae vitae*. Waldstein uses the example of the "Majority Report" of Paul VI's birth control commission, who employed a Baconian program identified as God's will, supplying a number of reasons supporting this position, including social changes in matrimony and family, but above all the duty to "humanize nature."[12] It was optimistically seen as an updating (*aggiornamento*) by "embracing a new loyalty to the Baconian project."[13] This mechanist, utilitarian view denies man's lofty nature as a unity, an incarnate or enfleshed spirit, created in the image of Christ.

For "a 'daring new' christocentric theological anthropology," Karol Wojtyla's *Theology of the Body* provides an antidote, as it establishes the theological foundation for *Humanae vitae*, and since he views his anthropology as being completed by his christology. In this chapter, we look to the *Theology of the Body* as a first step to restore the proper place of the human body and of nature. John Paul II offers Christian anthropology a path of renewal because it draws from the ecstatic dynamic within the Trinity, thus revealing man's fundamental role of self-gift.

Responding to the pulverization of man that he witnessed in Nazism and Communism in Poland and to the catechetical failure of *Humanae vitae* to

---

[12] "The story of God and of man, therefore, should be seen as a shared work. And it should be seen that man's tremendous progress in control of matter by technical means and the universal and total 'intercommunication' that has been achieved, correspond entirely to the divine decrees." Commission on Birth Control, "Majority Report," in *The Catholic Case for Conception*, ed. Daniel Callahan (New York: Macmillan, 1969), 150, quoted in John Paul II, *Man and Woman He Created Them: A Theology of the Body*, ed. Michael Waldstein, rev. ed. (Boston: Pauline Books & Media, 2006), 101.
[13] John Paul II, *Man and Woman He Created Them*, 101.

speak of the marital love of couples, Wojtyla wrote a treatise (*Love and Responsibility*), that was subsequently given in installments as a series of catechetical talks as pope during his General Audiences from 1979 to 1984. Since then, there has been increasingly greater recognition of the momentousness of this contribution and the need to mine its riches. He identifies the heart of human nature as "self-gift," finding its origin in the Trinitarian self-communication.

A. Theology of the Body

This chapter introduces the novice in theological anthropology to the significance of John Paul II's thought through commentators.

Wojtyla's Seven Major Works

1. 1948	*Faith according to St. John of the Cross* (doctoral thesis)
2. 1953	*Evaluation of the Possibility of Constructing a Christian Ethics on the Assumptions of Max Scheler's System of Philosophy* (habilitation thesis)
3. 1954-57	*Lublin Lectures* (philosophical lectures on the foundations of ethics in dialogue with Plato, Aristotle, Augustine, Thomas, Kant, Scheler)
4. 1957-59	*Love and Responsibility* (philosophical-theological treatise on love and marriage)
5. 1969	*The Acting Person* (philosophical account of the human person)
6. 1972	*Sources of Renewal: The Implementation of the Second Vatican Council*
7. 1976	*Sign of Contradiction* (retreat preached to Papal household)[14]

---

[14] John Paul II, *Man and Woman He Created Them: A Theology of the Body*, 77-78. Waldstein's updated work is a result of much research into the original titles and ordering, such that the reader has the text as envisioned by John Paul II, along with a new translation. It affords the reader a better overview of the trajectory of the *Theology of the Body*. Christopher West, in his 2007 edition of *Theology of the Body Explained: A Commentary on John Paul II's Man and Woman He Created Them* (Boston: Pauline Books & Media, 2007), appears to have revised his original structure to match that of Waldstein. Two other works come close to the category of "major works": *Primer of Ethics* and *Catholic Social Ethics*.

1. *John Paul II Saw the Need for a Theology to Undergird Marriage*

George Weigel noted that the development of this theme is better understood against the backdrop of what might be described as the leitmotiv of his pontificate, challenging the pulverization of the unique dignity of every human person (Nazism and Communism). Writing to his friend Henri de Lubac in 1968, he enunciated his belief that the crisis of modernity involved a "degradation, indeed… a pulverization of the fundamental uniqueness of each person." Whenever another human being was reduced to an object of manipulation, the "pulverization of the fundamental uniqueness of each person" was taking place. Another related grave threat to humanity was "utilitarianism," making "usefulness to me" the sole criterion of human relationships. For John Paul II, in developing the idea of human sexuality as an icon of the interior life of God, he was working out the implication of the very same concept of human dignity and freedom, for they were all of a piece.

In doing this, as George Weigel noted, John Paul II also gave a new footing to *Humanae vitae*. When he was elected to the papacy, Karol Wojtyla knew that the Church's effort to address the sexual revolution and its relationship to moral life, especially as focused on *Humanae vitae,* however correct it was on the moral issue of fertility, had been a pastoral and catechetical failure. For vast numbers of Catholics rejected its teaching, and many felt that their experience of sexual love had been ignored by religious leaders. This feeling of rejection led to the conclusion that the Church had nothing of consequence to say about any aspect of human sexuality. John Paul II felt it was time to set this explosive issue on a new footing, to provide a voice with which to address the challenge of the sexual revolution. Basing his catecheses on *Love and Responsibility*, he deepened the doctrine biblically and brought it to a world audience in 130 general audience addresses, spread over four years, that make up his *Theology of the Body*.[15]

John Paul II's *Theology of the Body* addresses do not make for easy reading, but they are compact theological and philosophical meditations, and repay careful study. George Weigel, the biographer chosen by the pope himself, has written that "Pope John Paul II's *Theology of the Body* has ramifications for all of theology" and that "he has proposed one of the boldest re-configurations of

---

[15] George Weigel, *Witness to Hope*, 334-335.

Catholic theology in centuries." John Paul II begins by going back to the beginnings in Genesis. In Gen 1, he finds a curious clue that is not explained: that God's creation of male and female is connected to His image and likeness: "in the image of God he created him; male and female he created them" (1:27). This is only clarified in Gen 2. First, he notes that, even with God and animals, Adam experienced "solitude," that he was incomplete and did not yet understand who he was. Then it was only when God created him a "helper," that great joy was experienced, and this was because they finally understood that the deepest meaning of human life is of giving themselves to each other unconditionally; follows from their being made in the image and likeness of God, whose very essence is love.

2. John Paul II's Debt to St. John of the Cross

Jumping over his comprehensive presentation to his conclusions, we note that Michael Waldstein concludes that John Paul II's vision can be synthesized in a triangle of three points: gift of self; paradigm of married love; and model and source is the Trinitarian communion:

> (1) Love implies a cycle of mutual giving, supremely the gift of self. (2) The paradigmatic instance of such self-gift in human experience is the spousal relation between man and woman. (3) The Trinity is the archetype of such love and gift from which the love between God and human persons as well as love between human beings derives as an imitation and participation.[16]

Michael Waldstein perceived that these three foundational elements find three points of contact with John of the Cross's *Living Flame of Love* (Stanza 3). The degree to which Karol Wojtyla leans on St. John of the Cross can be seen in Waldstein's summation of the link between Wojtyla's main philosophical work (*The Acting Person*) and Max Scheler's phenomenology.[17] While affirming that Wojtyla learnt much from Scheler and that one can trace many influences through the references to Max Scheler in the indices of Karol Wojtyla's works, his overall judgment of Scheler's phenomenology is negative. Though he employs the phenomenological method and many insights of Scheler, "The main agenda of *The Acting Person* (1969), however,

---

[16] John Paul II, *Man and Woman He Created Them*, 29.
[17] Karol Wojtyla, *Evaluation of the Possibility of Constructing a Christian Ethics on the Assumptions of Max Scheler's System of Philosophy* (German original, Stuttgart-Degerloch: Seewald, 1980).

is not dictated by Scheler, but by Wojtyla's roots in the spousal theology of St. John of the Cross, specifically in the key notion, 'gift of self.'"[18] A word should be said about Karol Wojtyla's use of phenomenology and faith. He is particularly interested in how faith becomes experience. Modern theology has evinced a turn towards experience, some in extreme forms, like that of Schleiermacher, and perhaps in post-Vatican II catechesis. However, Wojtyla sets the proper structure establishing the primacy of faith, by making faith the source and form of experience, and not the reverse. His is not the false mysticism that glorifies and exalts experience that is not anchored by faith and that seeks experiences and exalts the ego.[19] Wojtyla rejects the distorted approach that makes experience the measure of faith.[20] He establishes both the necessity of faith lived in personal subjectivity, but rooting that experience within the norms of faith, and in the context of the goal of union with God. Faith deeply transforms experience as a means to union with God: "Faith is *the only proximate and proportionate means* for communion with God."[21]

Even more so in *Love and Responsibility*, the original work (1957-1959) that attaches itself more immediately to the beginning of his formation, is the debt to the spousal personalism of John of the Cross apparent. Though John of the Cross does not explicitly or thematically discuss love between man and woman, his frequent use of bridegroom imagery in the soul's union with God contains a rich theology of marriage that Wojtyla made explicit. The core of Wojtyla's philosophical thought in *Love and Responsibility* is the understanding of gift of self as key element of spousal love that is central to John of the Cross: "It is thus clear that the spousal theology of St. John of the Cross ultimately shapes the agenda of *Love and Responsibility*."[22] This insight of Waldstein, that the spousal theology of John of the Cross shaped his thought, is a precious contribution. Illuminating too is the three-fold configuration: self-gift; paradigm of married life; and model and source is Trinitarian communion— this sets out the game-plan for human life. Wojtyla's Christian anthropology, based upon self-gift as the essence of life, which is an image

[18] John Paul II, *Man and Woman He Created Them*, 79.
[19] Karol Wojtyla, *Faith According to St. John of the Cross* (San Francisco: Ignatius Press, 1981), 16-17, quoted in John Paul II, *Man and Woman He Created Them*, 83.
[20] Ibid., 123, quoted in John Paul II, *Man and Woman He Created Them*, 83.
[21] John Paul II, *Maestro en la fe*, 2, quoted in John Paul II, *Man and Woman He Created Them*, 84.
[22] Ibid., 79.

of Trinitarian life, already provides an antidote for many anthropological deviations of our time: pulverization of human dignity, exploiting of spouses, extra-marital relations, contraceptive culture, same sex ideology, cloning, etc.

B. John Paul II's *Theology of the Body* Completed by Christology

1. The Postconciliar Rejection of Christ

As George Weigel affirms, the *Theology of the Body*, John Paul's theological anthropology, is only a first step that is completed with his christology: "In John Paul's understanding of the Council, everything else Vatican II did… is a further explication of these two great themes: Christ, the redeemer of the world, reveals the astonishing truth about the human condition and our final destiny; self-giving love is the path along which human freedom finds its fulfillment in human flourishing."[23] It is obvious today that christology itself has been weathering many challenges, some in very radical forms. As Angelo Cardinal Amato, astutely perceives that in this terrain we are not dealing with academic *quaestiones disputatae* (disputed teachings) but ones that threaten the very foundations of the mystery of Christ, such as His divinity, His virginal birth from Mary through the Holy Spirit, the reality of His Resurrection, and the universal efficacy of His Paschal mystery. There is a denial of the Christian originality of the figure of Christ for reasons of inculturation and inter-religious dialogue, sometimes to the point of completely annulling His work of universal salvation.[24] In the aftermath of this deviation, the SCDF issued *Dominus Jesus*.[25] Pope John Paul II's pontificate has helped to restore this christocentrism.

---

[23] George Weigel, *Witness to Hope*, 846-847.

[24] Angelo Amato, *Gesù, Salvatore Unico, Definitivo, Universale, e la Cooperazione di Maria all salvezza*, in *Maria nel mistero di Cristo, pienezza e compimento del regno* (Roma: Edizioni Marianum, 1999), 387-392.

[25] Cardinal Ratzinger, at the Press Conference to issue *Dominus Jesus*, said that, because of the dissolution of christology, "The result is that the figure of Christ has lost its character of unicity and universality." At the same conference, Msgr. Fernando Ocàriz (now Prelate of the Opus Dei prelature) spoke of how diffuse was a current interpretation that all religions were all equally ways to God and corrected this by recalling *Redemptoris Missio's* teaching that other religions rather contained "elements of religiosity that come from God…" and have the value of "preparation for the Gospel." Vatican.va website, accessed May 10, 2017, https://press.vatican.va/content/salastampa/it/bollettino/pubblico/2000/09/05/0518/01 756.html.

2. "Self-Gift" in John Paul II's Papal Documents Culminates in Christology

An examination of John Paul II's papal documents can point to the christological foundation for his Christian anthropology. The core and conclusion of John Paul II's *Theology of the Body* is that man is called to love, specifically to a "*communio personarum,*" a communion of persons, both with others and with God the Trinity, and love entails "self-gift." But "self-gift," though obviously a great insight, is not a typical nor obvious category that one would set at the heart of theology and faith.

Let us turn to a few other later papal documents to develop this understanding through Michael Waldstein, who wrote an excellent article, "John Paul II and St. Thomas on Love and the Trinity."[26] We find that some of John Paul II's papal documents have already elaborated upon, filled out, and summarized his thought on the *Theology of the Body*. Michael Waldstein begins by examining several of these texts of John Paul II, specifically, *Redemptor hominis* 10, *Dominum et vivificantem* 10, *Familiaris consortio* 11, as well as Vatican II's *Gaudium et spes* 22 & 24. Restricting this introduction to only one document, *Redemptor hominis* 10, we find John Paul II affirming the christological core: that "man cannot live without love" and links this need for love specifically to finding Christ; *that love is found and fulfilled by drawing close to Christ and appropriating His mysteries.*

This points to a deeper reality than being made in the image of Christ and to be conformed to Him; it points to a fulfillment of love in Christ, that our hearts long for and find an eternal spousality with Him. Here is a sublime text:

> Man cannot live without love. He remains a being that is incomprehensible for himself, his life is senseless, if love is not revealed to him, if he does not encounter love, if he does not experience it and make it his own, if he does not participate intimately in it. This, as has already been said, is why Christ the Redeemer "fully reveals man to himself." If we may use the expression, this is the human dimension of the mystery of the Redemption. In this

---

[26] Michael Waldstein, "John Paul II and St. Thomas on Love and the Trinity," *Anthropotes* 18 (2002): 113-138; 269-286 (the text is divided into two sections within the same volume).

dimension man finds again the greatness, dignity and value that belong to his humanity. In the mystery of the Redemption man becomes newly "expressed" and, in a way, is newly created. *He is newly created!...* "for you are all one in Christ Jesus." The man who wishes to understand himself thoroughly— and not just in accordance with immediate, partial, often superficial, and even illusory standards and measures of his being— he must with his unrest, uncertainty and even his weakness and sinfulness, with his life and death, *draw near to Christ*. He must, so to speak, enter into him with all his own self, he must "appropriate" and assimilate the whole of the reality of the Incarnation and Redemption in order to find himself.[27]

3. The Overall Plan of Faith is Centered on Christ

The reader can find a brief excursus in Kenneth L. Schmitz's *At the Center of the Human Drama*, where he explains more fully how John Paul II's *Theology of the Body* finds its completion in his christology (pp. 108-120). Asking the question rhetorically of what manner we should continue the ways in which Vatican II has set us, Pope John Paul II responds decisively: "Our response must be: Our spirit is set in one direction, the only direction for our intellect, will and heart is— towards Christ our Redeemer, towards Christ, the Redeemer of man."[28] The christocentrism of John Paul II is clear, presenting Christ as *"the centre of the cosmos and of history"* (RH n. 1).

III. Defending Man's Transcendence, the Man-Woman Bond, and Femininity (Luigi Giussani, Alice von Hildebrand)

A. Protecting the Person's Dignity through the Religious Sense

The anthropological deviations we have seen have their underlying cause ultimately in the loss of the sense of transcendence (loss of the divine), which brings with it tragic consequences. Msgr. Luigi Giussani, in his developed synthesis, pointed out that the key antidote is the religious sense, the "lived awareness of this relationship" to God. In fact, "religiosity is the single hindrance, limit, confine to the dictatorship of man over man":

---

[27] Pope John Paul II, *Redemptor hominis*, n. 10.
[28] Ibid., n. 7.

So here is the *paradox*: freedom is dependence upon God....

The human being— the concrete human person, me, you—once we were not, now we are, and tomorrow will no longer be: thus we depend. And either we depend upon the flux of our material antecedents, and are consequently slaves of the powers that be, or we depend upon what lies at the origin of the movement of all things, *beyond* them, which is to say, God.... Religiosity is the lived awareness of this relationship. Freedom comes through religiosity. Religiosity is the single hindrance, limit, confine to the dictatorship of man over man, whether we are referring to men and women, parents and children, government and citizens, owners and workers, party chiefs, rank and file. It is the *only* hindrance, the single barrier and objection to the slavery imposed by the powers that be.[29]

It is only "religiosity," the awakening of the heart to its thirst for God, that is the bulwark against all ideology (e.g., Nazism and Leninism). He quotes a text that points to this root cause of horrific genocides as ideology, the "multiplier of crime" (we recall the warning at Fatima about Russia spreading errors):

The Italian journalist, Alberto Ronchey, commenting on Solzhenitsyn, correctly recalled the fact that in Shakespeare, Macbeth was a criminal because he killed seven people: "In order to kill six million, or sixty million, one needs a multiplier: this multiplier of crime is ideology," an all-encompassing conception of the human being fostered by the ruling powers.[30]

And Msgr. Giussani points out that it is the Church alone that is the bulwark that defends the "absolute value of the person" and points to its source in God. Here he also synthesizes what we will see in the next chapter on evolution, that man is "not totally the fruit of the biology of the mother and father, not strictly derived from the biological tradition of mechanical antecedents"; what makes him free is the understanding of the paradox that "freedom is dependence upon God." Freedom is dependence upon God; a paradox, but absolutely clear.

---

[29] Luigi Giussani, *The Religious Sense*, trans. John Zucchi (Montreal: McGill-Queens University Press, 1997), 91-92. See also an Italian description in
http://english.clonline.org/default.asp?id=440&id_n=19380.
[30] Ibid., 92.

The Foundation of Freedom. The Church alone, in its tradition, defends the absolute value of the person, from the first instant of conception to the last moment of old age, however decrepit and useless the individual may be. And what is this defence of the human being's value based on? How is it that man has this right, this absoluteness whereby even if the whole world were to move in one direction he has something within that gives him the right to stay where he is…. The Catechism of Pius X affirms this: "the body is given by the parents, but the soul is infused directly by God"…. It directly depends on the infinite, which makes the whole world. *Only* this hypothesis allows me to proclaim that the world can do what it wants with me, but it cannot conquer, possess, grasp on to me, because I am greater than it is. I am *free*…[31]

B. Concupiscence Compromises Man-Woman Relationship

Given that the dignity of man was being created in the image of Christ and for self-gift (imaging the self-gift among the Trinitarian Persons), it is vital to protect it. Alice von Hildebrand, with wisdom and feminine intuition, offers much light in pointing out the strategy of the most insidious attacks on anthropology, especially against the false femininity that is extreme feminism. We see here the pernicious sources of the confusion in the contemporary crisis in human identity.

Concupiscence

First, von Hildebrand helps us to understand the present tensions between man and woman by looking at *concupiscence*. She distinguishes two aspects in God's design that depend on each other. Calling the creation of man in two genders with its call to love a "divine invention," she notes that his inherent makeup has two dynamics that must be harmonized: body-soul and man-woman. Sin has caused the cravings of the body to burden the soul, and what was noble has degenerated into self-centeredness.

Unless this first dynamic (concupiscence) is conquered, the second dynamic of the harmony between man and woman will be compromised.[32] The human

---

[31] Ibid., 90-91.
[32] Alice von Hildebrand, *Man and Woman: A Divine Invention* (Ave Maria, FL: Sapientia Press, 2010), xiii-xvii.

person is a "double mystery," foreshadowing the Mystery of mysteries, the Incarnation. In addition, von Hildebrand highlights the specific qualities of each gender that were present in the original unity: "We have mentioned briefly some of the characteristics of Adam: nobility, strength, chivalry, and objectivity. Eve, too, was given typically female gems: gentleness, empathy, warmth, devotion, and mystery. Sin ravaged these traits."[33] Great literature especially depicts the degradation of man to a brute and woman to a temptress.[34] As mentioned, the relationship between man and woman is compromised by the internal battle between body and soul: sin separated man from God, wounding his human nature, such that his mind is dulled and will is weakened, heart hardened, and he now suffers and dies.[35] The intimate sphere of love between couples has been damaged by sin and needs the healing of prayer to obtain God's grace. Couples are called to imitate Tobias' action towards Rebecca, in contrast to those of her previous seven husbands, one without lust: "Either God or Satan is in the bridal chamber."[36] She presents two opposite paths: "Where tenderness reigns, concupiscence recedes. Where concupiscence reigns, artificial contraception and abortion inevitably follows."[37] Von Hildebrand points out with remarkable clarity the path for renewal by overcoming concupiscence (spouse as object of pleasure), which converges with John Paul II's thought.

The Ever-Present Temptation of Choosing Self

Alice von Hildebrand treats in an article, given our state of concupiscence, of the recurring temptation to seek self. In the delicate example of the unitive aspect of marriage in the marital embrace, there can be a temptation to seek ecstasy or pleasure, when the first intention should be on self-giving to one's spouse, from which one will enjoy the concomitant pleasure, a helpful distinction for couples living in Christ. She makes the key analogy to Christian life in which we tend to set the goal as "beatitude," our happiness, our going to heaven. We should instead follow Jesus' injunction, "Seek first the kingdom of God and the rest will be given to you." That is, we should

---

[33] Ibid., 11.
[34] Ibid., 11-16.
[35] Ibid., 5.
[36] Ibid., 8-9.
[37] Ibid., 10.

seek first to love God above all things, to fulfill the first Commandment. She gives examples of many saints who loved God above all things, and were overwhelmed with God's graces and consolations, so much so that they would make holy "protest" against the superabundance given them.[38]

C. Discerning the Attacks on the Feminine-Beauty that Endanger the Family

1. Feminism's War on Femininity

Alice von Hildebrand then identifies how marriage and family are being attacked at its heart: femininity and motherhood. She brings her keen insights as a woman and a scholar to the dangers of extreme feminism. In her work, *Man and Woman: A Divine Invention*, she tells us that if we want to kill a person, we aim at the heart, and if we want to "destroy marriage, the family, the Church, and society in general, wage war on femininity," and that is precisely the agenda of contemporary feminism; to destroy all of these elements. She very openly states that this is the agenda of the devil, to be only be fought by supernatural means, namely, faith, prayer, and sacrifice.[39]

She enumerates the thoughts of a number of well-known authors who have openly criticized the feminist movement in its *distorted* form. Cardinal Ratzinger perceives that feminism is no longer Christianity but "another religion"; Chesterton notes that feminism dislikes the chief feminine characteristics, and that there is nothing more opposed to equality than identity; Kierkegaard perceives clearly the great danger: "no base seducer could think out a more dangerous doctrine for woman," and sees on the other hand that "as woman she can be everything for him [man]." Dostoyevsky sees disastrous consequences if the "admirable complementarity" between man and woman is abolished; Solzhenitsyn is very explicit that love without the spiritual side is not love, and that feminism is anti-natural and that it "does destroy the feminine and in so doing it also destroys mankind"; even Nietzsche, though we are right to reject his philosophy, is very frank in seeing feminism as a "masculinization of women"

---

[38] Alice von Hildebrand, "Love, Marriage, Sacrifice: A Reflection on the Meaning of Human Love and Marriage," *Inside the Vatican*, January 2016, 46-47.
[39] Alice von Hildebrand, *Man and Woman*, 19.

and is the enemy of femininity, and notes that "since the French Revolution, woman's influence has decreased in the very proportion that her rights and her pretensions have increased." While woman now apes man in seeking to assert her rights and to be exactly like him, we note that sculptor Adolf von Hildebrand sees the need for woman's feminine touch to develop man's human side. While man becomes inventors, creators, and producers, with a tendency to abstractions, there is a greater need to develop his own being: "through womanhood we develop our most human element into full sensibility; the rest of our being belongs therefore to the outer world."[40]

The war on femininity produces a different world, one of machines and techniques, in which "the feminine element is systematically eliminated." Language becomes more impersonal (e.g., multiple acronyms used in the media), and Gertrud von le Fort notes that "materialism, socialism, futurism have a masculine connotation. They are no longer in the fullest sense organic creations from a totality of polaric powers… Mysteries are no longer needed."[41] She also perceives the great contrast between the soul-less world of great advances in technology and the female element of "the personal, the living, the concrete, the heart."

Von Hildebrand perceives that, while modern technology has brought great wealth, it has also caused several great losses or deprivations: of *deep thought* (Plato teaches that ignorance of highest things causes ruin); of *symbolism*, such as no longer facing East (toward Christ) at Mass, which causes the loss of understanding of transcendent realities; of *nurturing love*, as our society has discovered the great tragedy of a lack of love, with consequences of despair and an inability to commit ("once marriages break down, families become cancerous"); of *silence*, which is the balm of the soul, and which enables *thinking*; of *personal contact*, as in the robotic world of hospitals with machines and scarce human contact, such that the soul is neglected, needing especially the empathy of a woman's heart. We can add that it *discourages vocations* and encouraged nuns to give up their vocations for more "productive" work.[42]

---

[40] Ibid., 19-26.
[41] Gertrud von le Fort, *The Eternal Woman* (Milwaukee: Bruce Publ. Co., 1954), 46, quoted in Alice von Hildebrand, *Man and Woman*, 27.
[42] Alice von Hildebrand, *Man and Woman*, 28-31.

2. War on Motherhood

Alice von Hildebrand recognizes that men and women entering fields traditionally reserved to one as justifiable in some cases. But she also believes that in many cases, "many women in our society have become disciples of Esau, who gave up his birthright for a mess of pottage."[43] With far more career women, the result is that many get married late and either do not have children or have them at a later age, with the result being an imbalance between youth and old age, that has created great economic stress. Here is her beautiful vision of the great vocation of wife and mother:

> Feminists forget that *sub specie aeternitatis* (under the aspect of eternity) to be wife and mother, to create a "home," to "be there," to give love, and to listen to the woes of little ones (and not-so-little ones) who crave for tenderness and affection is like being the sun illuminating a dark world. There are millions of children in our society who are disturbed because they are the victims of a motherless (and fatherless) youth.[44]

Even more striking are József Cardinal Mindszenty's tender words in regard to his mother, who accompanied him through his dark days of imprisonment:

> Motherhood is a call to love and service…. [she] carries life in her bosom, when she gives birth to it, and gives service from morning to night. She sacrifices her patience, love, health and life. She presses you to her heart— she watches over you. She teaches you to talk, to love and laugh. In the cold of winter, she warms your tiny fingers in her hands….
>
> When you lisp "mother" and she answers "My baby," even God must rejoice in His soul… There are sacrifices only a mother can make…. There is no other dignity which can crown woman with greater dignity than the dignity of motherhood, the greatest gift that a woman could receive. By her motherhood she even outranks man.[45]

Von Hildebrand does accept that some have extraordinary callings, such as St. Joan of Arc, but that these are exceptions. Plato wisely notes that truly

---

[43] Ibid., 32.
[44] Ibid., 33.
[45] József Cardinal Mindszenty, *The Mother* (Post Falls, ID: Lepanto Press, 2009), 55, quoted in Alice von Hildebrand, *Man and Woman*, 101-102.

worthy leaders will not be anxious to head the state, but rather they "will take the office as a stern necessity," that they should not covet the task.[46]

3. War on Beauty

Alice von Hildebrand also perceives a war on beauty. Few women are poets, but many great poets have been inspired by beauty, such as Dante, who has composed perhaps the greatest work of Catholic poetry in *Divine Comedy* that was inspired by Beatrice. In addition, physical perception of beauty is important for our spiritual life, according to Plato, because we are made of body and soul. Emphasizing the importance of exposing children to beauty, Plato writes:

> Then will our youth dwell in a land of health, amid fair sights and sounds and receive the good in everything; and beauty, the effluence of fair works, shall flow into the eye and ear, like a health-giving breeze from a purer region, and insensibly draw the soul from earliest years into likeness and sympathy with the beauty of reason.[47]

Von Hildebrand notes specifically that "modern architecture and modern churches have no soul," that we are practising "the cult of ugliness." There is great danger in getting used to ugliness, and "it is saddening that the danger either is not recognized, nor properly diagnosed, or underestimated."[48]

4. War on Spiritual Ecology (Sexless and Efficient Society)

Somewhat linked with this lack of beauty is also a lack of warmth of the heart, where the danger is also great: a war on spiritual ecology. The balance between masculinity and femininity gives a "spiritual ecology." Ratzinger points out that we have embraced the "cult" of efficiency (masculine), one that is stripped of holiness. For Von Hildebrand, we speak of ecological sins, *but much more dangerous and serious is the war waged upon femininity*:

> To create a "sexless" society is to destroy the ecological design of the human being and will inevitably lead to religious, moral, psychological, and physical disasters.

---

[46] Ibid., 34.
[47] Plato, *The Republic*, no. 401d, quoted in Alice von Hildebrand, *Man and Woman*, 36.
[48] Alice von Hildebrand, *Man and Woman*, 36.

To advocate new families made up of two fathers or two mothers must, to use the strong language of Léon Bloy, make the stars bellow. It is metaphysically impossible for two men or two women to complete each other, for the very plain reason that they have the same sex.

A denial of the basic metaphysical truth found in Genesis is an act of rebellion that is bound to have tragic consequences. Admirable as true friendship between women or men can be, it can never be a substitute for the admirable complementarity that God established between Adam and Eve. To deny this obvious truth is an abomination. We shall pay the price by creating a society in which madness is praised as a sign of "progress," the fruit of "scientific" discoveries— a society in which madness is politically correct.[49]

5. Beauty of the Supernatural

Yet another weakness is that original sin has blinded us to the beauty of the supernatural— a "supernatural blindness: a triumph of secularism."[50] Secular values, such as strength, physical beauty, success, power, have taken pride of place, and the slogan of the new aristocracy is "self-fulfillment." A key mark of secularism is its denial of any transcendence: it understands the world as the only valid reality, and consequently, "producing, inventing, accomplishing, improving, and changing seem more important than 'being.'"[51] This is at loggerheads with the Christian insight that producing is not what matters most, but what one is as a person.[52] In *The Lord*, Romano Guardini confirms this truth:

> Christianity has always placed the life struggling for inner truth and ultimate love above that intent on exterior action, even the most courageous and excellent. It has always valued silence more highly than words, purity of intent more than success, the magnanimity of love more than the effect of labor.[53]

---

[49] Ibid., 38.
[50] Ibid., 39.
[51] Ibid.
[52] Ibid., 40.
[53] Roman Guardini, *The Lord* (Washington, DC: Regnery Publ. Inc., 1996), 227.

6. *Mary, the Model, is the Solution*

We can add here that Alice von Hildebrand points to Mary (with her feminine dimension) as the model for, and in a sense *the solution* to, the problem. She notes perspicaciously that feminism arose in Protestant countries, convinced that this happened because they lost "a precious pearl: the devotion to the Mother of the Savior." Sigrid Undset's insight follows the same logic: that the terrible consequence of losing Mary as their role model is that they will inevitably lose the particular dignity of the feminine, and this is also seconded by John Saward.[54] Mary, with her purity, which is rooted in a living before the presence of God, can be a bridge that will bring reconciliation between men and women. Having given herself totally to God, her fecundity is such that as a virgin she has become the Mother of all. Mary is also a model because of her matchless humility, through which she has been raised higher than the angels, and teaches us her life of adoration and service. She also teaches us to be vessels of devotion, to have reverence. When Athens enjoyed its peak of greatness, Plato wrote that "Reverence was our queen and mistress." He pointed out that history teaches that lack of reverence leads to moral decadence.

Alice von Hildebrand noted the great insight that in Eastern Europe it was the *babushki* (grandmothers) who kept the faith burning during atheistic communism, as stated by Paul Evdokimov. The role of women is essentially *religious,* "their mission is related to eternity," when the works of men will be burned (2 Pet 3:10): "Only those wilfully blind can fail to perceive that the devil has achieved his greatest triumph since the victory in the Garden of Eden by convincing women of their inferiority and waging war on maternity."[55] An added benefit of going through Mary is, as St. Bernard points out, that the devil fears Mary more than he fears God, because of her humility, for which she has great power, "terrible as an army with banners" (Song of Songs 6:10). Furthermore, while she is not a theologian, it is Mary who destroys all heresies: "Rejoice, Virgin Mary! You alone in the entire

---

[54] A. H. Winsnes, *Sigrid Undset: A Study in Christian Realism* (New York: Sheed and Ward, 1953), 167; and John Saward, "Thanks for the Feminine," in *The Enemy Within: Radical Feminism in the Christian Churches* (Wicken, Milton Keynes, UK: Family Publications, 1990), 128, both quoted in Alice von Hildebrand, *Man and Woman*, 82.
[55] Alice von Hildebrand, *Man and Woman*, 92.

world have destroyed all heresy."[56] It is Mary, united with Truth in her womb and in her life, who will lead us to truth. But Mary can provide much more that even this (see below).

Synthesis

In seeking to establish a "new christocentric anthropology" by linking John Paul II's *Theology of the Body* with christology, since Mary already links ecclesiology to christology, we might incorporate a mediating role to Mary in theological anthropology because of the following elements.

First, Vatican II taught that Jesus and Mary are "indissolubly linked," and the Council Fathers set Mary within *Lumen gentium*, pointing to the truth that the Church is Marian in her essence.

Second, Charles Journet points out that, in the time of Christ's coming, the Church was only in Mary and the hierarchical powers are all centered in Christ Himself; thus the whole Christ was only Christ and Mary. The Church would never be holier, as a concentration of grace in our Lady gave the infant Church a complexion as a Marian Church.[57]

Third, Louis de Montfort, in *Secret of Mary*, cites Augustine as calling Mary the "living mould of God" (n. 16), teaching that "Mary is the great mould of God, fashioned by the Holy Spirit to give human nature to a Man who is God by the hypostatic union, and to fashion through grace men who are like to God" (n. 17).

Fourth, we can turn to Mary's vital role in the thoughts of Adrienne von Speyr and Hans Urs von Balthasar: (i) for von Speyr, Christ prepared His mother, so that, as she gave birth to and formed Him, she would generate and form His mystical body in her "form"; and (ii) von Balthasar describes in his Marian Principle that Mary mirrors the "feminine" form of Christ's receptivity to the Father. The Son's role is feminine before the Father's masculine role; receptivity is the height of holiness. If the goal of

---

[56] Office of the Blessed Virgin, seventh antiphon of Matins, in Guéranger, *Liturgical Year*, feast of Our Lady, Help of Christians (May 24): 8:538, quoted in Alice von Hildebrand, *Man and Woman*, 93.
[57] Charles Journet, *The Meaning of Grace* (New York: Scepter Publishers, 1996), 105.

anthropology is to become *ipse Christus*, we ought to be formed in Mary. Both these elements are treated in Chapter 14, "Mary, Morning Star."

As a first step toward a "'daring new' christocentric theological anthropology," we began with John Paul II's timely *Theology of the Body*, the foundation that is to be completed by his christology. An alternative path is to have recourse to Hans Urs von Balthasar's far more developed christology, since "Balthasar aims at nothing less than a christocentric revolution in theology."[58] That is, building upon the rich insights of Pope John Paul II's *Theology of the Body*, one could in the second step to incorporate christology consider looking to Balthasar's well-developed christocentric theological anthropology, where he depicts Christ as at once the form of the Father and of man.

---

[58] Aidan Nichols, *Scribe of the Kingdom: Essays on Theology and Culture*, vol. 2 (London: Sheed & Ward, 1994), 24.

CHAPTER 3

BRIDGING FAITH AND SCIENCE IN EVOLUTION

As believers we answer, with the creation account and with John, that in the beginning is reason. In the beginning is freedom. Hence it is good to be a human person. It is not the case that in the expanding universe, at a late stage, in some tiny corner of the cosmos, there evolved randomly some species of living being capable of reasoning and of trying to find rationality within creation, or to bring rationality into it. If man were merely a random product of evolution in some place on the margins of the universe, then his life would make no sense or might even be a chance of nature. *But no, Reason is there at the beginning: creative, divine Reason.* And because it is Reason, it also created freedom; and because freedom can be abused, there also exist forces harmful to creation. Hence a thick black line, so to speak, has been drawn across the structure of the universe and across the nature of man. *But despite this contradiction, creation itself remains good, life remains good, because at the beginning is good Reason, God's creative love. Hence the world can be saved.*[1] (Pope Benedict XVI, emphasis added)

Harmony between Faith and Science in Evolution

God created the universe in Christ as template, and thus it reflects His two-fold human and divine structure. As Augustine exhorts us to honour the twofold nature of Christ (*Commentary on John* 78, 3), so we should honour the two-fold nature of His creation. Any apparent conflict between faith and science in regard to evolution (e.g., the erroneous belief that the Church interprets the 7 days of creation in Genesis 1 literally) compromises this two-fold structure of Christ's creation and also constitutes a formidable roadblock to the credibility of the Christian faith and thus a hindrance to the work of the new evangelization. In the contemporary context, we wish to examine evolution because this cosmological horizon impacts all human scientific endeavors today (worldview of Western universities today) and because evolution finds parallels in other domains (e.g., salvation history). There is

---

[1] Benedict XVI, Easter Vigil Homily (Rome, April 23, 2011), Vatican.va, accessed August 18, 2018, http://w2.vatican.va/content/benedict-xvi/en/homilies/2011/documents/hf_ben-xvi_hom_20110423_veglia-pasquale.html.

already a formidable body of literature discussing the intersection of the two domains[2]; this chapter seeks to serve only as an introduction to bridging the domain of evolution and faith for evangelization.

This chapter has three steps: (I) <u>Framework</u>: establishing the truth that there are two autonomous domains of faith and science but that they need each other (Schönborn, Kasper); (II) <u>Mediating Link</u>: restoring reason (including hellenization of the faith, final causality) as the link between faith and science, as reason can then also be linked to the *Logos* in Jn 1 (Ratzinger, Gilson); and (III) <u>Working Hypothesis</u>: Teilhard de Chardin's vision as a possible Christian synthesis of evolution. An examination of the relation between the two orders ought to restore a sense of the magnificence of God's creation.

I. The Church's Vision of Faith and Evolution

Church Promotes Study of Evolution within Context of Harmony of Faith and Evolution

The Church views evolutionary processes as a substantial scientific theory that should be studied, but what she rejects are atheistic evolutionary theories. Evolution posits that the universe is not as it was from the beginning of its existence, but has evolved. As Stephen Barr, a theoretical physicist, affirmed: "Catholic theology has never really had a quarrel with the idea that the present species of plants and animals are the result of a long process of evolution— or with the idea that this process has unfolded according to natural laws."[3] This is clear if one consults Catholic sources, like the 1909 *Catholic Encyclopaedia*, a position reiterated by Pope Pius XII's *Humani generis*.[4]

We note that John Paul II wrote in a letter to the Pontifical Academy of Sciences that "New knowledge leads to the recognition of the theory of evolution as more than a hypothesis. It is indeed remarkable that this theory has been progressively accepted by researchers following a series of discoveries in various fields of knowledge." The 1994 *Catechism of the Catholic*

---

[2] A good introduction to the contemporary landscape is Avery Dulles' "God and Evolution," *First Things*, (October 2007); a solid introduction to contemporary theories is Robert J. Spitzer's *New Proofs for the Existence of God* (Grand Rapids, MI: Wm. B. Eerdmans Publ. Co., 2010).
[3] Stephen M. Barr, "The Design of Evolution," *First Things* 156 (October 2005): 9.
[4] Ibid.

Church itself gives a positive commentary on evolution[5], as does Pope Francis' recent *Laudato Si'* on environmental concerns for the planet. The Church has remained open to the possibility of an evolution of the human body, but maintains the immediate creation of the soul.[6] Within the Roman Catholic Church, there has been increasing attention given to an examination of the place of evolution in creation. There have been several recent Symposiums and studies held in Rome. Along with Pope Francis' encyclical, *Laudato Si'*, one should take note especially of his 2014 address to the Pontifical Academy of Sciences, in which he spoke strongly for the reality of evolution.[7]

Thus, what we have are two autonomous domains of faith and science, which also complement each other. Each specializes in its own domain, but must respect the limits of its methodology and expertise. For example, faith cannot do research on finding a cure for cancer or investigate the evolutionary process, which is the domain of science; and science is unable to see the human soul through a microscope, know the ethical limits of research (e.g., cloning), or contemplate the far more important object of the Creator God, as Christianity does through faith, Revelation, and theology. Thus the two domains need each other and must be brought into relation.

To reinforce this point, let us employ an image of the orders representing two arrows to synthesize our vision. If there is a Creator God, who provides

[5] "The question about the origins of the world and of man has been the object of many scientific studies which have splendidly enriched our knowledge of the age and dimensions of the cosmos, the development of life-forms and the appearance of man. These discoveries invite us to even greater admiration for the greatness of the Creator, prompting us to give him thanks for all his works and for the understanding and wisdom he gives to scholars and researchers" (CCC, n. 283).

[6] This position has been reiterated both by Pope Pius XII in *Humani generis* and by Pope John Paul II in his widely noted message to the Pontifical Academy of Sciences on Oct.er 22, 1996.

[7] (1) The SCDF, led by its Prefect, Cardinal Ratzinger, hosted the 1985 Symposium, *Evolutionism and Christianity*; (2) Pope John Paul II sponsored a week of study on science and religion at Castel Gandolfo from September 21 to 26, 1987; (3) In 2004, the International Theological Commission published *Communion and Stewardship: Human Persons Created in the Image of God*, which touches upon the subject; (4) Conference with Pope Benedict XVI at Castel Gandolfo in 2006: *Creation and Evolution*; (5) Symposium at Gregorian University (2009): III STOQ (Science, Technology, and Ontological Quest— Pontifical Council of Culture in collaboration with Roman Universities) International Conference: *Biological Evolution, Facts and Theories: A Critical Appraisal 150 Years after "The Origin of Species."* Other symposia have followed as well.

both Revelation (divine mysteries) and the human intellect (for investigating the universe's mysteries), then Revelation is like an arrow that descends from God and science is like an arrow that ascends to God. And since there can be only one truth (from the one God, who is Truth), then both arrows must meet.

And how do the arrows meet: through science using reason to ascend, and theology applied to Revelation also by reason to descend, but with faith ("faith seeking understanding"). And the key issue is whether or not one understands reason as limited to the empirical or in its fullness as past scholars have done (e.g., Aristotle, Plato). For the latter group, true reason should lead us to the divine.

Real Problem is a Rationalistic Ideology that Eliminates the Transcendent

Christoph Cardinal Schönborn's address at the November 2008 Pontifical Academy of Sciences meetings reaffirms the Catholic teaching that there is no conflict between the possibility of evolution and creation. The true problem is rather a "conflict between two diverse concepts of man and his rationality, between the Christian vision and a rationalism that pretends to reduce man to the biological dimension."[8] For science does not answer the greater philosophical question of origin nor respond to the need to know "that man is not the fruit of chaos, but that he 'has been thought of,' 'wanted' and 'loved' by the Creator."[9]

On another occasion, Schönborn made the distinction between evolutionism and the scientific theory of evolution: evolutionism is an ideology, where people such as Marx and Engels find the scientific foundation for their materialist theory,[10] as Louis Bouyer explains Father Stanley Jaki's insight:

---

[8] Christoph Schönborn, "Pope Benedict XVI on 'Creation and Evolution,'" (paper presented at Pontifical Academy of Sciences, Rome, November 2008), Pontifical Academy of Sciences website, accessed August 18, 2018,
http://www.casinapioiv.va/content/dam/accademia/pdf/acta20/acta20-schoenbornen.pdf.
[9] Ibid.
[10] Christoph Schönborn, "Cardinal Schönborn Proposes Evolution Debate" (Address at Meeting of Friendship Among Peoples, organized by the Communion and Liberation Movement in Rimini, Italy, August 25, 2006), Zenit.org, accessed October 30, 2015, http://www.zenit.org/article-16800?l=english.

As Father Jaki has recently emphasized in his Gifford Lectures, if at first sight the vision of the world provided by modern science seems to leave no place for God, his angels, or our souls— for anything spiritual or hypercosmic— this vision and science itself can be understood only if we remember that science necessarily assumes something beyond or outside its reach.

The transcendent element supports the coherence of the entire scientific undertaking, which would falter and dissolve irreparably if it were to persist in ignoring this silent but radiant presence behind everything scrutinized by science. It is a presence that also underlies, even more directly, the scientist's own capacity for fruitful endeavor. One may suspect that the repeatedly alleged "death of God" portends the imminent death of countless men undermined in their humanity by their excessive and exclusive self-confidence.[11]

A. *Communion and Stewardship*: Human Persons Created in the Image of God

Stephen Barr recommends the International Theological Commission's (ITC) *Communion and Stewardship: Human Persons Created in the Image of God* as a significant point of reference. One section, "Science and Stewardship of Knowledge," provides three valuable building blocks as a preliminary foundation. But the primary contribution here is the clarification of how evolution involving randomness can be reconciled with God's necessary action.

1. The Church Promotes the Study of Evolution but Rejects Atheistic Theories

While condemning a "discredited concordism" (a facile, superficial reconciliation), the document begins with a clear affirmation of our responsibility to examine evolution in the context of faith: "Christians have the responsibility to locate the modern scientific understanding of the universe within the context of the theology of creation" (n. 62). This statement implicitly draws upon the Church's long-held vision and mission

---

[11] Louis Bouyer, *Cosmos: The World and the Glory of God* (Petersham, MA: St. Bede's Publications, 1988), xi-xii. Fr. Jaki was a distinguished theologian and physicist, and a leading contributor in the philosophy and history of science, particularly in their relationship to Christianity.

to work for the harmony between faith and science. Yet, while the document notes the Church's acknowledgement of the value of scientific discoveries and openness to examining theories (such as the "big bang"), it is not a blanket approval of all current theories, pointing out ones incompatible with the faith. For example, it notes that Pope Pius XII's encyclical *Humani generis* rejected several theories of evolution that were "materialist, reductionist and spiritualist" and incompatible with the Catholic faith. This statement on John Paul II's message is more incisive:

> It follows that the message of Pope John Paul II cannot be read as a blanket approbation of all theories of evolution, including those of a neo-Darwinian provenance which explicitly deny to divine providence any truly causal role in the development of life in the universe. Mainly concerned with evolution as it "involves the question of man," however, Pope John Paul's message is specifically critical of materialistic theories of human origins and insists on the relevance of philosophy and theology for an adequate understanding of the "ontological leap" to the human which cannot be explained in purely scientific terms. The Church's interest in evolution thus focuses particularly on "the conception of man" who, as created in the image of God, "cannot be subordinated as a pure means or instrument either to the species or to society." (n. 64)

John Paul II "insists on the relevance of philosophy and theology for an adequate understanding of the 'ontological leap' to the human which cannot be explained in purely scientific terms." There are two limitations mentioned here regarding the limits of science: that "the human... cannot be explained in purely scientific terms"; and science is unable to explain the problem of the "ontological" or "macro" leaps in evolution.

The document already makes a valuable contribution: evolution cannot be explained without divine action, and philosophy and theology must be incorporated.

2. God Ordains Events Either by Necessity or by Contingency

Second, we come to the section of most interest in *Communion and Stewardship* n. 69, that addresses the key issue of our time: the relation between contingency and divine action. It is a basic tenet of "neo-Darwinian" theories of evolution that evolution occurs by pure contingency or randomness (chance). The document categorically argues that a position holding that "there can be no place in it for divine providential causality" is based upon a "misunderstanding of the nature of divine causality." It turns to St. Thomas Aquinas' clarification in this matter, that contingency can happen as a result of God's ordaining causality:

> The effect of divine providence is not only that things should happen somehow, but that they should happen either by necessity or by contingency. Therefore, whatsoever divine providence ordains to happen infallibly and of necessity happens infallibly and of necessity; and that happens from contingency, which the divine providence conceives to happen from contingency (*Summa Theologiae*, I, q. 22, a. 4, ad 1).

Properly understood, the discernment of a possible "incursion" by divine causality within contingency is beyond the powers of observation of the realm of science:

> In the Catholic perspective, neo-Darwinians who adduce random genetic variation and natural selection as evidence that the process of evolution is absolutely unguided are straying beyond what can be demonstrated by science. Divine causality can be active in a process that is both contingent and guided. Any evolutionary mechanism that is contingent can only be contingent because God made it so.[12] (n. 69)

The document bases this upon Thomistic categories of being and causality: if all things have a First Cause and thereby participate in God's being, "It necessarily follows that all things, inasmuch as they participate in existence, must likewise be subject to divine providence" (*ST* I, q. 22, a. 2).

3. Evolution Fits within Scholastic Theology's "Secondary Causality"

Third, if God is active in creation, what categories does this document employ to indicate God's action in evolution? Here too the document turns to another Scholastic category, "secondary causes" (e.g., parents' cooperating

---

[12] ITC, *Communion and Stewardship: Human Persons Created in the Image of God*, n. 69, vatican.va, http://www.vatican.va/roman_curia/congregations/cfaith/cti_documents/rc_con_cfaith_d oc_20040723_communion-stewardship_en.html.

in procreating children). For example, beyond participating in God's being (His *esse*), human beings also participate by being preserved in existence and also participate in God's collaboration in every action they do (*conservatio* and *concursus divinus* respectively):

> God is the cause not only of *existence* but also the cause of *causes*. God's action does not displace or supplant the activity of creaturely causes, but enables them to act according to their natures and, nonetheless, to bring about the ends he intends.

> In freely willing to create and conserve the universe, God wills to activate and to sustain in act all those secondary causes whose activity contributes to the unfolding of the natural order which he intends to produce. Through the activity of natural causes, God causes to arise those conditions required for the emergence and support of living organisms, and, furthermore, for their reproduction and differentiation. (n. 68)

Synthesis: Key Question of Design as Supporting Faith in Creation

The ITC's document proves valuable for the most difficult aspect to negotiate in the domain of evolution, namely, the thesis of pure randomness (chance, contingency). This tension became a flashpoint in the debate between Fr. George Coyne (former director of the Vatican Observatory) and Christoph Cardinal Schönborn of Vienna.

Fr. Coyne took exception to an editorial by Cardinal Schönborn for the *New York Times* which appeared to espouse "intelligent design" (a theory promoted by the Discovery Institute). For Fr. Coyne, intelligent design is neither science nor is it a proof of the existence of a Creator God.

In defending his position, Cardinal Schönborn quoted Fr. Coyne as stating that randomness fell outside of even God's providence. While we do not wish to enter the merits of the two figures' positions, we do need to establish parameters for the discussion of evolution.[13] Fr. Coyne's position argues

---

[13] George Coyne's position can be found in George V. Coyne, *Faith and Knowledge: Towards a New Meeting of Science and Theology*, ed. Gustav Teres (Città del Vaticano: Libreria Editrice Vaticana, 2007). Christoph Schönborn's response can be seen in his book, *Chance Or Purpose? Creation, Evolution and a Rational Faith*, ed. Hubert Philipp (San Francisco: Ignatius Press, 2007).

correctly that the presence of apparent design, an "intelligent design," cannot be adduced as proof for the existence of a Creator God. Empirical indications do not make one believe in a Creator God; only the infused gift of faith can lead one to believe— this is the domain of Revelation and faith.

Yet, on the side of Cardinal Schönborn's position, the ITC document, without alluding to this debate, removes any doubt through Aquinas' logic that contingency falls within the Creator's providence. The fact that the ITC document brushes by this debate points us in the direction of what matters: support for faith affirmations regarding creation and providence:

> Although there is scientific debate about the degree of purposiveness or design operative and empirically observable in these developments, they have de facto favored the emergence and flourishing of life. Catholic theologians can see in such reasoning support for the affirmation entailed by faith in divine creation and divine providence. (n. 68)

Our entire Catholic Tradition points in this direction. For example, the apostle Paul teaches, "For what can be known about God is plain to them, because God has shown it to them. Ever since the creation of the world his eternal power and divine nature, invisible though they are, have been understood and seen through the things he has made" (Rom 1:19-20).

We even find the idea of the Trinity's fingerprints on creation in Augustine (e.g., Trinity's creating results in the three-fold personal faculties of mind, will, memory).

This raises the whole question of the *analogia entis* ("analogy of being"), in which Hans Urs von Balthasar defended the Catholic position, diverging from the thought of Karl Barth, who denied any possibility of natural knowledge of God. In this conclusion, we have just surmounted the greatest concern: that evolution is compatible with creation.

B. Walter Cardinal Kasper: Six Points of Historical Development for Linking the Two Orders

Adding to this foundation that the ITC document provided, Walter Cardinal Kasper provides an invaluable overview, with a historical development that sheds light on the contemporary state of discussion. In his article, "The Logos Character of Reality," Cardinal Kasper uses six points to defend the "rationality" (role of reason) of our world and history and the necessity of linking of faith and science.[14]

First, he makes note that in recent times *the fathers of modern science were deeply religious men*, including Nicolas Copernicus, Johannes Kepler, Galileo Galilei, Albert Einstein, Werner Heisenberg, and many others, and saw traces of the divine Spirit giving order to the world.

Second, *rational scientific faith developed on the basis of the biblical faith of creation*.[15] What we conclude from this is that faith had always been the milieu of science, and that rationalism is a foreign virus.

Third, Cardinal Kasper observes a new rapprochement in our times. Since the middle of the twentieth-century, there has been a positive turn of events whereby both the natural sciences and theology came to see that they were operating at *two different levels*, putting to rest many conflicts: sciences dealing with the "how" and theology dealing with the "why." This is a significant step forward and consoling to those who believe in a Creator God.

Fourth, with this rapprochement, he then makes a critical point for our chapter thesis for moving forward: given the distinction between the two orders of faith and science, *there cannot be a lack of mutual relation*:

> Such an indifference would make faith in God a luxury without inner-worldly consequences. Liberal and existential Protestant theology drew this false conclusion. It withdrew from the world and reduced, or rather concentrated, faith in creation on the existential experience and concern. Yet, through such an immunization strategy, God became worldless and the world godless. That the world was created by God cannot, however, be simply without consequence for the way the world functions.[16]

Cardinal Kasper, with keen insight, raises the alarm about the dire fallout should Christianity choose to sever the relation between faith and evolution.

---

[14] Walter Kasper, "The Logos Character of Reality," *Communio* 15 (Fall 1988): 274-284.
[15] Ibid., 274-275.
[16] Ibid., 279.

The dropping of the "total Christian-theological interpretation" for the universe would leave a void, such that "one almost necessarily had to expand natural-scientific knowledge into a philosophy of nature and a world-view."[17] Because faith has abdicated its presence in the world of science, science came to explain everything, and evolution became the comprehensive paradigm for explaining the world: from the "big bang," to the origin of human life. But the difficulty is that these new scientific interpretations, though more refined than the old mechanistic theories, run counter to the Christian faith in creation, and a truce cannot simply be maintained. Cardinal Kasper strongly urges that we do not seek a God on the margins or in the gaps of our knowledge, but rather "in the middle of life and of the world, and to find him, as the mystics say, in all things."[18] He notes that in the world there is both contingency in God's creation in His freedom, and yet through His free creation, there is also great order and wonder and faithfulness on God's part. But again, he warns against separating the two orders, a harmony that the Nominalists have threatened. We recall that Vatican II's *Gaudium et spes* exhorted us to engage and be in the midst of the world. It is here that Teilhard de Chardin comes to the fore, engaging the world of science.

Fifth, he suggests the solution provided by Henry Newman for the justification of faith: "According to him, probability is the guide through life. Many probabilities gain an ultimate certainty in the light of faith, which then far transcends the logical power of our inferences."[19] Cardinal Kasper concludes:

> The relation between contingency and regularity is the basic problem of today's natural sciences. Natural laws merely stipulate general lines according to which something will take place, not however how it will happen in an individual case. The result is that the entire evolutionary process is, in spite of all necessity, extremely improbable. For that reason, the order of the world also remains ultimately wonderful precisely for the natural scientist.[20]

---

[17] Ibid.
[18] Ibid., 281.
[19] Ibid., 283.
[20] Ibid.

The theory of Relativity and Quantum theory both point to the necessity of considering the subject's standpoint: "the theological interpretation of the world is thoroughly analogous to the general reflections of today's scientific theory." The believer has no fear and wears no blinders; "the one who believes sees more."[21]

Sixth, Cardinal Kasper notes the historical separation of rationality of nature from the Creator as Reason (*Logos*): the world has order (reason) precisely because its Creator is Reason. The rationality of creation in the Genesis texts includes the creation of the world through a word (*logos*), "he spoke and it came to be," and through separation out of *chaos* comes a cosmos with *divine ordering* (i.e., reason). This rationality (order) of creating can be found in many other biblical texts (e.g., Psalms 8; 19; 96; 104; 135; 148). The New Testament deepens these insights by identifying the logos (word, meaning, order) with the eternal *Logos (Son)*: the world was created in, through, and for Him. The Church Fathers also took up the rational view of the world, but this was already anticipated in the ancient Greek world (e.g., Plato's *Timaeus*). *The Church had to fight over and over again to protect this rationality and goodness of matter, especially against Gnosticism.* "The rationality of reality is thus a Christian thesis and a Christian heritage."[22]

Summing up, the reversal that has come to pass requires consideration of a complex number of causes, including the trial of Galileo and Darwin's theory. God has since become a "dispensable hypothesis," and one could approach Him *deistically* (created but not involved with the world), or *pantheistically* (the divine submerged in the universe); *in both cases He becomes irrelevant or insignificant.*

Here, Cardinal Kasper has anticipated the reader's next burning question: having seen that randomness can be reconciled with creation, what could possibly constitute the all-important link for a rapprochement between theologians and evolutionary scientists? The role of reason is now more fully developed in the thought of Ratzinger.

---

[21] Ibid., 283-284.
[22] Ibid., 277.

II. Linking Faith and Evolution through "Reason" (Logos)

A. Cardinal Ratzinger Introduces Reason as Mediating Link

In a lecture delivered at the Sorbonne University in Paris in 1999 and subsequently published in 2004 as *Truth and Tolerance*, Cardinal Ratzinger, like Pope John Paul II and Cardinal Kasper, rejected evolution as the exclusive *philosophia universalis*, the basic philosophy that explains all reality without recourse to any other form of knowledge. But where does that leave us, where exactly are we located in the evolution spectrum? Like Pope John Paul II, Cardinal Ratzinger accepts the reality of micro-evolution, adaptations that take place primarily with non-rational creatures at the microscopic or microcosmic level, but affirms that there is not yet empirical evidence for macro-evolution, pointing to the work of Szathmary and Maynard Smith (two supporters of an all-embracing theory of evolution, but who deny the existence of any such evidence). That is, we may be getting too far ahead of ourselves in presupposing a vast evolutionary enterprise when substantial scientific evidence (missing links) is not yet at hand. Now we can address more fully the pivotal question allegedly raised by Fr. Coyne. Against the universally-held position in evolution of pure randomness, Cardinal Ratzinger introduces the principal category for bringing science and faith into harmony— "reason"— and then links it to the divine Logos. He centers the spotlight directly on the illogical argument that reason or rationality can derive from irrationality, which is itself a denial of rationality:

> The question is whether reason, or rationality, stands at the beginning of all things and is grounded in the basis of all things or not. The question is whether reality originated on the basis of chance and necessity (or, as Popper says, in agreement with Butler, on the basis of luck and cunning) and, thus, from what is irrational; that is, whether reason, being a chance by-product of irrationality and floating in an ocean of irrationality, is ultimately just as meaningless; or whether the principle that represents the fundamental conviction of Christian faith and of its philosophy remains true: "In principio erat Verbum" — at the beginning of all things stands the creative power of reason.[23]

---

[23] Joseph Ratzinger, *Truth and Tolerance* (San Francisco: Ignatius Press, 2004), 181.

The consequences of such a position are bleak. If the universe is a product of pure randomness, then the universe has no inherent structure, meaning, or purpose. This implies that life has no truths, morality, or destiny, which in reality does not correspond to our experience. On the positive side, if there is reason, structure, and purpose, it implies a "First Mover," who embodies these elements.

Now Cardinal Ratzinger makes a key second step, towards the Logos and to love. Christianity is *enlightened* because it maintains the primacy of reason, which is why it was "the obvious choice" in the ancient world. Here is the progression: the strength of the Christian faith is found in the rational view, then ethics within this vision, and finally *the concrete primacy of love, especially of a Love that suffers with us*. Cardinal Ratzinger's use of reason allows him to go the further step beyond reason *to love and to the Logos* that corresponds to our heart's desire:

> The orientation of religion toward a rational view of reality as a whole, ethics as a part of this vision, and its concrete application under the primacy of love became closely associated. The primacy of the Logos and the primacy of love proved to be identical. The Logos was seen to be, not merely a mathematical reason at the basis of all things, but a creative love taken to the point of becoming sympathy, suffering with the creature. The cosmic aspect of religion, which reverences the Creator in the power of being, and its existential aspect, the question of redemption, merged together and became one.[24]

The fundamental argument here is that *irrationality cannot give rise to rationality*. In his address to the plenary meeting of the Pontifical Academy of Sciences on October 31, 2008, he uses a beautiful analogy: "to evolve" is "to unroll a scroll" (think of Jesus unrolling a scroll at Nazareth), and that Galileo also viewed creation as a book that God wrote, as He wrote Scripture. There is inner logic, mathematics, phenomena, intelligible events, all that speak of the foundational presence of God.[25] And because a Creative Reason must exist,

---

[24] Ibid. 182.
[25] Pope Benedict XVI, "Address of His Holiness Benedict XVI to Members of the Pontifical Academy of Sciences on the Occasion of their Plenary Assembly" (Rome, October 31, 2008), vatican.va, accessed August 18, 2018, http://w2.vatican.va/content/benedict-

we can move to God's creative love (motive for creating), and the world can be saved: "Hence we can and must place ourselves on the side of reason, freedom and love."

As Pope Benedict XVI, he reiterated this truth of truths in the 2011 Easter Vigil homily— *we are loved into creation* (irrationality from pure randomness destroys this vision):

> If man were merely a random product of evolution in some place on the margins of the universe, then his life would make no sense or might even be a chance of nature. But no, Reason is there at the beginning: creative, divine Reason. And because it is Reason, it also created freedom... But despite this contradiction, creation itself remains good, life remains good, because at the beginning is good Reason, God's creative love. Hence the world can be saved. Hence we can and must place ourselves on the side of reason, freedom and love – on the side of God who loves us so much that he suffered for us, that from his death there might emerge a new, definitive and healed life. (partially quoted earlier)

To understand our present impoverished situation without reason in its fullness, it is helpful to retrace the historical origins and steps that have led to it. Cardinal Schönborn delineates this development: the origins with Bacon (Mechanism) and Descartes (Rationalism) were unified by Newton's physics, and were completed in the living organisms by the random mutations and chance of Darwin's theory. It is possible that the origins may go back further, to the Nominalists and their pioneers, who loosened the bonds between the Creator and the universe (see Leo Scheffczyk). *These misdirections or deviations have deprived us of "reason" in its fullness and ultimately of the Logos.*[26]

We must address two specific obstacles from the path toward full reason: three steps of de-hellenization in theology along with irrationality that distances us from the Word and love; and the removal of final causality from empirical science.

---

xvi/en/speeches/2008/october/documents/hf_ben-xvi_spe_20081031_academy-sciences.html.

[26] Christoph Schönborn, Foreword, in Étienne Gilson, *From Aristotle to Darwin and Back Again: A Journey in Final Causality, Species, and Evolution* (San Francisco, Ignatius Press, 2009).

B. First Obstacle: De-hellenization

Pope Benedict XVI points to the consequence of limiting reason to *the empirical by uprooting Greek philosophy*— a de-hellenization. Pope Benedict XVI's address to representatives of science at the University of Regensburg in 2006 provides us with a key to proceeding forward. The key and controlling statement was taken from Byzantine emperor Manuel II Paleologus to an educated Persian against conversion by violence: "not to act in accordance with reason is contrary to God's nature." But the foundation is the *necessary encounter between biblical faith and Hellenism, between faith and reason*, noting the call to Peter by a Macedonian to come to bring the faith and the need to translate the Old Testament into Greek, the Septuagint. Pope Benedict XVI's pointing out the necessity of Greek philosophy is a vital insight for the renewal between faith and evolution.

With great acuity, Pope Benedict XVI outlines *three steps* of de-hellenization in Christian history that have been inimical to the acting by reason: (i) the Middle Ages, beginning with *voluntarism* of Duns Scotus, separated reason from faith, by declaring that God's omnipotence makes possible our acting against reason; (ii) the eighteenth and nineteenth centuries, beginning with Adolph Harnack, proclaimed the need to *return to the pristine message of the Gospel* by removing the accretions to theology, like that of Hellenism, and instead ending up in a certain moralism (contradicting the Church's recognition of the bible as inspired in its original text); and (iii) the contemporary *multiculturalism* that argues that one must detach the faith from the Hellenistic culture in order to root it in each culture it encounters.

For the Pope, each step of de-hellenization was also a step that took away from the fundamental harmony between faith and reason, creating a breach between the two, and especially with contemporary science— to limit reason to the empirical and deny it of its breadth and grandeur.[27] The presupposition to this insight is the Church's belief that God, who in His providence inserted

---

[27] Pope Benedict XVI, "Faith, Reason and the University: Memories and Reflections" (Lecture, University of Regensburg, September 12, 2006), Vatican.va website, accessed October 30, 2015,
www.vatican.va/holy_father/benedict_xvi/speeches/2006/september/documents/hf_ben-xvi_spe_20060912_university-regensburg_en.html.

His Son into a concrete culture, enriched and strengthened this Judaic foundation of the Church historically with specifically Roman order and Greek philosophy.

In contrast to de-hellenization, Pope Benedict XVI finds three steps in Scripture toward the *Logos*: being (Exodus); "God of Heaven and Earth"; and *Logos*, Word or Reason, in John. Yahweh had first revealed Himself in Exodus as "I am [being]," and then subsequently deepened that revelation to "God of Heaven and Earth" (e.g., Ezra 1:2-4, Mt 11:25). But John's insight into the Trinity reveals the final stage: God as *Logos*, who is also Love. Without love, man does not truly arrive at his deepest reality, but he cannot do so unless he begins with reason, the structure of his being.

While love is the apex of the Christian life, it is based upon the foundation of *Logos*, of rationality, and the original *Logos* is the Son of God, who is the Formal Cause of all reality (Col 1, Eph 1, Jn 1). In the end, the bridge between heaven and earth, God and man, is the *Logos*, the Son of God. Through reason, there is a consistency in man, in his relation to others, his relation to reality, and his relation finally to God.[28]

C. Second Obstacle: Science Disregards Aristotle's "Final Causality"

Cardinal Ratzinger's concern about limiting reason to the empirical has its origin in an earlier problem noted by Étienne Gilson, one of the foremost Thomistic philosophers of the twentieth-century. He called for a restoration in science of a forgotten link, the "final cause." For Étienne Gilson, contemporary empirical science has shrunk its previous horizon, limiting reality to what can be perceived by the five senses, empirical verification; and has consequently failed partially in its understanding of reality.

Étienne Gilson affirms that Aristotle has not yet been surpassed in the understanding of reality as a whole, especially in regard to the four causalities, and the development of evolution has in fact vindicated Aristotle:

> He is reproached, sometimes bitterly, with having explained them poorly, but up to the present no one has explained them [causalities] any better [*plus*

---

[28] Ibid.

du tout]. Mechanist interpretations of these facts, which Aristotle formerly said had failed, have not ever been satisfactory; they have only displayed more and more the inevitability of the notions of organization and teleology invoked by Aristotle. Contemporary science itself attests to the unavoidable notions of this sort. This fact encourages us not to hold them as no longer applicable but rather to see in them [notions] constants of philosophy of nature, which itself, within limits accessible to historical observation, does not appear to have ever ceased to be what it is.[29]

Science today seeks only what is useful: only the efficient and material causes are worthwhile and necessary to postulate, and dispenses with the idea of final causality or goal. Reducing reality to the immediate of how things work without understanding the source or the why is short-sighted, limiting the scientist to the realm of the immediate and not hearkening to man's higher faculties and interiority that distinguish him from animals. *It is teleology or final causality that enables us to make the link to the Creator God.*

For Étienne Gilson, the first argument for restoring final causality to science is found in a characteristic of reality, especially living beings: art imitates nature and not nature art.[30] Where art requires many trials, and often without perfection, nature always arrives at the perfect product each time. That is to say, nature acts with greater perfection than man with all his skill and intentionality.[31] This implies superior final causality in living beings.

A second reason is found in living organisms, which are not homogeneous (e.g., a rock) but heterogeneous, and require some "organization" (*organisée*). To explain the organization of living organisms, it has been necessary since the time of Aristotle to have both the efficient-material causality and final causality. While the final cause is not perceptible through observation, its work is obvious.[32]

---

[29] Étienne Gilson, *From Aristotle to Darwin and Back Again*, 141.
[30] See Ibid., 156.
[31] Ibid., 114-115: "Without models or trials, nature succeeds in the first attempt or she definitively fails.... And she wills the parts in her willing of the whole. Like the God of Thomas Aquinas, nature does not will this in view of that, but she wills that this may be in view of that."
[32] Ibid., 144.

It is perhaps justifiable from a methodological perspective for empirical science to not need final causes, but that does not mean that they do not exist. Gilson employs the convincing argument about understanding a traveler seated on a train, that one can analyze the speed, distance, and energy expended. But this physical "explanation" bypasses the all-important personal dimension: why such a promising scientist has given up a potentially world-changing career. At the end of the day, the argument for pure chance in living beings is no explanation. To use our own example, an eagle, a formidable predator, has an impressive array of long-distance vision, deadly claws, rapid speed and silence, all coordinated by instinct, that affords the prey little chance. Étienne Gilson argues that

> there is no other alternative to final causality. "Finalism encompasses every doctrine which admits that there are facts in the universe which reveal direction".... On the contrary, we could find few scientists who would not consider that the best explanations, generally, are inspired by the principle that everything happens as if nature proposed to attain certain ends with a strict economy of means. (Maupertuis)[33]

Chance is not an explanation for this type of superb directedness. That is, the "how" question does not suffice: "Final causes have disappeared from science... but have they disappeared from the mind of scientists?"[34]

Synthesis

First, the obstacle of pure randomness, incompatible with Christianity, is surmounted, as God's creation can involve both randomness and necessity. Then Cardinal Ratzinger solidifies a clear principle: irrationality cannot give rise to rationality, so that order points to a creative Reason (transcendent). And third, creative Reason can only give rise to reason or rationality in creation. This means that rationality in creation has to be protected in all dimensions: no compromises with de-hellenization or voluntarism, no running to a manufactured pristine Gospel message or false multi-culturalism; and no avoidance of final causality.

---

[33] Ibid., 156-157.
[34] Ibid., 150.

What is at stake here? Pope Benedict XVI notes that the bridge between all reality is reason, which is also the bridge between man and God (*Logos*). Going back to the Regensburg address, if extreme voluntarism is correct, then God is free to act capriciously, and this would open the door to violence in the name of God. Instead, Catholics, while affirming that what we know is more unlike God than it is like Him, adhere to a link or an analogy of being. What we can know of God is subject to reason and rationality. From the side of empirical science and multi-culturalism, if we sunder the link between God and man, then man too can act capriciously; in the name of science he can disregard all metaphysical and theological reality. Pope Benedict XVI teaches that reduction of reason leads to reduction of man himself, for he deprives himself of deeper realities than the sensible world. In the Christian vision, man is not a mere animal, but an enfleshed soul made in the image of God, its destiny is divinization and possession by its Creator God. Now we perceive more clearly the tragic sequel.

III. Teilhard de Chardin's Vision as a Credible Christian Synthesis?

A. Is Teilhard De Chardin's Vision Scientifically and Theologically Sound?

In the face of numerous atheistic theories of evolution of neo-Darwinian provenance, Christians might despair at finding a Christian synthesis that is truly scientific in competence and yet also deeply christological (Logos). Part III makes a proposal to consider Teilhard de Chardin's vision as a possible working synthesis for faith and science. Walter Cardinal Kasper recommends de Chardin's synthesis pointing out that his "intuitions have been taken up in more differentiated ways and further developed philosophically by H. de Lubac, K. Rahner, and J. Ratzinger, as well as many others."[35] Ratzinger himself wrote: "The impetus given by Teilhard de Chardin exerted a wide influence [on the Council]. With daring vision it incorporated the historical movements of Christianity into the great cosmic process of evolution from Alpha to Omega…"[36]

---

[35] Walter Kasper, "The Logos Character of Reality," 281.
[36] Joseph Ratzinger, *Principles of Catholic Theology* (San Francisco: Ignatius Press, 1987), 334. He also praised him in his famous work, *Spirit of the Liturgy* (pp. 28-29).

Positive Reception by Key Scholars

For some Catholics, however, the doctrine of Pierre Teilhard de Chardin could still elicit uncertainty, if not unease, due in part to the presence of the Sacred Congregation for the Doctrine of the Faith's *monitum* ("warning") that the Church has placed on his writings that has not yet been removed. This is understandable given that, with new insight, the compatibility with the faith is to be examined (e.g., how original sin fits in). Then there is also the negative perception that some doubtful elements (e.g., Creation-centered spirituality, New Age movements) have co-opted his thought for their purposes.

Given that we must heed the Church's instruction that we seriously examine theories of evolution, the concerns with de Chardin can be allayed by considering a few pertinent factors:

(i) he is among the foremost scientists of his era, an accomplished paleontologist inducted into the *Académie des sciences* (1947);

(ii) highly regarded figures have praised his work: Cardinal Henri de Lubac holds de Chardin and his work in great esteem; Étienne Gilson recognizes his orthodoxy and holiness[37]; Bishop Fulton Sheen believes that Teilhard de Chardin will be recognized as the great spiritual genius of the twentieth-century[38]; Walter Kasper and Christoph Schönborn support his work;

(iii) de Chardin led an exemplary life, desiring to be a son of the Church;

(iv) it is not uncommon for highly regarded theologians to have their theology questioned (Aquinas, de Lubac);

(v) having undergone much criticism of his work, he asked the Lord that, if his work had been pleasing to Him, to allow him to die on Easter Sunday. He died on Easter Sunday 1955.

---

[37] Quote of Étienne Gilson ("faith so simple, so pure and so total"), in Ibid., 32-33.

[38] "It is very likely that within fifty years when all the trivial, verbal disputes about the meaning of Teilhard's 'unfortunate' vocabulary will have died away or have taken a second place, Teilhard will appear like John of the Cross and St. Teresa of Ávila, as the spiritual genius of the twentieth century." Fulton Sheen, *Footprints in a Darkened Forest* (New York: Meredith Press, 1967), 73.

New Paul: Evangelizer of Science Calling for a New Cosmology

We now look to Henri de Lubac to help "explain" him (*Teilhard Explained*). One can sweep aside any concerns about Teilhard de Chardin's orthodoxy and fidelity to Christ and the Church for these reasons.

First, Henri de Lubac compares the spirit and mission of Teilhard de Chardin to the Apostle Paul, with Part One entitled "Missionary and Disciple of St. Paul." De Chardin in his earlier life had been riveted by certain Christological texts of Paul and John and constantly meditated upon the cosmic Christ. Like Paul who wished to bring Christ to the Gentile world, de Chardin wished to bring Christ to the new frontier of technology and science, realizing that Christianity suffers death, not only by dissolution (destroying doctrine) but also by estrangement and separation (e.g., from the world of science): "When truth is no longer fruitful, it is close to death."[39]

Second, for Teilhard de Chardin, the world had for the first time in its history lost consciousness of God: "Humanity had momentarily lost its God," and the problem with the Church in our times is that "we have *ceased* to be contagious."[40]

Third, while he recognized that Christianity never had difficulty working within a static framework, he also recognized the necessity, as well as the urgency, for Christianity to transpose herself into each new era: "What must Christology become if *it is to remain itself?*"[41] It was quite evident to de Lubac that Teilhard de Chardin's entire work is "one vast proof— renewed in a scientific perspective— for the immortality of the human soul and the existence of God…"[42]

Fourth, regarding docility to the Magisterium, like Paul, who wished to meet with Peter and the Apostles, de Chardin also desired to have Rome review all his writings, and he considered Rome the axis of the world.

---

[39] Henri de Lubac, *Teilhard Explained*, 20.
[40] Ibid., 12.
[41] Teilhard de Chardin, Letter of Dec. 9, 1933, quoted in Ibid., 19.
[42] Henri de Lubac, *Teilhard Explained*, 41.

The Core of the Difficulty: the Immense Enterprise of Synthesizing Faith and Science

But what is the difficulty? He is attempting the staggering synthesis between faith and science. Bishop Fulton Sheen described the vastness of his project:

> No one attempted a synthesis of the new departments of advanced knowledge until the time of Chardin. What Aristotle had done in pre-Christian times, what Thomas Aquinas did in the Middle Ages— and both on the basis of the old astronomy— what Descartes attempted in philosophy, Teilhard did but without appeal to astronomy. He introduced two changes: in place of astronomy as the basis of the universe, he used evolution; instead of making it like a solar system, he saw all sciences and all knowledge, from biology and paleontology up to theology, as a cone or a series of cones, one inside the other.[43]

Readers of Teilhard de Chardin with a philosophical or theological background may discern some difficulties with "this great effort of integration, sublimation, and synthesis." There were indeed difficulties of formulation and terminology, and he never pretended to formulate a complete theology.[44]

But Henri de Lubac argues that embarking on such an enterprise is precisely why Teilhard de Chardin is our model of missionary fervor. He was possessed of a fire like Paul, and in the face of the world of atheism, *to move forward in spite of lacking the full wherewithal*, and have men recognize "the basic orientations veiled beneath inadequate expressions."[45]

B. Briefly Introducing Teilhard de Chardin's Synthesis

Bishop Fulton Sheen outlines the overall trajectory of Teilhard de Chardin's thought thus. Earlier figures like Plato and Aquinas sought a synthesis, but within the earlier cosmological framework of a planetary system that was static, pristinely created by God. But science in various disciplines have

---

[43] Fulton Sheen, *Footprints in a Darkened Forest*, 75.
[44] Henri de Lubac, *Teilhard Explained*, 33.
[45] Henri de Lubac identifies Teilhard de Chardin as a "true believer," unlike the generalities (e.g., "overture to the world" and "implicit Christianity") which are sometimes stripped of the good meaning they can have which become a "pretext for venturesome speculations" in which one can no longer recognize the Christian treasure (Ibid., 34).

discovered that the world from the beginning has in reality been in flux (e.g., geology, astronomy, species). Because the old cosmology no longer matches the reality of the universe, he insists upon a new cosmology, a new way of understanding the universe.

The overall project involves an evolution, like a series of cones, in four stages (cosmogenesis, biogenesis, anthropogenesis, Christogenesis), with divine intervention for each macro-leap for each ascent, and with divine activity acting as "Alpha and Omega," within and above respectively.[46]

While Teilhard de Chardin stoutly defends the reality of evolution and the need for a new cosmology, unlike proponents of atheistic or materialistic theories of evolution, *he decries the exclusion of a divine Creator.* The basic fallacy is that one cannot climb in evolution from the lesser to the greater (the Law of Entropy refutes this) and also miraculously and precisely arrive at the new level of consciousness. As Bishop Fulton Sheen describes, one can build a super-computer that can unravel all the processes of evolution but cannot make it conscious:

> Teilhard contended that the mere physical and chemical forces of and by themselves do not manufacture any new energy. On the contrary, they have a tendency to disintegrate unless sustained from without....
>
> ... There had to be an Alpha Point at the beginning of the universe which explains everything that will unfold in an orderly fashion, as an author has the plan of his book in mind before he writes it. Every word, paragraph, and chapter are the unfolding of this original idea. The Alpha Point explains the origin of self-consciousness....
>
> As the unfolding of evolution has not only an Alpha Point; it also has an Omega Point. There is a target for the arrow and a bow which shoots it. A little architect exists on the inside of everything to make it what it is.... The Omega is not the end product of natural evolution; it is "the prime mover ahead... the principle that at one and the same time makes this cosmic coiling irreversible and moves and collects it."[47]

---

[46] Fulton Sheen, *Footprints in a Darkened Forest*, 75-77.
[47] Ibid., 76-77.

Teilhard de Chardin Identifies the Omega Point as the Christ of Revelation

Rather than approach the world from theology, philosophy, or contemporary science, he chose paleontology. In ascending evolving complexity, if man (consciousness) is the point of convergence of the universe, he can *only be explained by a greater point of convergence, which is both immanent and yet beyond the evolutionary ladder.*

It appears that de Chardin's path is inclusive of the *whole reality of man*; and that science must be completed by philosophy, which in turn is completed and elaborated by Revelation: "The Christian need merely meditate on the *Credo* to find in the Revelation which he admits the unhoped-for realization of the dream at whose threshold he is logically conducted by philosophy."[48]

This can be explained thus. In order for man to exist, *there has to be an Omega Point, which from his faith he deduces to be the Incarnate Word, that is immanent by becoming concrete, and thus recenter the universe.* Through grace, we recognize that the Omega of reason is identical to the universal Christ of Revelation.[49] *He views materialistic evolutionary theories as inadequate*— "Christianity would have been snuffed out"[50]— and that the transformism of evolution more seriously understood would lead to the two perspectives (Christianity and evolution) being put together. In a very striking statement, he sweeps away any concern for the incompatibility of the two orders:

> Not only does the Christological tradition through experience show itself capable of tolerating an evolutionary structure of the world; but even more, contrary to all previews, it is at the heart of this new organic and unitary milieu, in favor of this particular orientation of space linked with time, that it develops most freely and fully. It is there that it assumes its true form.... Christianity and evolution are not two irreconcilable visions, but two perspectives destined to fit together and complement each other.[51]

---

[48] Teilhard de Chardin, *Mon Univers* of 1924, *Oeuvres*, vol. 9, 81, quoted in Henri de Lubac, *Teilhard Explained*, 58.

[49] Henri de Lubac, *Teilhard Explained*, 59.

[50] Ibid., 60.

[51] Teilhard de Chardin, response to an enquiry of the *Esprit, Catholicisme et Science* (1946), *Oeuvres*, vol. 9, 238-240), quoted in Ibid., 61.

Questions of methodology arise at this point. Teilhard de Chardin's methodology begins with observation of the phenomena (empirical science); yet his approach goes beyond the concept of the "positive sciences" in vogue today, and is more akin to the ancient Greek and Medieval physics, that includes all reality (synthesis), a method that would not be accepted by most adherents of modern science.[52] Norbert M. Luyten, O.P., points out the reason for de Chardin's expansion, that the object has to be enlarged to accommodate both: "[He] has transcended the methodological frameworks in which both the sciences and philosophy seemed to be enclosed… that he realized very early that 'in order to advance science and prevent it from petering out…. its object *must be enlarged and its methods changed,* and a *more profound and more synthetic study* attained.'"[53]

The Sad World without the Transcendent and Adoration

On returning to Paris in 1945, Teilhard de Chardin reacted very strongly to the pessimistic and atheistic existentialist wave engulfing Europe. Realizing that modern man lacking the Transcendent is "sad," he wished to relieve man of this sadness and tedium. His is an optimism, like that of Aquinas, that flows from saying "yes" to creation with a "certain zest for existence," "a zest for Being."[54] *Without the historical wedded to the Transcendent in the materialist evolutionary view, the option that lies before is a low sky that suffocates, man needs an outlet to escape "total death"*: "To know that we are not imprisoned. To know that there is an outlet, and air, light, and love, in some measure, on the other side of total death. To know this without delusion or fiction!"[55] Thus man is faced with a choice, to stay within a self-enclosed world or to find the outlet, to choose between "the alternative of the attitude of the Titans and Prometheus, or the attitude of Jacob; the attitude of 'revolt' or 'adoration'; of 'haughtily Power' or 'evangelical sanctity'; of 'arrogant autonomy' or 'loving excentration'; of the rejection or acceptance of Omega."[56]

---

[52] Henri de Lubac, *Teilhard Explained,* 62.
[53] Teilhard de Chardin, *Teilhard de Chardin et la pensée catholique, Colloque de Venise,* 19, quoted in Ibid., 63.
[54] Henri de Lubac, *Teilhard Explained,* 67-68.
[55] Teilhard de Chardin, *Le goût de vivre* (1955, *Oeuvres,* vol. 7, 246),), quoted in Ibid., 69.
[56] Henri de Lubac, *Teilhard Explained,* 70.

C. Evaluation

The basic question we must ask is, does Teilhard de Chardin's system work: does it conflict with the evidence, or is it a viable system that needs some modification (de Lubac's conviction)? The fundamental difficulty is verification of a synthesis that involves the divine. From an initial examination, we find that de Chardin's synthesis does indeed incorporate all the key elements desired: it incorporates evolution (with randomness) within the divine creative action; it establishes two autonomous orders (faith and science), yet that are linked; it includes final causality (end goal); it is based on reason, more concretely on increasing complexity that attains consciousness (anthropogenesis); and it is based on faith in the Logos, with a long evolution upward to Christ's Incarnation (Christogenesis).

The second question concerns the reception of his thought. Cardinal Kasper affirms that many scholars have employed his vision. For example, Cardinal Schönborn praised the approach of Teilhard de Chardin, that it is far removed from contemporary widespread materialistic concepts of "evolutionism." While recognizing the shortcomings of the approaches on both sides (faith and science), Cardinal Kasper left no question about the necessity of de Chardin's work and the importance of his legacy:

> For our subject, *it is important that Teilhard de Chardin dared a venture that was at the same time full of risks and yet necessary.* He incorporated the way that the Christian faith viewed the Incarnation of God in Jesus Christ as an inspiring vision into his research and his thought as a natural scientist. Conversely, he was constantly opening up his activity as a scientific researcher toward the great horizon which had been unlocked for him by his Christian faith. It is true that faith and science should be distinguished from each other. *Yet it is also true that they ought not to be separated….* Through his work, Teilhard de Chardin helped many scientists to overcome the prejudice that faith cramps science.[57] (emphasis added)

---

[57] Christoph Schönborn, *Chance or Purpose?*, 142-143.

Synthesis

The universe was created in the Incarnate Word (Col 1, Eph 1), and its logic and order reflects the Logos (Jn 1). The new Christ comes to see that science is studying the one Logos from below, and that the universe teeming with mystery points to Him, to whom Teilhard de Chardin's writings sing a hymn.

CHAPTER 4

A THEOLOGICAL MENTOR

> By this light set in the mind's eye Thomas [Aquinas] saw me and there gained the light of great learning. Augustine, Jerome, and my other holy doctors, enlightened by my Truth, understood and knew my Truth in the midst of darkness. I am referring to Holy Scripture, which seemed darksome because it was not understood. This was no fault of Scripture, but of the listener who failed to understand. So I sent these lamps to enlighten blind and dense understandings. They raised their mind's eye to know the truth in the midst of darkness, and I the fire, the one who accepted their sacrifice, carried them off and gave them light...[1] (God speaking to St. Catherine of Siena)

God revealed to St. Catherine of Siena that some saintly doctors of the Church (Augustine, Jerome, and Aquinas) were given special missions to give light to the world (see above). These "lamps" were, so to speak, the extensions of the one Light, who is Christ, and brought His light to address the darkness of each age. Consequently, this chapter seeks to make use of this concrete method of God by choosing a great theologian or figure (lamp) as mentor in one of three Golden Ages of the Church, with the ideal being the theological path of Ratzinger, who gained familiarity with all three Golden Ages of theology to bring about renewal in the Church today. A renewed theology cannot be overemphasized, as it constitutes the foundation of the Church (e.g., God providing the Church Fathers) and also of mysticism and spirituality. The vast importance of Vatican II for the Church and for the new evangelization highlights the importance of a renewed theology. The new Christ armed with such a strong foundation is better prepared to present the faith and answer questions.

But the novice lay person may find this theological panorama a dense forest or a maze, and we wish to point to key landmarks (3 Golden Ages), choosing from one of these Ages, and especially choosing a theologian as mentor, and how to access these resources.

---

[1] St. Catherine of Siena, *Dialogue, Classics of Western Spirituality* Series (New York: Paulist Press, 1980), n. 85, 155-156.

I. Path to Renewal in Theology

A. Preface

1. Poor Postconciliar Theological Formation and Busyness

Let us learn from the wisdom of John Paul II, who combined first-rate scholarship with a contemplative spirit. First, the importance of personal study for bishops is highlighted by Pope John Paul II:

> The responsibilities that weigh on a bishop's shoulders are many. I have discovered this for myself and I know how hard it is to find time for everything. Yet this experience has also taught me the great need a bishop has for recollection and study. He has to have *a profound theological formation, constantly updated, and a wide-ranging interest in thought and culture. These are treasures* that all thinking people share. For this reason I would like to say something about the importance of reading in my life as a bishop.[2] (emphasis added)

If we superimpose this for everyone, it would read like this: "[The new Christ] has to have a profound theological formation, constantly updated, and a wide-ranging interest in thought and culture," and he concludes that "These are treasures that all thinking people share"— note "all thinking people." Second, each one can learn from the inter-connectedness or "harmony between faith, reason, and the heart" of Pope John Paul II. That is, it must generate a sense of wonder through our hearts:

> In my reading and in my studies I always tried to achieve a harmony between faith, reason, and the heart. These are not separate areas, but are profoundly interconnected, each giving life to the other. This coming together of faith, reason, and the heart is strongly influenced by our sense of wonder at the miracle of a human person— at man's likeness to the Triune God, at the immensely profound bond between love and truth, at the mystery of mutual self-giving and the life that it generates, at our reflections on the succession of human generations.[3]

---

[2] John Paul II, "Books and Study," in *Rise, Let Us Be on Our Way* (New York: Grand Central Publishing, 2004), 93.
[3] Ibid., 97.

The Confusion of the Post-Conciliar Years

Since priests have a unique role in forming and leading others, let us briefly address their particular context. We note that in the wake of Vatican II, theological formation at many seminaries in the West exposed seminarians primarily to the speculations of prominent contemporary theologians, without first being given a sound and comprehensive foundation. One priest who completed his seminary years in the 1980s left with the hollow sense that he had been introduced to the penthouse of theology (theological speculations) without ever having been given the foundation of the theological structure: no formation in the foundational theology of Thomas Aquinas, nor of the rich patrimony of the Church Fathers (the fonts). In the domain of Scripture, the New Testament course was a collaborative effort of a theological consortium, but with the exclusive focus on the Historical-Critical Method— and there was no hint that there were three "spiritual senses" (senses imbued by the Holy Spirit) beyond the literal sense as taught by the *Catechism of the Catholic Church*.

One encountered speculative theories that in many cases proved to be incompatible with the faith: the theory of an immediate resurrection of the body after death, removing the terminology of "sacrifice" from the Eucharist for fear that it might offend contemporary ears. The theological worldview was described as "evolutionary," such that the old scholastic distinctions and patristic insights were no longer useful, and one had to create a new theology. The domain of scriptural exegesis was diagnosed to be especially confusing. So tumultuous were these post-conciliar years that one lay professor who obtained her doctorate at a prominent Catholic university found that a number of her colleagues who studied Scripture there in the post-conciliar years were losing their faith.

Busyness Hindering Theological Reading

Second, today's busy priest faces a difficulty, one captured by an observation of Bishop Fulton Sheen. Having arrived at a parish rectory for a stay, Bishop Sheen happened to glance at the bookshelf in the pastor's office. He wittily observed that he could tell when the priest was ordained, as there were no new books acquired beyond a certain year (presumably, the year of his ordination). The conclusion, of course, was that the pastor did not continue theological reading, which is a phenomenon that is not unusual today, especially given the shortage of priests and their busy schedules.

The priest may also not perceive the value of theological reading, seeing it mainly as something needed only for his formation days at the seminary. However, he ought to consider two benefits. First, we note that in many professional disciplines, there are annual renewal courses that practitioners have to take if they wish to maintain their professional licenses (e.g., dentistry). Would we want to take on a medical doctor who never keeps abreast of new drugs and procedures that could help his patients? Second, the priest is a spiritual doctor of souls, and theological reading overflows into areas of preaching and spiritual direction (e.g., in Confession), but can also elevate his spiritual life. When a senior priest shared with a young priest that his theological reading would find its way into his homilies and influence the way he thought and even his spiritual life, the young priest (who has a doctorate in science) echoed that sentiment from his own experience:

> My personal experience has been that theological reading has helped me as a priest. I find that it gives me a good grounding for preaching, sacramental work, etc., in such a way that, without giving the people a theological treatise, the theology and teachings of the Church become more "second nature" in my preaching. That comes from regular theological reading and study.

2. Vatican II's "Return to the Fonts"

For a renewal in theological reading, we have to take the path laid out by the Second Vatican Council. We begin theological renewal by hearkening to the Council's counsel to "return to the fonts [sources]," principally Scripture and the Church Fathers (and the Liturgy). Because the new Christ is unlikely to have time to go to the sources, he can look to contemporary theologians who can mediate the sources of Scripture and the Fathers. Nevertheless, it is good to lay out the ideal preparation of going to the "primary sources" (the original authors).

Looking to the Council, we find that *Dei verbum* teaches that these fonts are the vital and perennial foundation of the Church's faith. Paul Paniccia noted that this was the principal way Vatican II went about the process of renewal: "The way that various interweaving themes ultimately permeated most of the documents was due, among other things, to the Council's move away from predetermined concepts and categories in order to look at issues afresh, and *frequently to return to sources*" (emphasis added).[4]

We wish to follow the Council to renew our theology so as to re-evangelize the Church. The fruitfulness of returning to the fonts can be seen in some of the key figures who prepared the way for the Second Vatican Council. This includes Henry Cardinal Newman with his turning to the Church Fathers, as well as the theologians of *La Nouvelle Théologie*, whose return to Scripture and the Fathers was called *ressourcement*, "return to the sources" (it anticipated Vatican II).

The former papal liturgist, Archbishop Piero Marini, identified at a symposium the Church's three "sources":

> The Church's treasure, as we well know, consists firstly of Scripture in which is contained a Word of God that asks to be brought continually into the light of our today. However besides Scripture the Church also has the treasure of Patristic tradition and the Liturgy from which to draw in order to rediscover her truest dimension as a pilgrim community.
>
> Scripture, the Fathers and the Liturgical sources, are not simply testimonies of past history, a subject of archaeological interest, they are testimonials in the deepest sense of the word of a "story" between God and his people. They are the knots in the woven fabric of which we are the newest threads striving to interlace with one another to form new cloth.[5]

Archbishop Marini was addressing in his conference primarily the liturgy. Perhaps the most signficant point of his discourse was recalling Jesus' words in Mt 13:52 about bringing out things old and new. Archbishop Marini notes that this text of Matthew "is quoted in the Preamble of the new Roman

---

[4] Paul Paniccia, "Principal Themes of Vatican II," Vatican II— The Voice of the Church, accessed July 23, 2016, http://vatican2voice.org/4basics/themes.htm.

[5] Piero Marini, "Returning to the Sources: A Service to the Liturgy" (Symposium, Salesian Institute of the Sacred Heart, Rome, March 23, 2006), accessed August 28, 2018, http://www.vatican.va/news_services/liturgy/2006/documents/ns_lit_doc_20060323_ritorno-fonti_en.html.

Missal as a conclusion to justify and explain the revision of that important liturgical source." He adds, "In this manner the Church while remaining faithful to her office as teacher of truth safeguarding 'things old,' that is, the deposit of Tradition, fulfills at the same time another duty, that of examining and prudently bringing forth 'things new.'"

Now Archbishop Marini cautions that the point of the exercise is not to return to a certain archaeologism, finding a supply of "pre-packed patterns to repropose," "but [is] rather a journey which probes deep and goes to the essential."[6] The Preamble to the Missal teaches that we should go beyond the immediate inheritance to see the Church's entire past and how the "Holy Spirit endows the people of God with a marvellous fidelity in preserving the unalterable deposit of faith, even amid a great variety of prayers and rites."[7] Archbishop Marini also notes that this treasure (fonts) of the Church is a place of encounter and communion between us, the people of today and the first witnesses, who were given the responsibility of transmitting the faith.[8]

Given the theological deviations that took place after Vatican II, along with the return to the fonts, we wish to explicitly reaffirm *Dei verbum*'s delineation of the three pillars of the Church: the two sources of divine Revelation, Scripture and Tradition, guided by the Magisterium (DV 10):

> It is clear, therefore, that sacred tradition, Sacred Scripture and the teaching authority of the Church, in accord with God's most wise design, are so linked and joined together that one cannot stand without the others, and that all together and each in its own way under the action of the one Holy Spirit contribute effectively to the salvation of souls.

To dispense with one or another pillar is like removing one or more legs from a stool with three legs; one falls. Catholic theology differs from Protestant and Evangelical theology in that they mainly follow the *sola Scriptura* (Scripture alone) rule.

---

[6] Ibid.
[7] *Roman Missal*, revised in keeping with decrees issued by the Second Vatican Council and promulgated by Pope Paul VI, Preamble 9.
[8] Piero Marini, "Returning to the Sources."

B. Three Recommendations

1. Immersion in One Great Theologian as Mentor

Poor theological formation and the need to grow in theological knowledge can be addressed in one of two main ways. The first is the path of some scholars who choose an encyclopaedic approach, a more synthetic one, drawing from a number of theologians but not necessarily becoming deeply expert in any one. This is a praiseworthy path that has value and benefits. However, the drawback of an encyclopaedic approach is that it lacks sounding the depths and vision of a great figure of the Church. With this approach, scholars are likely to have stereotypical critiques of great scholars (all can be open to critiques, but the key question is whether the theologian's teachings conform to the faith).

The difficulty with such a lack of depth is that, unless one is fully immersed in a theology, one can easily misjudge that theology. For example, one often hears that Augustine was theologically pessimistic regarding sin and redemption, without considering his theological context of responding to Pelagius. Augustine's writings are so vast and comprehensive that even heretics can look to him for support; instead, one must look to his overall trajectory, to master it to some extent, otherwise one may end up with a superficial assessment. Likewise, to assess the theology of a great theologian of von Balthasar's stature and extensive writings is difficult without engaging the whole arc of his thought.

There is a far superior method, and it flows from the wisdom of a saying, "Beware the man who knows one book"— he is formidable. The ideal approach to scholarship is the immersion in the thought of one of the Church's greatest scholars, preferably of the calibre of a doctor of the Church, rather than being familiar with many competent theologians. Not only does one choose from among the greatest, one should also choose a saintly theologian who is a true son or daughter of the Church (*sentire cum Ecclesia*) and is saintly (e.g., Augustine, Aquinas, Newman), such that these saintly luminaries become essentially theological and spiritual "mentors," revealing their profound vision and even spiritual secrets to those who persevere. Jean-Pierre de Caussade writes tellingly of the importance of faith:

> One grain of pure faith gives more enlightenment to a simple soul than Lucifer ever gained by his vastly superior intelligence. A simple soul, faithfully fulfilling its duties, contentedly obedient to the suggestions of grace and being gentle and humble with everyone, possesses knowledge worth more than the most profound intellectual penetration of the unknown.[9]

This principle of a dominant and saintly mentor is how God forms saints (think of the Desert Fathers Abbas guiding disciples)— this is the principle of religious orders. Religious like St. Maximilian Kolbe are formed by one dominant model, St. Francis of Assisi. St. Catherine of Siena says that God teaches us above all through the doctors and confessors of the Church:

> The way that he [Christ] taught… has been verified by the apostles and proclaimed in the blood of the martyrs. It has been lighted up by the doctors, attested to by the confessors, and committed to writing by the evangelists. All of these are living witnesses to the truth in the mystic body of holy church. They are like lamps set on a lampstand to point out the way of truth, perfectly lighted, that leads to life.
>
> And how do they tell you? With proof, for they have proved [experienced] it in themselves.[10]

There is another choice that sometimes needs to be made: the immersion into the thought of a perennial doctor of the Church or a current theologian. The president of a Catholic patristic institute shared with a well-published dogmatic theologian colleague how he envied the latter's familiarity with contemporary theologians, to which the dogmatic theologian expressed disbelief, exclaiming how he and his fellow colleagues would give their right arms to have the patristic scholar's deep knowledge of Augustine. Similarly, a patristic scholar gave a doctoral thesis candidate, torn between choosing a Church Father and a contemporary theologian as subject for his thesis, this counsel: "It is better to study deeply a great Church Father with perennial value than be conversant with a theologian whose theological light might soon be eclipsed."

---

[9] Jean-Pierre de Caussade, *Abandonment to Divine Providence* (Toronto: Image, 1975), 115.
[10] St. Catherine of Siena, *Dialogue*, n. 29, 69-70.

2. Theological Renewal in the Path of Joseph Ratzinger

Among contemporary theologians, Joseph Ratzinger, who described his theological influences in *Milestones*, offers what can be an exemplary path for the priest aspiring to develop a theological foundation. Ratzinger shares with us a description of true scholarship in one of his professors:

> Next to the exegetes, however, those who had the greatest influence over me were Söhngen and Pascher…. He [Söhngen] belonged to that dynamic current in Thomism that took from Thomas the passion for truth and habit of asking unrelenting questions about the foundation and the goal of all the real; but all of this he consciously placed in relation to the questions that philosophy asks today…. Being the child of a mixed marriage and deeply concerned with the ecumenical question on account of his origins, Söhngen took up the debate with Karl Barth and Emil Brunner. He also ventured out with great competence into the mystery theology founded by Odo Casel, the Benedictine monk from Maria Laach….
>
> Characteristic of Söhngen above all was the fact that he always developed his thought on the basis of the sources themselves, beginning with Aristotle and Plato, then on to Clement of Alexandria and Augustine, Anselm, Bonaventure, and Thomas, all the way to Luther and finally the Tübingen theologians of the last century. Pascal and Newman, too, were among his favorite authors. What particularly impressed me about him was that he was never satisfied in theology with the sort of positivism that could usually be detected in other subjects. Rather, he always asked the question concerning the truth of the matter and hence the question concerning the immediate reality of what is believed.[11]

This description of Professor Söhngen points to four elements of a true scholar that mirror his own bent: passion for truth; setting questions in the context of the debate today; going to the sources and having a historical context; and avoiding positivism and seeking the truth whatever it is.

While the new Christs as well as priests do not have to be scholars, they ought to cultivate a similar bent towards theological reading in general. For Joseph Ratzinger, it all begins with an over-riding search for truth. There are several

---

[11] Joseph Ratzinger, *Milestones: Memoirs 1927-1977* (San Francisco: Ignatius Press, 1998), 55-56.

elements in his personal development: having the standard foundation in Thomas Aquinas, looking to the fonts or sources (Scripture and Fathers), making Scripture the soul of theology, conversing with contemporary Protestant thought, being influenced by great seminal thinkers (e.g., Guardini, Newman, Augustine, Bonaventure), and above all, finding all this culminating in the liturgy.

3. The Three Golden Ages of Theology that Helped Form Ratzinger

A second step is to lay a strong foundation by choosing a representative of one of the three Golden Ages of Catholic theology. The contour of the three Golden Ages of theology follows the history of the Latin Church (historical divisions of Patristic, Medieval, Modern, and Contemporary). First, no one disputes that the Patristic age (Western and Eastern Fathers) has become the perennial foundation of the Church (see *Dei verbum*). Second, neither can one dispute that a second Golden Age is the Medieval period of the Scholastics: Peter Lombard (*Sentences*), Thomas Aquinas (*Doctor communis/angelicus*), Albert the Great, Bonaventure (*Doctor seraphicus*), Duns Scotus (*Doctor subtilis*), and many others. Third, one can argue convincingly that the period leading up to the Second Vatican Council flourished with great theological minds provided by the Holy Spirit.[12] While immersion in Scripture is the first priority, we are recommending doing this through the great figures.

It is precisely these three Golden Ages that have been the primordial matrix for Cardinal Ratzinger's theological formation. For the priest's renewal in theological reading, it is suggested that he follow Ratzinger's path of three golden ages. His influences were mainly: Augustine (Patristic), Bonaventure (Medieval), and Guardini, Newman, von Balthasar, de Lubac, and others (Contemporary).

Rather than present open-ended options, we wish to propose specific figures to the new Christ seeking a mentor: from the Patristic age, we recommend the foremost of the Western Fathers, Augustine; from among the medievals, we recommend Thomas Aquinas, because he provides a vital foundation;

---

[12] One could argue that there is a fourth age, the post-Reformation period, which flourished, though perhaps not as brightly (Bellarmine, Cajetan, etc.).

from among contemporary theologians, two theologians steeped in the Fathers are recommended here: von Balthasar and de Lubac.

The new Christ should understand why this heavy emphasis is given to choosing as mentor only from among the greats and specifically a saintly theologian who has a special mission. It has to do with the nature of theology, the *logos* (science) of *theos* (God). Von Balthasar lamented the divorce in the Middle Ages of theology from mysticism and spirituality, such that theology has become pure scholarship, separated from faith and holiness. He believes that the "study of God" (theology) should be filled with *fire and light*. This means that theology should immerse the student in divine mysteries, should elevate and inspire him. It follows Rudolf Otto's famous insight from *The Idea of the Holy* that an encounter with the holy has two opposite movements: the *mysterium tremendum* and the *mysterium fascinosum*, an awe-filled mystery and a very alluring mystery. When this encounter with the holy is lacking, the new Christ fails to be "fed" and lacks the capacity to influence others. The theologian mentors recommended here have this fire and light. The mentor ideally should mediate the fonts of Scripture and the Fathers.

C. Concrete Reading Plan for Today

Outstanding Saintly Theological Mentor

For a plan for theological reading today, here are a few suggestions, summarizing what we have seen. First, it is recommended here that one selects from among the very greatest of theologians as *theological mentor*. A priest doctoral student was counselled by a Jesuit professor (a former member of the International Theological Commission) to "read the best," and as mentioned, the company we keep forms us: "Tell me who your friends are and I will tell you who you are." Therefore it is recommended that one chooses a theologian who is at the level of a doctor of the Church.

But it is recommended that one also look for sanctity in a prospective mentor (just as sanctity was one of the four requisite traits of the Church Fathers). For example, the brilliant theology of Cardinal Newman is surpassed only by his saintly life; and perhaps, his theology is an expression of that profound life.

Adopt a Contemporary Great with Familiarity of the Patristic or Medieval Periods

Second, while it is ideal for a scholar to be exposed to all three Golden Ages discussed, the new Christ is unlikely to have the time nor the energy to do so. Nevertheless, exposure to the Patristic or Medieval periods provides a strong theological foundation. One way to gain some familiarity with one of the two older Golden Ages is by adopting *a contemporary author* who specializes in a theologian of one of these ages (e.g., Augustine, Aquinas). Not only might a contemporary theologian's theology be more accessible to the priest, the latter may find that he either is not capable of understanding their original insights (e.g., Thomas' categories) and original languages, or does not have time to read their primary texts (e.g., Augustine's vast corpus).

For example, those who desire to access specifically the Church Fathers but lack the time might consider the great theologians whose work is built upon the Church Fathers: Henri de Lubac, Hans Urs von Balthasar, Jean Daniélou, Joseph Ratzinger, Antonio Orbe, etc. Those who wish to access Scholastic Thomism could consider Reginald Garrigou-Lagrange's works. The author's preference is the path taken by Vatican II, Cardinal Ratzinger, and the "New Theology" (*La Nouvelle Théologie*) of renewing theology through return to the fonts of Scripture and the Fathers, but mediated through a contemporary theologian, such as Henri de Lubac and Hans Urs von Balthasar. Nevertheless, he finds that the theology of Thomas Aquinas serves as a much-needed foundation for all theology.

Deep Familiarity with Vatican II Documents and the Catechism

In addition to immersing one's self deeply in one great author, a third suggestion is to gain deep familiarity with the *Vatican II documents*, especially the major ones. Since the Council truly is the work of the Holy Spirit and constitutes a primary reference for our times, each new Christ should consider reading all the principal documents, and seminarians should do so before ordination. We remember the fine example of John Paul II, who regarded the primary role of his pontificate to be to implement the teachings of Vatican II. We might also consider good commentaries that illuminate the Council texts, including the set produced by the Gregorian University consortium, edited by René Latourelle, *Vatican II: Assessment and Perspectives:*

Twenty-Five Years After (1962-1987), as well as Joseph Ratzinger's *Theological Insights of Vatican II* and de Lubac's *Vatican Council Notebooks*. It goes without saying that all should also read the *Catechism of the Catholic Church*. To navigate one's way in the contemporary theological landscape, one could look to Tracey Rowland's work mentioned earlier, *Catholic Theology*.[13]

Reading Program for Scripture

Because of the centrality of Scripture, it behoves all in the Church to gain intimate knowledge of this font. The first recommendation is we read through the entire Bible. Since it is rather arduous to read through the bible from beginning to end, as one scholar recommended, we could select three points in the bible (two in the Old Testament and one in the New Testament) of which one reads a brief portion each day. One helpful resource that systematically organizes this approach is "Read the Bible and the Catechism in a Year," published by *Coming Home Network International*.[14]

For reading works on Scripture, one might begin with Vatican II's *Dei verbum* and Pope Benedict's *Verbum Domini: Post-Synodal Apostolic Exhortation on the Word of God in the Life and Mission of the Church*.

Among books on Scripture, we recommend: the three volumes by Pope Benedict XVI, *Jesus of Nazareth*; the four volumes by Adrienne von Speyr, *John*; Romano Guardini, *The Lord*; Fulton Sheen, *The Life of Christ*; Henri de Lubac, *Scripture in Tradition*, *History and Spirit*, and *Medieval Exegesis*; Ignace de la Potterie, *The Hour of Jesus*; and Albert Vanhoye, *Old Testament Priests and the New Priest*.

---

[13] It helps the priest to recognize a number of contemporary emphases within theology today. These include: man as the image of God, especially in Christ (GS 22); deformation of this image through sin; the question of the supernatural (especially bridging nature and grace); eschatological perspectives; the awakening of the sense of the Church in the Christian, and a special emphasis on theological anthropology (e.g., the human person). Since Vatican II, theology has made a concerted effort at certain emphases: the integration of various theological disciplines, incorporating a Trinitarian background, restoring a salvation-historical horizon, a renewed eschatological emphasis, rediscovery of the human person and work of the Holy Spirit, the role of the laity, reading "the signs of the times," along with previously mentioned "return to the fonts," including Scripture and the Church Fathers, and a renewed understanding of Mary's role.

[14] http:www.chnetwork.org (email: info@chnetwork.org). One can order pamphlets online.

II. Three Golden Ages

A. First Golden Age: Patristic

> The bride of the incarnate Word, the Church taught by the Holy Spirit, is concerned to move ahead toward a deeper understanding of the Sacred Scriptures so that she may increasingly feed her sons with the divine words. Therefore, she also encourages the study of the holy Fathers of both East and West and of sacred liturgies. (DV 23)

The text of *Dei verbum* above highlights the importance of study of the Church Fathers. For the sake of brevity, we will not examine the vast literature on Scripture (see Chapter 10, "Preaching Christ in the New Evangelization"). An added benefit of studying the Church Fathers is that they were the first interpreters of Scripture (the closest), and because their theology and entire Christian life found its culmination in to the liturgy.

1. Return to the Church Fathers

It is helpful for the new Christ to have some background in the Church Fathers. As *Dei verbum* pointed out, the Fathers constitute a perennial foundation for the Church. In the Second Vatican Council's exhortation to "return to the fonts," the font of the Church Fathers is key, as it assists us to understand how to approach the other two fonts of Scripture and Liturgy. In addition, renewal of theology often begins with a return to the font of the Church Fathers, as seen with Newman, de Lubac, and Ratzinger. The Church Fathers are so foundational for theology that it would be good to review some basic facts in summary fashion.

Who are the Fathers? The author now summarizes from sources. The Fathers are considered privileged witnesses of Tradition, a unique and very precious "*locus theologicus*" (theological font). The title "Father" is employed in the Old Testament for immediate witnesses of the great events, like Abraham, or the patriarchs of the Old Testament, and in the history of the Church, for bishops and pastors of the flock, to Council Fathers, to eminent teachers of doctrine, to founders of religious orders, abbots, etc.

There are 4 traits found among the Church Fathers: (i) orthodoxy in doctrine; (ii) antiquity: the great heirs of ancient cultures (in the West, up to Boethius, Gregory the Great, Isidore of Seville, or even to Bede and Bernard; in the East, up to John Damascene; as well as the Syrian, Persian, Armenian, etc., Fathers); (iii) sanctity of life; and (iv) approbation by the Church in which they lived and died. Therefore, the Church Fathers are those who have contributed a decisive element to the Church's life, either in faith, in discipline, or in general attitude. They were in a sense inspired, raised up, enlightened, guided and strengthened by the Holy Spirit.

The Special Value and Historical Importance of the Fathers

The Church of the Fathers possessed something quite special and privileged. That period represents the moment when the deposit of apostolic faith was given an exact form by excluding certain interpretations. The historical role of the Fathers consists in this: they gave a particular human form and expression to our faith in a cultured society. This was done also by the first four Ecumenical Councils.

The Fathers determined the fundamentals of belief (Trinity, Christology), they forged the elements of the whole Christian language, they laid the foundations of Church discipline, and they fixed the forms of liturgical celebrations. Thus they affected the Church's forms at the decisive moments of its life. They also added the exegetical tradition and patristic spirituality, our present belief therefore is entirely biblical and entirely patristic.

The Fathers did all this "*in medio ecclesiae*" as true sons of the Church. Though they had their own personal geniuses, their paternity belongs less to the individuals than their collective personality. We speak of them in plural: the Fathers. Their period belongs to the Church's youth. They are very close to the pristine quality of the scriptural and primitive Christian doctrine. Ratzinger calls them the first interpreters of Scripture. They are still in direct contact with Christian fundamentals. They manifest a sense of freshness and fullness. They are still members of the undivided Church.[15]

---

[15] The author does not recall from which sources these summaries have been made, there possibility that it was influenced by Yves Congar's *Tradition & Traditions*.

Characteristic Features of the Fathers

The Church Fathers are not just examples of eminent doctrine and holiness of life, but more— they were pastors. Their aim was basically to build up the Church, answering the need of the Church in their time. Their writings are sermons or catecheses, refutations, exhortations, homilies, manuals. They had local responsibilities, but also universal concern. They were committed to proclamation, exposition and defense of the Christian mystery. They were bishops or monks, their work was blended with prayer, fasting, penitential exercises and the life of divine union. They were in immediate contact with spiritual realities. Patristic theology had the quality of totality.[16]

The Fathers always see the unity of faith and Christian life: mysteries coexist, cooperate with one another in a kind of circumincession (perichoresis). Their theology is concentrated: theocentric, christocentric, pneumatocentric, ecclesiocentric, mysteriocentric. Their thoughts unite in a single vision of God, Christ, the Church, and the sacraments.[17] It is commonly held that their teaching is sound when there is a consensus among the Fathers.

2. Augustine

There are clearly several major Eastern Church Fathers that would make for very fruitful reading (e.g., Origen, the Cappadocian Fathers). In the West, however, Augustine needs no introduction, and the profile just given on the Fathers portrays him. But he is dominant in the West, since the Latin Church has followed the theological track of this Western "Doctor of the Church." It has been noted that his theological output surpasses that of all the other Western Church Fathers combined. One senses something of his theological brilliance by the sheer staggering number of works and doctoral theses devoted to his theology. Thomas Aquinas himself, as have many others, depended on Augustine as the most significant "authority."

---

[16] Ibid.

[17] This section has been drawn mainly from Attila Miklósházy, "Apostolicity" (Lecture 8, "Ecclesiology," St. Augustine's Seminary at the Toronto School of Theology, University of Toronto, 1976).

Reading Program for Augustine

But where do we begin? In general, one should normally read the biography of the theologian, as it tends to inform his theology. Fr. George Lawless, a former long-time professor at the Patristic Institute "Augustinianum," made the following recommendations for how best to introduce the neophyte to Augustine's work.[18] He suggested reading Augustine's works, but the author has slightly modified his order to place the biography and the introduction to Augustine's thought first:

> ➢ Biography: Gerald Bonner, *Augustine*
> ➢ Introduction to Augustine's thought: John Rist, *Augustine: Christian Thought Baptized*; (also recommended is Augustine Trapè, *St. Augustine: Man, Pastor, Mystic*)
> ➢ (i) *Confessions*; (ii) *Sermons*; (iii) *City of God* (Chs. 19, 22, pp. 10-on)
> ➢ *Commentary on John* (either from the Carol Harrison series from Durham, England, or *Augustine in the 20th Century*)
> ➢ Allan Fitzgerald, ed., *Augustine Through the Ages: An Encyclopedia*

Reading Program for the Church Fathers in General

An accessible introduction to the Fathers are Cardinal Ratzinger's profiles of many early figures: *Jesus, the Apostles, and the Early Church*; *Church Fathers and Teachers: From Saint Leo the Great to Peter Lombard*. For a more systematic study of the Fathers, one standard text series is *Patrology* (edited initially by Johannes Quaesten, then later volumes by Angelo Di Berardino, published by Christian Classics, 1994). Some well-known theologians have offered works on specific Church Fathers (e.g., Balthasar's *Cosmic Liturgy: The Universe According to Maximus the Confessor*) or works built upon the Fathers in general (e.g., Henri de Lubac's *Catholicism*). Appendix 1 provides a more comprehensive list.[19]

---

[18] Augustinian Order Website: http://augnet.org/default.asp?ipageid=559; Bibliographical Collection concerning Augustine and his legacy: http://www.findingaugustine.org. The most common and most complete (but uncritical) edition of Augustine in Latin is the seventeenth century Maurist edition of Augustine's Opera Omnia which is reprinted in volumes 32–47 of J. P. Migne's *Patrologiae Cursus Completus, Series Latina* (Paris 1844–64) [PL].

[19] Find critical texts in Italian on Mary in the Patristic and Medieval eras: *Testi Mariani del Primo Millennio* and *Testi Mariani del Secondo Millennio* (Città Nuova), a key editor of which was Luigi Gambero, of the Pontifical Theological Faculty "Marianum."

B. Second Golden Age: Medieval

1. Aquinas: "A Blazing Torch Shedding Light"

While the Medieval Age comprises many theological luminaries, we will address specifically Thomas Aquinas because of his great influence in the Church. To begin, we note the secret of Thomas was prayer more than human study, through infused grace: "Thus he learned more through prayer than through human study." More generally, it is holiness that allowed him to gain such light: "This is a vision through infused grace that I give to the soul who loves and serves me in truth. By this light set in the mind's eye Thomas saw me and there gained the light of great learning."[20] God revealed to St. Catherine of Siena that St. Thomas was given a special mission: "So I sent these lamps to enlighten blind and dense understandings"[21]; "He was a blazing torch shedding light within his order and in the mystic body of holy Church, dispelling the darkness of heresy."[22]

> Consider the glorious Thomas. With his mind's eye he contemplated my Truth ever so tenderly and there gained light beyond the natural and knowledge infused by grace. Thus he learned more through prayer than through human study. He was a blazing torch shedding light within his order and in the mystic body of holy Church, dispelling the darkness of heresy.[23]

The Church has greatly lauded the theology of Thomas Aquinas: "We exhort you, venerable brethren, in all earnestness to restore the golden wisdom of St. Thomas, and to spread it far and wide for the defense and beauty of the Catholic faith, for the good of society, and for the advantage of all the sciences" (Leo XIII, *Aeterni Patris*, 31). John Paul II himself noted the importance of Aquinas for his studies: "Later, during my theological studies in Rome, I took a deep interest in the *Summa Theologiae* of Saint Thomas Aquinas."[24]

---

[20] St. Catherine of Siena, *Dialogue*, n. 85, p . 155.
[21] Ibid., nn. 84-85, 155.
[22] Ibid., n. 158, p. 339.
[23] Ibid.
[24] John Paul II, "Books and Study," in *Rise, Let Us Be on Our Way*, 95.

Since his death (1226-1274 AD), St. Thomas' doctrine has constituted the primary theology of the Church until the period of the Second Vatican Council. Where Augustine was primarily inspired by Neoplatonism (through Plotinus), Thomas employed the categories of Aristotle, as depicted in the famous painting of Raphael's *School of Athens*, with Plato's hand pointing upwards to ultimate reality of forms, and Aristotle's hand pointing downwards, to the reality we can experience by our senses.

While Thomas' theology does not give the overarching arc of salvation history, as does Augustine's *City of God*, it provides great light in giving a comprehensive, systematic theology, with many categories and distinctions (in general, Scholasticism is more analytic). This affords much clarity and light to the Church (e.g., in sacramental theology and in metaphysics). As such, an introduction to the vision and theology of Thomas Aquinas is indispensable, though one should go beyond to return to the sources (e.g., de Lubac) and also look to contemporary insights (e.g., John Paul II).

Other medieval authors are also well-worth considering. We point to the example of Joseph Ratzinger, who wrote his habilitation thesis on the theology of St. Bonaventure. The so-called "dark ages" were populated by many other luminous intellects, such as Bernard of Clairvaux, Peter Lombard, Hugh of St. Victor, Anselm of Canterbury, Albert the Great, and Duns Scotus, to name but a few.

2. Reading Program for Aquinas

The reader should be made aware that there was a reaction by some theologians in the twentieth-century (e.g., de Lubac, von Balthasar, Rahner) against what is called Suárezian Thomism, with the belief that Francisco Suarez's version of Thomism deviates from the true trajectory of Thomas. Tracey Rowland, in *Catholic Theology*, sees these theologians as welcoming the sound appropriations of Thomism, including those of Josef Pieper, Étienne Gilson, Alasdair MacIntyre, and Servais Pinckaers, representing more recent Neo-Thomist revivals (e.g., biblical).[25] Nevertheless, the author has found

---

[25] Tracey Rowland offers a fine exposition of the different streams of Thomism, especially the revivals in the contemporary landscape in "Hallmarks and Species of Thomism," in *Catholic Theology* (New York: Bloomsbury T & T Clark, 2017), 43-89.

fruit from reading older Thomist authors, such as Reginald Garrigou-Lagrange and Charles Journet. When reading theological works, the ideal is to read the primary sources, the original texts by the author. But without the time or the necessary background, the priest may find negotiating the *Summa Theologiae* of St. Thomas daunting, and he would be well-served to look to summaries or commentators. Among the accessible authors, we find:

> - Biographies: G. K. Chesterton, *St. Thomas Aquinas: The Dumb Ox*; James A. Weisheipl, *Friar Thomas d'Aquino: His Life, Thought, and Works*; Louis de Wohl, *The Quiet Light*.
> - Summaries: Edward J. Gratsch, *Aquinas' Summa: An Introduction and Interpretation* (see also *Principles of Catholic Theology: A Synthesis of Dogma and Morals*, that includes chapters by Gratsch).
> - The literal English translations of the *Summa Theologiae* (or the Latin original) are preferred. One contemporary language translation is by Timothy McDermott, *Summa Theologiae: A Concise Translation*.
> - Accessible Scholastic Thomism interpreters: Reginald Garrigou-Lagrange, *The Three Ages of the Interior Life*, vol. 1 and *Everlasting Life*; Charles Cardinal Journet, *The Meaning of Grace*. The older Scholastic Thomistic interpreters lack modern emphases (e.g., eschatological), but offer a good foundation.
> - As mentioned, other highly regarded older Thomists include Josef Pieper, Étienne Gilson, and Jacques Maritain, and one might prefer some more current Thomists, such as Pinckaers and MacIntyre.

C. Third Golden Age: Contemporary

Great twentieth-century theologians have observed that the Thomistic background, while essential, must give rise to a new theology that speaks to our age, as Thomism itself succeeded Augustinianism. The majority of contemporary theologians have taken new paths: including *La Nouvelle Théologie*, Rahner's transcendental Thomism, Lonergan's epistemology, Karol Wojtyla's use of Max Scheler's phenomenology (while employing a scholastic foundation), etc.

1. Nineteenth-Century Theologians: John Henry Newman

Because of his link to the Second Vatican Council, we briefly mention John Henry Newman. Pope Paul VI, in an address to the members of Rome's

Newman Symposium in audience in 1975, spoke of Cardinal Newman's anticipating the Second Vatican Council and his importance for our time:

> Many of the problems which he treated with wisdom— although he himself was frequently misunderstood and misinterpreted in his own time— were the subjects of the discussion and study of the Fathers of the Second Vatican Council, as for example the question of ecumenism, the relationship between Christianity and the world, the emphasis on the role of the laity in the Church and the relationship of the Church to non-Christian religions. Not only this Council but also the present time can be considered in a special way as Newman's hour, in which, with confidence in divine providence, he placed his great hopes and expectations.[26]

Many contemporary theologians, including Joseph Ratzinger, have been influenced by this great figure. Those who have turned to Cardinal Newman have been rewarded by rich insights and spiritual formation. One should also note the work of the great nineteenth-century theologian, Matthias Scheeben.

2. Twentieth-Century Theologians: Hans Urs von Balthasar and Henri de Lubac

It is the conviction of the many universal renewal movements beginning about a century before the Second Vatican Council were the work of the Holy Spirit preparing the Church for Council, which, in turn was a providential springboard for evangelization in the Third Millennium (Pope John Paul II's belief).

The Church has not seen a class of such brilliant theologians in centuries, perhaps not since the time of Aquinas. The theologians generally noted within the Roman Catholic Church include: Karl Rahner, Henri de Lubac, Jean Daniélou, Yves Congar, Hans Urs von Balthasar, Bernard Lonergan, not to mention seminal thinkers like Odo Casel and Teilhard de Chardin. One can extend this list to others, including Karol Wojtyla, Joseph Ratzinger, Walter Kasper, Louis Bouyer, and Reginald Garrigou-Lagrange and Marie-

---

[26] Pope Paul VI, Address to Newman Symposium, Rome, 1975. *L'Osservatore Romano*, Weekly Edition in English, April 17, 1975, I.3.

Dominique Chenu (Thomists).[27] We should not also note the work of great Protestant theologians, like Karl Barth.[28]

Four contemporary theologians, von Balthasar, de Lubac,[29] Daniélou, and Congar are recommended, all incorporating renewal movements and contemporary advances (e.g., biblical, patristic, trinitarian, christocentric, recovering mystical dimension). The author also highly recommends Joseph Ratzinger, whom Robert Cardinal Sarah in an interview speculated could very well one day be declared a doctor of the Church. Anyone choosing Ratzinger as mentor would be well served by beginning with his autobiographies (*Salt of the Earth; Milestones; Last Testament*) and his *Jesus of Nazareth* series.

(i) Henri de Lubac

Henri de Lubac enlisted in France during World War I, fighting at the front for three years and sustaining a head wound that would affect his health for the rest of his life. He led a renewal in theology by a return to the sources (*ressourcement*) with *La Nouvelle Théologie*, that would influence Vatican II, and sought a new unity with exegesis, dogmatic theology, and spirituality. He founded the *Communio* Journal with von Balthasar, Ratzinger, and others. After the publication of *"Surnaturel"* in 1946, some Neo-scholastic theologians claimed he held unorthodox theological positions and he was forbidden to teach for eight years. Rehabilitated in 1958, he became a member of the Academy of Moral and Political Sciences. Pope John XXIII asked him to help prepare Vatican Council II, then he took part in the Council itself, from 1962-65. He helped prepare the ground for Vatican II

---

[27] While the theological contribution of Pope John Paul II is significant, especially his Theology of the Body, his primary work is within the philosophical domain. This applies also to Étienne Gilson and Jacques Maritain. And this does not yet include the theologians within the Reform (e.g., Karl Barth, Jürgen Moltmann) and the Orthodox tradition (e.g., Vladimir Lossky, Johannes Zizioulas).

[28] Resources include: *Key Theological Thinkers: From Modern to Postmodern*, ed. Staale Johannes Kristiansen & Svein Rise (Surrey, England: Ashgate Publishing Ltd, 2013); Fergus Kerr, *Twentieth-Century Catholic Theologians: From Neoscholasticism to Nuptial Mysticism* (Oxford: Blackwell, 2007); James J. Bacik, *Contemporary Theologians* (Chicago, IL: The Thomas More Press, 1989); Patrick Granfield, *Theologians at Work* (New York: The MacMillan Co., 1967).

[29] Tracey Rowland offers a very short profile of both the methodology of Henri de Lubac and Hans Urs von Balthasar in *Catholic Theology*, pp. 106-111, that is elaborated more comprehensively in the full Chapter, "The *Communio* Approach," pp. 91-137.

(especially *Lumen gentium* and *Dei verbum*), and worked on *Gaudium et spes* with Wojtyla, and was made a Cardinal deacon in recognition of his theological contributions.

Henri de Lubac forged a friendship with Pope John Paul II at Vatican II and had high regard for him, which was reciprocated. Visiting the Catholic Institute of Paris in 1980, Pope John Paul II, catching sight of him, interrupted an address to say, "I bow my head before Father de Lubac." His insights are profound: his love of the Church (see *Splendor of the Church*), the breadth of his vision (e.g., *Catholicism* influenced the Ratzinger as student), not to mention his influence on his students, von Balthasar and Jean Daniélou.

Among the books of Henri de Lubac recommended are:

> Introductions: Hans Urs von Balthasar, *The Theology of Henri de Lubac* and Rudolph Voderholzer, *Meet Henri de Lubac: His Life and Work*. See also a chapter in Fergus Kerr's *Twentieth-Century Catholic Theologians*. For a brief theological introduction, see Tracey Rowland, *Catholic Theology*, pp. 106-109, 134-136.

> Books to start that are entrancing: *Catholicism: Christ and the Common Destiny of Man* and *The Splendor of the Church*.

> Other books recommended: Ecclesiology: *The Motherhood of the Church*; Atheism: *The Drama of Atheist Humanism*; Scripture: *Scripture in the Tradition* and *Medieval Exegesis* and *History and Spirit: The Understanding of Scripture According to Origen*; Grace: *The Mystery of the Supernatural* and *Brief Catechesis on Nature and Grace*.

(ii) Hans Urs von Balthasar

Fergus Kerr, the current editor of *New Blackfriars* (theological and philosophical review of the English Dominicans), in *Twentieth-Century Catholic Theologians*, a survey of Catholic theologians who shaped theology before, during, and after the Second Vatican Council, affirmed that Hans Urs von Balthasar was "widely regarded as the greatest Catholic theologian of the century."[30] Many have been influenced by von Balthasar, including Pope John Paul II, Pope Benedict XVI, and some scholar prelates, among others, Cardinal Marc Ouellet, Cardinal Christoph Schönborn, and Cardinal Angelo Scola. For a brief theological introduction, see Tracey Rowland, *Catholic Theology*, pp. 101-121, 127-129, 134-136. Von Balthasar's contribution has been recognized by the last two popes. Pope John Paul II gave von Balthasar a Cardinal's hat in recognition of his theological contribution,[31] and both he and Ratzinger were friends of, and influenced by, his theology. Pope Benedict XVI, retiring to Castel Gandolfo upon retirement, brought with him von Balthasar's *Glory of the Lord* series.

Perhaps the most impressive aspect of von Balthasar's life is how much he has been overlooked. One of the most difficult decisions he had to make was the decision to leave the Society of Jesus after long discernment to later found the Community of St. John. He himself chose to work as a university chaplain over a promising teaching career at the Gregorian University in Rome. He was never invited to be a *peritus* (theological expert) at the Second Vatican Council, and was largely overlooked in that period. And he, along with his collaborator, Adrienne von Speyr, has been attacked on some fronts: latent apocatastasis (universal redemption) and their thought on Jesus' descent on Holy Saturday. It is customary for many great theological figures to receive opposition to their teachings, which may be signs of God's favour: the opposition of Bishop Tempier to the teaching of Thomas Aquinas; the silencing of Henri de Lubac and Teilhard de Chardin; the shutting down of St. Pio of Pietrelcina; the response to Pope Benedict XVI's address at Regensburg.

There is a possibility that von Balthasar may have a significant role to play in God's providential plan. In God's divine providence, Augustine's theology has ruled the day until the time of Thomas; since Thomas, Thomism has been the mainstay within Catholic theology (though not evenly or universally). Each theology has ruled for about some seven hundred years. Of the three

---

[30] Fergus Kerr, *Twentieth-Century Catholic Theologians*, 121.
[31] One might consider reading the chapter by Brendan Leahy, "John Paul II and Hans Urs von Balthasar," in *The Legacy of Pope John Paul II*, eds. Gerald O'Collins & Michael Hayes (London: Burns & Oates, 2008).

transcendentals (timeless and universal attributes of being), Augustine has developed the "good" (through the will), Thomas has focused on the "true" (through the intellect), and now Balthasar as developed an entire treatise on the "beautiful" or glory (through the heart). This pattern of succession from Augustine to Aquinas and beyond should be kept in mind. One might supplement the reading of von Balthasar with the works of his collaborator, Adrienne von Speyr (mystic). Her writings (e.g., her 3-volume commentary, *John*) are so luminous that they recall the writings of the Church Fathers. For reading von Balthasar's texts, it is recommended that one begins with his shorter works.

> ➤ Stratford Caldecott and Aidan Nichols offer fine brief online profiles.[32]

> ➤ A recommended introduction with contributions from different balthasarian experts is *Hans Urs von Balthasar: His Life and Work* (ed. David Schindler). Shorter introductions include John O'Donnell, *Balthasar;* Aidan Nichols, *The Word has been Abroad: A Guide through Balthasar's Aesthetics.*

> ➤ A compilation of representative texts is presented in *The Von Balthasar Reader* (eds. M. Kehl, W. Loser).

> ➤ One might begin with *Love Alone is Believable*, as love is at the heart of his theology; and *Mysterium Paschale: The Mystery of Easter.*

> ➤ Shorter works include: *Prayer, New Elucidations, The Office of Peter and the Structure of the Church, Truth is Symphonic, Mary for Today, Dare we Hope that all be Saved, Theology of History.* The priest and deacon might be interested in a collection of homilies, *You Crown the Year.*

> ➤ The crown of Balthasar's work is his famous trilogy: *Glory of the Lord, Theodrama, Theologic.* There is also a second series, *Explorations in Theology.*

---

[32] Stratford Caldecott, "Introduction to Hans Urs von Balthasar," http://www.christendom-awake.org/pages/balthasa/introduc.html; Aidan Nichols, "An Introduction to Balthasar," http://www.christendom-awake.org/pages/balthasa/introan.html. Both are found on the Christendom Awake website and accessed July 19, 2018.

Appendix: Theological References

It is helpful to have a few standard theological references. One might consider acquiring one of two recently published Latin-English versions of the Church's teachings: *Enchiridion Symbolorum: A Compendium of Creeds, Definitions and Declarations of the Catholic Church* and Norman P. Tanner, ed., *Decrees of the Ecumenical Church* (2 vols.). Priests with some interest in Canon Law might find the annotated Latin-English version informative: *Code of Canon Law Annotated*. The International Theological Commission has now published a second volume of its proceedings: *International Theological Commission: Texts and Documents 1986-2007*. The Church Fathers have four major critical series: *Corpus Scriptorum Ecclesiasticorum Latinorum* (CSEL); *Corpus Christianorum, Series Latina* (CCL); *Bibliothèque Augustinienne, Oeuvres de Saint Augustin* (BA); *Nuova Biblioteca Agostiniana, Opera di S. Agostino* (NBA).[33]

References for Augustine

William Harmless of Creighton University ("Augustine and the Latin West") suggests some bibliographical aids to the study of Augustine: Allan Fitzgerald, ed., *Augustine Through the Ages: An Encyclopedia* (1999): "An excellent reference work on Augustine, over 900 pages, surveying every aspect of his life, writings, theology, and influence. The best place to begin one's research on Augustine." Other particularly helpful secondary sources include: Robert Dodaro & George Lawless, eds., *Augustine and His Critics: Essays in Honour of Gerald Bonner*; Carol Harrison, *Augustine: Christian Truth and Fractured Humanity*, Christian Theology in Context— an excellent survey of Augustine's theology organized thematically; Gerald Bonner, *St. Augustine: His Life and Controversies*, 3rd ed.— a classic that is a little dated; Peter Brown, *Religion and Society in the Age of St. Augustine* (1972, reprint: Eugene, OR: Wipf & Stock, 2007).[34] There is a fine critical and expanding series in English: *Augustine in the 20th Century* (ed. Edmund Hill).

---

[33] "St. Augustine," Stanford Encyclopedia of Philosophy, s.v. "Bibliography," accessed August 28, 2018, http://plato.stanford.edu/entries/augustine/#Aca.

[34] William Harmless, S.J., Creighton University, "Augustine and the Latin West." This website is no longer accessible:
http://moses.creighton.edu/harmless/bibliographies_for_theology/Patristics_6.htm.

CHAPTER 5

SANCTIFICATION FOR MINISTRY

The Church since the Council has to a large extent put off her mystical characteristics; she has become a Church of permanent conversations, organizations, advisory committees, congresses, synods, commissions, academies, parties, pressure-groups, functions, structures, and restructurings, sociological experiments, statistics: that is to say, more than ever a male Church... May not the reason for the domination of such typically male and abstract notions be because of the abandonment of the deep femininity of the Marian character of the Church?[1] (Hans Urs von Balthasar)

I. Obstacles to Evangelization

"Male Functionalist" Church

The goal of Baptism is to become a new Christ, whose task is to allow Jesus Christ to act in him to evangelize the world (that is, Christ's words at the Ascension to evangelize the world applies to all Christians). But in our task of evangelization, it is vital that we identify what hinders evangelization, that is, the principal obstacles. And it is the conviction of Henri de Lubac that Hans Urs von Balthasar's diagnosis of the deepest problem of our time is the most accurate. Where the heart of Christ was led like a child in each moment by the Holy Spirit, von Balthasar perceived a "male functionalist" culture today, with a predilection to activism and to seek to control and accomplish things through human effort (see quotation above).

Von Balthasar brings into play a profound insight: holiness entails the theologically feminine dimension: abandonment or receptivity. We find this theologically feminine (receiving) dimension in Jesus and Mary before the Father. Von Balthasar pinpoints the model of the heart of Jesus: He gave up sovereignty of His own will and sought only the Father's will:

---

[1] Hans Urs von Balthasar, *Elucidations*, trans. John Riches (San Francisco: Ignatius Press, 1998), 109-110.

Christ's mode of time is an expression of the fact that *he renounces sovereignty over his own existence*. Both as a whole and in all its details, that existence is to become a *monument to the Father* in this world. *His life must speak of the Father and not of himself*. That is why he does not round off the meaning of his life, but leaves it to the Father to shape it from moment to moment and fill it with his meaning. He does not provoke the situations which form his life, but leaves it to the Father to place him in them.[2] (emphasis added)

Christ lets go sovereignty of His own existence and allows the Father to take charge. Christ does not fall into the temptation of living as a *worker* for God, but lives as *a child of God*. This is the *foundation of foundations* of the new apostle of Christ in the new evangelization— he or she must allow Christ to take over within.

We see this receptivity in the one who is most like Christ, Mary. Mary is the model par excellence of surrender and of receptivity—for the Church is Marian in her essence. The more Marian she becomes, the more Church she becomes:

> Without mariology, Christianity threatens imperceptibly to become inhuman. The Church becomes functionalistic, soulless, a hectic enterprise without any point of rest, estranged from her true nature by the planners. And because, in this manly-masculine world, all that we have is one ideology replacing another, everything becomes polemical, critical, bitter, humorless, and ultimately boring, and people in their masses run away from the Church.[3]

When the new Christ usurps the Father's role by seeking to control and take charge, "everything becomes polemical, critical, bitter, humorless, and ultimately boring, and people in their masses run away from the Church" (*Elucidations*, 72). Like Jesus before the Father, each new Christ is to be the receiver (not the initiator or doer) who offers his yes to God's Providence in self-surrender. It is an ever-present temptation of the new apostle of Christ to focus on ministry and not be a child of God, who keeps his eyes on the Father's holy will.

---

[2] Hans Urs von Balthasar, *A Theology of History* (San Francisco: Ignatius Press, 1994), 51.
[3] Hans Urs von Balthasar, *Elucidations*, 112-113.

This chapter is comprised of three parts: I. Obstacles to evangelization; II. Companionship with Christ in four dimensions; III. A program for priests in Cardinal van Thuan's Ten Rules, among other practical suggestions.

A. Two Examples of Activism from Cardinal van Thuan and Dom Chautard

The first obstacle to sanctification for evangelization is activism. One religious, with deep insight, said that "Busyness is the tool of Satan." We present life-changing discoveries by two great figures of the Church: Francis Cardinal van Thuan and Dom Jean-Baptiste Chautard. The first example of Cardinal van Thuan arose when he was chafing in his prison because, as a vibrant young bishop, he was not able to minister to his flock in Saigon over-run by the Communist Viet Cong regime:

> Alone in my prison cell, I continued to be tormented by the fact that I was forty-eight years old, in the prime of my life, that I had worked for eight years as a bishop and gained so much pastoral experience and there I was isolated, inactive and far from my people... (1700 km)

> One night, from the depths of my heart I could hear a voice advising me: "Why torment yourself? **You must discern between God and the works of God**. Everything you have done and desire to continue to do, pastoral visits, training seminarians, sisters and members of religious orders, building schools, evangelizing non-Christians. All of that is excellent work, the work of God but it is not God! If God wants you to give it all up and put the work into his hands, do it and trust him. God will do the work infinitely better than you; he will entrust the work to others who are more able than you. You have only to choose God and not the works of God!"[4]

To the troubled heart of Archbishop van Thuan, incarcerated and unable to shepherd his flock, the Lord spoke interiorly and set before him the vital choice in ecclesial ministry: "You have only to choose God and not the works of God." The decisive lesson given by God to the great Vietnamese archbishop is to choose God over His works: "All of that is excellent work, the work of God but it is not God! If God wants you to give it all up and put the work into his hands, do it and trust him…. You have only to choose God

---

[4] Francis Cardinal van Thuan, Duong Hy Vong: Nguyen van Thuan, accessed August 27, 2018, http://www.nguyenvanthuan.com/tenrules.html.

and not the works of God!" It is especially priests and religious who can easily fall into this trap in ministry, becoming attached to a ministry and finding their identity in it, instead of finding it in being unconditionally and infinitely loved as a child of the Father.

The second example is from an outstanding book that inculcates the primacy of the interior life and not human works or talents: Dom Chautard's *Soul of the Apostolate*. After long experience, this saintly and influential abbot in France came to see the greatest and most pernicious crisis of his times: "Heresy in Good Works! Feverish activity taking the place of God; grace ignored; human pride trying to thrust Jesus from His throne; supernatural life, the power of prayer, the economy of our redemption relegated, at least in practice, to the realm of pure theory…"[5]

He himself had experienced this truth in his life when, because of his tremendous human gifts, his superior sent him to Paris to save a financially-failing community, but he failed. All of his "native ability and eloquence and learning and economics proved useless. Finally he threw himself down in prayer at the shrine of our Lady of Victories." Just half an hour later, a total stranger came up to him and offered his help, and he learned the lesson of the "relative worth of natural activity, and activity based by and based on prayer."[6]

He had great success in a magazine for French priests sent to the Front during the First World War, and he learned from much experience the source of all our strength: prayer and mortification. This is what he perceived during the persecution of the Church in France— "a glaring inconsistency in the reaction of a certain type of priest":

> He observed that some priests, some organizers of Catholic Action, imagined that they could fight political enemies with more or less worldly and political weapons. In defending the Church against state persecution, they thought the most important thing was to gain and preserve political and social power. They believed that these gains could best be consolidated by a great material expansion. They expended all their efforts in running

---

[5] Dom Jean-Baptiste Chautard, *The Soul of the Apostolate* (Charlotte, NC: Tan Books, 1946), 10.
[6] Ibid., ix.

newspapers, holding conventions, publishing pamphlets and magazines, and above all, they measured the growth of Catholic life by the number of new school buildings, new Church buildings, new hospital buildings, new orphanages, new social centers... as if the Church of God were built exclusively of bricks and mortar! Such apostles tended to congratulate themselves when they had raised large sums of money, or when their Churches were filled with great throngs of people, without reference to what might be going on in the souls of all those who were present. To the eyes of the Cistercian Abbot, a man who had learned his wisdom close to God, in the silence of the cloister, before the Tabernacle, there was a deep-seated and subtly pernicious error in all this....

But they were not the one essential thing. And those who had become entirely absorbed in this work of more or less material growth, seemed to have lost sight of the fact that the Church is built of living stones. It is built of saints. And saints are made only by the grace of God and the infused virtues and the gifts of the Holy Ghost, not by speeches and publicity and campaigns which are all doomed to sterility without the essential means of prayer and mortification. Dom Chautard saw, no doubt, that all this came from the subtle infection of Modernism and kindred heresies, bred of contact with a purely materialistic and secular culture.[7]

This entire text is quoted here as it may represent the malaise of our times too. The "heresy of works" is always with us, an infection "bred of contact with a purely materialistic and secular culture." It forgets that the Church is built of *saints*. He later points to the secret of fruitfulness:

"Those who pray," said the eminent statesman Donoso Cortes, after his conversion, "do more for the world than those who fight, and if the world is going from bad to worse, it is because there are more battles than prayers." "Hands uplifted," said Bossuet, "rout more battalions than hands that strike."[8]

This temptation of Cardinal van Thuan to choose the works of God and not God manifests itself within the Church's ministry in many diverse ways. A dedicated bishop can with conviction affirm that "A bishop should be out with his flock" is a necessary and praiseworthy outlook for a bishop, one

---

[7] Ibid., xi-xii.
[8] Ibid., 35

115

preached by Pope Francis. But it can also mask the temptation to be always running, to find one's identity in action and movement— work. The difficulty is that the first priority cannot be the pastoral work but holiness, and *nemo dat quod non habet* ("no one gives what he does not have"). As mentioned earlier, John Paul II gave us a blueprint for the Church in the third millennium in *Novo millennio ineunte*: the primary task of the parish priest is to bring people to holiness. He also gave us a shining model. He always went out, especially seeking the youth, yet what dominated in him was not action and "movement" but contemplation and union with God; he always seemed to be "in God." There is a world of difference between choosing God and choosing His works: there are many works that are good but they may not be God's will. The temptation can also arise in lay groups. A common temptation for a devout Catholic engaged in evangelization is to think that holiness is about running from one conference to another and being busy with prayer meetings and the ministry of inner healing, that is, focusing on the "works of the Lord" instead of focusing on being a child of God.

B. Examples of Relying Primarily on Human Effort

The temptation just expressed of focusing on the works of God instead of on God is often found with a related temptation: to substitute human effort for divine workings. Derek Prince, the Evangelical author of *Blessing or Curse*, discovered this truth when a community with which he was working fell apart spectacularly because of this failure. Out of this debacle came some hard-earned wisdom and insight. With inspired insight, he wrote that, where human effort and not God's work is dominant, we are doomed to failure, and the following priorities will result:

> Theology will be exalted above revelation;
> intellectual education above character building;
> psychology above discernment;
> program above the leading of the Holy Spirit;
> eloquence above supernatural power;
> reasoning above the walk of faith;
> laws above love.[9]

---

[9] Derek Prince, "Legalism, Carnality, Apostasy," in *Blessing or Curse: You can Choose* (Grand Rapids, MI: Chosen, 2006), 103.

116

Two Examples

The text above truly captures the temptations of our age. Within the Catholic Church, there is a deep need today for evangelization, and with it comes a very tempting and powerful pull to a very horizontal or human focus: theology, intellectual education, psychology, programs, eloquence, human reasoning, and laws. Here are two examples.

First, we see some fine Church programs in North America, especially for youth, such as the transplanting of the Steubenville weekend program with a large turnout of youth, a truly blessed event. But there can be a temptation to rely primarily on these big events that give us a temporary "high," but do not translate into daily sanctification. As one parish priest commented, "Who will accompany these youth for the rest of the year?" More than the big events, the young need to learn the daily deep encounter with Christ, finding Christ in the sacraments and prayer, in the fulfillment of the duties in their state of life, and to listen to the inner promptings of the Holy Spirit. The author of this book has been helped by a precious counsel given him in the first year of priesthood by his spiritual director: "When you preach, many will hear you; but if you wish to touch and change hearts, you have to do so one by one in the confessional."

A second example involves promoting priestly vocations. A diocese might be able to provide a full-time vocation director and have many good programs: vocation discernment weekends, high school visits, individual diaconate ordinations in parishes, large-scale dinners that feature transitional deacons. All of this is praiseworthy, but still secondary to our Lord's instruction: "The harvest is plentiful, but the laborers are few; pray therefore the Lord of the harvest to send out laborers into his harvest" (Mt 9:37-38).

Our Lord calls us first to prayer: such as the desire of bishops to invite a monastic order into the diocese to serve as a contemplative dynamo; and inviting families to pray together, especially the Rosary (Mother Teresa taught that the family that prays together stays together). This temptation is Derek Prince's diagnosis of putting "program before the leading of the Holy Spirit," or temptation to big action, much movement, much emotion. We recall that Elijah found Yahweh, not in the earthquake, fire, or strong wind, but in the gentle breeze.

C. Three More Pitfalls: Priority on Ministry, Numbers, and Changing Others

Having looked at the temptation to choose the busyness of works and not God and to rely primarily on our human efforts, let us examine more fully the fruitfulness of holiness within ministry. The early Church evangelized the then-known world with little but the power of faith and the cross. In a similar vein, Msgr. Georges Chevrot's work, *The Eight Beatitudes: Reflections on the Sermon on the Mount*, reminds us of the powerful impact our faith should have on the world in the face of overwhelming opposition, and the prior requirement of conquering ourselves before seeking to conquer the world.

1. Incapacity to Lead Nations to Christ Indicates a Lack of Holiness

Msgr. Chevrot makes a point of staggering importance: our growth in faith (holiness) should have *a temporal effect; if it doesn't, we lack holiness.*[10] He begins with two characteristics of the Christian faith. First, the Christian faith is a collective and communal faith, in its present state and in the glorious Communion of Saints in heaven, such that for Jesus there is no such thing as "isolated Christians." Second, this new community follows the same path as the Hebrew nation, *called to lead other nations to God* but also dispersed after exile as a result of their infidelity, but bringing their faith to other lands: "The society of Jesus' disciples would be Israel's successor, forming the new people of God, a people without frontiers, composed of all races and in which all tongues would be mingled. The Church, as he would call it, would have to lead and guide humanity toward the total realisation of its destiny."[11] And while the kingdom of God cannot be identified or reduced to political institutions ("not of this world"), it must have a temporal effect:

> Quite on the contrary, the temporal effect of the Gospel will be all the more profound when it stays on its own plane, which is that of the world's sanctification. For human progress is a by-product of the holiness of men. Do you not notice a coincidence between the number of evils that afflict our epoch and a certain loosening of public morality?[12]

---

[10] George Chevrot, *The Eight Beatitudes: Reflections on the Sermon on the Mount*, trans. J. Ardle McArdle (Manila: Sinag-tala Publishers, 1998), 30-32.

[11] Ibid., 30.

[12] Ibid., 30-31.

Msgr. Chevrot's diagnosis is critical for our times, that "human progress is a by-product of the holiness of men"; and the opposite, *the progress of evil, is a result of a failure of holiness*. Chevrot goes on to describe the wonderful progress of technology, which should increase our happiness, but where instead we witness great evils. The progress in science is willed by God, *but there has not been a concomitant progress in sanctity to accompany it*:

> Let us not complain that there are too many scientists; our unhappiness springs from the fact that there are not enough saints, that conscience has not progressed at the same speed as science…. "Science cannot be stopped any more," said an eminent physician, Prince Louis de Broglie… but neither should one hinder the progress of conscience by minimising its demands, or the flight of virtue by deifying our instincts, or faith in God whose loving authority helps the believer to fulfill all his duties. Our world needs holiness; it needs men who take the Gospel as a rule of life.[13]

Msgr. Chevrot points to the false paths. He condemns the caricature of the Christian who is concerned solely with his place in heaven, which falsifies the Gospel, as Christ gave the golden rule of love of neighbour and called those blessed who sympathised with human suffering (Mt 25:31-46; Beatitudes). In answer to those who accuse Christians of not being concerned about their fellow men, he points out instead a revealing insight— it is precisely those who deny God who become inhuman: "the facts teach that it is when they have rejected God that they become inhuman, and that in claiming to abolish heaven they make a hell on earth."[14]

2. Reliance on Numbers When the Lord Employs a Few Chosen Ones

Second, having established the prior need for sanctity, that is expressed by love in action, Msgr. Chevrot affirms another dimension for evangelization. There can be another objection to this work of evangelization, that Christians are "only a drop in the bucket," and can't fight the overwhelming odds.

Msgr. Chevrot points out the revealing insight of how God in the history of the world has always used the *weak minorities* for His mission:

---

[13] Ibid., 31-32.
[14] Ibid., 33.

History replies to them that every time man rose again from the mud, it was the action of the chosen few that brought it about. To save the human-race, God always relied on the weak minorities: long ago, on the twelve sons of Jacob; later on, on the twelve Galileans. Instead of securing for himself the co-operation of the powerful empires of Chaldea and Egypt, he set apart a tiny people swamped in the midst of idolatrous nations. Even in the heart of the Jewish people infidelities and apostasies multiplied, but it was enough for God that seven thousand men— a laughable proportion— did not bend their knees before Baal... that "the remaining few" listened to the prophets, that fifteen thousand men agreed to rebuild Jerusalem, whom Esdras their leader called "a remnant to be saved"... Jesus in person only converted a "little flock" to his cause, but he meant it to be a little group of intrepid men (Luke xii. 32)....

On the morrow of the Ascension only one hundred and twenty disciples were waiting in Jerusalem for the descent of the Holy Ghost, yet it was enough to bring three thousand of the faithful rallying to the infant Church on the evening of Pentecost.[15]

Msgr. Chevrot reminds us of God's logic: "For my thoughts are not your thoughts; nor your ways my ways" (Isa 50:8). Where we look for quantity, God looks for quality, making use of figures like Francis of Assisi, Vincent de Paul, Charles de Foucauld, and Thérèse of Lisieux.

There is a temptation to be disheartened by the overwhelming opposition to the new evangelization. Msgr. Chevrot's insight should spur us to action: "In truth, for the realisation of his greatest plans, God only uses some weak instruments, but if they docilely follow his lead, through them he transforms the world."[16]

3. Seeking to Change Others Instead of First Changing Ourselves

The final point brings us full circle to the first point. If God can employ the weak minority to transform the world, then everything rests upon *not seeking to change first the world but ourselves*: "'The world can change, if you change,' ... If you become the new man, the new world will be possible; and you have in

---

[15] Ibid., 33-34.
[16] Ibid., 34.

the Gospel all the enlightenment and all the vigour to create, one from the other, the new man and the new world" (Fr. Gratty).[17] This is summarized by *Victor sui, dominus mundi* ("he who conquers himself, conquers the world").

Two Examples of the Power of the Interior Life
Dom Chautard gives examples of the difference an interior life makes, and here we present two. The first drawn is a congregation of women religious who were catechists under the direction of a religious priest, a man of prayer whose life story has been written. There was a dynamic and vibrant young teaching nun who was drawing many students to the school. This priest recommended to her shocked superior that she replace her with another nun, as he noticed that the young nun was depending primarily on her teaching (human) gifts. To quell her anxiety, the priest suggested that they do this as a temporary experiment. Another competent but deeply interior nun took her place, and with time, while the children progressed in their studies, there was a noticeable depth of tranquility and prayerfulness.[18]

The second example is the inspiring figure of Father Allemand, who founded in Marseilles a youth movement for students and workers and died in the odour of sanctity. The secret of his ascendancy?— "beauty of soul":

> This movement still bears the name of the founder, and for more than a century it has continued to enjoy a remarkable success. And yet, from the natural standpoint, this priest had few gifts. Half-blind, shy, devoid of any talent as a speaker, he was, humanly speaking, incapable of the prodigious activity his work called for.
>
> A certain lack of proportion in his features should, ordinarily, have aroused derision in young people, but the beauty of soul that was reflected in his looks and in all his bearing prevented it. Thanks to that beauty, the man of God gained a great ascendancy over these energetic youths, by which he dominated them and gained their esteem, respect, and love.
>
> Fr. Allemand wanted to build on no foundation but the interior life, and he was strong enough to form a nucleus of young men, at the center of his movement, men of whom he did not hesitate to ask, to the extreme limit

---

[17] Ibid., 35.
[18] Dom Jean-Baptiste Chautard, *The Soul of the Apostolate*, 158-160.

permitted by their condition, a complete inner life, uncompromising custody of the heart, morning meditation, and so on. In a word, he asked the complete Christian life, in the sense in which it was understood and practiced by the Christians of the earliest times.[19]

D. Contemporary Diagnosis: Predominantly Relying on Human Effort and Living at the Human Level

The author has come to this personal conviction: **that the primary weakness of the Church today is perhaps a living predominantly at the human level and thus relying on human effort.** We have just read of God's constant appeal that we are not heeding: Dom Chautard's diagnosis of the "heresy of good works"; Jesus' words to Cardinal van Thuan, "Do you want God or the works of God"; one religious sister's perception that "busyness is the tool of Satan" and receiving a vision of the Church as a ship listing to the side of action (away from contemplation); and especially von Balthasar's diagnosis that we are going through a dark night of a "male functionalistic world" of relying on busy human action (playing God instead of receiving from God as Jesus and Mary did).

While there is need for a "both… and" of divine and human dimensions, we may have gone overboard towards the human. Perhaps that which captures this best is the lesson just described of the lesson learned by a well-known Evangelical pastor, Derek Prince, that the cause of the spectacular falling apart of his parish community was reliance on human effort.

Note that holy people (e.g., John Paul II, Benedict XVI, St. John Vianney) often lack knowledge of basic everyday things: how to drive a car, intricacies of the use of computers, of the latest cultural fads or trends, etc.; but they have the pearl of great price, they are not Marthas but Marys ("one thing that is necessary"). When we make the supernatural (vertical) dimension secondary, we end up giving the predominant focus to the human (horizontal)— **everything human takes on an inordinate importance.** It is a preference for the human multiplicity of "Jerusalem" and not the hidden simplicity of "**Nazareth.**"

---

[19] Ibid., 151-152.

The following might be symptoms of living human predominance (Jerusalem) over the leading by the Holy Spirit (Nazareth):

➢ constant <u>fretting about troubles in the Church and in the world,</u> e.g., CNN (the Holy Family focused primarily on doing God's will and did not concern themselves unduly with the Roman rule as the Jews did);

➢ assessing world events primarily by <u>human standards</u> (e.g., that Pope Benedict XVI failed in prudence at Regensburg, not seeing that God may have desired him to experience the cross of opposition— St. Ignatius of Loyola diagnoses laxity (lukewarmness) when everyone loves us, or alternately we can say that the devil attacks only those who hinder his work);

➢ diligently <u>battling contemporary issues</u>, e.g., secularism, euthanasia (without relying primarily on the power of the Holy Spirit— see how the Holy Spirit was the "general" that led the Church in battle in the Acts of the Apostles);

➢ praiseworthy zeal in trying to convert people through <u>evangelization</u> (but without the primary focus on **conquering ourselves**— *victor sui, dominus mundi*, "the one who conquers self conquers the world";

➢ seeking to <u>convert people in large numbers</u>, e.g., through homilies, TV (and not one-by-one in a confessional or in individual encounters, which was Jesus' preferred method);

➢ seeking to foster vocations and faith life primarily by <u>programs and warm personality</u> (rather than primarily by the power of the Holy Spirit in prayer: "pray therefore the Lord of the harvest," Mt 9:38);

➢ finding fulfillment in <u>external acts of virtue, piety, and penance</u>, e.g., a faithful plan of life (i.e., in my personal fidelity and not above all in my interior abandonment to God's will);

➢ a love for <u>holding meetings</u> and of running to <u>conferences</u> (and not living the stillness of Nazareth);

➢ <u>proclivity to rules and excessive hankering for public approval</u> (contrast the Pharisees' obsession with rules and public respect to the liberty of spirit of Jesus, who lived a higher pleasing the Father in the Spirit);

➢ constant eagerness to <u>travel</u> (saints, like the Holy Family, often remain in one place; think also of the material poverty of our past generations);

➢ undue attachment to <u>social life</u> (Fulton Sheen had no social life because he was too busy bringing souls to God) and to constant chatter and media exposure with <u>cell phones</u> (we note John Paul II's interior silence)

Explanation through the Marian principle

What Jesus and Mary lived was docility to the Holy Spirit (feminine or Marian dimension), through which they act by the Holy Spirit's power. Hans Urs von Balthasar's frames the Church's charisms in two primary dimensions: Petrine and Marian. The Petrine (hierarchy) represents God the Father's theologically masculine role of giving holy things, and the Marian (baptized) represents the Son's feminine dimension of receiving (surrender or saying yes to) everything from the Father. Pope John Paul II says that the Marian principle is more foundational than the Petrine and is the pattern for all baptized and, and even Peter and the hierarchy must live their feminine receptive baptismal dimension of being led by the Holy Spirit. That is, the Church is Marian in her essence; it is the universal call to surrender to the Holy Spirit's action, resulting in holiness and contemplation; to be primarily sons/daughters of God and secondarily His workers.

People run after saints

Here is the test to know if we are growing in the Marian dimension: people will come seeking us (for counsel, Confession, healing, etc.), the way they sought St. Andre Bessette, Fr. Solanus Casey, St. John Vianney, Padre Pio, etc. One co-worker of St. John Vianney said to him, "other missionaries run after sinners, even into foreign countries, but as for you, it is the sinners who run after you.'" In addition, the saints' exponential influence perdures till the end of the time (e.g., St. Therese of Lisieux). **Our present crisis is a crisis of a paucity (scarcity) of saints, because of which we fail to be "contagious"** (salt that has lost its corrosiveness). We are running around doing evangelization without sanctification. Blessed Dina Bélanger tells us that Jesus shared His disappointment in many priests: "My priests should be other Christs… Many among them possess eloquence and human learning but they lack the fundamental science, holiness." The example of the early Church is instructive: they lacked wealth, education, and influence, and yet conquered the world for Christ; for the Holy Spirit was powerful in them in the higher "Mansions," the apex of which was the dark night of persecution and martyrdom: "you will be brought before kings and governors for my name's sake" (Lk 21:12-19).

II. *Sanctification through Companionship with Christ*

Before the new Christ looks toward the evangelization, he has to sanctify himself. Sanctification entails receptivity (feminine dimension), allowing Christ to possess him. This section presents: (A) <u>Preparation</u> for the transformation of the Sixth Mansions from the feminine receptivity of poverty in faith, hope, and love; (B) The <u>transformation</u> of the Sixth Mansions from companionship with Christ; (C) The <u>strengthening</u> of intimacy with Christ before the Blessed Sacrament. Mary is our model here.

A. <u>Preparation</u>: Faith, Hope, and Love for Receptivity in Poverty

The twelve apostles went forth in poverty only with the Holy Spirit, the experience of Christ's love, and faith and hope.[20] The new Christ too allows Christ to possess him and to act in him ("but Christ who lives in me," Gal 2:20). St. Margaret Mary Alacoque once confided to another Sister that Jesus was always trying to teach her, "Let me do it." Mother Catherine Mechtilde de Bar teaches us that lack of humility and emptiness of self prevent God from invading us and filling us with Himself and His graces:

> God asks for nothing better than to fill us with himself and his graces, but he sees that we are so full of pride and self-satisfaction that it prevents him from communicating himself to us. For if souls are not founded upon true humility and self-contempt, we are incapable of receiving God's gifts, because our self-love would devour them. So God is obliged to leave us in our poverty, darkness, and sterility to make us realize our nothingness. This is how necessary the virtue of humility is. (*Adorer et adhérer*, 113).

This greater efficacy of faith, hope, love, and poverty derives from the fact that it *participates in the receptivity of the Marian dimension referred to by von Balthasar*. St. Thérèse teaches us its power in her experience of God's "absence" in the dark night before her death by making more acts of faith, hope, and love in her last year than in all her life. These theological virtues and poverty enable *God to work in us*. St. Thérèse teaches us the power of this poverty-receptivity:

---

[20] We note that Joseph Cardinal Ratzinger emphasized "faith" in *The Ratzinger Report* and Gerhard Cardinal Müller emphasized "hope" in *The Cardinal Müller Report* (San Francisco: Ignatius Press, 2017), x.

Thérèse is marvelously free from herself and marvelously free for God. Her soul is wide open to the invasions of divine love. We, in fact, prevent God from coming to us and "flooding our souls with waves of his tenderness," because we do not open to him the place he wants to occupy. Only when poverty is united with confidence, is God able to realize in us the desires of his love.... "Merit does not consist in doing or in giving much, but rather in receiving, in loving much.... Let us allow Him to take and give all He wills."[21]

1. Poverty: Emptiness Allows God to Act in us (St. Thérèse)

The higher Mansions of St. Teresa of Jesus' interior castle are attained through surrender to the invasion and action of the Holy Spirit (St. John of the Cross calls this loving inflow "contemplation"). Beyond the need in our age for restraint from materialism, there is need to capture an even deeper, inner poverty, what Mother Teresa described as "giving God permission" (giving Him the reins within us). Fr. Paul-Marie of the Cross describes beautifully how St. Thérèse chose to be powerless like a child before God the Father, not even relying on her merits as would a little child. Her words below describe the power of this path of spiritual childhood, the path of unlimited confidence (theological virtue of hope) in complete poverty as a child:

> Moreover, having learned from experience about this *motherly* goodness of God, and knowing that the smaller the child, the more it can count on merciful help and attentive care, Thérèse intended to remain little, that is to say, she would no more be concerned about her powerlessness; on the contrary, she would rejoice in it.... She does not count on her works, or on her merits, she "keeps nothing in reserve," and she is not to be discouraged even about her faults.[22]

But it contains a deeper secret in this response to Sister Marie of the Sacred Heart (eldest sister) about Thérèse's desires for martyrdom: the sheer poverty and confidence as a little child allows for "the workings of this consuming and transforming love":

---

[21] St. Thérèse of Lisieux, *Correspondence*, LT 142, pp. 794-795, quoted in Paul-Marie of the Cross, *Carmelite Spirituality in the Teresian Tradition* (Washington, DC: ICS Publications, 1997), 65.
[22] Paul-Marie of the Cross, *Carmelite Spirituality in the Teresian Tradition*, 62.

Dear Sister, how can you say after this that my desires are the sign of my love?... Ah! I really feel that it is not this at all that pleases God in my little soul; what pleases Him is that He sees me loving my littleness and my poverty, the blind hope that I have in His mercy.... That is my only treasure, dear Godmother, why would this treasure not be yours?...

Oh, dear Sister, I beg you, understand your little girl, understand that to love Jesus, to be His victim of love, the weaker one is, without desires or virtues, the more suited one is for the workings of this consuming and transforming Love.[23]

Poverty is a stripping that allows the new Christ to depend more deeply on Christ through the theological virtues of faith, hope, and love. The simplicity of poverty brings many fruits: freedom of spirit, overcoming self-interest and bringing solicitude for the flock, making room for the workings of the Holy Spirit, and a certain influence upon those to whom he ministers.

Here are some practical suggestions for living poverty for priests and religious. There is a poverty in obedience to the Church and her teachings and norms; the poverty in giving up one's will in allowing the bishop or superior to choose one's assignment; the poverty of material things, perhaps choosing to look after our clothing and possessions so that they last; the poverty of choosing to sacrifice travel (many religious get only a home visit annually or every few years); the poverty of trusting in providence by not anticipating the future in anxiety or not focusing on the crises but looking at Jesus; the poverty of zeal in not being concerned about our retirement but working zealously for Christ's flock; the poverty of humility in not seeking to be recognized and be popular; the poverty of daily fidelity in the little things in a hidden way; the poverty of self-knowledge that we are nothing before God and to not be troubled by our sins or defects; the poverty of abandoning ourselves to God in the face of trials; the poverty of the cross by accepting illness, reverses, misunderstanding, superiors who lack discernment, desolations or dark nights.

---

[23] St. Thérèse of Lisieux, *Correspondence*, LT 197, p. 999, quoted in ibid., 65.

2. Faith: A Vigorous and not a Timorous, Resigned Christianity (Georges Chevrot)

The first element required of faith is a Christ-like fiery zeal and willingness to suffer. Msgr. George Chevrot shares something of his own fiery zeal, reminding us that "Our Master does not want a closed Christianity where the warm intimacy of the small gathering, a few privileged people would apply themselves to the observance of the Christian virtues, inaccessible to the great mass of men."[24] Instead, He desires the salvation of all men and receives even those who seem most unworthy, but whose grace is capable of transforming and purifying them. Our Lord's disciples must go out to the ends of the earth, to all cultures, flowing from the infinite love God has for all. Calling us to a vigorous Christianity, he exhorts us not to limit ourselves to patient endurance of the attack of the adversaries, but *to go on the offensive to speak out when necessary and expose ourselves to criticism and opposition.*[25]

In particular, Msgr. Chevrot mentions two types of Christianity that are falsifications of Christ's work that we must avoid in our work of evangelization. The first is a *resigned* Christianity. Those who preach it argue that Christianity is no longer incisive or biting. Msgr. Chevrot responds to the contrary:

> But is this not because they have pulled its teeth? The Gospel is a salt that attacks all metals, provided that it is not made insipid. Otherwise, they fatalistically accept injustices here below. "They are unbeatable," they say, "they will never be overcome. Evil is too strong." This defeatist mentality is the same as doubting the divine personality of the Saviour and his most formal promises. A Christian believes that evil is not more powerful than good and that God is stronger than Satan. He believes in the final overthrow of evil and devotes himself to hasten it.[26]

Thus, the apostle of Christ believes in the infinitely superior power of God and in this divine promise, "I have conquered the world." The end is assured. Chevrot teaches us to not simply confine ourselves to bowing our heads in

---

[24] George Chevrot, *The Eight Beatitudes*, 212.
[25] Ibid, 213.
[26] Ibid., 213-214.

endurance of evil, but to *combat injustice* wherever we meet it, renouncing our tranquility and putting up with mockery and insult. And even more, the apostle will *make reparation* for the wrong done, to take the place of the ones who have run away and neglected their duties.[27] Msgr. Chevrot also warns us against the danger of a *timorous* Christianity, which is an adulteration:

> One cannot but be struck by Jesus' insistence to forewarn his disciples against every feeling of fear. When he warned the Twelve once more that the preaching of the Gospel would earn them enemies, as it did to him, he hastens to tell them: "Fear not. Do not be afraid of those who kill the body, they cannot kill the soul…"

To train them to face danger, he sleeps in the boat peacefully during a tempest. When the apostles were struck with fear and roused Him, He ordered the waves to calm down with a simple gesture, but surprisingly reprimanded them, "Where is your faith?" He seeks to teach them not to fear: "The disciples are worried because they are a mere handful around the Saviour, but this is not the cause for despair: 'Do not be afraid, my little flock. Your father has determined to give you his kingdom.'"[28] Our Lord wishes to reach all, but we note that, to do so, He often uses the few, "the little flock." Msgr. Chevrot teaches that we should not be afraid to tire ourselves out for the Gospel and to avoid the example of the slothful servant in the parable who hid his talent. To combat fear, we must have faith, having the same lot as Jesus did:

> Let them have confidence in him and they will know how to face up to malevolence and danger. Adversity ought not to dismay them. It is not an accident, but a normal condition of disciples who take up their vocation seriously. "All those who are resolved to live a holy life in Christ Jesus will meet with persecution" (II Tim. iii. 12), wrote St. Paul in the twilight of his life…[29]

He notes that *Jesus only blessed the Christians who were reviled and persecuted* (Eighth Beatitude). But this does not refer to those who are attacked for their own defects, such as rebuking unjustly, indiscreet zeal, seeking personal glory, or

---

[27] Ibid., 214.
[28] Ibid.
[29] Ibid., 215.

the impetuous apologist lacking humility and meekness, making himself odious (as St. Peter pointed out in 1 Pet 2:20; 3:13-14). In great contrast to human expectation, those who have suffered do not seek our pity; instead, we find that the Twelve left the Sanhedrin after their whipping *rejoicing* and that Paul tells us, "I cannot contain myself for happiness, in the midst of all these trials of mine" (2 Cor 7:4).

Many others who have suffered for Christ have reiterated this joy, including St. Francis of Assisi, who found perfect joy in suffering without having deserved it, *"to share the sorrows of the blessed Christ."*[30]

3. Hope: Confidence in Weakness (St. Thérèse)

Along with faith, hope and confidence are very prominent in the life of St. Thérèse of Lisieux, who saw all her great desires (hope) fulfilled. She had desired to become a great saint and to evangelize all the earth but was but a young, humble religious sister. She came to see the power of *great desires* that she believed God put in her and, in her exclusive focus on love for Christ and for Christ's flock, she looked with confidence to Christ for everything:

> I read some tales of chivalry, but it wasn't long before God made me realise that the true glory is that which is eternal and that, to achieve it, there is no need to perform outstanding deeds. Instead, one must remain hidden and perform one's good deeds so that the right hand knows not what the left hand does. When I read stories about the deeds of the great French heroines - especially of the Venerable Joan of Arc, I longed to imitate them and felt stirred by the same inspiration which moved them. It was then that I received one of the greatest graces of my life, for, at that age, I didn't receive the spiritual enlightenment which now floods my soul. I was made to understand that the glory I was to win would never be seen during my lifetime.
>
> My glory would consist in becoming a great saint! This desire might seem presumptuous, seeing how weak and imperfect I was and still am, even after eight years as a nun, yet I always feel the same fearless certainty that I shall become a great saint. I'm not relying on my own merits, as I have none, but I put my hope in Him who is goodness and holiness Himself. It is He alone

---

[30] Ibid., 215-217.

who, satisfied with my feeble efforts, will raise me to Him, will clothe me with His infinite merits, and will make me a saint. I did not realize then how much one had to suffer to be a saint, but God soon showed me this through those trials I have already written about. [31]

She came to see that Christ's love would not fail her and do everything for her: "I'm not relying on my own merits, as I have none, but I put my hope in Him who is goodness and holiness Himself. It is He alone who, satisfied with my feeble efforts, will raise me to Him, will clothe me with His infinite merits, and will make me a saint." Herein lies the power to conquer hearts and evangelize all. It does not require great acts, but great confidence and poverty of spirit. Perhaps this is why Jesus chose for the Divine Mercy image, "Jesus, I trust in you."

4. Love: Experience of Christ's Love (von Balthasar)

Finally, Christian faith is not primarily about a set of doctrines and precepts, but that the Christian heart is won over by the experience of the infinite and personal love of Jesus. The lives of the saints are witness to this truth, as we have seen in St. Thérèse very powerfully (her prayer of oblation of love). One specific way our Lord employs from time to time to engender greater love for Him is His appearing to the saints in His crucified form.

This truth of the necessity of the experience of God's love as the first foundation is demonstrated theologically in Hans Urs von Balthasar's famous Trilogy (*The Glory of the Lord, Theodrama, Theologic*) in his description of Christ's salvific work. Von Balthasar teaches that God did not come primarily as a Teacher (the true) or as a Saviour (the good), but came to give Himself, to be a revelation and irradiation of the Trinity (Trinitarian love). So, to live the first two transcendentals of the true (e.g., doctrine) and the good (e.g., morals), we have to see the beauty or glory (third transcendental) within them. And the glory of God is revealed in Christ, the "form" of God, and above all in His kenotic love on the cross, His descent (love in self-

---

[31] St. Thérèse of Lisieux, *The Autobiography of St. Thérèse of Lisieux: Story of a Soul*, trans. John Beevers (New York: Image/Doubleday, 2001), 37-38. John Clarke's translation (Washington, DC: ICS, 1996), 72.

emptying).[32] So embracing Christ in His kenotic love is the key to the true and the good. We find this wonderfully illustrated biblically in the life of the apostle Paul, who suffered much for Christ ("I will show him how much he [Paul] must suffer for the sake of my name," Acts 9:16), and what drove Paul is revealed in these tender words: "He loved me and he gave himself up for me" (Gal 2:20).

Thus the work of the new Christ's sanctification begins with one thing— his personal experience of the love of God. The regional diocesan seminary in Toronto had been blessed for many years by the presence of the Hungarian Jesuit, Attila Miklósházy. This saintly bishop had endured much: his father died in his arms after being shot, he himself was arrested once and released, imprisoned and escaped, saw much bloodshed during the Budapest uprising, fled Hungary to pursue his vocation, and remained a lifelong exile from his native land. An inspiring sharing with seminarians of his heroic life in Communist Hungary culminated with a profound counsel to the seminarians: "If you have not yet had deep experiences of God's love, beg the Lord to grant them to you." His counsel likely revealed the strength (God's love) from which he himself drew the courage and joy of his own self-gift, his oblation.

B. Transformation: Companionship of Christ in the Sixth Mansions (St. Teresa of Jesus)

The theologically feminine dispositions of faith, hope, and love in poverty open the way for the actual transformation that comes from companionship of Christ, especially in the Sixth and Seventh Mansions. When Christian faith declines, as it has in our age, we should do an examination of conscience to discern the cause. St. Teresa of Jesus points out the reason why we disciples of Christ fail to influence the world— we fail to attain the higher Mansions, the stages of which constitute the interior journey for all human beings.

We find key insights of St. Teresa mediated through Sr. Madeleine of St. Joseph. She highlights St. Teresa's teaching on how a person reaching the

---

[32] Staale Johannes Kristiansen, "Hans Urs von Balthasar," in *Key Theological Thinkers: From Modern to Postmodern*, ed. Staale Johannes Kristiansen & Svein Rise (Surrey, England: Ashgate Publishing Ltd, 2013), 258.

Sixth Mansions exercises *tremendous influence in the world,* for it is *Christ at work within*:

> Supernatural understanding is that sovereignly efficacious act of the Holy Spirit which takes hold of the soul through its faculties of perception and puts it into direct contact in love, with him "who is." It is this understanding which reveals Christ, which establishes the soul in a relationship of perfect dependence on his action, and makes possible the intimate unity which he desires in view of the union achieved in the sixth Mansions....
>
> Today is it not more necessary than ever to do this? If everyone, or at least those who guide others, lived sufficiently by Christ to deserve to see him, to touch him, to listen to him in the Spirit of love, how much easier communion in him would be between East and West, between Catholic and Protestant theologians, between Christians of all shades of thought.[33]

Sr. Madeleine points out that even the lofty Fifth Mansions are still somewhat unstable. Progress to the Fifth Mansions is already remarkable progress within St. Teresa of Jesus' *Interior Castle,* for it is the entry into the unitive stage, where the power of interior progress can be strongly experienced. Though already in the Fourth Mansions one experiences deeper forms of prayer and liberation, it is in the Fifth Mansions that one experiences what St. Teresa images in the transformation of the silkworm (caterpillar) into a butterfly. Nevertheless, the butterfly (Fifth Mansions), though vastly superior to the silkworm, is still rather weak, like a kite blown by the wind. This is partly because the lower faculties are not yet subject to the will, which is corrected in the Sixth Mansions. Sublime graces are indeed attained in the contemplative Fourth and Fifth Mansions; yet, it is the *Sixth Mansions upwards that help bring true, lasting change in the world.* The great power in the Sixth Mansions derives from direct contact with Jesus, the One who awakens, as He awoke Lazarus and the daughter of Jairus. He now penetrates our human psyche and touches our emotional and affective life, as it were, by *direct contact*:

> Because this manner of working is characteristic of Christ, it characterizes the New Testament. Saint Peter says so on the day of Pentecost, the

---

[33] Sr. Madeleine of St. Joseph, *Within the Castle with St. Teresa* (trans. Carmel of Rochester, reprinted by Carmel of Lafayette in honour of the 5th centenary of the birth of St. Teresa of Jesus), 171-172.

threshold of a new era, in the discourse we referred to above: "It is what Joel the prophet spoke of." For it is the time of the visible approach of the Spirit, in which, as he promised, Jesus is going to manifest himself.[34]

What all this leads to can be captured by these words of St. Teresa of Jesus: "The more the soul advances, the closer does this good Jesus bear it company." The Father's plan is that we be "with" His Son:

> The Father's intention is for us to be "with" his Son, and all his works are directed toward procuring that end. Above all, supernatural creation [Baptism] makes us sons of God who tend to imitate the eternal Son according to our nature, for God has "predestined us to share the image of his Son" (Rom. 8:29). The Incarnation renders man's presence to the Incarnate Son possible; the Redemption unites him to the Son because of a joint obligation; and the gift of grace makes Christ present by a direct communication of the filial character.
>
> In practice, the summit of this divine plan is found on the level of the Sixth Mansions. There, the circle of our supernatural vocation begins to close. The joining of the soul and Christ Jesus takes place in a complete psychological reality. When Jesus said to Saint Teresa, "It is I," he was accomplishing his last promise: "Know that I am with you!" And, in the same action, he realized his eternal dream.[35]

The great failure of many to progress and to influence people is precisely because we do not go through Christ and seek His intimate company:

> Our Lord himself has strong words on this point: "The Holy Spirit," he says, "will prove the world wrong about sin... in that they refuse to believe in me" (John 16:8-9). This is the sin of the infidels, of the atheists, of the deists. It is also the error, offensive to the Savior, of those Christians who would like to find God without Christ, of those who think, for example, that little St. Thérèse speaks too much of Jesus, that here was the mentality of a child, while the spiritual giants have a different style.[36]

---

[34] Ibid., 159.
[35] Ibid., 157-158.
[36] Ibid., 159.

Many make slow progress because they go directly to "God," as if the Father had not sent His Son and made the Son our path and our Bridegroom. Each new Christ should be like the haemorrhaging woman who, touching the hem of Jesus' clothing, was the only one in the crowd who "had achieved real contact, calling into action the miraculous power of His Sacred Humanity."[37] In ascending the Mansions, Jesus becomes the predominant focus. Rather than going to God through zeal and harsh asceticism, there is "more spiritual greatness in lisping the name of Jesus," to converse and keep company with Him:

> At the risk of startling some readers, we could say that there is more spiritual greatness in lisping the name of Jesus in the context of the Sixth Mansions and on the foundations which they suppose, than in turning oneself purely toward God through harsh asceticism…. To pretend to go to God in another way is to condemn oneself to not enjoying substantial results: it is the poverty of non-Christian spiritualities, however venerable they may be.

> These sometimes heroic attempts resemble the blows of the rod of Moses on the rock. The water springs up, it is true, but those who drink of it do not enter into the real Promised Land. The Lord did not say: "Strike the rock," but: "Order the rock to yield its waters" (Num. 20:8-11). What does this mean? Saint Paul informs us that the Rock is Christ (see 1 Cor. 10:4); it is not easy to engage in conversation with him. If we want to address someone we must adapt ourselves to his language.

> Many would more willingly perform works of zeal and penitence than maintain, without growing weary, such a conversation with this poor and humble Master who is so glad to speak of his cross. "It is a great art," says the *Imitation*, "to know how to converse with Jesus, and to know how to keep Jesus!"[38]

C. Strengthening: Intimacy with Christ before the Blessed Sacrament

In their work of sanctification, amidst the many challenges, Christ's disciples have a powerful and consoling external presence and aid: the presence of the Lord in the reserved Blessed Sacrament. The lives of saints witness to its

---

[37] Ibid., 157.
[38] Ibid., 159-160.

power, as we note, for example, the consolation and strength it lent to the great English convert, Robert Hugh Benson.

To give a specific example, let us take note of the great consolation Henry Cardinal Newman received from it over and over again in his life. It was his friend Richard Hurrell Froude, high Anglican, who "taught Newman two central beliefs that he carried to the end of his life, namely, the doctrine of the Real Presence and the devotion to the Blessed Virgin."[39] In the many difficulties Newman faced, it was the reserved Blessed Sacrament that became his consolation, which is a consoling example for all priests:

> Yet as the reserved Sacrament had been his chief comfort during the weeks spent in the Hope-Scott household, that was likewise the case during his prolonged absences in Dublin when he was trying against such heavy odds to found the Catholic University in Ireland.[40]
>
> Newman not only found in the Blessed Sacrament the strongest moral support of his personal life, but he sought to explain, both to Catholics and to those outside the Church, aspects of her Eucharistic doctrine and practice that puzzled them.[41]

The new Christ before the Blessed Sacrament becomes in a certain way like a sentry at his "post." How many people in moments of crises, such as Cardinal John O'Connor as a military chaplain abroad, during his dark nights, have knelt in anguish before the Blessed Sacrament, begging for help and interceding for others. According to the author of *In Sinu Jesu*, the Lord has called for renewal in the Church, beginning with priests dedicating time before the Blessed Sacrament.

Adoration before the Blessed Sacrament and its Link with the Trinity

We summarize an article by a hermitess on the sublimity of the Blessed Sacrament: "Behold I am with You Always: When we Adore His Son in the Blessed Sacrament, 'God Takes us to Himself.'" In her reflections on John

---

[39] Wilfrid Ward, *The Life of John Henry Cardinal Newman*, I (London: Longmans, Green and Company, 1912), 323.
[40] Ibid., 335.
[41] Ibid., 337.

14-17, she sets the Blessed Sacrament as the fulfillment of Jesus' words, "I will not leave you orphans but will come to you… I will remain with you always" (Jn 14). This is not a moral presence, for the entire Paschal drama has led to a re-ordering of the universe to "'contain,' in a more personal way, the veiled substantial presence of the Godhead."

With a deep theological, contemplative background, she makes profound points regarding adoration of the Blessed Sacrament:

➢ Since Christ now sits at the right hand of the Father, when we adore the Blessed Sacrament, "we ourselves sit at the Father's right hand as adopted sons";

➢ Through the Blessed Sacrament, "[W]e can now have a window into infinity because we can see His Risen and Ascended glory, and the very countenance of the Father";

➢ The Old Testament experiential contact "is still distinct from contact with God's essential, (super!) substantial, ontological [Eucharistic] presence";

➢ "Here we have direct contact with the Father's house in the Substance of the Godhead, God's inner life, the *ad intra* Infinity";

➢ "The special place Jesus has prepared for us while we sojourn on earth is kneeling before His Eucharistic Presence in silent adoration, where He very powerfully takes us to Himself";

➢ "Hours of physical proximity to the Eucharist in adoration are arguably the most powerful agent of the interior life";

➢ "When looking at the Eucharistic Face of Jesus… and therefore the countenance of the Father, whatever we ask in Jesus' name He will do."[42]

---

[42] Hermitess, "Behold I am with You Always: When we adore His Son in the Blessed Sacrament, 'God Takes us to Himself,'" *Inside the Vatican* (May 2017): 43.

III. Program: Cardinal Van Thuan's 10 Rules, Other Norms

From his experience in prison, Cardinal van Thuan composed a program of ten rules that can serve as a program for each priest.:

1. I will live the present moment to the fullest
2. I will discern between God and God's works
3. I will hold firmly to one secret: prayer
4. I will see in the Holy Eucharist my only power
5. I will have only one wisdom: the science of the Cross
6. I will remain faithful to my mission in the Church and for the Church as a witness of Jesus Christ
7. I will seek the peace the world cannot give
8. I will carry out a revolution by renewal in the Holy Spirit
9. I will speak one language and wear one uniform: Charity
10. I will have one very special love: The Blessed Virgin Mary[43]

Particular Concrete Suggestions for the Parish Priest

John Paul II in *Novo millennio ineunte* teaches that the goal of the parish is to sanctify the parishioners— to make them saints. Since the priest cannot give what he doesn't have, he must *first sanctify himself* before seeking to sanctify the parishioners.[44] Suggestions include the following:

- go through Mary to Jesus in everything;
- be intensely eucharistic, such that the Mass is the center of the priest's day and the Blessed Sacrament is his spiritual hearth;
- find a holy and experienced spiritual director (it is difficult to become holy without the aid of a holy spiritual director);
- weekly Confession should be his transforming power;

[43] Francis Cardinal van Thuan, Duong Hy Vong: Nguyen van Thuan, accessed January 31, 2016, http://www.nguyenvanthuan.com/tenrules.html.
[44] Fr. Stephen Rossetti offers valuable insights in this area. He lists ten steps to holiness: cease any serious sin; renew the sacrament of Penance; pray more; dive deeply into the Eucharist; love the Church; practice gratitude; embrace your crosses; relax and trust [God is looking after His Church]; and abandon yourself to God. These are taken from the slide presentation, *Our Journey into Joy: Ten Steps to Priestly Holiness* (Fall Recollection at St. Augustine's Seminary, November 1, 2015). But they are also elaborated upon in the book with the same title: Stephen J. Rossetti, *Our Journey into Joy: Ten Steps to Priestly Holiness* (Notre Dame, IN: Ave Maria Press, 2009).

➤ priestly fraternity should be his strong support;

➤ continue theological reading (adopt a theological mentor) and prepare homilies before the Blessed Sacrament;

➤ the joys and sorrows of the parishioners become those of the priest, as their spiritual father and shepherd. He should see interruptions (arising from the needs of his flock) as part of his work.

Of these suggestions, let us give singular prominence to weekly Confession in the words of St. Josemaría Escriva: "Go weekly to the holy sacrament of Penance... Our radical transformation into Christ takes place in the sacrament of mercy"[45]; "Jesus Christ our Lord was moved as much by Peter's repentance after his fall as by John's innocence and faithfulness.... He seeks us out, just as he did the disciples of Emmaus... He sought Thomas... Jesus Christ is always waiting for us to return to him..."[46] Weekly Confession, besides remitting sin, is a great aid to sanctification, constituting, with daily celebration of the Mass, the twin pillars of the interior life.

When seeking to sanctify parishioners, the following suggestions come to mind:

➤ First, we can consecrate the parish to Mary. Then, we can also recommend consecration to our Lady to parents of their children at Baptism and couples of their marriage. There ought also to be devotion to the parish's patron saint as well as fostering the veneration of saints.

➤ Second, before focusing on being welcoming and improving the music, the liturgy itself, especially the Mass, has to be the primary means of evangelization and sanctification. Scott Hahn was converted through the Mass, and people were transformed from attending Padre Pio's Masses.

➤ Third, consider having perpetual or partial adoration of the exposed Blessed Sacrament at our parishes.

➤ Fourth, the first preaching has to be the example and life of the priest. Praying before the tabernacle can be a witness to the people.

---

[45] St. Josemaría Escrivá, *Hoja informativa*, n. 5, p. 6.
[46] Idem, *Christ is Passing By* (Manila: Sinag-Tala Publs., 1974), no. 75, 118

➢ Fifth, the preaching must flow from theological riches of the Church (e.g., Church Fathers). Instead of always using everyday examples (e.g., marital love) for love, why not first point to the infinite love of Christ for us on the cross, or the intra-Trinitarian love among the three divine Persons?

➢ Sixth, we can look to tap into the richness of the new charisms provided by the Holy Spirit in the Church in our time, such as the Charismatic Renewal, the lay charisms (e.g., Charismatic Renewal, Opus Dei, Focolare, Communion and Liberation, Madonna House, Taizé, etc.).

➢ Seventh, we seek to find ways to enable the parishioners to experience God's love. The priest must above all be a "spiritual father," the people experiencing Christ's personal love in and through him (parish as family).

Appendix: A description of Msgr. Georges Chevrot:

> The Morins were devoutly Roman Catholic, and the church was an integral part of family life. Although Invalides was within the parish of the nearby Basilica of Sainte-Clotilde, Yvette and her parents and grandfather chose to attend Saint-François-Xavier church… Their preference stemmed largely from their friendship with, and admiration for, Saint-François-Xavier's charismatic Monsignor Georges Chevrot. A well-known and widely respected priest and a prolific author on religious topics, he had also created a Church youth movement to which Yvette had belonged for most of her adolescence. In addition to emphasizing equality and social justice, Chevrot imbued his young charges with a love of their nation's history and the role of the Church in that history. Nor was Chevrot's patriotism merely intellectual, for when the clouds of war once again gathered over France he would prove himself more than ready to turn words into action— as would those who revered him.[47]

---

[47] Stephen Harding, *Escape from Paris: A True Story of Love and Resistance in Wartime France* (New York: Da Capo Press, 2019.

PART II: EVANGELIZATION

PRESENTING CHRIST ANEW

"I came to cast fire upon the earth; and would that it were already kindled"

(Lk 12:49)

CHAPTER 6

LOVE OF CHRIST'S CHURCH AND MISSION

> Praised may you be, Mother of love at its most lovely, of healthy fear, of divine knowledge and holy hope…. Without discouraging us from any task, you protect us from deceptive myths; you spare us from the aberrations and the aversions of all churches made by the hand of man…. Living Ark, Gate of the East! Unflawed mirror of the activity of the Most High. You who are the beloved of the Lord of the Universe, initiated into His secrets, and who teaches us what pleases him! You whose supernatural splendour never fades, even in the darkest hours! It is thanks to you that our darkness is bathed in light! You through whom the priest goes up every day to the altar of God, who gives joy to his youth…. Each day you give us him who is the Way and the Truth…. Holy Mother, unique Mother, immaculate Mother! O great Mother! Holy Church, true Eve, and sole true Mother of all the living.[1] (Henri de Lubac)

Preface: from Christ to the Church

Let us review in outline the itinerary of the disciples of Christ who follow His very path. Through Baptism, they become new Christs with Christ's new presence in His Mystical Body, the Church. The mission of Jesus is prolonged in that of his own apostles whom He sent out. They must preach the Gospel and heal the sick (Lk 9:1f.), that which was the personal mission of Jesus. They are the workers sent into the harvest of the Master (Mt 9:38; see Jn 4:38); the servants sent by the King to bring the guests to the nuptial banquet of His Son (Mt 22:3). These messengers will have the same end that He had: "He who listens to you listens to me, he who rejects you rejects me. And he who rejects me, rejects the One who sent me" (Lk 10:16); "… he who receives me, receives the One who has sent me" (Jn 13:20). The mission of the apostles is, in fact, rooted in a strict path of that of Jesus: "As the Father has sent me, so I am sending you" (Jn 20, 21). This expression clarifies the profound sense of the final mission of the Twelve: "Go out into the world and preach…" Because of this mandate, they proclaimed the Gospel (Mk 16:14), made disciples of all the nations (Mt 28:19), and brought their witness even to the farthest ends of the world (Acts 1:8).

---

[1] Henri de Lubac, *Splendor of the Church* (San Francisco: Ignatius Press, 1999), 277-278.

The apostles accomplished their mission thanks to the power of the Holy Spirit, since "the Consoler, the Holy Spirit that the Father will send in my name, He will teach you all things" (Jn 14:26; see 15:26; 16:7). This context situates Pentecost as the initial manifestation of this mission of the Spirit that will last for all the time of the Church (Acts 1:8). The mission is, therefore, a task that belongs to the entire Church in virtue of her essential character, that is, insofar as she is the community of salvation of Christ, and in virtue of her place in salvation history, being situated between the Ascension and the final Parousia. From this is derived the Church's catholicity as an expression of this essential and universal mission that belongs to her. For this reason, each situation in the world that appears as a challenge to her catholicity becomes for her an irresistible call to mission. The *Catechism of the Catholic Church* defines evangelization as fulfilling the mandate of Jesus Christ to "make disciples of all nations" (Matthew 28:19), so that all might respond to the Father's love and be saved through communion with Jesus and His body, the Church.[2]

The new Christ, as a prerequisite for engaging in the new evangelization, should have a profound love of the Church and deep sense of her splendour. He cherishes her individual images, like facets of a diamond, marvelling at the divine shining forth in her human qualities: as People of God, Body and Bride of Christ, Temple of the Holy Spirit, reflecting Trinitarian communion, etc.

To this end, we offer three discourses on the Church. I. Charles Cardinal Journet's depiction of the superior divine power of grace given within the visible Church (covenanted graces by contact) that renders us like unto Christ and impels us to the Trinity and to co-redeem the world. II. Hans Urs von Balthasar explains how this happens when each person, through personal surrender as with Mary and the apostles, become universal "Church-persons" who live the Trinitarian perichoresis (being for others). III. Henri de Lubac, as a "Church-person," teaches us how to love the Church's divine dimensions while being prudent with and charitable toward her human limitations.

---

[2] The author has drawn this section from a source but cannot recall which source.

I. Covenanted Graces Make Us Like Christ and Impel Us to the Trinity and to Co-Redeem (Charles Journet)

Charles Cardinal Journet provides a very helpful panorama of the five existential states (phases) of grace in salvation history. (1) The first existential state is the age of Adam or paradise before the Fall, otherwise known as the age of the Father. (2) The second existential state has to do with Christian grace anticipated in the Gentiles (Natural Law) and the Mosaic Law. (3) The third existential state is Christian grace of derivation by contact with the arrival of Christ. (4) The fourth existential state is that of grace by derivation, either by contact (covenanted Christian graces) and at a distance (uncovenanted graces, outside the Church). (5) The fifth existential state is that of Glory, of beatifying and transfiguring grace.

Here we will examine only the third existential state of grace (age of Christ), which is also essentially that of the Church till the end of time. We see that Christ's grace fulfills and far surpasses that of the Old Testament. Cardinal Journet offers a Thomistic discourse, depicting the splendour of grace given within the Church that surpasses the grace of Baptism by desire. It depicts the ineffable grace given within the Church that is already an anticipation of the heavenly grace. Here Cardinal Journet, provides, as it were, a crash course on how the teachings and sacraments are given through the Church's hierarchical charism, simply summarizing Cardinal Journet's thought.

A. Grace by Derivation from Christ (Succeeding Grace by Anticipation)

There are two basic ages of Christ's grace as described by Cardinal Journet: *graces by anticipation (before Christ) and graces by derivation (with Christ's arrival)*. In the third existential state of grace (Christ), the Church was only in Mary and there were no hierarchical powers, for these are all centered in Christ Himself. Jesus promised to hand them on to His apostles. There was the Bridegroom, Christ, and the Bride, His Church, that consisted solely then of the Virgin Mary. The Church would never be holier than it was at that time, at a concentration of grace in our Lady which gave the infant Church a complexion as a Marial Church. At Pentecost, the Church, which from the time of the Incarnation was definitely established in Christ, reached

145

fulfillment in His body by a kind of pressure exerted by the Holy Spirit on the grace of Christ to make it flow out on mankind. To the end of time, the Holy Spirit will pour out Christ's grace to His Church.[3]

At that time, Christ was constituted mediator of all graces. Before Christ, grace came directly from God, who gave it in view of the future merits of Christ's passion (Christian grace by anticipation). Beginning with Christ, all graces passed through the sacred humanity of Christ— they are Christ's grace by *derivation*, so that Christ's humanity is the "organ of the divinity," which St. Thomas calls the "instrument conjoined to His divine person." It is because all graces pass through His sacred humanity that Jesus could say to the infirm woman, "Who has touched me?"[4]

The graces by derivation with the coming of Christ are themselves of two types: graces of *contact*, grace that is derived from direct contact with Jesus; and graces given at a *distance*. An example of grace of contact is Jesus' healing the man born blind by putting clay on his eyes, an example of grace given at a distance is the healing of the 10 lepers who were cured on the way back from meeting Jesus.

The reason for the mystery of the Incarnation is that we might have contact with Jesus. God could simply have sent His graces from heaven, as He did in the days of Adam. Since the Fall, man's balance is upset, and he is in a way under the dominion of the things of *sense*. They are a temptation to him, and yet he needs to be able to rise beyond them. So God willed to make of this dangerous thing (sense) a means of salvation for us, to free us from our prison walls; therein lies the whole mystery of the sacramental system. Since man's faith is impaired, he needs to be touched by the hand of the divine healer, by human contact, that could be seen and felt. In heaven, this immediate contact will no longer be necessary because man's state will no longer be impaired.[5]

---

[3] Charles Journet, *The Meaning of Grace*, 105.
[4] Ibid., 106.
[5] Ibid., 106-107.

B. The Ineffable Power of Christ's Grace that Makes Us like Christ

Cardinal Journet describes grace by derivation as fully "Christian," *making us fully like Christ.* And, *since grace is correlative with the indwelling of the Three Divine Persons*, its strict identification with the Redeemer *makes this indwelling more profound, more interior, and more intense.* It gives us a new mode of access to the divine Persons (Jn 7:38). The Holy Spirit did dwell in the just men of the Old Testament, and in Adam, and in the angels, but he did not dwell in them *so intimately and so powerfully.* It was necessary for Christ to accomplish His work of Redemption and to enter into His glory. And once the whole course of the Redeemer, the Head, had been run, the Holy Spirit would come down at Pentecost with *this new intimacy and po*wer. Christ would be the dispenser of the new grace, a New Law, which would be the pre-condition of the new mode of indwelling of the three Divine Persons: "… and My Father will love him, and we shall come to him, and take up our abode with him" (Jn 14:23).

Since the time that our nature was wounded (Fall), we have had need of *mediation.* With the Incarnation, mediation attained its fullness, and since God, who could perfectly well have given this directly from above, became incarnate and made the heart of Jesus the source of grace and forgiveness, the words of forgiveness now come from a voice on earth. The source of forgiveness has come into time and space. *Grace was never more intense than at the moment of the visible mediation, and never had it overwhelmed man so powerfully.* Mediation, then, is not a screen, but a channel.[6]

Let us make a few helpful distinctions. Abraham received the grace that was powerful and profound but it was only grace by "anticipation," while the least of Christians have a superior grace that comes to them by "derivation." Our dispensation with Christ's coming is superior to Abraham's. Augustine affirmed, "Abraham was better than I am, but my state is better than his." John the Baptist had a grace far greater than any of us; but he belongs to the age of the expectation of Christ, he is the finger pointing to Christ.[7]

---

[6] Ibid., 107-108.
[7] Ibid., 108-109.

The Church's Hierarchy Acts in Christ's Place through Teaching and Sacraments

When Jesus left this world, He established these graces of contact through the Church, by setting up on earth hierarchical powers (apostolic college), both jurisdictional (teaching) and sacramental: "Go and teach all nations, baptizing them in the name of the Father and of the Son and of the Holy Spirit" (Mt 28:19). It is Christ's voice that continues to instruct us (teaching) through time; and Christ's hands, stretching through time and space, that continue to touch us by the sacraments. We may say that *the powers of jurisdiction and the sacramental power of order belong to the hierarchy*, and the grace that she possesses, which is fully Christian and makes us like Christ, issues from the hierarchy. This grace is fully Christian for two reasons: it is oriented, since the power of jurisdiction gives directives, grace must operate on a prescribed course; and secondly, it is sacramental.

Grace needs to be oriented (by teaching). Whenever it really lives in a soul, it wants to be active. It seeks out ways to submit its understanding to God to ask what it must believe so as to please Him. The virtue of faith is never deceived, but the believer himself may often be. The believer, without knowing it, may clutter his faith with things opposed or alien to it, and it is always dangerous to be deceived about these. God tells us that, by His Holy Spirit, Jesus would continue teaching us through those who have jurisdiction.[8]

Journet teaches that the powers of jurisdiction are oriented in two distinct ways:

1. Teaching

(i) *Bridegroom's voice*: First, the Church, by her powers of proclaiming what Christ taught, speaks as the echo of the Bridegroom's voice. It is truly God's voice that she brings to us, and she is assisted *absolutely, infallibly, unalterably,* to orient the grace within us. This happens when she defines a doctrine, declares that something is part of Revelation. You may not find this doctrine stated explicitly in Scripture, but you will find a principle that, developed

---

[8] Ibid., 109-110.

homogenously in the course of time, has given us the truths like those of the Immaculate Conception and of the Assumption, revealed truths contained implicitly in the deposit of Revelation. They require of us an obedience of faith, a *theological obedience*, for it is on God's authority that I believe, not on that of the Church. We disobey the Church when she speaks with the Bridegroom's voice: for example, disobedience in regard to the dogma of the Immaculate Conception, though not a sin for a Protestant, is theological for Catholics and one is guilty of heresy, which can make a shipwreck of one's faith.

(ii) *Church speaks as Spouse*: The second type of teaching is when the Church, by her canonical power, speaks in her own name as Spouse. She herself decides, for Jesus gave her His power: "He that hears you hears me, and he that despises you despises me" (Lk 10:16). The apostles and the Church, speaking with the Bridegroom's voice, also have to settle a number of problems or matters that are not of the faith, or at any rate, are not so yet. For example, Pope Pius XII condemned Polygenism in *Humani generis*. He wrote about this in an encyclical, and so it is not yet defined as a truth of faith.

This is the voice of the Spouse. When the Church speaks on such matters, she is assisted to orient the grace within us, not in an absolute manner, but *prudentially*. Here we are no longer on the first plane (voice of the Bridegroom). The Church is putting forward her own ideas, but she makes her voice heard as the voice of the Spouse. When the Church gives us prudential directives, whether in papal encyclicals or in episcopal utterances, what is required of us is an attitude of "intellectual" obedience in the case of doctrinal propositions, and of "practical" obedience in disciplinary matters. Obedience here is not theological, but of the moral order. We sin *mortally* by disobeying these. It is not a sin of heresy but a sin of disobedience, against the virtue of prudence.

The prudential assistance given to the canonical powers to orient grace is of various degrees: fallible or infallible. At the end, the grace of the New Testament is oriented by *the voice of Christ, which speaks to us, in different accents, through the powers of jurisdiction*— emphatic and clear in the pronouncements of the declarative power; subdued yet recognizable, in those of the canonical power.[9]

2. Seven Sacraments

Second, in addition to being oriented by the hierarchy's jurisdiction, the grace that derives wholly from Christ is sacramental. As God took Eve from the side of Adam, so He raised up from the second Adam in His sleep on the cross the second Eve, the Church. The sacraments flow from the side of Christ, water symbolizing Baptism and blood symbolizing the Eucharist: Baptism is the entry into the life of grace, the Eucharist is its consummation, the greatest of the sacraments. Thus, *the sacraments are, as it were, the prolongation of Christ's humanity*, like a mist rising from the earth after rain, spreading over it and making it fertile. Those who do not belong to the Church, even if they know nothing of Christ, if they are in good faith and have a real desire for God, loving Him more than they love themselves, are justified; which means that they have received grace in a hidden manner, the same grace as we have. They, however, lack something of particular excellence: the special complexion given to grace by the sacraments, which makes it, instead of being just Sanctifying Grace, a grace that is *fully Christian, sacramental grace*. In those outside the Church, grace is as if in a foreign land, a place of *exile*; whereas the sacraments communicate to us not only the grace of Christ but also *the modalities it has in His heart*.

Three Qualities of Christian Grace Prepared in the Heart of Jesus

(i) Connatural: In the heart of Jesus grace is in His own chosen territory, as in its *connatural place*, specially prepared for it. Since the soul of Christ is so close to the person of the Word, grace finds its true home and there unfolds itself in perfect freedom. Grace brings a kind of enlargement, the liberty of the children of God. It is transmitted to them as already humanized in the heart of Christ; it enters them unforced, it becomes connatural to them.

(ii) Filial: As Jesus is the Son of God by nature, the grace that fills His heart has a wonderfully *filial quality*. When He communicates it to us by the touch

---

[9] Ibid., 110-114.

of the sacraments, it is to make us *fully children* by adoption of His Heavenly Father. Sacramental grace is a grace by which we are made Christ's brethren at the same time as it makes us children of the Father. If the Holy Spirit would have instead become incarnate, grace would have a different complexion, but it would not have been filial to the extent revealed in Gal 4:4-6: "... that we might receive the adoption of sons.... 'Abba, Father.'" Those who lived before Christ were indeed *children of God, but not with the same intimacy* proper to the New Law.

(iii) The grace received by the sacraments is *plenary*, grace in its perfect flowering. Consequently it is capable of producing a sevenfold result— the seven sacraments.

The Sublime Grace Poured out in the Seven Sacraments

To bring out the connection among the seven sacraments, we can compare the phases of natural life with those of the supernatural. There are *birth, growth, and nourishment*, corresponding to Baptism, Confirmation, and the Eucharist respectively. This would suffice for the fullness of Christian life in the individual were there no sin, and against sin two remedies are provided: Confession, which is able to restore life to the soul, and Anointing of the Sick, in case, at the moment it is to appear before God, there still remains some weakness, a lack of transparency to the divine. Lastly, on the supernatural plane, man lives in society. The organization for this society is provided for by the sacrament of Holy Orders, and His continuation by matrimony, raised to the dignity of the sacrament, with two ends, one earthly, the other heavenly, to increase the number of the elect.

In addition, three of the sacraments imprint on the soul an ineffaceable character, which is a power of validly performing the acts of Christian worship. Those without the powers of Holy Orders can recite the words of consecration over bread and wine, but nothing happens; but a priest, even in the state of mortal sin or if he be a heretic, can consecrate the species. An unbaptized person making a Confession would receive an invalid absolution, since only Baptism enables one to receive the other sacraments validly. Confirmation gives one the formal power to confess Christ openly by continuing the witness that Christ came into the world to give to the truth.

151

Here then we have three ineffaceable sacramental characters. An apostate priest forbidden to say Mass and exercise the ministry is still a priest. Likewise, an apostate is not rebaptized, for one is baptized once and for all. Regarding marriage, as long as one of the two parties to a marriage is living, a second union is invalid. And as long as the same illness continues, Anointing of the Sick is not repeated.

So three of the sacraments (Holy Orders, Baptism, Confirmation) imprint a *character* and two (matrimony and Anointing of the Sick) a *mark*, which is not indelible but temporary. Apart from the "character" or "mark" given by five of the sacraments, all seven give or increase grace. Two are instituted to give grace to those who are without it, Baptism and Confession; for that reason, they are called sacraments of the dead. The others give increase of grace in those who already have it, and thus are the sacraments of the living.

The fullness of grace makes us like Christ when received through the sacraments. We note first that the effect of grace is not, like that given to Adam, to eliminate, but since derived from Christ, to illuminate suffering and death. Jesus did not eliminate suffering and death for Himself, but illuminated them; and the grace of the Redemption causes us to follow in His footsteps.[10]

C. Covenanted Grace Impels Us to the Trinity and to Co-Redeem the World

Cardinal Journet describes that, in Baptism, the grace that was in Jesus Christ flowed over me and began to exert in my soul an impulse similar to an impulse in Him. In the grace of Christ there are, as it were, <u>two forces</u>: *one, of glory, impelling Him toward the Trinity; the other, of the cross, urging Him to redeem the world.* The germ of baptismal grace may be choked up by my whole line of conduct, but in itself, it tends, if I do not oppose it, to perfect itself by the other sacraments, and to produce in my life effects like those produced in the soul of Christ. Redemptive in Christ, *it will be co-redemptive in me, summoning me to the great trials and the great deliverance as spoken of by St. John of the Cross.*

---

[10] Ibid., 114-121.

Confirmation causes me to confess the faith in close unity and profound continuity with the witness borne by Jesus to the truth. I shall testify to the faith, not just as a freelance, but with a love of the kind that emanates from that of the Redeemer confessing the truth in the world.

The Eucharist is the sacrament of the consummation of the spiritual life; what Baptism has sown in the soul, the Eucharist develops to maturity. The real aim of the Eucharist is not primarily to avoid sin, which is true enough, but to perfect the spiritual life. The most genuine Holy Communions are those of the saints.

The sacrament of Confession gives a special grace of purification and, in consequence, a hunger for the Eucharist. That is the proper effect of Confession.

Anointing of the Sick prepares the soul for departing to eternity. It purifies it from the remains of sin, that is, from all the weaknesses left by original sin and actual sins, even though forgiven. It prepares the soul for the great meeting with God.

Matrimony gives those who receive it the power to love one another, not only with a mutual human love— itself a great thing— but as members of Christ. It will give to each of the partners a particularly tender respect for the grace of Christ in the other, or, at least, for the other's call to receive the grace of Christ, which brings with it the indwelling of the holy Trinity. If each party respects this in the other, the character of their love will be completely Christ-like, mirroring His love for the Church.

The person who receives the sacrament of Holy Orders exercises his power as Christ's instrument, *according to the intensity of grace in him, to administer them with the heart of Jesus Himself.* Thus, grace, in passing through sacraments, is enriched with various modalities and hues, like light passing through a window of seven different colors.

These different sacramental modalities of sanctifying grace constitute the splendour of the Mystical Body. They are present already in the least of the justified Christians, but in this life they show their power only in the great saints. The sacramental grace, as seen in the saints, is alone fully Christian and makes us like Christ. Only at the end of the world will the full beauty of the Church be revealed, beauty that will never come to an end.[11]

Cardinal Journet's vision is sublime. Such is the third existential state of grace, that of grace by derivation from Christ. Such grace, on the one hand, oriented (teaching) by the powers of jurisdiction in the hierarchy assisted by Christ and, on the other hand, enriched by its passage through the sacraments of the New Law, is thereby enabled to be fully Christian and to make us like Christ. This grace, first prepared in the heart of Christ with three qualities (filial, connatural, plenary),[12] impels the baptized to the Trinity and to co-redeem with Christ.[13]

Those outside the visible do also receive sanctifying grace (e.g., Baptism by desire) but not with such power, and the grace they receive should lead them to receive the fullness of divine filiation within the Church. For the Church is the Sacrament of Christ (LG Ch. 1), that prolongs the presence of Christ in the world and in history.

The pervasive power of the grace by contact (covenanted) within the Church can be seen just by looking at the flowering of sanctity in the twentieth-century alone: saintly popes (e.g., Pius XII, John XXIII, Paul VI, John Paul II, Pope Benedict XVI); saintly bishops (e.g., Francis van Thuan, Fulton Sheen, John O'Connor), theologians (e.g., Romano Guardini, Henri de Lubac, Yves Congar); founders (e.g., Chiara Lubich, Luigi Giussani, Josemaría Escrivá, Pierre-Marie Delfieux, Catherine Doherty, Dorothy Day, Kiko Argüello, Andrea Riccardi); and blesseds and saints of the twentieth-century numbering over three hundred and forty four.[14] This covenanted grace has the goal of forming us into "persons" reflecting the three Persons of Christ in their *ekstasis*: existing in and for each Other.

---

[11] Ibid., 120-121.
[12] Ibid., 115-116.
[13] Ibid., 119.
[14] "Chronological list of saints and blesseds in the twentieth century," *Wikipedia*, accessed July 18, 2018,
https://en.wikipedia.org/wiki/Chronological_list_of_saints_and_blesseds_in_the_20th_century.

II. The Church-Person Mirrors the Ineffable Trinitarian Persons in *Being for Others* (perichoresis)

Cardinal Journet teaches us that grace of contact, prepared in the heart of Christ and received within the Church, impels us to the Trinity and to co-redeem the world, making us like unto Christ. Von Balthasar goes further to teach us how this happens: the mission of each person in the Church is to become universal "persons," as an extension of the Trinitarian Persons.

For the heart of all reality is the communion of Three Persons, and the essence of the Church is to be an extension of this communion, built up especially of isolated individuals who become public persons, and whose influence radiates like ripples into the Church.

Part II thus addresses how the devout Christian can have much influence in the Church from an expropriation of self and living on earth the Trinitarian communion centered on Mary (to be developed more fully in Chapter 11). The following is but a summary of Stephan Ackermann's fine article, "The Church as Person in the Theology of Hans Urs von Balthasar."[15]

A. From Isolated Individuals to Realsymbolic Persons (Universal Mission)

Von Balthasar deepens the concept of personhood in relationship to the Trinity. Public "persons" in the sense that von Balthasar develops are above all the saints. First among the saints is Mary, the obedient handmaid and mother of the Lord. First, what binds together all the early Church figures around Jesus is the fact that each embraced and carried out the personal mission that fell to him within the context of Christ's mission. They were thus able to move from being isolated individuals to being "persons," each with his own distinctive human and theological profile. The lay person engaged in evangelization can take great comfort from their example.

A second point of significance is that, because these persons share in a particularly close way in Christ's universal mission, they are to a certain extent

---

[15] Stephan Ackermann, "The Church as Person in the Theology of Hans Urs von Balthasar," *Communio* 29 (2002):238-249.

themselves *universalized*; they experience a simultaneous opening and broadening of their person. Increasing personalization is accompanied by *progressive socialization*. In embracing mission, each person becomes ever more himself, though not simply for his own sake, a "deprivatization":

> If the mission is accepted and carried out, it de-privatizes the "I," causing the latter's fruitful influence (through grace) to expand into the whole "Mystical Body" of Christ. In this way, there is a mutual interpenetration of the diverse missions and the persons who identify themselves with them: this is what is meant by the *communio sanctorum*.[16]

These persons are not, however, either "functionalized" or "depersonalized" in the process, but while growing increasingly less private, they are all the while becoming more deeply personal. Indeed, in a certain way they become *super-personal, paradigmatic, prototypical, or archetypical* for all who, in faith, recognize and embrace their mission from God.

The origin of the Church then does not lie in abstract ideas or principles, but in concrete persons whose lived-out, divine missions have allowed them to become ecclesial principles themselves— *realsymbols* (symbols that contain the reality symbolized) in and for the Church.

B. Four Fundamental Missions

Hans Urs von Balthasar illustrates these ecclesial principles by synthesizing them into four fundamental missions of experiences of the Church ("Marian principle" in chapter 14):

> 1. The *marian* mission of handmaidenly being-at-the-disposal-of-the-other….; 2. The *petrine* mission as the embodiment of the objective and official dimension of the Church; 3. The *johannine* mission of a love for Christ that mediates between the marian and the petrine dimensions; and finally, 4. the *pauline* mission, which presents in its purity the experience of "Catholic unity in the midst of diversity."[17]

---

[16] Hans Urs von Balthasar, *Theodrama III: Dramatis Personae* (San Francisco: Ignatius Press, 1990), 349.

[17] Hans Urs von Balthasar, *The Office of Peter and the Structure of the Church* (San Francisco: Ignatius Press, 1986), 290-296.

These four fundamental missions cannot be reduced to a single category (although the Marian encompasses the others), nor are they separated by neat boundaries. Rather, von Balthasar understands the relationship among the four as a manner of "a mutual osmosis," analogous to the circumincession (*perichoresis*, inter-penetration) among the Persons of the Trinity. Insofar as persons participate in Christ's mission, they are taken up into the inner-Trinitarian processions themselves! Through this participation they become *realsymbols* (communicates the very presence of that which it symbolizes) of the unity in diversity of the ecclesial communion.

These great expanded figures within the Christological constellation have a super-personality that opens up the possibility for a host of additional personal missions, which take their place within the space marked out by the four primary missions above. The effective range of these missions can vary greatly, from extraordinary, to hidden, to ordinary; what matters is the readiness in accepting.

C. Expropriation Leads Us to Become Ecclesiastics with a *Sentire Ecclesiae*

We see here the perfection of what the Bible calls "discipleship." When a person is obedient to the call to follow, when one gives one's "Yes" of faith, one is lifted out of one's human (and sinful) narrowness and is enlarged to the dimensions of the mission of Christ and the Church.

For von Balthasar, there is no system for explaining how a person's expropriation of oneself and one's appropriation of God is simultaneous with a discovery of one's own personal self. This can only be grasped as a theological paradox.

The result is what, since the time of Origen and Ambrose, has traditionally been called the *anima ecclesiastica* (Church-soul):

> "[T]he more selflessly and un-egotistically a Christian serves and commits himself to God's work in the world in Christ, the more he is at the disposal of God, the Church, and his neighbor, the more his heart is open to the needs of others, the more Christ's desire to save all becomes important to him, even outweighing his own personal salvation and well-being, the more

universally his prayer to God includes all humanity, even the most "reprobate," the more he presents himself to God and places his life, and perhaps his death, if necessary, at the disposal of the saving will of God, by that much more will he be fruitful in the kingdom of grace... by that much more will his existence become universal and accessible to all; by that much more will he grow to the dimensions of the Church and identify himself with her intentions, becoming, as the Fathers say, a "man of the Church," an "*anima ecclesiastica.*"[18]

Von Balthasar goes one step further. With respect to consciousness of the individual, this means that there is a point where a "thinking *with* the Church" [*sentire cum ecclesia*] becomes the "thinking *of* the Church" [*sentire ecclesiae*], and "love *for* the Church" becomes the "love *of* the Church." The consciousness of the individual and the consciousness of the Church *interpenetrate*. This does not dissolve the individual into a greater whole nor does the growing socialization eliminate the point where the individual is alone with himself; in fact, to the degree that acceptance of one's personal mission involves a "decision from the depths" regarding one's life, it can only be born from the solitude of the I.

If, in the soul conformed to the Church, there exists not only a "thinking with the Church," but indeed a "thinking of the Church," then there can be individual persons whose inward attitude enables them to act *as* the Church, "in the person of the Church," as Augustine and the Fathers say.

Peter, for example, stands "in the person of the Church," when, despite his horror, he allows Jesus to wash his feet, thus turning all worldly hierarchy (master-slave, God-man, saint-sinner) on its head. Mary of Bethany, listening to Jesus and anointing his feet, embodies the faithful, loving Church in her "Yes" to the way of Jesus— a "Yes" that is "fundamentally open *a priori*, disposing itself of nothing but holding itself ready in all things and allowing itself to be formed."[19]

---

[18] Hans Urs von Balthasar, *Kirche im Ursprung*, 121, quoted in Stephan Ackermann, "The Church as Person," 245.

[19] Idem, *Explorations in Theology III: Creator Spirit* (San Francisco: Ignatius Press, 1993), 225.

D. Church Formed Around Mary and her Paradigm

Particular attention is reserved for Mary: she is, according to von Balthasar, the "Church in origin" and its intact core:

> In her unconditional "Yes" to the Incarnation of the Son of God in her womb, Mary embraced her personal mission perfectly, and so became a unique theological person. Obviously, Mary pronounces this "Yes" only analogously to, and derivatively from, that of the Son (in whom mission and person are eternally one). Her unqualified "Yes" is made possible by the fact that she is conceived without original sin (*immaculata conceptio*): in other words, due to her (christologically and soteriologically) unique grace of "pre-redemption" and preservation through the cross of Christ, her readiness for faith in, and obedience to, the will of God is not diminished through sin. Because Mary is thus equal to her vocation as *Theotokos*, she becomes the "personal center" of the Church, the "fulfillment of the idea of the Church," the "*realsymbol*" of the Church.[20]

The Church first arises not from the calling of the apostles but rather already from the Incarnation of God in the Virgin's womb. The primordial cell of the Church is the chamber of Nazareth, Mary herself. In her acceptance of the divine task, Mary becomes not only the primordial image of the Church as a whole, but the type of each individual Church-soul.

Who, then, is the Church? Von Balthasar addresses this question again and again throughout *Sponsa Verbi* with a breathtaking inner consistency: it is built by Mary and on her expropriation to allow God's salvific work:

> "Who is the Church?" According to the answer given, the Church in her deepest reality is the unity of those who, gathered and formed by the immaculate and therefore limitless assent of Mary, which through grace has the form of Christ, are prepared to let the saving will of God take place in themselves and for all their brothers.[21]

At another point von Balthasar employs for the same discussion the striking image of "widening, interpenetrating ripples" that appear in water:

---

[20] Stephan Ackermann, "The Church as Person," 246-247.
[21] Hans Urs von Balthasar, *My Work in Retrospect* (San Francisco: Ignatius Press, 1993), 63.

When, for example, someone throws in a handful of pebbles. If there is a larger stone, it sends its ripples through the others without destroying them, even as it is also affected by the other smaller stones in its own sphere.... How far the effect of the ripples spreads in each case... depends on two factors: the "size" of each mission and the quality of the answering reception.... among all the circles the greatest is Mary's, whose radius extends through all the others and encloses them in itself; she is, in other words, co-extensive with the Church, insofar as the Church is the "Bride without spot or wrinkle."[22]

The Triune Model of Openness for Perichoresis ("being for another")

What this means is that within the space of the Church, persons do not exist as unrelated atoms, but mutually pervade each other, analogously to the *perichoresis* (being for others) of the Persons of the Trinity.

This becomes possible to the degree that persons in the Church *open themselves to Christ and, in him, to the whole triune life, and thus also to each other.* In their openness to God, persons are transformed at their deepest level by the Trinitarian mode of life, which is pre-existent through and through, as we are in the *pro nobis* ("for us") that characterizes the mission of Jesus on behalf of man. This being-for-another in grace can expand so far (e.g., in the saints) that it becomes "mutual osmosis" or "circumincession" in faith and good works (culminating in the "exchange of merits"). In sum, von Balthasar's spirituality becomes ecclesiology:

> Balthasar's theological understanding of the Church as person does not involve some kind of "ecclesial hypostasis" located somewhere next to or above the concrete community of believers, nor mere pure theological or spiritual piety. On the contrary: to speak of the Church in personal terms is to capture the reality of ecclesiology. This reality is the particular unity of the Church, which is not a unity of monism, but of "perichoresis." It is thus inconceivable without personal distinction. Balthasar's personal understanding of the Church weaves together the unity and distinction, identity and difference of ecclesial *communio* in the closest possible way. At its most profound level, the personal understanding of the Church is

---

[22] Idem, *Kirche im Ursprung*, 122; quoted in Stephan Ackermann, "The Church as Person," 247-248.

nothing other than the ecclesiological concretization of the words of Jesus: "that they may all be one even as thou, Father, art in me, and I in thee, that they also may be in us, so that the world might believe that thou hast sent me" (Jn 17: 21).[23]

In sum, each person is to become an extension of the three Trinitarian Persons after the model of Mary and the three apostles named, which involves an expropriation and expansion of the personal self to become a public person, love for the world.

III. The Disciple of Christ as a "Church-Person"

The Church is Christ's Bride and Mystical Body. The disciple of Christ seeking a model for love of the Church can find an inspiring example in Henri de Lubac, who sought to be a son of the Church. After being wrongfully silenced for eight years by the Church authorities, prohibited from teaching and publishing, de Lubac manifested no bitterness, resentment, or critique. Instead, his first publication on his return, *Splendor of the Church*,[24] was a sublime meditation, that manifested his love for the Church and his identity as a son of the Church. His work appears to be an unveiling of his heart, revealing his love for the Church to his readers.

The following is but a summary of one chapter from *Splendor of the Church,* "Ecclesia Mater," which describes the love that each Catholic should have for the Church and the call to be a *"vir ecclesiasticus,"* a "Church-person." Underlying de Lubac's vision is the sacramental understanding of the Church as mirroring the two natures of Christ: with a human element that is weak and changeable, united to a divine element that is all-holy and divine. Thus, he is able to help the "ecclesiastic" *negotiate* the difficult path of being faithful while being open and charitable. It can help when one finds apparent failure or difficulties with representatives of the Church, as de Lubac did with the Church's authorities. This chapter of *Splendor of the Church* was introduced in *New Christ: Divine Filiation.*

---

23 Stephan Ackermann, "The Church as Person," 248-249.
24 Henri de Lubac, *Splendor of the Church* (San Francisco: Ignatius Press, 1999).

The Church is Full of the Trinity

Henri de Lubac begins with a profound Trinitarian insight. He explains how the Church is "full of the Trinity." God made us to be brought together into the heart of the life of the Trinity, a recapitulation and regeneration into the unity of the Trinity, that brings together the family of God; a mysterious extension of the Trinity in time, a life of union that we already have begun participating in at Baptism. The Church is full of the Trinity, with a relationship to each one of the three divine Persons, and is the very realization of that communion which is so much sought for, whose dimensions are vaster than the universe, such that all past and future and earth to heaven are present to us. Those to whom she has united to God are truly the soul of the world, the soul of humanity.[25]

A. *"Vir Ecclesiasticus"* *("Church-Person")*

Henri de Lubac then moves from the love of the Trinity to its consequence, unity with and love of the Church. It is necessary to restore its breadth and dignity, specifically, to be a man of the Church, a *vir ecclesiasticus*: "For myself, I desire to be truly ecclesiastic," said Origen, who thought that there was no other way of being a Christian in the full sense.[26] It is not sufficient to be loyal and obedient and to perform exactly what is demanded by his profession of the Catholic faith, but that the Church steals his heart. The *vir ecclesiasticus* will love the Church's past, not as nostalgia, for he knows that Christ is always present, today as yesterday, right up to the consummation of the world, to continue Christ's life, to find there a great and living permanent force. Thus the "Church-person" accepts the Magisterium as the absolute norm, believing both that the Father has revealed in His Son all that is to be revealed, and yet that divine thought must adapt the understanding of the mystery of Christ at each epoch, in the Church and through the Church.

The Church follows the direction of the Holy Spirit, with the inseparable three-fold channel of Scripture, Tradition, and the Magisterium by which

---

25 Ibid., 237-239.
26 Origen, *In Lucam*, nom. 2, p. 14, quoted by Henri de Lubac, *Splendor of the Church*, 241.

the Word reaches him. Total loyalty to the Magisterium does not keep him from an in-depth contact with Scripture or the Church's Tradition, which includes a loving knowledge of the classics of his faith, and, by keeping company with those who fought for Christ, will acquire something of a Catholic ethos. Beyond the many non-essential things which change with time and space, he sees also the continuity that exists at an even deeper level of reality, while giving special attention to certain facts and periods (first martyrs, monasticism, etc.). That is, the Catholic Tradition becomes fully intelligible only to him who keeps in the line of its axis and studies it from the inside. A culture of this type will entail avoiding certain temptations: touring Tradition as if touring monuments and esoterism (instead of Catholic solidarity), letting the cause of Christ to become secondary.[27]

The "Church-person" will not hesitate in joining battle for the defence and honour of the faith, at the risk of displeasing many and being misunderstood, ready to give any man a reason for the hope that is in him, being of a deeper faith as a real son. Like Newman, he will not be tempted "'to break in pieces the great legacy of thought thus committed to us for these latter days' by men like St. Irenaeus, St. Athanasius, St. Augustine, and St. Thomas."[28]

Yet, while he defends the faith, he will have an openness in charity and understanding of unity in diversity. Fidelity to the Church will not turn into hardness, contempt, or lack of feeling, and will not destroy his friendliness. He will want to "leave every open door through which minds of different kinds may reach the same truth,"[29] seek the much-to-be-desired moderation, and avoid over-zealousness to respect the plan of God. While seeking to elucidate for the men of this time the things necessary for salvation, he will take care not to let the mystery of faith be degraded to an ideology or make the Gospel a scientific objective. He will hold himself apart from all coteries and all intrigue, seek to be "charitable rather than

[27] Henri de Lubac, *Splendor of the Church*, 241-247.
[28] Ibid., 247-248.
[29] Étienne Gilson, *Jean Duns Scot*, 1952, 627, quoted in Henri de Lubac, *Splendor of the Church*, 249.

quarrelsome," in distinction from every faction or sectarianism, and be no friend of the itch for controversy. He will respect the legitimate diversity in the multi-form wisdom of God, viewing reduction of everything to uniformity as marring the beauty of Christ's Bride.[30]

Even if these diversities become divergences, he will not start to worry and lose patience. Instead, he will try to keep the peace and retain a mind bigger than his own ideas, allowing others freedom while avoiding making himself the incarnate norm of orthodoxy, for he will put "the indissoluble bond of Catholic peace above all things and will hold it a black mark to tear the seamless robe even by the smallest 'schism of charity.'" Since he is a member of the Body of Christ, he will be responsive to what affects the other members, suffering from the evils inside the Church, seeking greater holiness, always directing his accusations against himself first and foremost.

Yet, he will not resign himself to settling down in the all-too-human, nor blinding himself to the faults and sufferings within the Church. For a reforming impulse is natural to the Church, which will require the discernment of spirits, avoiding the impulse to repress but to redirect. A man of the Church will want to always remain open to hope, to be full of rejoicing in his sufferings, and his attitude be eschatological like that of Paul.[31] De Lubac appears to be describing his own life and openness.

B. Obedience

The person of God does not stop at mere obedience. He loves obedience in itself, and will not be satisfied with obeying "of necessity and without love," but an obedience that involves a receiving of the Spirit of God, a dispossession of or dying to ourselves. True obedience submits our thoughts and desires to the obedience of Christ. François Fénelon justly says: "It is Catholicism alone which teaches, fundamentally, this evangelical poverty; it is within the bosom of the Church that we learn to die to ourselves in order to live in dependence."[32] This obedience is perhaps the

---

[30] Henri de Lubac, *Splendor of the Church*, 250-252.
[31] Ibid., 252-257.
[32] François Fénelon, *Entretien avec le chevalier de Ramsay*, in A. de Campigny et al., Les Entretiens de Cambrai (1929), 136, quoted in Henri de Lubac, *Splendor of the Church*, 258.

most secret point in the mystery of faith and that which is hardest of access to a mind which has not been converted to God, and appears to be an intolerable tyranny.

The Church commands only because she obeys God; obedience is the price of freedom, for she is not a human institution: "He thanks God for having given him that Magisterium in the Church and experiences a foretaste of the peace of eternity in placing himself under the eternal law by the obedience of faith."[33] He will accept all the acts of the hierarchy, never adopting an argumentative attitude and "will not countenance any contest with those who represent God, any more than he would with God himself."[34]

Knowing that the Spirit of God never abandons the Church as a whole, the baptismal instinct of the child responds with a leaping joy to the demands made upon it by its Mother (Church). Even in the day-to-day matters, he will not spend any longer than he can help over considerations at the human level; he will have confidence in his superiors and make it his business to see their point of view from the inside, and see in them Christ Himself. It is certain that it will be wrong to disobey, and thus he will not abandon the responsibilities with which the superior has been invested by his office or circumstances.

Ultimately, all he has to do is to take his place in the divine plan by which God leads him through His representatives and he cannot fail to share in the infallible security of Providence. He can never forget that the salvation of mankind was accomplished by an act (Christ's) of total self-abandonment.[35] He will not reduce obedience, which is conformity with the obedient Christ, to a virtue which is primarily of social importance. He must in principle maintain a certain distrust with regard to his own judgment, that even with the best of intentions he can still grossly deceive himself, and that he must first and foremost be a submissive member, quick and docile in response to the direction of the Head.

---

[33] Henri de Lubac, *Splendor of the Church*, 260.
[34] Ibid.
[35] Ibid., 260-263.

As a community, the Church is first a hierarchy, not some ideal and unreal Church but this hierarchical Church herself, to whom we owe a filial obedience. She is a Mother who has not just brought us to birth but guards us and keeps us together in a maternal heart. And every true Catholic will have a feeling of tender piety towards her: "He who has not the Church for Mother cannot have God for Father" (Cyprian, Augustine). The elaborating of this obedience to others cannot be taken upon by a precise explanation of how the Church's authority works, but from showing the splendour of the Catholic vision, to show her true character from within; and moreover, how they will hear today the voice of their Lord through us, in the spiritual fruitfulness of sacrifice and by displaying some of the great miracles of Catholic sanctity.[36]

C. The Church as Mother

Against the accusations of tyranny, the Catholic calls the Church his Mother: "The Roman Church is the object par excellence of accusations of tyranny; she is even sometimes— absurdly— put on a parallel with the various systems of political absolutism. And she is also the primary object of the objections of many Christians, who nevertheless recognize the necessity of a visible authority."[37]

He sees the see of Rome as the master of the whole household of Christ, the "Holy See," the "Apostolic See." He sees that Peter was given charge of both lambs and sheep, that Christ Himself prayed that Peter's faith might not fail, that he was given the keys of the kingdom and the command to confirm his brethren. He realizes that Peter personifies the whole Church and that this visible foundation in no way prejudices that unique foundation which is Christ, and that Peter lives, presides, and judges perpetually.

The Catholic has not lost the sense of the totality of the Church in submitting himself to the power of the Pope, for we do not deny the existence of a circle when we know that it has a centre, and it is not abolishing of the body when we say that it has a head. The Pope's

---

[36] Ibid., 264-267.
[37] Ibid., 267.

infallibility is that of the Church herself, which can involve weighing Tradition, Scripture, the *sensus fidelium*, which infallibility is not derived from the bishops or other members. Thus he will always see in Peter the fullness of power of the Church, holding to Ambrose's words, "Where Peter is, there the Church is" —where is found the centre of Catholic truth and unity, the support of his faith and the guarantee of his communion.[38]

The Church is of absolute necessity in the plan of God. It is the Church who daily teaches the law of Christ, giving us His Gospel and helping us to understand its meaning: "It is hard to imagine where the Gospel would be or what state it would have reached us in if, *per impossibile*, it had not been composed, preserved, and commented on within the great Catholic community…"[39]

St. Francis de Sales, for example, tells us that, while Scripture is entirely adequate to teach all things, without Tradition and the Magisterium of the Church, we would not be able to determine the meaning which it ought to have. Scripture must be read in the Church: "The Church is always the paradise in the midst of which the Gospel wells up like a spring and spreads out into four rivers to make the whole earth fruitful."[40] If the Church does not produce in us its fruition of life (sanctity), the fault is ours.

We owe, therefore, our praise to this great Mother of ours: (i) for the divine mystery which she communicates to us through the twofold and ever-open door of her doctrine and her liturgy, (ii) for centres of religious life, (iii) for the interior universe she discovers to us and guides us, and (iv) for purifying our worship by unmasking and dispersing the illusions which deceive us. This wonderful Mother gives us a myriad of benefits; we owe her so much. Above all, she forms us into new Christs for the Church and the world.[41]

---

[38] Ibid., 267-273.
[39] Ibid., 273-274.
[40] Ibid., 275.
[41] Ibid.

APPENDIX

THE 1985 EXTRAORDINARY SYNOD FINAL REPORT:
4 AXES

The mission of the Church from Vatican II to *Redemptoris Missio* (1990) can be summarized in the 1985 Extraordinary Synod Final Report. The Synod deals of a great synthesis, departing from the reflection made on the mystery of Christ and the Church, that directs us to the fonts of ecclesial renewal: the Word of God and the liturgical celebration, to direct these towards the mission of the Church in the world. Reading the signs of the times, it provides four axes to approach evangelization, each with two aspects in tension (like Christ's two natures).[42]

1. *Christological Axis*: Christ's continuing departure and return

The synodal text interprets the theology of the cross in the key of the Paschal mystery, given that it is "in this paschal perspective that one affirms the unity of the cross and the Resurrection." Here one is not speaking of pessimism, but of the reality of Christian hope, since

> The Church and Christians cannot "situate themselves" in the Paschal Triduum: their place is neither before nor after the cross, but from both places: from one place (that however must not remain fixed) but then sent back to the other place and inclined toward the other.[43]

This theology of the cross re-situates the theology of creation and of the Incarnation, the most traditional pivots for speaking of the mission in the world, at times seen in a way that is too "linear," and gives to it a perspective that is more "dramatic" for the image of the Paschal mystery, seen here in Ratzinger's description of the liturgy as an anticipation of the Parousia: "The Parousia is the highest intensification and fulfillment of the Liturgy. And the Liturgy is Parousia, a Parousia-like event taking place in our midst" (*Eschatology*, 202-203).

---

[42] The author cannot remember the source for this material in Part II.
[43] Hans Urs von Balthasar, *Mysterium Paschale*, in *Mysterium Salutis*, vol. 6 (Brescia: 1980), 403.

2. *Anthropological Axis*: Inculturation respecting dignity but purifying culture

The attention to man, in his history and in his culture, brings, according to the formulation of the Synod, a constant *"aggiornamento"* ("updating") and a need for "inculturation" that maintains the true human values, especially the dignity of the human person, peace, and freedom from oppression, from misery, and from injustice. From this comes the necessity of evangelizing the culture itself, or more precisely, the cultures, by means of the Good News.

To attain this articulation, the synodal text makes reference to the classical perspective of grace as purifying (*gratia sanans*, of which St. Augustine spoke) and as elevating (*gratia elevans* of the Scholastics of the XIII century), since "Integral salvation is obtained only if these human realities are purified and elevated through the grace of familiarity with God, through Christ, in the Holy Spirit" (D. 3, EV 9, 1812).

3. *Dialogical Axis*: Dialogue in mission

The dialogue with the non-Christian religions and with non-believers is another central point of the mission of the Church today: "Nor shall divine providence deny the assistance necessary for salvation to those who, without any fault of theirs, have not yet arrived at an explicit knowledge of God, and who, not without grace, strive to lead a good life" (LG 16).

While the Church now departs from the starting point of dialogue, she insists nevertheless that dialogue must never be opposed to mission:

> Dialogue must not be opposed to mission. The authentic dialogue tends to make the human person open and communicate his interiority to his interlocutor. Furthermore, all Christians have received from Christ the mission of making disciples of all nations (Mt 28:20). In this sense, God can make use of dialogue between Christians and non-Christians and with non-believers as a means to communicate the fullness of grace. (D. 5, EV 9, 1814)

4. *Diaconal Axis*: The service of the poor, oppressed, and marginalized

Like Jesus' constant care of the sick and needy, the history of the Church, beginning with the early Church, manifests that continued solicitude:

> After the Second Vatican Council, the Church has become more aware of her mission at the service of the poor, the oppressed, and the marginalized. In this preferential option, that must not be understood as exclusive, shines the true spirit of the Gospel. Jesus Christ has declared the poor as blessed (Mt 5:3; Lk 6:20) and has Himself desired to be poor for us (2 Cor 8:9) (EV 9, 1815). This formulation, that comes from the Third General Conference of the Latin-American Episcopate of Puebla in 1979, has become paradigmatic and has been taken up again in a modified way by John Paul II, above all, in the encyclical *Sollicitudo rei socialis* of 1987. (nn. 42 f.)

The synodal text concludes this point with an inseparable connection of the relation between salvific mission and human advancement:

> The mission of the Church is not reduced to a monism, in whatever form that can be understood. Certainly, in this mission, there is a clear distinction, but not a separation, between the natural and supernatural aspects. This duality is not a dualism. It is necessary, therefore, to set aside and overcome the false and useless oppositions, for example, between spiritual mission and the *diakonia* [service] to the world. (EV 9, 1816)

This dual aspect has as point of reference the Christological axis, even without citing it explicitly, given that the language used clearly recalls that of the Council of Chalcedon, that speaks of the two natures of Jesus Christ united in the one sole person "without confusion or separation" (*inconfuse et indivise*, DS 301). In this manner, the diaconal axis renders possible the recovery of the "primacy of Christ over the cosmos" (ITC, *The Consciousness of Christ concerning Himself and His Mission*, 1980) and sets in turn the Church in its proper place, understood as the sacrament of communion with God and with all for the universal mission of the salvation of the world and of history (LG 1, 9, 48, 59; SC 5, 26; GS 42, 45; Ag 1, 5).

CHAPTER 7

THE LAY MISSION OF SANCTIFICATION OF THE WORLD

> However, I have listened to many discussions on the subject of the laity
> and I have come away from all these discussions with the impression that
> what we need is a study of the whole question, in all its ramifications, in
> which consideration is given not only to the form of witnessing and that
> spiritual mission (apostolic mission) which are peculiar to laymen, but also
> to those modalities peculiar to their interior life, to their spiritual trials, to
> their prayer (liturgical as well as private), and to their progress toward union
> with God and the perfection of charity, which is evidently what must come
> before all else, since progress toward perfection is prescribed to all: *estote
> perfecti*...[1] (Jacques Maritain)

Catholics unaware of twentieth-century developments are likely to see the
new evangelization as being accomplished principally by priests and religious.
But the call to witness and to sanctify the world flows from one's Baptism,
through which one becomes Christ's *other self*, the *new Christ*. The prominent
twentieth-century Catholic lay philosopher, Jacques Maritain, even before
Vatican II, had long discerned the mission of the laity in the world and felt
that the Church needed to study their mission and sanctification (see
quotation above). At the request of Pope Paul VI, in preparation for his
closing address to Vatican II Fathers and prior to the promulgation of *Lumen
gentium*, Maritain was commissioned to produce a memorandum, "The
spiritual Mission of the Laity," now published.[2]

The Lay Mission of Evangelization through Holiness

The Second Vatican Council's *Lumen gentium* set the Church on a new lay
path. It begins with the "People of God" as a whole (Ch. 2), then highlights
the laity and holiness in "Laity" (Ch. 4), and the "Universal call to holiness"
(Ch. 5). The Council teaches that the work of evangelization belongs
primarily to the laity, who are present in every sector of society. It is
principally the laity then, not priests and religious, who are to imbue society
with the Christian ethos, and the role of the consecrated souls to facilitate

---

[1] Jacques Maritain, "The Spiritual Mission of the Laity," *Communio* 14 (1987): 195.
[2] Ibid., 193-202.

that, especially through sanctification. Thus the laity it to accomplish evangelization principally through the fruitfulness from conformation to Christ, i.e., holiness: "They must follow in His footsteps and conform themselves to His image seeking the will of the Father in all things":

> Thus it is evident to everyone, that all the faithful of Christ of whatever rank or status, are called to the fullness of the Christian life and to the perfection of charity…. They must follow in His footsteps and conform themselves to His image seeking the will of the Father in all things. They must devote themselves with all their being to the glory of God and the service of their neighbor. In this way, the holiness of the People of God will grow into an abundant harvest of good, as is admirably shown by the life of so many saints in Church history. The classes and duties of life are many, but holiness is one… (LG 40, 41)

Pope John Paul II himself, in *Novo millennio ineunte*, stated in no uncertain terms that the goal of the parish is holiness: "First of all, I have no hesitation in saying that all pastoral initiatives must be set in relation to holiness. Was this not the ultimate meaning of the Jubilee indulgence, as a special grace offered by Christ so that the life of every baptized person could be purified and deeply renewed?" (NMI 30). This clear goal of holiness implies that "all pastoral initiatives" serve this goal. The priest especially must not fall into the trap of seeking a "vibrant" parish with many programs and activities, but to first of all make his parishioners saints, and he has to remember that he himself cannot give what he does not have. Thus the priest must become holy and his role is to form and sanctify the laity for their mission of sanctification of the world.

We present three aspects to develop the lay mission in the world. A foundation can be built upon Hans Urs von Balthasar's insights into the role of lay mission (especially holiness) and Jean Mouroux's vision of the baptized as a "priest," a mediator called to co-create and co-redeem the world with Christ, through work, contemplation, and consecration through the Eucharist. Second, a special gift of the Holy Spirit, blessed by the Church, is St. Josemaría Escrivá's inspiration of a lay spirituality to sanctify oneself, work, and the world. Third, we embrace the significant contribution of the ecclesial lay movements for evangelization.

I. An Introduction to the Lay Mission

A. Von Balthasar Illuminates the Lay Mission within the Call to Holiness

(i) The Christian Lay Spirituality is Fundamental

We turn to Brendan Leahy for insights from Hans Urs von Balthasar. Von Balthasar's vision offers three key insights as background to this theme. First, for him, the lay spirituality is the fundamental spirituality of being or living as Christians. It is the first and most fundamental thing, and comes before the question of hierarchy or organization. John Paul II himself sees the Marian profile (baptismal) as more foundational than the Petrine (hierarchical) profile. For Chiara Lubich, foundress of the Focolare movement, what is important is to be a Christian, a follower of Christ, to live His commands, including the law of love and His last prayer for unity. This is the common vocation to be discovered and lived by all Christians. Priesthood or hierarchy is a further calling to service for the sake of the Church within that basic calling of Baptism. Von Balthasar locates the lay mission within holiness and Mary.[3]

(ii) Holiness, the Saints, Founders, and Charisms

Second, the fundamental call of Baptism is to holiness. Within the Church, it is the explosive energies of holiness (saints) that bring about change. Von Balthasar sees the theological significance of saints as a continuing of Mary's role in the formation of the Church. Although the saints' great efficacy is posthumous, while alive, they are "regenerative energies in the Church," causing hearts and structures to change.

The saints radiate the Church as a communion of holiness, not as an institution: as such, their holiness breaks through the prejudices that people continually erect around the institutional aspect of the Church, because it shows the transcendental significance of this aspect, their appeal being irresistible. They are living commentaries on Scripture and canonical forms

---

[3] Brendan Leahy, *The Marian Profile: In the Ecclesiology of Hans Urs von Balthasar* (New York: New City Press, 2000), 182-183.

for Church life. They are the living Tradition, and the Magisterium's infallibility is mirrored not so much in concepts as in a lived infallibility of holiness.

On a pastoral level, they bring advantages: (a) many aspects of the Church do not speak to people today, hence the importance of models that live out holiness in the present; (b) mere changes in the structures are not solutions to issues facing the Church today. New forms may make their appearance, which have a fresh, distinctive stamp, and are truly the work of the Holy Spirit (e.g., new ecclesial movements).[4]

For von Balthasar today, the new interpretation of the Gospel in the new lay charisms is a breathtaking adventure. Apart from their regenerative energies, there is also the prophetic dimensions of new charisms that open up new collective experiences within the Church. These charisms are endowed by the Holy Spirit to respond to challenges in each era of history by raising up new forms of discipleship for the upbuilding of the Church (e.g., Taizé, Comunità San Egidio). The founders and others who have a special mission from God proceed "like lightning from heaven and light up some unique point of God's will for the Church." The Church must receive them and herself embody their message.[5]

The saints manifest a new type of conformity to Christ inspired by the Holy Spirit and therefore a new illustration of how the Gospel is to be lived, a new interpretation of revelation. Their charisms are linked with Mary, because the Holy Spirit overshadowed her at the Annunciation and again at Pentecost. The Marian charism is the fundamental charism. If we want to look for a dawn to the difficulties of today, then we need to look to where Christianity appears as a "breathtaking adventure." The movement of genuine renewal can be traced back to an outpouring from a prophetic, charismatic, or mystical source.[6]

---

[4] Ibid., 170-174
[5] Ibid., 184-186.
[6] Ibid., 172-173.

(iii) Marian Mysticism: the Hour of the Laity

Third, the sanctity of Mary is the sanctity of the laity. When we reflect on Mary's sanctity, we don't say of Mary that she practiced certain forms of penance or had particular attitudes. Her life unfolded first in the privacy of her home and of her village, and then she followed Jesus, participating actively in the fulfillment of redemption. It is said in the Gospel that she was docile to the plans and to the will of God. In this lies her sanctity, a way to sanctity which is open and good for all, especially the laity. Von Balthasar discerns that this is the hour of laity.[7]

For von Balthasar, in general, the Church needs above all a Marian mysticism. The charism of mysticism is not some vague psychological phenomenon, but has a specific meaning with its supreme problem of union between the essential One and what is essentially multiple.

The particular insight into the Gospel that is granted is intended for the whole Church and to be lived with a Marian *anima ecclesiastica* (Church mind). There is a "double moment" in mysticism: *the solitude of being "thrust" into the very bosom of God; and being directed back toward the community in order to build up that communion* through the novelty of the interpretation of revelation given.[8]

We find this in many saints: Abraham prepared in the wilderness; the Israelites in the desert for forty years; John the Baptist prepared in the desert before his ministry; Paul sent to Arabia before beginning his preaching; the Holy Family in the obscurity of Nazareth before Jesus' ministry; St. Thérèse in the hiddenness of Carmel, now bearing great fruit in the world; Fr. Pierre-Marie Delfieux went into the Sahara desert for two years before founding the Monastic Fraternities of Jerusalem.

This is an eminently Marian movement, an expression of Mary's continuing ecclesial receptivity as partner of the Word and image of the Church.

---

[7] Ibid., 182-183.
[8] Ibid., 174-176.

B. Man's Priestly Mediation of World to God in Three Levels (Jean Mouroux)

The French theologian, Fr. Jean Mouroux presents a very helpful three level gradation of work itself (it offers a basic background to St. Josemaría Escrivá's vision): *homo faber*; contemplation; and consecration through the Eucharist.

1. Sanctification of Work as Homo Faber

First, man is to "subdue the earth" (Gen 1): he is *homo faber*, the worker, the artisan, etc. To "subdue" is to put his *stamp* on it, give it a human face and figure, integrate it with his own life and so fulfill it. He invents means and instruments only to realize his spiritual aims. The Christian engaged in such labour seeks to release the energies and riches of nature, to rid the earth of briar and thorns, to penetrate it with intelligible intentions and results, and thus make all things sing together. In the eyes of God, all the efforts of scientists, engineers, farmers are to humanize the world and to make it better than it ever was.[9]

2. Sanctification by Contemplation

But the activities of organization are inferior to those of man's interior life. Deeper than work, which is only a means, is contemplation, which is already an end. Surrounded as he is by God's holy reality, he has to discover its intelligible significance, to taste its spiritual savour, and to discern the beauty that comes from above. These, however, are not just abstract signs of God's presence. Things exist, they are rich with creative generosity, and abound with being and with goodness.

(a) Sometimes man will contemplate reality simply as *existent*, in all the beauty that comes of its very existence (e.g., St. Francis of Assisi). (b) As with St. Francis, we may also contemplate reality as *brotherly* ("brother sun, sister moon"), that is, to see it as an image of ourselves since it is born of the same Father. So deep is the brotherhood between these two creatures, that every human soul finds itself spontaneously in tune with the whole creation. (c)

---

[9] Jean Mouroux, *The Meaning of Man* (New York: Image Books, 1961), 38-39.

And the Christian will contemplate reality as *divine*, the direct reflection and loving call of God.[10]

3. Sanctification of the World through Consecration (Eucharist)

But the Christian does not merely contemplate creation, he also consecrates it to God. He must either adore it or present it to God. Man's final role is to bring about the return of all things to God by adoring, through them, Him who created them: "Bless the Lord, all you works of the Lord." In point of fact *this return is not to be effected save through Christ.* He it is who stands at the source as Exemplar; He it is who redeemed it and made it penetrable by grace; He it is who makes use of it to bring His own life to mankind; He it is who consecrates it to God; and this consecration is the Eucharist. Irenaeus teaches that Christ commanded His disciples to offer up to God the first fruits of His own creatures in the Eucharist. The Church alone offers this pure oblation to the Creator in offering Him with thanksgiving some small part of His creation. The world, tainted by sin but saved by Christ, returns to God at the Mass.

Many days were needed and much labour and weariness to bring corn and grape to fruition, and make of them bread and wine; and thus all human labour is resumed and offered and sanctified in the Eucharist. God's holy creation is present before us in bread and in wine, and they have become the Body and Blood of Christ. Since they become the Body and Blood of Christ, they are not simply sanctified but also sanctifying. It communicates to us the very Principle of all life and all sanctity (God). It is spiritualized under our eyes, vanishes into its Creator, passes to God like the Sacred Humanity itself, it is by this that we pass to God.[11]

> We may bring this to a point and say: the world, tainted by sin but saved by Christ, returns to God at the Mass. The bread and wine are fruits at once of the earth and of human effort: the Host and the Chalice represent the whole creation and all the toil of man…[12]

---

[10] Ibid., 39-44.
[11] Ibid., 44-46.
[12] Ibid., 45.

Jean Mouroux's Structure is Developed in and Surpassed by St. Escrivá's Vision

St. Josemaría Escriva's new rich charism develops this structure much more deeply. Fr. Jean Mouroux perceives that man's role as creation's head and priest (Gen 1:26-28) is to present it to the Creator. But since creation is wounded, he also has to redeem it with and in Christ. Furthermore, man does not separate himself from the world for contemplation and consecration, but sanctifies and elevates it in the midst of the world. But St. Escrivá presents a vaster overarching vision in which it is the lay baptized, who finding God in the "secular" world, sanctifies his work, self, and world, and recapitulating all to God through and in the midst of *work* itself: "We are instruments of God cooperating with him in the true *consecratio mundi*; or, to put it more exactly, in the sanctification of the world from within, from the very heart of civil society."[13]

> For many years now, ever since the foundation of Opus Dei, I have meditated and asked others to meditate on those words of Christ which we find in St John: "And when I am lifted up from the earth I shall draw all things unto Myself" (John 12:32). By His death on the Cross, Christ has drawn all creation to Himself. Now it is the task of Christians, in His name, to reconcile all things to God, placing Christ, by means of their work in the middle of the world, at the summit of all human activities.[14]

St. Escrivá, while implicitly including Mouroux's basic structure, goes far beyond to give a comprehensive battle plan to engage the world. (1) Where Mouroux focuses on humanizing the world, St. Escrivá's focuses on sanctification of work: finding God in the midst of ordinary life, perfecting our work, and offering all to God and for the salvation of souls. (2) Where Mouroux concentrates on finding the divine in the world, St. Escrivá highlights a "supernatural outlook," but through the profound awareness of one's divine filiation, and adds sanctification of oneself through the work, with human virtues (and a plan of life). (3) Consecration through the Mass is enriched by the Opus Dei's spirituality of placing themselves and their daily work on the paten at Mass, to become a victim like Christ through the Mass.

---

[13] Idem, Address, February 14, 1940, quoted in José Illanes, *The Sanctification of Work: Aspects of the Teaching of the Founder of Opus Dei*, trans. Michael Adams (New York: Scepter, 2003), 72.
[14] St. Josemaría Escrivá, *Conversations with St. Josemaría Escrivá* (New York: Scepter, 2007), 88.

Thus the sanctification of the world requires activity, word, and witness. It is the priest's role to help form the baptized but to allow them their full freedom to engage the world in infinitely varied forms as God inspires them.

II. St. Josemaría Escrivá: Sanctification through Work

A. Lay Spirituality of Work (St. Escrivá Anticipated Vatican II)

To summarize, in the charism of St. Josemaría Escrivá de Balaguer, the Holy Spirit has provided a new charism of sanctification of work for the laity in the world, one that in a refined fashion integrates Jean Mouroux's three levels of *homo faber*, contemplation, and consecration, while finding resonance with St. Thérèse of Lisieux's "little way" and the passionate love of the world of Teilhard de Chardin. The Prelature of the Holy Cross and Opus Dei was founded by Fr. Escrivá after receiving a divine inspiration in 1928. Scholars in the twentieth-century had pointed to the need to develop a theology of work. Scholars, like John O'Grady on Scriptural foundations ("The Biblical Doctrine of Work"), have diligently developed specific aspects, and papal documents, especially *Laborem exercens*, bring the Church's teachings on work up to date. But the vision of St. Escrivá anticipated this theology, and is perhaps the first and only spirituality of work that gives a comprehensive path of transformation of society through sanctification of work. Much of what follows is taken from Fr. José Luis Illanes' *The Sanctification of Work*.

Opus Dei's Spirit and Vatican II

St. Escrivá's successor, Alvaro del Portillo, among others, have noted that he was "one of the great precursors of the Second Vatican Council."[15] José Luis Illanes points to the coincidence of the teaching of the Magisterium with the spirit that animated Opus Dei since its foundation.[16] He notes the progress

---

[15] Alvaro del Portillo, "Mons. Escrivá de Balaguer, testigo de amor a la Iglesia," in *Palabra* 130 (Madrid, 1976) 205-210; quoted in José Illanes, *The Sanctification of Work*, 9.

[16] José Luis Illanes himself, in *The Sanctification of Work* (135-142) argues that it was St. Escrivá's spirituality of work that has likely prepared the way for the current developments in the theology of work (e.g., as in *Gaudium et spes*), and that without a proper spirituality of work like that of St. Escrivá, a theology of work will tend to end up in one of two opposite tendencies: a lack of appreciation of the true secularity, the goodness of the world and daily life (and fleeing the world), or a human vision of work that is not fully Christian (not Christ-centred).

made with the insertion of this lay spirituality within Vatican II documents, such as LG 31 affirming that the laity is called to live in the middle of temporal structures and find their means of holiness there: "Work— that is, man's job— is presented as something that is deeply inserted into the supernatural sphere,"[17] to be a leaven in society:

> But the laity, by their very vocation, *seek the kingdom of God by engaging in temporal affairs and by ordering them according to the plan of God.* They live in the world, that is, in each and in all of the secular professions and occupations. They live in the ordinary circumstances of family and social life, from which the very web of their existence is woven. They are called there by God that by exercising their proper function and *led by the spirit of the Gospel they may work for the sanctification of the world from within as a leaven.* (LG 31, emphasis added; see also LG 40-41)

Newness: A Lay Spirituality, God in the Midst of Daily Life and Work

We note the helpful observations of two Church figures. Albino Cardinal Luciani, soon to become John Paul I, published an article, "Seeking God through Everyday Work." He made the key distinction regarding St. Escrivá's contribution as going beyond St. Francis de Sales' "spirituality for lay people" to a "lay spirituality":

> Monsignor Escrivá... went further than Francis de Sales in many respects. St. Francis proclaimed sanctity for everyone but seems to have taught only a "spirituality for lay people" whereas Monsignor Escrivá wants a "lay spirituality." Francis, in other words, nearly always suggests the same practical means as used by religious, but with suitable modifications. Escrivá is more radical: he goes as far as talking about "materializing"— in a good sense— the quest for holiness. For him it is the very material work itself that must be turned into prayer and holiness.[18]

Sebastiano Cardinal Baggio, prefect of the Sacred Congregation for Bishops (1973-84), declared that Escrivá's work and message constituted a new chapter in the history of Christian spirituality: "What continues to be

---

[17] José Luis Illanes, *The Sanctification of Work*, 16.
[18] Albano Luciani, *Il Gazzetino* (Venice), July 25, 1978, quoted in Illanes, *The Sanctification of Work*, 10.

revolutionary in the spiritual message of Monsignor Escrivá de Balaguer is his practical manner of directing men and women of every condition of life to Christian holiness." He identifies three aspects characteristic of the newness of the Opus Dei spirituality that provide us with a synthesis:

> (1) The Christian laity should not abandon or despise the world, but should remain within it, loving and sharing the life of ordinary men and women; (2) while staying in the world, they should learn to discover the supernatural value of the normal circumstances of their lives, including the most prosaic and material details; (3) as a consequence, everyday work, the activity that occupies and fills the greatest number of hours of ordinary people, can and should be sanctified and used as a means of Christian apostolate.[19]

Cardinal Luciani and Cardinal Baggio highlight a key point of St. Escrivá: there are not two adjacent worlds, but God is found in the very midst of ordinary life, and holiness is accomplished through our work. In a famous homily given at the University of Navarre in Pamplona in October 1967, speaking at an open-air Mass on the university grounds, St. Escrivá pointed out that the world corresponds to the different parts of a church building (the world in a wider sense has become the Church):

> He waits for us every day, in the laboratory, in the operating theater, in the army barracks, in the university chair, in the factory, in the workshop, in the fields, in the home, and in all the immense panorama of work. Understand this well: there is something holy, something divine hidden in the most ordinary situations, and it is up to each one of you to discover it. (*Conversations*, nn. 113-114, p. 177)

He caps this off with a sublime image. Seeing the mountains touching the sky in the distance, and playing on the double meaning of *cielo* in Spanish for sky and heaven, he said extemporaneously, "Heaven and earth seem to merge, my sons and daughters, in the horizon. But where they really meet is in your hearts, when you sanctify your everyday lives" (*Conversations*, no. 116, p. 179). The world, though wounded, is the playground of God.

---

[19] Sebastiano Baggio, *Avvenire* (Milan), July 26, 1975, quoted in Illanes, *The Sanctification of Work*, 11.

Historical Development Towards a New Vision

The previously mentioned work of José Luis Illanes, *The Sanctification of Work*, offers much elaboration.[20] He discerns a historical development beyond the past common place temptation in theology to have a dualistic vision of the world. Today in contrast, (i) from the dogmatic and cosmic perspective, work in the world is now viewed as a prolongation of the work of the Creator; and (ii) from an anthropological consideration, through the help of aids (spiritual exercises and liturgy), we are called to not separate union with God and ordinary life, "but through the very performance of their tasks, which are God's will for them, actually promote the growth of their union with him" (*Apostolicam actuositatem*).[21]

Fr. Illanes notes that this language would have been inconceivable a few years earlier, as seen in the little mention found in Tanqueray's classic, *The Spiritual Life* and no mention at all in Reginald Garrigou-Lagrange's *The Three Ages of the Interior Life*. He pointed out the reasons for this: the monastic influence on spiritual life, with its prism of being cut off from the world; and the rupture of the secular and ecclesiastical worlds, aided by atheistic and deistic ideologies, especially from that which separated, and even set in opposition, work life from Christian life.[22]

Fr. Illanes highlights key emphases of St. Escrivá: holiness is not the preserve of priests and religious but is the vocation for all baptized; man is called to work (in Genesis 1, but also a teaching found throughout Scripture), which has been sanctified by Jesus' work at Nazareth; sanctifying work is part of the restoration of Christ after the rupture by Adam's sin; and that work could be sanctified and made a path to holiness: "Opus Dei... is based on each member sanctifying his work" (Address, November 21, 1965).[23]

Fr. Illanes' research has led him to the conclusion that there was a void of a defined "secular" (lay) theology of work. Work was often viewed in a negative

---

[20] In another manuscript by the author to be published (*New Christ: Divine Filiation: "You are my Son, the Beloved*), concrete aspects of St. Josemaría Escrivá's vision of sanctifying work were also introduced.

[21] Vatican II, *Apostolicam actuositatem*, no. 4.

[22] José Luis Illanes, *The Sanctification of Work*, 18.

[23] Ibid., 25-37.

perspective as an ascetical instrument (e.g., to overcome idleness), or as continuing the work of creation (without including Christ's redemption), or as ministry, focusing on Christ's three years of ministry (without looking at Christ's sanctification of work at Nazareth), or as bringing religious fruits from outside into the world, e.g., the Dominican's *contemplata aliis tradere*, "give to others the fruit of contemplation."[24]

B. Awareness of Divine Filiation

The key for St. Escrivá is Baptism, which is the most fundamental vocation (more than priesthood or religious life), for it is a vocation to be children of God, as he puts it, "other Christs," and "Christ Himself." The work of evangelization has to proceed from the tender identity as a divinized son or daughter of the Father, as it is divinely with Christ. The heart of the Opus Dei charism derives from the life-changing mystical experience that St. Escrivá had while travelling on a streetcar in Madrid of God as Father and he as son— divine filiation— an experience that marked him forever and which he associated as the heart of the Opus Dei spirituality. This experience of divine filiation brings a deep sense of God's closeness and Fatherly concern: "It's necessary to be convinced that God is always near us. Too often we live as though our Lord were somewhere far off— where the stars shine. We fail to realize that he is by our side— always. For he is a loving Father."[25]

Unlike this common perception of God far above and above all, it reiterates that He is a loving Father and we are His divine children by Baptism, our divine filiation. The consequence is a sublime, filial outlook. God does not contemplate us at a distance in an indifferent fashion; instead, "all human history is governed by 'an outpouring of love from the Blessed Trinity' (*Christ is Passing By*, nn. 84, 85)."[26] This awareness of divine filiation brings with it many consequences: "It gives an intimate, confident filial tone to prayer; it creates in the soul a happy, optimistic, daring attitude, which is able to take on big ventures without being put off by possible difficulties; it is the basis

---

[24] José Luis Illanes, "Opus Dei and the Evaluation of Work: Notes for a History of Spirituality," in *The Sanctification of Work*, 25-58.
[25] St. Josemaría Escrivá, *The Way* (Manila: Sinag-Tala, 1982), n. 267, pp. 87-88.
[26] José Luis Illanes, *The Sanctification of Work*, 100.

of fraternity and of a spirit of service."[27] Divine filiation is a joyful, consoling mystery; everything is seen as coming from the Father's hands. This is a "sense" that is a *vivid and deep awareness,* that gives a capacity to notice the presence of God and make one seek to please Him. It permeates one's entire existence, and only then does it produce all its spiritual fruits. *Divine filiation and contemplation form one thing.*

This summarizes St. Escrivá's idea that, when one's faith is alive, the everyday things are not without meaning, the little things become a path to God:

> For a Christian whose faith is alive, the things around him, the things that happen to him, are not meaningless or opaque events… they are calls, invitations from God, because "our Lord is calling us constantly in a thousand little events of each day" (March 24, 1930). "There is something holy, something divine, hidden in the most ordinary situations, and it is up to each one of you to discover it…" "The Holy Spirit, living in your soul in grace— God with you— is giving a supernatural tone to all your thoughts, desires, and actions" [*The Way*, n. 273]…. The contemplative life, awareness that God is our Father, fills one's horizon and creates in the soul a realization that it is worthwhile to give oneself completely, to launch out energetically to fulfill God's plan: "Be a little child; the greatest daring is always that of children."[28]

While the impulse to accomplish extraordinary things for God is good, that is not the core of this path. It rather invites one to see God in the ordinary life, "in even the unimportant events of daily work, in simple, natural family life and relationships with friends and colleagues— in the little things of everyday."[29] Fr. Illanes recommends reading the chapter, "Little Things" in *The Way*, where one sees its key position in Christian life, distinct in lay spirituality: "'You have mistaken the way if you despise the little things.' 'Do you really want to be a saint? Carry out the little duty of each moment: do what you ought and concentrate on what you are doing' (*The Way*, nn. 816, 815)."[30]

---

[27] Ibid., 100-101.
[28] Ibid., 103-104.
[29] Ibid., 104.
[30] Ibid., 104-105.

St. Escrivá makes use of a beautiful analogy of how precious to a father is the offering of the little trinkets of his child, and how love makes precious "these childish things— these insignificant little things— become 'big things' for our love is big: that's our style— out of love to make the little things of each day, each moment, something heroic."[31] Thus, within divine filiation, *it is filial love that transforms the little offerings*. And these offerings are not from just the special moments, but in all events of life. A lively faith enables us to see God in the ordinary things, and a lively charity influences even the insignificant or contemptible action; it is "capable of incarnating the love of God. 'Do everything for Love. In that way there will be no little things: everything will be big.'"[32] This message is to be *shouted from the rooftops*: Christ wishes to become incarnate in our things, to vivify our actions from within. Christ is interested and interests Himself in the little things of our everyday.

A consequence of this that St. Escrivá insists upon is the importance of going all the way, of giving everything a serious commitment, and avoiding mediocrity. Jesus does not want "halves," He wants *everything*; and for this we must *fall in love*.[33] The reader might see convergence between St. Escrivá's teaching on finding the ordinary world and work suffused with God's divine presence and the teaching of Jean-Pierre de Caussade's highly-recommended *Abandonment to Divine Providence*.

C. Sanctifying Your Work, Sanctifying Yourself in Work, and Sanctifying through Work

1. "Sanctifying Your Work"

St. Escrivá synthesizes the work of sanctification in the following maxim: "*sanctifying your work, sanctifying yourself in your work, and sanctifying through your work*." The first, "sanctifying your work," has two dimensions: (i) *technical perfection* (professionalism, no shoddy work, attention to detail); and (ii) *offered to God and for the salvation of souls* (in God's presence and in fulfillment of His will). It includes all the relationships and social dimensions such that a person is always serving, of use to society and the world, but above all bringing them

---

[31] Ibid., 105. See St. Josemaría Escrivá, *The Way*, nn. 852-901 for spiritual childhood.

[32] St. Josemaría Escrivá, *The Way*, no. 813, p. 279.

[33] José Illanes, *The Sanctification of Work*, 107.

closer to God. It stands in contrast to the lay person who is only interested in his own family and work life and no more. The dignity of work is based on *love*: "Work is born of love; it is a manifestation of love and is directed toward love" (*Christ is Passing By*, no. 48). As mentioned, it entails emphasis on or sanctification of the little things. Work is not a third element— we achieve holiness and apostolate precisely *through work*.[34]

This presupposes that we have a "supernatural outlook." No possession can be compared to God, and losing Him makes life contemptible and all our actions fruitless and purely humanistic:

> Well, this, along with all the follies of the heart satisfied, is worth nothing, is nothing and less than nothing compared… with this God of mine!— of yours! Infinite treasure, pearl of great price, humbled, become a slave, reduced to the form of a servant in the stable where he chose to be born… in His Passion and in His ignominious death… and in the madness of Love that is the blessed Eucharist. (*The Way*, no. 432).

> If life's purpose were not to give glory to God, how contemptible, how hateful it would be. (*The Way*, no. 783).

> If you lose the supernatural meaning of your life, your charity will be philanthropy; your purity, decency; your mortification, stupidity; your discipline, a whip; and all your works, fruitless. (*The Way*, no. 291)

2. "Sanctifying Yourself in Your Work"

Second, "sanctifying *yourself* in your work" does not mean "being sanctified while you work," but being sanctified by means of work. It is moving from the work done to the person doing the work, namely, the ethical, ascetical, or mystical sphere. Working with competence presupposes: (i) The whole host of *human virtues*: "Human virtues constitute the foundation for the supernatural virtues" (Homily 1952); "If we accept the responsibility of being children of God, we will realize that God wants us to be very human. Our heads should indeed be touching heaven, but our feet should be firmly on the ground…. and He [Jesus], I insist, wants us to be both very human and very divine, struggling each day to imitate Him who is *perfectus Deus, perfectus*

---

[34] Ibid., 78-87.

homo, perfect God and perfect man (*Friends of God*, nn. 74-75)"; "We must be very human, for otherwise we cannot be divine."[35]

(ii) There is a second dimension of "sanctifying yourself," namely, a *contemplative life*.[36] Lay people called to sanctify themselves in the world are tempted to see that their sanctification is accomplished in spite of the world and the work. But St. Escrivá teaches that we must sanctify ourselves with and through work, through contemplation, a *constant dialogue* with God without fleeing the world. For him, there is a unity between work life and life in God so that work impregnates prayer and prayer impregnates work: "A Christian life should be one of constant prayer, trying to live in the presence of God from morning to night…" (*Christ is Passing By*, no. 116); "we live in the street, that's where our call is: we are contemplatives in the middle of the world" (May 31, 1954); "We have to turn work into prayer and have a contemplative soul" (October 15, 1948).[37]

While this is a very demanding exercise, it is very attainable and by all lay people in any task. It does require formal prayer times of blessed solitude to root in ourselves this sense of presence of God. In prayer times, we can speak of God's interests, but also bring all the details of our life[38]: periods of prayer "will lead you, almost without being aware of it, to contemplative prayer. Your soul will pour forth more acts of love, aspirations, acts of thanksgiving, acts of atonement, spiritual communions…. You will find yourself referring everything you do to your Father God" (*Friends of God*, no. 149). For St. Escrivá, "contemplation" does not mean the sense of extraordinary phenomena, but *a deep, affective, lively sense of the presence of God* that fills us and gives meaning to the events of everyday life[39]:

> In our work, done facing God— in his presence— let us pray without ceasing, for when we work as our spirit asks us to, we put into practice the theological virtues that crown Christian living. We practice faith, through our contemplative life, in this constant conversation with the Trinity

---

[35] St. Josemaría Escrivá, *Christ is Passing By*, n. 166.
[36] José Illanes, *The Sanctification of Work*, 87-99.
[37] Ibid., 92.
[38] Ibid., 94-95.
[39] Ibid., 96-97.

present in our soul. We practice hope when we persevere in our work "knowing that, in the Lord, you cannot be laboring in vain" (1 Cor 15:58). We live charity, trying to put love of God into all our actions, spending ourselves in generous service to our fellow men, to all souls.[40]

This contemplative life requires *detachment*: "'The spirit of poverty, of true detachment from the goods of the world: and the spirit of humility, detachment from human glory, from power: these are the sweet fruits of the contemplative soul in everyday work' (January 9, 1932)."[41] In 1967, St. Escrivá reminded those who were receiving doctorates at the Roman university of the Holy Cross that they were not to seek to give orders, but to serve and become carpets for others: "You are going to serve. You're going to be the last of all, putting yourselves on the floor as soft carpets [door mats] for the others to walk on." His life manifested the desire to be last.

3. "Sanctifying [others] through your work"

The third dictum of St. Escrivá's motto is "sanctifying through your work" (bringing the world to God). The apostolate means a whole range of things, involving *three elements: activity, word, and witness*:[42]

> Lay people have their own way of contributing to the holiness and apostolate of the Church. They do so by their own free will and responsible action within the temporal sphere, to which they bring the leaven of Christianity. Giving Christian witness in their everyday lives, spreading the word that enlightens in the name of God, acting responsibly in the service of others and thus contributing to the solution of common problems: these are some ways in which ordinary Christians fulfil their divine mission (*Conversations*, n. 59, p. 88).

How can we perceive the power of sanctifying work and self to sanctify the world? St. Escrivá meditated long on John 12:32, "And when I am lifted up from the earth, I will draw all things to myself." He applied it to the mission of the baptized thus: "If you put me at the center of all earthly activities, he

---

[40] St. Josemaría Escrivá, Address, October 15, 1948, quoted in José Illanes, *The Sanctification of Work*, footnote 40, 97-98.

[41] Ibid. quoted in Illanes, *The Sanctification of Work*, 86-87.

[42] José Illanes, *The Sanctification of Work*, 111-121.

[Jesus] is saying, by fulfilling the duty of each moment, in what appears important and what appears unimportant, I will draw everything to myself."[43] The Christian is thus an *alter Christus, ipse Christus*, "Christ himself," is already drawing all things toward God. It is an approach in which "Christ crowns all activities," allowing the Holy Spirit to enter deeply into our souls to fill them with new life, an approach from within that sanctifies all human activities. Like the apostles, we hear the mandate at the Ascension addressed to ourselves, to bring the good news to the ends of the earth, to be an "apostle of apostles," who themselves in turn will encourage others to make Jesus Christ known to everyone (*Christ is Passing By*, n. 147): "Christ himself is telling you, is begging you."[44] We must avoid the temptation to say that this work is not for me and that I am not capable of it, and that I can leave it to others. In our exemplary sanctification of everyday, work with warm human qualities, and people will approach you, ask questions, and we will thus become a leaven in society, a burning coal to warm it:

> Just live your ordinary life; work at your job trying to fulfill the duties of your state in life, doing your job, your everyday work, properly, improving, getting better each day. Be loyal; be understanding with others and demanding on yourself. Be mortified and cheerful. This will be your apostolate. Then, though you won't see why, because you're very aware of your own wretchedness, you will find that people come to you. Then you can talk to them, quite simply and naturally— on your way home from work, for instance, or in a family gathering, on a bus, walking down the street, anywhere. (*Friends of God*, n. 273)

> In this way, through the consistency of his life and using natural, simple words, arising out of the context of his work, and in the midst of it, the Christian will be the leaven that ferments all the dough; he will be a burning coal that warms the ways of the earth with the divine fire he bears in his heart; he will be the stone fallen into the lake, which causes one circle and it another and another... bringing Christ's name to the ends of the earth.[45]

(i) The first element of apostolate is *activity*. He cautions us against a certain caricature of Christianity in which the search for holiness is an absorbing

---

[43] St. Josemaría Escrivá, *Christ is Passing By*, n. 183, p. 287.

[44] José Illanes, *The Sanctification of Work*, 119.

[45] Ibid., 119-120.

activity that gets in the way of our daily occupations. More specifically, he rejects any separation of holiness from the apostolate, and condemns this as arising from either a false interior life (individualistic pietism, e.g., "me and Jesus") or a naturalist approach that thinks of service in a purely earthly sense, that does not open up to our divine destiny. Holiness instead "will make you more of a brother to your brother"; personal holiness and apostolate are really two sides of the same coin. And the highest service we can offer is telling people about God. Through Baptism, we have been grafted on to Christ and become "other Christs," and through Confirmation, a new apostle with a capacity to carry on the battle in Christ's name. As mentioned, every Christian should hear the words of Jesus to the apostles, "Go, preach the Gospel," as addressed to himself. This "apostolate" (sent like an apostle) "is giving ourselves to others, to reveal Christ to them and lead them to God the Father" (*Christ is Passing By*, n. 49).

But the orientation toward apostolate for the Christian layperson has a particular tonality. Being in the middle of the world, he seeks to *penetrate all secular structures, and to show a fraternity* that has a supernatural meaning. This brotherhood of the children of God "'is the great solution offered for the problems of the world: to release men from their shell of selfishness: at the same time to guarantee... their rightful personality and true freedom... in a word, to open up for men the divine paths of the earth' (March 11, 1940)."[46] This apostolic concern is not something separate from everyday work, but rather coincides with everyday work. Here, one's work becomes a source of opportunities for meeting Christ. One's work situation does not change as such; *the change rather takes place inside our souls now that Christ has come aboard*, as the Lord came aboard the apostles' boat, and we allow Him to act in us.

(ii) The second element of apostolate, *word*, begins with recognizing Christ in others and seeking to serve Christ in others: "No man or woman is a single verse; we all make up one divine poem, which God writes with the cooperation of our freedom" (*Christ is Passing By*, no. 111, p. 171).[47] This life among men involves relationships and friendships. We go about "showing forth God and bringing people to Him, the nucleus of the apostolic endeavor,

---

[46] Ibid., 109-110.
[47] Ibid., 111-112.

is expressed in simple, natural, and ordinary words."[48] The Christian does not have a Church mandate, but acts by virtue of his Baptism. It is primarily an apostolate of *friendship*. It begins by our example, through which others begin to ask *questions* of us. The apostolate that leads others through example that inspires questions in warm friendship is captured well in this text:

> Why are you so happy? How do you manage to overcome selfishness and comfort-seeking? Who has taught you to understand others, to live well, and to spend yourself in the service of others? Then we must disclose to them the divine secret of Christian existence. We must speak to them about God, Christ, the Holy Spirit, Mary. The time has come for us to use our poor words to communicate the depth of God's love, which grace has poured into our souls....

> The Christian apostolate— and I am talking about an ordinary Christian living as simply one more man or woman among equals— is a great work of teaching. Through real, personal, loyal friendship, you create in others a hunger for God, and you help them to discover new horizons— naturally, simply. With the example of your faith lived to the full, with a loving word which is full of the force of divine truth. (*Christ is Passing By,* nn. 148-149, p. 228).

(iii) The third element of apostolate is *witness*. This is not our apostolate but Christ's apostolate. We carry out apostolate beginning with *example*. It is to cause the effect that Christ had on the disciples at Emmaus, "Did our hearts not burn within us as he talked to us on the road?" It is the path of making Christ present into all the spheres in which they are present such that they can see "the Master in the disciples":

> But he wants the vast majority to stay right where they are... the factory, the laboratory, the farm, the trades, the streets of the big cities and the trails of the mountains....

> Every Christian should make Christ present among men. He ought to act in such a way that those who know him sense "the fragrance of Christ." Men should be able to recognize the Master in his disciples. (*Christ is Passing By,* n. 105, pp. 162-163)

---

[48] Ibid., 112-113.

Thus, it is not about "doing apostolate" as in taking a few hours to do charitable works or doing a few pious practices, but working in an exemplary manner. We seek to be the best in our profession, and to have competence, and to use *professional prestige* as "Your 'bait' as a 'fisher of men.'" Professional work becomes, like the Gospel parable teaching, a lamp to enlighten our colleagues. St. Escrivá expanded the sense of "apostolate" to go beyond charitable works and apologetics. Faith and charity at work enables the Christian to unify his life (unity of life): "Your apostolate must be the overflow of your life 'within'":

> Everything has its beginning, he tells us, in the center of our soul, once the Christian recognizes the richness, depth, beauty— and demands— of God's love. "Your apostolate must be the overflow of your life 'within'" … From this interior life, this relationship with God, is born the desire to speak about God and make Him known— and, with it, the call to back up faith with deeds; the decision to do God's will; the effort to overcome our defects; the decision to love in spite of personal weakness; perseverance; beginning again after any falls; joy…. And then the circle is closed, because this simple example, which stems from ordinary life, provokes conversation with others, a dialogue about the meaning of life: apostolate in the form of the word that makes Christ known.[49]

There is thus a *close link between witness and word*. Our words, or passing on of the "good news," are much more powerful when they are backed up by example, which inspires questions in others about our life. Since there is no Church mandate, "example is essential"— this was *Christ's way. Practicing virtues and loving with deeds are already apostolate.* We imitate Christ, "Jesus began to do and teach" (Acts 1:1)— first action, then teaching. Then the example is directed towards word, words that can convey something that example is unable to do, the infinite love of God.[50]

D. Synthesis

St. Escrivá describes his vision as "unity of life": the laity are called to live as citizens of the world, loving passionately all that is good in the world, while

---

[49] José Illanes, *The Sanctification of Work*, 116-117.
[50] Ibid., 114-120.

at the same time, living these earthly realities as citizens of heaven, with a deeply contemplative spirit. He sees one reality with two dimensions: human and divine, both to be perfected; and we collaborate in Christ's recapitulation of the fallen universe (Eph 1). St. Escrivá's renewed vision comprises several elements: begins with divine filiation (the baptized as a child of God); unconditional self-gift and giving glory to God; context is life within the secular world; sanctifying work and offering it to God, principally through doing it with perfection (professionally); supernaturalizing it with contemplation; and offering it within the Eucharist; all accomplished within an apostolate of witness and friendship. Of all the effects of grace, it is charity on which St. Escrivá puts primary emphasis, even over work done professionally: "to show the charity of Christ and its concrete expression in friendship, understanding, human affection, and peace."[51] The model for his vision was the early Christian community's lived faith in the world. We note two points. First, it is easier to understand this charism if we view it against St. Escrivá's life. Second, we note that this introduction omits key elements, such as personal freedom.

St. Escrivá's charism is seen in greater clarity as first lived out in Christ: His divine filiation ("You are my beloved Son") overflows into the witness and word in life ("Jesus began to do and teach") and into His apostolate ("For God so loved the world that he gave his only Son"), amidst His influence in a myriad of relationships ("How often would I have gathered your children"— apostles, Mary-Martha-Lazarus, Nicodemus, Mary Magdalene, centurion, woman at well, etc.), drawing all into the Father's embrace ("to unite all things in him"). But this must be seen as already having been lived in His work as a carpenter at Nazareth, and we can see the three levels at Nazareth: "sanctifying your work" in how Jesus lived family life and did His carpentry vocation with perfection, made His work into a prayer and offered it to the Father; "sanctifying yourself through your work" in how Jesus lived heroically the human virtues and deep dialogue with the Father; and "sanctifying through your work" in how Jesus drew in those around Him and sought to bring the world to God.

---

[51] St. Josemaría Escrivá, *Friends of God*, n. 166.

III. The Holy Spirit's Gift of the New Lay Charisms

A. New Way of Consecration Lived in the World by Lay Charisms

The Holy Spirit has in our time provided a new way of consecration or sanctification while living in the world. In each era, the Holy Spirit has provided movements that have brought about great renewal in the Church. In the Early Church, the Holy Spirit provided the Church Fathers and the Desert Fathers in the Patristic period. Then came Benedict, Anthony of Egypt, and others in a vast monastic movement that accomplished great good. Then the twelfth century saw the beginning of a movement out of the secluded monastery and into the world, of Mendicant orders, specifically Franciscans and Dominicans, which would later be followed by a proliferation of congregations, orders, and institutes, including those secular institutes that live an intermediate lifestyle or vows/promises. The sixteenth century saw even greater involvement in the world with religious institutes, such as the Jesuit order.

The twentieth-century has brought another movement, a new phenomenon, lay charisms, whose members now live in the world and are comprised mainly of laity (including Focolare, Opus Dei, Communion and Liberation, Neocatechumenal Way), as well as a fresh breath of the Holy Spirit in spiritualities like the Charismatic Renewal. As the Church has seen great renewal through Francis and Dominic, so the Church looks forward to a new outpouring of the Holy Spirit through Chiara Lubich, Josemaría Escrivá, Luigi Giussani, and others. Thus there has been an overarching movement toward the world: desert, monasteries, mendicants, religious institutes, and now lay movements.

We notice a growing phenomenon of the widespread and fruitful influence of new lay movements among priests: an Italian missionary priest in Hong Kong spiritually fed by the Focolare charism; an American Dominican priest as well as a Portuguese diocesan priest associated with Communion and Liberation; diocesan priests becoming affiliated with Opus Dei's "Priestly Society of the Holy Cross" as well as the Madonna House Associate Priest Program; a diocesan priest attracted to the spirituality of the Jerusalem Monastic Communities; and diocesan priests engaged in the Charismatic

194

Renewal. Pope John Paul II clarified their status, indicating that, the lay charisms, which are the work of the Holy Spirit, are "co-essential" with the institutional dimension and help to renew the Church:

> I have often had occasion to stress that there is *no conflict or opposition* in the Church between the institutional dimension and the charismatic dimension, of which movements are a significant expression. *Both are co-essential* to the divine constitution of the Church founded by Jesus, because they both help to make the mystery of Christ and his saving work present in the world. *Together they aim at renewing* in their own ways the self-awareness of the Church, which in a certain sense can be called a "movement" herself, since she is *the realization in time and space of the Father's sending of his Son in the power of the Holy Spirit.*[52] (emphasis added)

B. Welcoming the Lay Charisms

Instead of being wary of lay movements, we ought to embrace and collaborate with them, as they are privileged instruments of the Holy Spirit in the new evangelization, learning from the universal approach of John Paul II. He saw these movements as "one of the most significant fruits of the new springtime of the Church that burgeoned with the Second Vatican Council":

> The Pope sees these [ecclesial or "new communities"] movements as one of the most significant fruits of the new springtime of the Church that burgeoned with the Second Vatican Council, and as "a motive of hope for the Church and for humanity" today, a work of the Spirit that makes the Church a stream of new life flowing through the history of mankind.

> In our increasingly secularised world, in which the faith of many is sorely tested, and is frequently stifled and dies, the movements and the new ecclesial communities, which are bearers of unexpected and powerful newness, are "the response, given by the Holy Spirit, to this critical challenge at the end of the millennium, [a] providential response."

---

[52] "Message of Pope John Paul II for the World Congress of Ecclesial Movements and New Communities," Vatican.va website, accessed August 28, 2018, https://w2.vatican.va/content/john-paul-ii/en/speeches/1998/may/documents/hf_jp-ii_spe_19980527_movimenti.html.

As John Paul II sees it, the lay associations in the Church are opening up a phase that is rich in expectations and hopes.[53]

Yet, there can be resistance to new movements because of occasional tensions. The parish priest can become leery of these new movements, as they stand outside of the parish structure and perhaps lead away from it, and also because of occasional episodes of conflict.

A woman once expressed concerns about one of these lay charisms, citing examples of difficulty at two of their parishes in the world. The priest responded that new movements can have, as Pope Benedict XVI said, "childhood diseases," but that the only question she should ask is that expressed by the wise Gamaliel to the Sanhedrin: "but if it [plan] is of God, you will not be able to overthrow them. You might even be found opposing God!" (Acts 5:38-39). The only question she should have asked was, "Is this of God?," and we can only know this through the Magisterium of Mother Church.

For example, a priest who has had a bad experience during the earlier and less stable period of the Charismatic Renewal within the Catholic Church might be tempted to write them off. In the Church's history, many heretics have erred because they relied on their interior subjective assessments without conforming them to the exterior judgment of the Church (see Robert Benson's *Friendship with Christ*).

Beyond this brief introduction, we simply point to the three "Congresses of Ecclesiology Movements and New Communities" under three popes (1998, 2006, 2014), as well as annual meetings with the Pontifical Council for the Laity with founders, leaders, or delegates of these groups at an international level. For a brief introduction to this phenomenon, we recommend the 1998 "Message of Pope John Paul II for the World Congress of Ecclesial

---

[53] Stanislaw Rylko, *Directory: International Associations of the Faithful,* Pontifical Council for the Laity,
http://www.vatican.va/roman_curia/pontifical_councils/laity/documents/rc_pc_laity_doc_20051114_associazioni_en.html.

Movements and New Communities."[54] To get some sense of the richness they offer today, a fine work is Bishop Brendan Leahy's *The Marian Principle: In the Ecclesiology of Hans Urs von Balthasar* (part V, pp. 163-198). A very helpful compendium is the Proceedings of the First Congress of Ecclesiology Movements and New Communities, produced and published by the Pontifical Council for the Laity: *Movements in the Church, World Congress of Ecclesial Movements, 27-29 May 1998.*

The author's experience is that association with some strong spirituality within the Church can enrich one's spiritual life and strengthen the apostle for the new evangelization: lay groups (e.g., Militia Immaculata, Legion of Mary), Third Orders (e.g., of Missionaries of Charity, Jerusalem Monastic Community), new lay charisms (e.g., Focolare, Communion and Liberation, Opus Dei, Neocatechumenal Way, Madonna House).

---

[54] Pope John Paul II, Vatican.va, https://w2.vatican.va/content/john-paul-ii/en/speeches/1998/may/documents/hf_jp-ii_spe_19980527_movimenti.html.

CHAPTER 8

EVANGELIZATION IN THE PATH OF CHRIST

Just like her daughter Saint Thérèse of the Child Jesus, the first Teresa burned with the desire to be a doctor, a missionary, an apostle; she longed to make God's name known and His kingdom come in every part of the world. A zeal much like that of her father Elijah entered her prayer and made it a prayer of fire. Her writings are in their own way another form of this zeal, and they show us that she was constantly "filled with the ardent desire of being useful to souls." She was "grief-stricken at the loss of so many souls" (*Foundations*, 1, 7). She "would have given a thousand lives to save one soul" (*Way*, 1, 3). She spent her time "occupied in prayer for those who are the defenders of the church and for preachers and for [theologians]" (*Way*, 1, 3). She wrote: "I tried to please the Lord with my poor prayers and always endeavored that the Sisters would do the same and dedicate themselves to the good of souls and the increase of his church…"[1] (Paul-Marie of the Cross)

The Second Vatican Council's Decree on the Missionary Activity of the Church, *Ad gentes divinitus*, establishes at the very outset the fundamental principle: "The pilgrim Church is missionary by her very nature, since it is from the mission of the Son and the mission of the Holy Spirit that she draws her origin, in accordance with the decree of God the Father" (n. 2). *Ad gentes divinitus* reminds us that the Church is "missionary in her essence," that she loses her very identity when she loses her missionary fervour.

A. Contemporary Masculine Rationalism of the *Homo Faber* (Man the Maker)

Let us highlight once more von Balthasar's spiritual diagnosis of the world, which Henri de Lubac affirms is the most penetrating to be found. Von Balthasar sees much that is positive at work in the world, but in commenting upon the atheistic humanism of our contemporary world scene, suggests that we are living through a kind of collective dark night. Among the features is a predominance of a "masculine" rationalism of the *homo faber*, which has

---

[1] Paul-Marie of the Cross, *Carmelite Spirituality in the Teresian Tradition*, 43.

shaped a culture to see natural things as material for manufacture. Even the human spirit is in danger of becoming material for mere self-manipulation through the various sciences. There is a loss of "wonder" of being, and once devoid of philosophy and of ethics, we risk becoming victims of a pure positivism of "making" and "having."

Karl Barth comments that we run aground on the sandbanks of a technological rationalism. Precisely because the Church's foundation is in the mystery of God's plan, the Church's consciousness and mission are closely bound with humankind's consciousness and need to rediscover "mystery."[2]

B. Ever-Present Temptation to Look Back to a Golden Age or Rest on our Laurels

In *The Eight Beatitudes*, George Chevrot points to an ever-present temptation to complacency in contradiction to the principle established by *Ad gentes divinitus*. For example, there is a natural tendency within Christianity to look backwards to the golden eras when Christianity was a force: the Constantinian peace, to Christendom in the Middle Ages, and, more recently, to the period in the early twentieth-century when Christianity was part of the fabric of Western culture.

But an examination of Jesus' path and His mandates as well as a closer scrutiny of the course of the history of the Church reveal a different path and a different program. In many ways, we are like the Jews of Jesus' time, who longed nostalgically for the time of David's monarchy or later for the period of Solomon's Temple:

> After the Saviour's resurrection some are still hoping that he will re-establish the ancient kingdom of Israel (Acts. i.6). They dream of a temple that slavishly copies the strong administration of King Solomon, of a powerful and respected political machine which would unite all people in serene submission to the laws of God, in short, of a well-framed and solidly-laid kingdom. For one last time Jesus will undeceive them. Settled conquerors? They are dreaming of a restoration when God is charging them with a creation; they are content to patch where they must construct. They

---

[2] Brendan Leahy, *The Marian* Principle, 194. See H. U. von Balthasar, *Elucidations*, 100-113.

turn their eyes to the past but the Master forces them to look forward, to the farthest ends of the earth, to the last day of the world. The final orders he gives them can be summarized in one word: "Go!" (Matt. xxviii. 19; Mark. xvi. 15). They are marching orders. Christianity is a movement.[3]

The Church's history reveals that God acts to ensure that this does not happen. Whenever Christianity becomes a force and then is tempted to rest on her laurels (e.g., Middle Ages), God finds a way to break that down so that we can return to our essence: a "movement," a missionary Church:

> Certainly a society is only durable on condition that it is organized; this is why the church appears to us as an institution. But the Holy Ghost who guides her keeps her from atrophying in the ease of repose. Every time in her history that she was just about to become established in the political or social framework of an epoch, these supports suddenly gave way, or else the church was persecuted, and she was compelled to find again, in insecurity, her missionary ardour. The church is not an establishment, she is a movement; her function is "to renew the face of the earth."[4]

In the fragility of our own times, Msgr. Chevrot's words on the Holy Spirit's way of constantly rebuilding can be reassuring. In this light, Chevrot reminds us that we are a "movement" and identifies our work with fire (Holy Spirit descending at Pentecost in the form of fire): "Our Gospel is a fire, the fire lit by Jesus Christ, which must gradually set the world alight."[5] This explains why the mandate to bring the world to Christ were His last words to the eleven apostles before His Ascension: "Go therefore and make disciples of all nations…" (Mt 28:18-20).

Evangelization today has not changed in its essence. It still follows the path of Jesus, delineated here in three steps: 1. Personal encounters with Jesus that lead to a response of gift of self; 2. Jesus' universal desire to embrace all ("make disciples of all nations"); 3. This ardent desire to save all leads to the identification of victimhood that brings forth the fruits in evangelization. This chapter therefore does not provide practical how-to counsels for making the parish thrive (other books address this), but goes to the fundamental level

---

[3] Georges Chevrot, *The Eight Beatitudes*, 10-11.
[4] Ibid., 11.
[5] Ibid.

of the transformation of the new Christ's heart in the path of Jesus and the apostles according to the following Church figures: captivated by the beauty of an exceptional presence (Luigi Giussani); radical universality of the Church-man's heart (Henri de Lubac); and the desire to save all that leads to victimhood (Hans Urs von Balthasar).

I. Evangelization through an Encounter with Christ

A. Greatest Need Today is a Personal Encounter with Christ (Luigi Giussani)

The new Christ engaged in the new evangelization can feel overwhelmed and helpless before the mass abandonment of participation in the Catholic faith and in the face of the increasing spread of secular and relativistic culture and legislations. He might do well to glean insights from a revealing experience of this crisis and a life spent in addressing it by Msgr. Luigi Giussani.[6] A fateful meeting with teenagers on a train in 1954 would change the course of Msgr. Giussani's life. When asked how their faith in Christ influenced their vision and life, the youth were stumped. It was clear that, though they were baptized and raised in the Catholic faith, their faith was formal, consisting of rituals and traditions that did not touch their worldview and their everyday moral and faith life:

> It wasn't that they didn't have any faith; or that they had formally rejected the Church that first introduced them to it. They were not apostates. It was simply that none of it seemed to matter very much. It had no real or immediate relevance to their lives; it awakened no sense of urgency in their hearts. No fire in the belly. The year was 1954, and the young priest, a wonderfully exuberant Italian by the name of Luigi Giussani, never got over the experience. "I found them so unaware of the most elementary things," he was to write years later, "and so indifferent to them, that I felt an uncontrollable desire to share my experience with them. I wanted them to have, as I had had, the experience of the 'beautiful day.'"

---

[6] This section partly draws from retreat conferences to seminarians at St. Augustine's Seminary in which Dr. John Zucchi introduced the thought of Luigi Giussani, founder of the Communion and Liberation movement in the Church. Dr. John Zucchi is its national coordinator in Canada and a professor at McGill University in Montreal.

That journey on the train changed his life. Also the lives of countless young people for whom he would harness all that he had to offer in order to bring Christ to their world. To enable them to experience the beautiful day that had first enraptured him. Passion for Christ having become the transformative experience of his life, he was determined to infuse the lives of others, especially the young, with that same passion. "I would like to share with you," he told them, "the stunning wonder (the Italian word is *stupore*) which, vibrating at the heart of my existence, has made it possible for me to grasp the profound rationality which moved me as a man to take up the study and pursuit of God."[7]

Msgr. Giussani desired to share his experience of the "beautiful day" of encountering Christ, and his resulting passionate love for Christ. Moved by this train experience, he subsequently requested and received permission to leave his seminary assignment to work at a high school. Over the years, he studied the problem of this formalized faith, seeing its influence in the Church in the 1950s before the collapse of the institutionalized faith, and he sought to revitalize the faith with his new-found insights. Priests are inclined to preach doctrine and moral precepts to non-practising Catholic students in a class, especially of the Sunday Mass obligation, with little effect. Similarly, a Catholic debating with a proponent of abortion can only point to its moral bankruptcy, which usually leads the latter to stronger opposition. Msgr. Giussani speaks a different language, because he appeals not to the mind but to the heart. He saw with clear insight that which was needed was not primarily ethics nor doctrine but a personal experience— an encounter with the living Christ.

Here is a summary of how Msgr. Giussani himself explained it during a retreat for Communion and Liberation university students.[8] Among different Gospel scenes, the central scene was a meditation of the first encounter of Andrew and John with Christ, when they asked Jesus, "Where are you staying?" and Jesus responded, "Come and see," and they stayed with him

---

[7] Regis Martin, "Recalling Luigi Giussani's Passion for Christ," *Crisis Magazine*, accessed August 28, 2018, http://www.crisismagazine.com/2014/in-search-of-the-beautiful-day-luigi-giussanis-achievement. This article by Regis Martin is an excellent introduction to Msgr. Luigi Giussani's life and insights.

[8] Luigi Giussani, "Riconoscere Christo" (Esercizi spirituali degli universitari di Comunione e Liberazione, Fraternità di Comunione e Liberazione, Rimini, 1994).

that day. This encounter of both disciples with Jesus turned their world upside down, eventually leading them to leave all for this new world of friendship with Christ. A history of *sharing this encounter* would ensue. Andrew told his brother Simon that they had found the messiah, and the apostles and other disciples would later leave everything behind to follow Jesus. Others meeting Jesus would stay in their homes, but all would share their encounters of Christ with others, and they in turn would tell others, until someone down the ages would tell Don Giussani's mother, who in turn would tell him; and now he was telling others. Thus the story of Christianity is centred around an "event," an encounter with the One for whom we were made and who fulfills all the attractions of our hearts, and who leads us to share this encounter with others. Msgr. Giussani has just sketched the path of the apostles, and therefore the path of the Church— being captivated by meeting Christ.

This path is summed up in Msgr. Giussani's *Generating Traces in the History of the World: New Traces of the Christian Experience*. The first three chapters reveal the sequence just mentioned of the path taken by the Church: "The Christian Event as an Encounter with Christ"; "The Event Goes on in History"; and "A New People in History for the Human Glory of Christ."[9]

In this book, we find an elaboration of an encounter with what he calls an "exceptional Presence," that gives us insight into the heart of Msgr. Giussani's thought:

> While religious experience springs from the need for meaning that is awakened by the impact of the real, faith is the recognition of an exceptional Presence that corresponds totally to our destiny, and the adherence to this Presence. Faith means to recognize that what a historical Presence says of itself is true. Christian faith is the memory of a historical fact: a Man said something about Himself that others accepted as true, and that I, too, accept because of the exceptional way in which that fact still reaches me. Jesus is a man who said, "I am the way, the truth and the life." It is a Fact that happened in history: a child, born of woman, registered in the Bethlehem birth register, who, once He had grown up, announced He was

[9] Luigi Giussani, Stefano Alberto, & Javier Prades, *Generating Traces in the History of the World: New Traces of the Christian Experience* (Montreal & Kingston: McGill-Queen's University Press, 2010).

God: "The Father and I are one." Paying attention to what that Man did and said to the point of saying, "I believe in this Man," adhering to His Presence, and affirming what He said as the truth: this is faith.[10]

The Beauty of the "Exceptional Presence" Captures our Hearts

Regarding this attraction of the heart for the One, we can find a fitting summary in Cardinal Ratzinger's homily of his long-time friend, Msgr. Giussani. At Msgr. Giussani's funeral, he made a key statement: "[H]e understood that Christianity is not an intellectual system, a collection of dogmas, or moralism; Christianity is instead an encounter, a love story; it is an event."[11] Cardinal Ratzinger pointed to the manner in which God reached Msgr. Giussani's heart in this love story: beauty, especially "Beauty itself," had ravished his heart:

> Father Giussani grew up in a house that was—to use his words— poor in bread but rich in music, so that from the very beginning he was touched, or, better, wounded, by the desire for beauty. He was not satisfied, however, with just any ordinary beauty, with beauty however banal; he sought rather Beauty itself, infinite Beauty, and thus he found Christ. In Christ he found true beauty, the path of life, true joy. Already as a boy, together with other youths, he started a community by the name of Studium Christi. Their plan was to speak of nothing but Christ, because everything else seemed to be a waste of time. Later, of course, he was to overcome this one-sidedness, but the substance for him would always remain the same: only Christ gives meaning to the rest of our life. Fr. Giussani kept the gaze of his life, of his heart, always fixed on Christ. It was in this way that he understood that Christianity is not an intellectual system, a collection of dogmas, or moralism. Christianity is instead an encounter, a love story; it is an event...[12]

Like Augustine, he was captured by Beauty. It is an encounter with Christ's love that would transform the person, and that person cannot hide it; all he has to do is be himself.

---

[10] "The Religious Sense and Faith," section 5, Ch. 1, Ibid.
[11] Joseph Cardinal Ratzinger, "Funeral Homily for Msgr. Luigi Giussani," *Communio* 31:4 (Winter 2004): 685.
[12] Ibid.

B. Encounter with Christ Leads to Self-Gift in Mission

Cardinal Ratzinger explained that this meeting of Christ in his heart has a demand— it called for a self-gift on Msgr. Giussani's part, as it does for all who meet Christ (as happened to Pope Francis at the age of seventeen):

> The Lord says, "Whoever seeks his own life will lose it, and whoever loses his life will find it."

> Father Giussani truly desired not to have life for his own sake: instead he gave life, and it is precisely in this that he found it not only for himself, but for so many others. He lived out what we heard in the Gospel. He did not wish to be served but to serve. He was a faithful servant of the Gospel. He gave away all the wealth of his heart, he gave away all the divine wealth of the Gospel that permeated him. By this service, by giving his life, this life of his has borne rich fruit, as we can see in this very moment. He has truly become the father of many and by guiding people not to himself but to Christ he has truly conquered hearts, he has helped to make the world better, he has helped to open up the doors of the world to heaven.[13]

Thus, in this second step, the encounter with Christ brings about a mission, or, as Msgr. Giussani would always say, "the encounter coincides with the mission." Dr. John Zucchi explains it this way: "When we meet a presence [Christ] that truly corresponds with our deepest desires, when we recognize that presence for what it is, then we want to tell the world about it." It can take the form of accompanying others, which has to do as well with his understanding of community.

For Msgr. Giussani, "To be in community is not an exterior 'getting along,' a simple convergence from the outside. To be in community is *an interior dimension, at the origin of each action.*"[14]

> To share my life with others in this way becomes a *collectivity*. 4. Instead, the emergence of these people by my side, those who surround me and whom I meet, are that aspect of the Creator's will that involves the greatest commitment. Thus, I must accept these people. By accepting them, they

---

[13] Ibid.

[14] Luigi Giussani, *The Journey to Truth is an Experience* (McGill-Queen's University Press, 2006), 26.

become mine, part of me, become me: "love thy neighbour as thyself." It is precisely in this manner that *community* is born, as the continuous outcome of this initiative of acceptance on my part, of tireless commitment to the presence of others, to the surprising and mysterious sign of the Other, just as is my presence to myself. Sharing my life with others then is something that springs from within me, a gesture that expresses me, a gift of myself, a *relationship of love*.[15]

Community, as Msgr. Giussani explains it, flows from being loved by Jesus and leads to giving away one's life. It is a dimension of the human person; it is already intrinsic to the person, but entails a getting together from the inside. Dr. Regis Martin summarizes our insights about this original event, that began with the encounter of the shepherds, thus:

> In other words, what formed the centerpiece of the entire enterprise was a recognition regarding the basic reasonableness of faith. That belief in God, belief in Christ and the gift of the Spirit sent to renew the face of the earth, far from imposing arbitrary or impossible demands, succeeded in speaking directly to the mind and heart of men everywhere. Is it not the same heartbeat, Fr. Giussani would repeatedly ask, that animates man wherever he may be found? "Christ's message is so much in keeping with what man longs for," he would argue, "that the individual who hears it cannot help being struck by it."
>
> Here was evidence of Giussani's distinctive genius, i.e., his untiring, unremitting insistence upon the universality of *"the religious sense"*— that is, the elemental human longing to know the meaning of everything, and so to dwell amid the precincts of an indestructible joy and freedom, truth and beauty. Here was nature's secret warhead for the explosions of grace to follow. That the proposal of Jesus Christ uniquely and comprehensively corresponds to the deepest desires of the human heart. Awareness of that fact would furnish the impetus giving birth to the ecclesial movement called *Communion and Liberation*.[16]

Where the new Christ is inclined to evangelize people by presenting doctrinal truths or moral precepts, the apostles' zeal for mission flowed from their encounter with the overwhelming presence and love of the person of Christ. This logic derives from the truth that man is made for Christ and has his

---

[15] Ibid.

[16] Regis Martin, "Recalling Luigi Giusanni's Passion for Christ," *Crisis Magazine*.

destiny in union with Him: "the elemental human longing… to dwell amid the precincts of an indestructible joy and freedom, truth and beauty. Here was nature's secret warhead for the explosions of grace to follow." Msgr. Giussani is pointing to the need for the beauty of the encounter with Christ's love to reach hearts (not truth for the mind and good for the will), especially of the youth.

The Church needs to target the heart, to awaken hearts to Christ's presence (religious sense), as the apostles Andrew and John experienced— for the heart to taste love and seek to give one's heart in response— this is where evangelization begins. This requires a sea-change in the Church's approach, a deeper approach than simply being welcoming in the church vestibule and spending money on music. One can ask how people can experience the apostles' encounter with Christ today, and perhaps it can be mediated partly through an encounter with the beauty of the face of Christ in the priest and the Church. Here are three suggestions.

C. Three Suggestions for the Priest that also Applies to All

(i) First, the faithful must experience Christ's love in the priest. The priest can imitate Fr. Giussani in the beauty of his *apostolate of friendship*, of deep concern and love for each person he met. How many people have recounted being transformed from experiencing the warmth of his personal love, such as a troubled priest who spent months with him, and who was then led to found houses for drug addicts in South America. The priest reaches hearts, not principally in preaching to large congregations but in the one-on-one encounters, especially in the confessional. Francis Cardinal Nguyen van Thuan learned to put primary emphasis on personal contact:

> Make use of the only effective method— personal contact. Enter into the lives of others, to understand and love them. Developing personal relationships is more effective than preaching and writing. Contact between one person and another— "heart-to-heart" exchanges— is the secret of perseverance and success.[17]

---

[17] Francis Xavier Nguyen van Thuan, *The Road to Hope: A Gospel from Prison* (Boston: Pauline Media, 2001), no. 994, p. 229.

(ii) Second, the priest might seek the attractiveness (beauty) of *holiness*. We see an example of the warmth of the saintly personality of Msgr. Giussani in the personal friendship with Cardinal Ratzinger, that included monthly meetings. The temptation is to seek to convert by much preaching and to foster parish vibrancy in numerous parish activities, which Dom Chautard calls the "heresy of good works." Ethnic parishes can have marvellous community activity and participation, but do they also have many Confessions, prayer before the tabernacle and devotion to our Lady, concern for evangelization and the poor; all indicators of the deeper spiritual life? The attractiveness of holiness draws people, as France sought Fr. Vianney.

(iii) Third, the priest can focus on *ways of reaching hearts through beauty* (*Communion and Liberation* highlights beauty): the beauty of celebrating the Mass that recalls Calvary and the heavenly liturgy (as Padre Pio did); the beautiful encounter with Christ through the compassion of the priest in the Tribunal of Mercy (Confession); the depth of the priest's supernatural outlook and recollection (vs. activism); the Christ-like beauty of his kindness and his simplicity of life (poverty); the filial beauty of devotion to the Church, our Lady, and the saints; the warmth of the fire that is the Blessed Sacrament; the beauty of the faith drawn out in homilies (Church Fathers) and through the introduction to profound Catholic writings; the depth of parishioners yearning to be contemplative (presence of the Blessed Trinity within their souls) and sacrificial in redemptive suffering (e.g., illness).[18]

Captivated by the beauty of this "exceptional Presence" that is Christ, the first apostles were armed with two dispositions of their divine Master: Part II. H. de Lubac's truly universal outlook to embrace all ("I have become all things to all men, that I might by all means save some," 1 Cor 9:22); and Part III. Hans Urs von Balthasar's desire for the salvation of all ("I came to cast fire upon the earth; and would that it were already kindled!", Lk 12:49).

---

[18] As a reference, we note a worthwhile article by Paul Coady that examines Avery Dulles' six models of evangelization: personal witness; verbal testimony; Christian worship; community; inculturation; and works of charity. Paul Coady, "The New Evangelization- Part II: The Dulles/Bayerley Models of Evangelization," *Missions Today,* vol. 70:2 (Spring 2002): 8-11. Coady writes that Dulles used as his primary source for these models Fr. Timothy E. Bayerley's *The Great Commission: Models of Evangelization in American Catholicism.*

II. Universalism: The Power of the Holy Spirit to Unite

A. Henri de Lubac's Universal Outlook Depicted in *Catholicism*

The new Christ cannot simply concern himself with some specific apostolate and the priest cannot concern himself only with his parishioners, preaching only to the choir. Imitating the apostles' path to become all things to bring all to Christ, all new Christs seek to be universal. Possibly no contemporary theologian is so marked by this universality than Henri de Lubac, one of the great theologians of the twentieth-century, a co-founder of the Catholic international theological journal, *Communio*, and teacher of Jean Daniélou and Hans Urs von Balthasar. Joseph Ratzinger himself as a theological student read de Lubac's *Catholicism* and its universality and breadth changed his theological outlook.

It had a similar effect on Hans Urs von Balthasar, as described by Antonio Sicari. Von Balthasar, who, writing on the occasion of Henri de Lubac's ninetieth birthday, pointed out that this theological breadth derives from the Holy Spirit: "It remains only for me to say that I learned from you from my years of study at Lyons until today: something about the Holy Spirit. The Spirit, you taught me, can unite much more than we are accustomed to think."[19] Von Balthasar himself was influenced by this breadth of the Spirit that "can unite much more than we are accustomed to think."

Thus universality through the Holy Spirit comprises a double dynamic: the vertical movement by the gifts from on high breaking upon all humanity; and a horizontal movement, spreading out in every direction to recreate bonds between peoples and overcoming all barriers, but which has its living and personal center in Christ. Henri de Lubac's breadth reflects the universal heart of Christ and of the apostles.

We see concrete examples of Henri de Lubac's desire for unity in his universal concern for the "distant ones" (from the faith) in *Catholicism* (the following

---

[19] Hans Urs von Balthasar, *Il Padre de Lubac*, Milan, 1986 reprint, quoted in Antonio Sicari, "*Communio* in Henri de Lubac," *Communio* 19 (Fall 1992): 450.

section is a summary).[20] He treats of inculturation which as we know has to do with culture; but more deeply with *koinonia* (communion), since it has to do with catholicity or universality, which embraces all, while rejecting the evil elements. He points to the opposing approach: are the religions that Christianity comes in contact with, with customs, social and intellectual life, morality, which all bear their imprint, to be put off like a cloak? Must everything be jettisoned to give place to the Gospel? There are some who desire this, asserting that everything in false religions is bad, contains lies and perversions of the truth, and what we see before us is a city of Satan, which must be razed to the ground. This was the reasoning of Tatian and Marcion, as well as the extreme Jansenists. Such an attitude is unfair, since no reality is totally evil, and since the seed of the Word has already penetrated:

> Human nature… is certainly sick, infirm, but it is not totally depraved. Human reason is weak and wavering, but it is not entirely doomed to error, and it is not possible for the divinity to be entirely hidden from it. "The seed of the Word is innate in the whole human race." The divine likeness in it may be dimmed, veiled, disfigured, but it is always there…. False religions, therefore, are religions that stray from the truth or become engulfed in error, rather than religions whose whole direction is misleading and whose principles are wholly false. They are based on childish ideas more often than on evil ones…. The Creator and the Redeemer, the Church adds, are one and the same God; therefore there can be no conflict between their works…. The Word that became incarnate to renew and complete all things is also he who "enlighteneth every man that cometh into this world"…. Just as he did, his messengers come not to destroy, but to accomplish; not to lay waste, but to raise up, transform, make holy. And even the moral decay that they encounter requires not rejection but rectification.[21]

B. The Model is the Immanent Method of Matteo Ricci

Thus Henri de Lubac points out that Christ's way is to be open to the good in other cultures: "not rejection but rectification." Faith spreads to *distant cultures*, with local differences, and there is a spontaneous reaction that

---

[20] Henri de Lubac, *Catholicism: Christ and the Common Destiny of Man* (New York: Sheed & Ward, 1950).
[21] Ibid., Ch. IX, 147-148.

eliminates whatever is unwholesome in them. But the missionary apostolate also becomes more conscious of the rules that govern it and reproduces them in its method, as we see with Matteo Ricci:

> But the principle appears most clearly in the missionaries of the modern period: Mathew Ricci, who without playing the oriental, "educated himself so cleverly and so whole-heartedly that he had the sentiments and the appearance of an oriental"; his follower in India, Robert de Nobili, who made himself a Brahmin among the Brahmins: the very diversity of their methods bear witness to the unity and purity of the Catholic spirit by which they were inspired, even as it is still today the inspiration of their successors. In the eighteenth century the same spirit is shown all through the Instructions of Propaganda to the bishops sent to China, and it may be found again in the formal teaching of recent popes, *Maximum illud* of Benedict XV (1919), *Rerum Ecclesiae* of Pius XI (1926).
>
> The twofold desire willingly to entertain whatever can be assimilated and to prescribe nothing that is not of faith, although it is acknowledged and systematically employed, is by no means the calculated plan of cunning men in search of a successful method, as has been sometimes suggested…. But it can only be done at the cost of a systematic, persevering effort that love alone makes possible. For it requires of the apostle not only a continual adaptation of self, like St. Paul who, becoming all things to all men, did not speak before the Areopagus as he spoke to his fellow-countrymen. Much more than a mere outward adaptation is required: a whole inner transformation, a real exodus from the secret places of the soul: "leave your country, your family and your father's house, to go to the place that I shall show you." Such a method demands also an enduring patience, for it is impossible without a deep study of the peoples who are to be converted, their customs, morals and beliefs.[22]

For de Lubac, the method of Fr. Matteo Ricci has been a light for the Church: "to entertain whatever can be assimilated and to prescribe nothing that is not of faith," to become all things to all out of love, requiring adaptation, a whole inner transformation, and an enduring patience combined with a deep study of the culture.

---

[22] Ibid., 151-152.

One can only imagine what the faith of China would be today had Ricci been allowed to continue his program. Thus, there are two ways of being strict: the unjust way that arises from a lack of understanding that increases evil; and a second way that is a requirement of love itself, and increases good, and "because it is Catholic, makes its own and completes all man's genuine thinking, which of itself is always fragmentary and mean in some degree."[23]

This path above is the method of *immanence*, the most traditional of all, and its application is not confined to discussion and books. An unobtrusive work of art can epitomize much patient negotiation, the method in the humble chapel of El-Abiodh, continuing among the Mohammedans Charles de Foucault's silent vigil. How pressing is the need for such an effort at understanding when it concerns those features of a civilization whose chief fault is merely that they are unfamiliar to us. The Church's ambition is to gather the whole human family together, and she has nothing in common with our cheap pretensions. As Charity's ambassador she lays no claim to cultural imperialism. It is the Church's mission to purify and give fresh life to the outstanding varieties of spiritual experience, to deepen them and bring them to a successful issue *by means of the supernatural revelation that she holds in deposit*. The Church cannot forgo this pre-eminently *world-wide mission* so as to be in the exclusive service of one or another form of civilization. Here is de Lubac's sublime synthesis of the way of the Church (it recalls the *Letter to Diognetes*):

> For she knows that, apart from the fact that no human achievement has been promised eternity, all races, all centuries, all centres of culture have something to contribute to the proper use of the divine treasure which she holds in trust…. She is mindful of those providential harmonies which prepared the resources of Greece and Rome for her first expansion, and… she believes in fresh providential harmonies for her further expansion. At periods of fearful conflict she still has hope, though it be in her humblest members, and a fresh assimilation is prepared in the silence of prayer and study. The story of a few Dominicans kidnapping Aristotle… is not an isolated case… she is too painfully conscious of the impoverishment caused by the great schisms not to seek compensating factors. Why should she desire to change flexible and vigorous structural unity for a drab uniformity?

---

[23] Ibid., 152.

... As she is the only ark of salvation, within her immense nave she must give shelter to all varieties of humanity. She is the only banqueting hall, and the dishes she serves are the product of the whole of creation. She is Christ's seamless coat, but she is too— and it is the same thing— Joseph's coat of many colours.... She knows that the various customs hallowed by her "confirm the unanimity of her faith," that this visible catholicity is the normal expression of her inner riches, and her beauty is resplendent in its variety...[24]

C. The Church is Universal in her Breadth

Thus, for de Lubac, she is the Catholic Church; neither Latin nor Greek, but universal. To see in Catholicism one religion among others, one system among others is to mistake its very nature, or at least to stop at the threshold. Catholicism is religion itself. It is the form that humanity must put on in order to finally be itself. It is the only reality which involves by its existence no opposition. It is therefore the very opposite of a "closed society." Like its Founder, it is eternal and sure of itself. And the very intransigence in matters of principle, which prevents its ever being ensnared by transitory things, secures for it a flexibility of infinite comprehensiveness— the very opposite of the harsh exclusiveness which characterizes the sectarian spirit. The Church is at home everywhere, and everyone should be able to feel himself at home in the Church. The temptation to interpret the Church otherwise has become stronger. After a period of triumphant optimism, which linked the destiny of Europe to that of Christianity, it has now come about a mood of disillusion links the destiny of Christianity to that of a Europe supposedly in a decline:

> In the long run, we are told, Christianity must recognize that there are certain great religions which it cannot penetrate. All over the world spheres of influence have been allotted, definite positions taken up.... To leave one system of belief in order to enter another is a change of civilization rather than of religion. Ultimately Christianity will have to accept this proof that it is linked with a culture and ways of thought that are not universal.[25]

---

[24] Ibid., 155-156.
[25] J. Schlumberger, *Sur les frontières religieuses*, 22 (1935), quoted in H. de Lubac, *Catholicism*, 157-158.

This is a disastrous and fatal idea, encouraged by all too many failures in the past and by all too many suggestions in the present; it can only be overcome by a great spiritual asceticism.

The Church, trusting in the Holy Spirit that leads her, trusts also all the peoples that she comes to free— this is no sign of *naïveté*. She realizes that not all cultures are at the same cultural level, that not all afford the same possibilities. But she knows too that all men are one in community of their divine origin and destiny, and this suffices to give her confidence in the face of all the theories engendered by pride and egoism.

The most efficacious way, to bring out the hidden truth and to avoid extinguishing the good that would break forth, lies in a systematic desire to *study sympathetically* those forms that are most remote from us, and within that, it is at the highest reaches that humanity must be understood; the depressions will always be explored soon enough.

At the Same Time, the Church Avoids Syncretism

Yet Henri de Lubac warns that the Church must avoid syncretism and a human religion. The Church is not syncretistic any more than it is naïve. Syncretism is artificial, generally the work of rulers or literary men, and presupposes declining faith. It is an insult to the living God. In the energetic language of the prophets, syncretism is fornication: it is barren in the spiritual order, and lowers and vulgarizes all elements it combines.

While the Church has rejected Gnosticism, a representative of the syncretist system, such uncompromising boldness has not hindered her in carrying out her work of assimilation with a breadth of vision that is more clearly manifest every day. It is equally unfitting to speak of liberalism, of tolerating error, or making the salt of the Gospel savourless. For if Christianity must be shown with all its exigencies, it must also stand out in all its purity and it would be working to obscure the gentle severity of the Gospel:

> And if it is once understood that the work of conversion consists, fundamentally, not in adapting supernatural truth, in bringing it down to human level, but, on the contrary, in adapting man to it, raising him up to the truth that rules and judges him, we must especially beware, as of

blasphemy, of confusing ourselves, its servants, with it— ourselves, our tastes, our habits, our prejudices, our passions, our narrow-mindedness and our weaknesses with the divine religion with which we are so little imbued. We must give souls to God, not conquer them for ourselves.[26]

St. Paul's great example is the most fitting of all to secure against the mistakes to which we are liable in this connection. In the face of St. Peter's imprudent concessions, he refuses to change the Gospel to please other men because then he would be unfaithful to Christ.

The key is the guidance of the Holy Spirit: "The Holy Spirit who guided the Apostle is the same who still guides the Church, and speaks by the voice of the modern Popes. The path to which it commits us is the only safe one. To follow it is neither naïveté, nor syncretism, nor liberalism; it is simply Catholicism."[27]

Thus the disciple of Christ marries total fidelity to Christ's teachings with the enveloping breadth of His love that invites all: Samaritan woman at well, centurion, Pilate, Good Thief, even Judas. De Lubac himself showed remarkable openness towards figures who were regarded as "distant" within the Church, including Teilhard de Chardin.

If the Holy Spirit is marked by openness ("can unite much more than we are accustomed to think"), then *openness is a mark of holiness and possesses power to evangelize*: with liturgy, being open to our Lady and the saints; with solemn rubrics, seeing Calvary being mystically present at Mass; beyond pastoral methods, seeking first a deepening union with Christ in reparation; beyond the parish, identifying with the forty-five million plus refugees; beyond a traditional spirituality, being open to the richness of the new lay charisms; building on Aquinas, but open to contemporary theological developments; having exterior virtues, being even more open to interior virtues (e.g., obedience, abandonment); and possessing priestly dignity, yet becoming, like St. Escrivá and Cardinal van Thuan, a door mat to bring all to Christ.

---

[26] Henri de Lubac, *Catholicism*, 159.
[27] Ibid., 160.

III. Desiring All be Saved Leads to Vicarious Identification

A. "Dare We Hope That All Men Be Saved"— Identification

It appears that Henri de Lubac's universality and breadth has been passed on to his former student, Hans Urs von Balthasar, who poses the ultimate and controversial question on openness: *Dare We Hope That All Men Be Saved?*[28] Von Balthasar, along with Adrienne von Speyr, had been accused by some of adhering to the heresy of universal restoration (*apocatastasis*), that all will be saved, including Satan and the fallen angels. Von Balthasar's book is a defence of his intuition against these accusations.

Von Balthasar Received Ecclesial Approval

Is von Balthasar a heretic? Discernment in the Spirit teaches us not to get lost in the myriad of details by first setting the discussion into the big picture of his status and reception within the Church. In this context, we should first take note of the support his overall theology has received, including the approval of two Popes. He was given the Cardinal's hat in recognition of his theological contributions by Pope John Paul II. It was recorded that Pope Benedict XVI, after his retirement, left the Conclave behind to go temporarily to Castel Gandolfo, and took with him von Balthasar's *The Glory of Lord* series. An Ontario newspaper's article theorized a link between Pope Francis's words to von Balthasar. We note also that von Balthasar enjoys the support of a number of key Cardinals who espouse his theology (including Marc Ouellet, Angelo Scola, Christoph Schönborn). Fergus Kerr, a Thomist, in his survey of *Twentieth Century Theologians*, concluded that Balthasar was clearly the greatest twentieth-century theologian.

Second, we note that the history of the Church shows that theologians who come up with new theologies are often initially condemned: St. Thomas Aquinas by Bishop Tempier (Paris), Henri de Lubac silenced for eight years, and Teilhard de Chardin with a monitum by the Vatican that is still in place. Finally, a theologian can freely and legitimately contest specific elements of

---

[28] Hans Urs von Balthasar, *Dare We Hope 'That All Men Be Saved?'*, trans. D. Kipp and L. Krauth (San Francisco: Ignatius Press, 1988).

Hans Urs von Balthasar's self-defence (where others can support the same points), but we may become stuck in a theological quagmire in debating the specific details. Let us instead examine von Balthasar's overall thrust.

Von Balthasar's Arguments

His specific arguments are several. To begin, he vehemently rejects the charge of this heresy of universal restoration (*apocatastasis*), bluntly condemning it. His defence begins with Tradition, pointing to the good company of theologians and saints who support his position, as well as to the Holy Father's defence of von Speyr. Second, his key concern is that many have implicitly transformed "real possibility" to "objective certainty" of people being damned to hell (the Church never declares a specific person to be in hell). He decries having "knowledge" of people in hell, especially when we exclude ourselves from that possibility; a hell for others but not for ourselves. Third, von Balthasar's way begins with that of utter helplessness before, and confidence in, God's mercy: that man's part in his baptismal faith is simply an utter throwing of himself into the mercy of Christ, and, while Christ's part is as judge, His is a judgment that goes beyond justice to love. Thus, no one must judge himself; all that is required is an acknowledgement of one's frailty and sinfulness, and the trust in the love of the Judge, our Saviour.

For von Balthasar, theology has historically taken a wrong turn and that has distorted the present theological outlook. The Western Church has with great wisdom followed the theological track of Augustine, but unfortunately also took on Augustine's sin-context in his fight against the theologically-"optimistic" position of Pelagius. Our recent theology, within this pessimistic sin-context horizon, tends to see God as presenting before us the two choices of salvation and damnation, all the while examining the minutiae of how God's freedom works with man's freedom in salvation. Von Balthasar teaches us to return instead to the original Pauline vision of predestination in Christ, where God from all eternity had planned to send His Son to make all into sons and daughters in the one Son. There is only one plan, and one destination— heaven; it is not God holding out heaven or hell as two possibilities. There can be great confidence, even with human freedom, as the Father's plan of predestination is efficacious because of the ineffable depths of the Son's kenosis (descent) of love.

218

B. Von Balthasar's Argument is not Intellectual but Pastoral— *Vicarious Love*

Why is von Balthasar making a fuss about the distinction between knowing and hoping— because it is love that leads to hope. This is not merely a theoretical debate; this is the question of all questions, the only concern that ultimately matters— *the salvation of mankind* (Mt 10:28; Lk 12:5). Von Balthasar is not having an intellectual debate, but is arguing with passion for a disposition of heart for all Christians: to have the very disposition of God the Father. To the author of this book, von Balthasar is really arguing, "Dare we *love enough* to hope that all men be saved?" It is the opposite of being an armchair coach sitting comfortably at home, arguing the merits or faults of a quarterback, while not paying the price on the field.

We illustrate this paternal instinct from the true story of a permanent deacon who gave public testimony of the account of his daughter, who had become involved with drugs and ended up on the streets, and how at some point he even had to mortgage his house in order to pay for a jail bond. He never gave up on his daughter, who eventually returned home and died soon after, having reconciled with God in Confession and with the family. He always hoped because he loved.

What is presented is a paradox, with two dimensions: on the one hand there is the definite reality of hell, which is already populated at least by the fallen angels; on the other, we must not limit God's love, for we do not think like He does. Again, would a father with ten sons, two of whom have become cocaine dealers and murderers, not hold out hope to the end that they will come back, arguing that you will always lose some?

If God is infinite love, does He not hold *hope* for all His children? What is required is not an intellectual but an existential posture: not an indifferent debate about who will be saved (not intellectualizing), but having a heart like that of Christ, that is moved by love, and that is profoundly disturbed by the possibility of some going to hell, and throws oneself into the fray (like St. Catherine of Siena).

219

The indications of the Gospel, it would appear, suggest that some will indeed go to hell, but the apostle of Christ does not intellectualize at an abstract level of debating numbers of the damned but his heart finds the loss of His children unbearable and acts like Moses and Paul in vicarious offering.[29]

Objections may still arise. What about free will? Here we have to keep in mind that in God's original creation there was no opposition between man's will and God's will. When God frees the human will from its attachments, it freely gives itself to God, who works within the inner core of that mercy, as in Augustine's saying about a man committing suicide: "Between the bridge and the water, the mercy of God can get in." What about the virtue of justice? To this, von Balthasar responds that God judges us but within His overarching mercy. Some argue that God must treat the devils and mankind equally; but we remember that the devils have acted out of malice, while man acts out of weakness and ignorance. Again, at the end of the day, the key is Christ's kenosis. When one struggles with the horrors of the atomic bomb on Hiroshima or of the rape of Nanking in China, one cannot find resolution and peace at the human level; but there is consolation in the knowledge at the vertical level that the Son of God as man went beyond all evil, that in the end His love can conquer all— His Resurrection is the pledge of God's victory over evil. Thus evil and sin are not whitewashed or explained away, but taken with the utmost seriousness, in which God Himself descends to take all evil on Himself, and in which love and mercy (not revenge) have the last word. Pope John Paul II discusses this briefly in *Crossing the Threshold of Hope*, ending with hope because "Before all else; it is Love that judges" (p. 187).

Love Leads to Identification in Vicarious Suffering

Thus what ultimately undergirds such a profound "hope" is found implicitly in this work by von Balthasar, but more explicitly in his other works. It lies in the kenosis of Christ. Jesus has gone to such depths of "hell" for us, far outstripping all the guilt of the evil of all the sin of the world. The love of God triumphs in Christ's identification with us: He becomes "sin" for us, He becomes one with our guilt. His kenosis goes infinitely beyond the debt to

---

[29] Ibid., 204-221.

be paid. His infinite merits on the cross parallel His largesse in creating: where one earth is sufficient for all humanity, He created millions of galaxies that reflects His magnanimity. Adrienne von Speyr provides the ultimate insight. Here we understand the centrality von Balthasar placed on Christ's kenosis. She writes that the cross was at the center of Jesus' thoughts and is the key to understanding all mysteries, including that of the Trinity:

> All his [Jesus] thoughts revolve around this [mystery of cross] ever since he assumed a human body. Whoever wants to understand him must immerse himself in the act of suffering which is the redemption…. Even the mystery of the Trinity and the other mysteries, those of heaven and the beyond, first come really alive for a person when they are illumined by the Cross. A trinitarian piety which tried to put the Cross on the side would soon be sterile.[30]

Beyond Christ's kenosis, the key to understanding von Balthasar's work is suggested by how he concludes his defence. There we find a number of figures presented who enter into Christ's kenosis in vicarious victimhood: Moses offered to be destroyed as propitiation for the Hebrew people; Paul offered to be "accursed" (damned) for the salvation of others; St. Catherine of Siena said that she would rush to its gates to do everything to prevent that from happening and asked Jesus to visit the wounds of the Church on her body; and Edith Stein spoke of how God would not violate our freedom but would "outwit" us, using every means at His disposal.

Those who "Dare to love enough to hope that all men be saved" do not sit back and intellectually analyze who will be saved and how our freedom is engaged for salvation and damnation. In imitation of their Master, they rush into action and "identify" with those who stray, and take upon themselves the burden in vicarious sacrifice. We note too that contemporary theologians have moved away from the early belief that most would be damned toward the opposite. The oft-quoted words of Jesus spoken to Julian of Norwich (whom Pope Benedict XVI used as a model) offer hope in regard to salvation:

> All shall be well, and all shall be well, and all manner of things shall be well. God loved us before he made us; and his love has never diminished and

---

[30] Adrienne von Speyr, *Handmaid of the Lord* (San Francisco: Ignatius Press, 1985), 38.

never shall. If there is anywhere on earth a lover of God who is always kept safe from falling, I know nothing of it, for it was not shown to me. But this was shown: that in falling and rising again we are always kept in that same precious love.[31]

C. Victimhood is the Measure of Fruitfulness in Evangelization

The Cross at the Apex of Sanctity

The logic of Jesus' persecution follows all his great disciples: "where I am, there shall my servant be also" (Jn 12:26). As a rule they always encounter opposition, sometimes even from within the Church: the apostles opposed by the Jewish authorities; mendicant orders' existence threatened by the secular clergy; St. Ignatius of Loyola and St. Josemaría Escrivá opposed in their new foundations while in Rome; Padre Pio made incommunicado for a few years because of false information that he was a fake; St. Marguerite d'Youville opposed by Church authorities; and St. Mary McKillop unjustly excommunicated by her bishop.

Those God prepares for a special work can have intimations of the cross. Cardinal van Thuan, the Vietnamese archbishop of Saigon who had been imprisoned for thirteen years and whom John Paul II called a "living martyr," on his first visit to Lourdes while in Rome for studies, felt the words of Mary to Bernadette being applied to himself: "'I do not promise you joy and consolations on this earth, but trials and sufferings.' I had the deep impression that these words were also addressed to me." And later during the years in prison, he came to understand that the greatest identification with the cross, as well as the most powerful intercession for the world, happens through the Mass.

Christ's immolation in the Mass is incomplete without our immolation:

> Like the Curé of Ars and Padre Pio, in each of our Masses we have around us the entire world with all those places where "God cries," with all sinners and with all the sufferings of humanity. Let us hear with our ears, let us

---

[31] Julian of Norwich, *The Revelations of Divine Love*, Classics of Western Spirituality (Mahwah, NJ: Paulist Press, 1977), Chapter 32 quoted by Pope Benedict XVI, General Audience, Wednesday, 1 December 2010.

suffer in our hearts, let us allow the Spirit to pray in us with "inexpressible groanings" (cf. Rom 8:26). Let us unite everything to Jesus crucified, who is there on the altar. Let us identify ourselves with him.[32]

The great mystics St. Teresa of Jesus and St. John of the Cross confirm this path of the cross for each person in the stages of the interior life. In various texts of the apex (Seventh Mansions) of *The Interior Castle*, St. Teresa of Jesus intimates that the crown of spiritual life is the cross:

> "I feel certain that these graces (seventh mansions) are sent to strengthen our weakness, that we may imitate him by suffering much."
>
> "His majesty can bestow no greater favour on us than to give us a life such as was led by his beloved Son."
>
> "Those nearest Christ our Lord bear the heaviest cross." "To be truly spiritual… is to be branded with his mark, which is the cross."
>
> "During the brief time this life lasts… let us give our Lord every sacrifice we can, both interior and exterior, and he will deign to unite it to his own."[33]

D. The Cross in the Life of Henry Cardinal Newman

Regarding the cross, the new Christs can look to the example of the towering figure of Henry Cardinal Newman, whom Pope Paul VI spoke of as anticipating the Second Vatican Council and important for our time. We find the great paradox of fruitfulness and the cross, and his "white martyrdom" may be the foundation for the tremendous influence he has in the Church.

John Tracy Ellis describes something of the pains endured by this sensitive soul.[34] Already in the final sermon of September 1843, in St. Mary's church, Littlemore, when he left for the Catholic faith, one senses the "poignancy of his grief in separation from so much that he had held near and dear."[35] But this was only the beginning of his arduous journey: the unfamiliarity of the new faith, practices, and surroundings; a sister who refused to speak to him

---

[32] Francis Xavier Nguyen van Thuan, *Testimony of Hope: Spiritual Exercises of Pope John Paul II* (Boston, MA: Pauline Books and Media, 2000), 94-95.

[33] Sr. Madeleine, *Within the Castle with St. Teresa*, 207-208.

[34] John Tracy Ellis, "The Eucharist in the Life of Cardinal Newman," *Communio* 4 (1977): 22.

[35] Ibid., 325.

after his entering the Catholic Church; the civil libel suit brought against Newman by an ex-Dominican, Giacinto Achilli (which lasted 18 months with much worry and expense); tension between his Birmingham Oratory and the London Oratory and the policies of their superior, Frederick W. Faber, that ultimately led to a break; the lack of guidance from Paul Cullen, Archbishop of Dublin, the bishop of Newport; Thomas Brown, who delated him to Rome as a heretic; and fellow converts, Manning and Talbot, at the Roman Curia, who misrepresented and demeaned his efforts.

Something of the darkness that covered the soul of Newman is captured in the following text:

> Circumstances have brought a special temptation upon me of late. I have now been exerting myself, labouring, toiling, ever since I was a Catholic, not I trust ultimately for any person on earth, but for God above, but still with a great desire to please those who put me to labour. After the supreme judgment of God, I have desired, though in a different order, their praise. But not only have I not got it, but I have been treated, in various ways, only with slight and unkindness. Because I have not pushed myself forward, because I have not dreamed of saying: "See what I am doing and have done"—because I have not retailed gossip, flattered great people, and sided with this or that party, I am nobody. I have no friend at Rome, I have laboured in England, to be misrepresented, backbitten and scorned. I have laboured in Ireland, with a door ever shut in my face. I seem to have had many failures, and what I did well was not understood. I do not think I am saying this in any bitterness.

> "Not understood"—this is the point. I have seen great wants which had to be supplied among Catholics— especially as regards education,— and of course those who laboured under those wants, did not know their state,— and did not see or understand the want at all—or what was the supply of the want— and felt no thankfulness at all, and no consideration towards a person who was doing something towards the supply, but rather thought him restless, or crotchetty, or in some way or other what he should not be. This has naturally made me shrink into myself, or rather it has made me think of turning more to God, if it has not actually turned me.

> It has made me feel that in the Blessed Sacrament is my great consolation, and that, while I have Him Who lives in the Church, the separate members

of the Church, my Superiors, though they may claim my obedience, have no claim on my admiration, and offer nothing for my inward trust. I have expressed this feeling, or rather implied it, in one of my Dublin Sermons, preached in 1856. (Occasional Sermons, pp. 64, 65, p. 57 edition 4).[36]

As it was the crown of Newman's life, Calvary has to be the summit of the new Christ's life and ministry as well. The apostle of Christ has to be immersed in the mystery of suffering both to be fruitful and to deepen his understanding of the mysteries of the faith. For if "the blood of martyrs is the seed of the Church" (Tertullian), then perhaps the "blood" of the new Christ is the seed for the new evangelization.

The three dimensions of this Chapter were lived out by John Paul II: an encounter with him made you feel as if you were the only person in the room; he went far and wide to reach all, especially the youth; and, he embraced his many crosses (e.g., losing entire family). Blaise Pascal points to our task: "Jesus will be in agony until the end of the world, we must not sleep during that time" (alternative translation: "till then we may not rest").[37]

---

[36] Wilfrid Ward, *The Life of John Henry Cardinal Newman*, vol. I (London: Longmans, Green and Company, 1912), 576-577, quoted in Tracy Ellis, "The Eucharist in the Life of Cardinal Newman," *Communio* 4 (Winter 1977), 325.

[37] Blaise Pascal, *Pensées* (Hammondsworth, England: Penguin books, 1966), 313.

CHAPTER 9

COSMIC LITURGY IN THE NEW EVANGELIZATION

> The liturgy should put us face to face with God in a personal relationship of intense intimacy. It should plunge us into the inner life of the Most Blessed Trinity.[1] (Cardinal Sarah)

Robert Cardinal Sarah speaks of a liturgical reform needed after the postconciliar crisis, not primarily from adaptation to the needs of the listener, which is secondary, that begins again from the essence of the liturgy and produces the fruits such as a face to face intimate encounter with God and being plunged into "the inner life of Trinity."[2] The young Joseph Ratzinger, during his period of study for the priesthood, was blessed with renowned professors who trod a new path with three renewals: returning to the fonts of the early Church, making Scripture again the heart of theology, and recognizing the historical aspect of theology. Through this introduction to a new theological world, it was the liturgy above all that captured his heart and dominated his theological vision (as the fundamental act of response to God). Like Cardinal Ratzinger's patristic emphasis on the liturgy, we seek to recover the vision of the Church Fathers, whose overall Christian outlook was manifestly liturgical:

> Ever since my childhood, the Church's liturgy has been the central activity of my life, and it also became, under the theological instruction of masters like Schmaus, Söhngen, Pascher, and Guardini, the center of my theological work…. I was not interested in the specific problems of liturgical study, but in the anchoring of the liturgy in the fundamental act of our faith, and therefore also its place in our entire human existence."[3]

We shall attempt to enter something of the newness of the liturgy, especially regarding its cosmic character.

---

[1] Robert Cardinal Sarah, "The Liturgy 'Plunges us into the Inner Life of the Trinity," *Inside the Vatican* (June-July 2019): 33.

[2] Ibid., 30, 31, 34.

[3] Joseph Ratzinger, *Teologia della Liturgia*, Preface, vol. 1, *Opera Omnia* (Rome: Libreria Editrice Vaticana, 2008), English translation of excerpt by Sandro Magister, "In the 'Opera Omnia' of Ratzinger the Theologian, the Overture Is All about the Liturgy," *Chiesa*, accessed August 28, 2018, http://chiesa.espresso.repubblica.it/articolo/208933bdc4.html?eng=y.

To this end, Part I examines "The Sublime Nature of the Liturgy," examining the link of the liturgy with the Paschal mystery and eternity. Part II examines how "The Eucharist Propels the New Evangelization," recovering the Eucharist as the main dynamism in evangelization. Part III discusses "Liturgical Renewals to Advance the New Evangelization," including avoiding post-Vatican II deviations.

I. The Sublime Nature of the Liturgy

A. The Eternal Sacrifice Descends in the Liturgy to Lift us into Eternal Love

Let us attempt to get a glimpse into the nature of the liturgy through Joseph Ratzinger's *The Spirit of the Liturgy*, which links the two triads of salvation history and liturgy.[4] The liturgy is the mediating link between time and eternity, the dynamism that unites time and eternity, that makes eternity present in time and propels time into eternity. Beyond the "specific problems of liturgical study" (e.g., rubrics), what dominates is the *overarching cosmic nature* of the liturgy that captured the heart of Joseph Ratzinger:

> The fundamental intention of the work is that of placing the liturgy above the often frivolous questions about this or that form, in its important relationship, which I have sought to describe in three areas that are present in all of the individual themes. In the first place, there is the intimate relationship between the Old and New Testament; without the relationship with the Old Testament heritage, the Christian liturgy is absolutely incomprehensible. The second area is the relationship with the world religions. And finally, there is a third area: the cosmic nature of the liturgy… is celebrated within the vastness of the cosmos, it embraces creation and history at the same time. This is what was intended in the orientation of prayer: that the Redeemer to whom we pray is also the Creator, and so there always remains in the liturgy love for creation and responsibility toward it.[5]

Cardinal Ratzinger highlights above all "the cosmic nature of the liturgy, which represents something beyond a simple meeting of a larger or smaller

---

[4] Joseph Ratzinger, *The Spirit of the Liturgy* (San Francisco: Ignatius Press, 2000), 53-61.
[5] Joseph Ratzinger, *Teologia della Liturgia*, Preface, vol. 1, *Opera Omnia*, in Sandro Magister, "In the 'Opera Omnia' of Ratzinger the Theologian, the Overture Is All about the Liturgy," *Chiesa*.

circle of human beings; the liturgy is celebrated within the vastness of the cosmos, it embraces creation and history at the same time." Even more, it is an intermingling of time with eternity, or more precisely a vision of the liturgy driving all of salvation history, impelling it in a revolution towards co-redeeming with Christ in the Holy Spirit and toward the Trinity. For the liturgy is already a proleptic Parousia, a "coming" back (John's "going and coming") of Christ already in this life:

> The Parousia is the highest intensification and fulfillment of the Liturgy. And the Liturgy is Parousia, a Parousia-like event taking place in our midst.... And so light falls on a further aspect: the interweaving of the present and future which constitutes the specific mode of Christianity's presence in the world and its openness to what is to come. The dethronement of the world elements, the fading of sun, moon and stars, has already taken place, and yet it is still to come. The trumpet of the Word is already summoning us, and yet it is still to be sounded. Every Eucharist is Parousia, the Lord's coming, and yet the Eucharist is even more truly the tensed yearning that He would reveal His hidden Glory. The deepening of the idea of the Parousia achieved in the Fourth Gospel is not, therefore, when compared with the Synoptic tradition, something different or strange.... We can simply note here that "going," related to the Cross, and "coming," related to the Resurrection, interpenetrate in an inward way. As the Crucified, Jesus continues to be One who goes away. As the Pierced One with outstretched arms He continually comes....

> It [Parousia] becomes an interpretation of the Liturgy and Christian life in their intimate connection as in their continual going beyond themselves. The motif of the Parousia becomes the obligation to live the Liturgy as a feast of hope-filled presence directed towards Christ, the universal ruler.... In His Cross, the Lord has preceded us so as to prepare for us a place in the house of the Father. In the Liturgy the Church should, as it were, prepare for him a dwelling in the world. The theme of watchfulness thus penetrates to the point where it takes on the character of a mission.[6]

Liturgy as Parousia (second coming of Christ) "becomes an interpretation of the Liturgy and Christian life..." How is this ineffable intermingling of time

---

[6] Joseph Ratzinger, *Eschatology: Death and Eternal Life*, Dogmatic Theology 9 (Washington, DC: Catholic University of America Press, 1988), 203-204.

and eternity possible? Ratzinger begins by responding to these two stereotypical objections: given that Christian worship is a cosmic liturgy that embraces heaven and earth, "Is the whole world now not his sanctuary?"; and more to the point, "Can there be any other holy time than the time for practicing love of neighbour, whenever and wherever the circumstances of our life demand it?" This appears to be a common temptation today (God is everywhere, and social justice and compassion are all that matters respectively), to which Ratzinger responds that such a question "overlooks the 'not yet' that is part of Christian existence and talks as if the New Heaven and New Earth had already come."[7]

B. Two Inter-linked Triads: Salvation History and Liturgy

Cardinal Ratzinger's foundation of the sublime nature of the liturgy is built upon three stages of salvation history by which he explains the three levels of liturgy. In the first triad of salvation history, he points to the Church Fathers' description of three stages in fulfillment of salvation history of *shadow, image, and reality*. The "shadow," which represents the Old Testament period, has been fulfilled by the coming of Christ, symbolized by "image": "The night is far gone, the day is at hand," as Rom 13:12 describes, which is strikingly captured by the tearing of the veil in the Temple, denoting the passing from the Old Testament to the New Testament dispensation.

But, as St. Gregory the Great puts it, this "image" of our present time only represents the first fulfillment, that is still only the time of dawn, when darkness and light are intermingled; the sun is rising, but it has still not reached its zenith. The time of the New Testament, our time, is a peculiar kind of "in-between," a mixture of "already and not yet," and must more and more burst open in preparation for the final fulfillment, the third stage, "the reality" in heaven. This idea of the New Testament as the between-time in salvation history, as image between shadow and reality, gives liturgical theology its specific form as a between-time as well. It becomes clearer when we apply the above three levels to how worship operates at three levels to receive the grace of Christ's coming: institution, Eucharist, and fulfillment.

---

[7] Joseph Ratzinger, *The Spirit of the Liturgy*, 53.

These three represent Christ's sacrifice or Pasch; the sacrifice of the temple replaced by the Eucharistic sacrifice; and the final fulfillment in eternity respectively (introduced in *New Christ: Divine Filiation*):

Salvation History	Liturgy
Shadow	Christ's sacrifice
Image [between-time]	Liturgy
Reality	Eternal fulfillment

In the second triad of the liturgy, Ratzinger is saying that it makes present Christ's sacrifice, but, this grace received is only the beginning of glory (fulfillment). First, he notes that the liturgy was what Jesus gave us in His words and actions at the Last Supper. These words and actions form the core of Christian liturgical celebration, which was further constructed out of the synthesis of the synagogue and Temple liturgies, the sacrificial actions of the Temple now replaced by the Eucharistic Prayer.

But this liturgical level does not stand on its own (mere ritual), but has meaning only in relation to something that really happens, to a reality that is substantially present (e.g., Mass perpetuating Calvary); otherwise it would lack real content, like bank notes without funds in the bank to cover them. The Lord could say that His Body and His Blood were "given" or "shed" only because He had in fact given His body and shed His blood.

The difference between His sacrifice on Calvary and ours (Mass) is that His Body is not the ever-dead corpse of a dead man, nor is the Blood the life-element rendered lifeless. No, sacrifice has become gift, for the Body and the Blood given in love have entered through the Resurrection into the eternity of love, which is stronger than death: "Without the Cross and Resurrection, Christian worship is null and void, and a theology of liturgy that omitted any reference to them would really just be talking about an empty game."[8]

He then explains that how the sacrifice of Calvary can be made present continually— because the sacrifice has been drawn up into eternity. The foundation of reality that undergirds Christian liturgy is found in the word *semel* (*ephapax* in Greek), "once for all." The epistle to the Hebrews vigorously

---

[8] Ibid., 55.

contrasts Christ's "once for all" sacrifice to the multitude of repeated sacrifices in the Old Covenant, which, like facts of the past, like dates in history books, could have nothing contemporary about them.

However, the exterior act of being crucified is accompanied by an interior act of self-giving (the Body is "given for you"), "No one takes it [my life] from me but I lay it down of my own accord" (Jn 10:18). It is no ordinary spiritual act, but one that takes up the bodily dimension in itself, that embraces the whole man; indeed, it is at the same time an act of the Son of God: "the obedience of Jesus' human will is inserted into the everlasting Yes of the Son to the Father."

> As St. Maximus the Confessor showed so splendidly, *the obedience of Jesus' human will is inserted into the everlasting Yes of the Son to the Father.* This "giving" on the part of the Lord, in the passivity of his being crucified, draws the passion of human existence into the action of love, and so it embraces all the dimensions of reality— Body, Soul, Spirit, Logos. Just as the pain of the body is drawn into the pathos of the mind and becomes the yes of obedience, *so time is drawn into what reaches beyond time. The real interior act,* though it does not exist without the exterior, *transcends time, but since it comes from time, time can again and again be brought into it.*
>
> That is how we can become contemporary with the past events of salvation. St. Bernard of Clairvaux has this in mind when he says that *the true* semel *('once') bears within itself the* semper *('always').* What is perpetual takes place in what happens only once…. The *ephapax* ('Once For All') is bound up with the *aiōnios* ('everlasting'). "Today" embraces the whole time of the Church…. Here is the real heart and true grandeur of the celebration of the Eucharist, which is more, much more than a meal. In the Eucharist we are caught up and made *contemporary with the Paschal Mystery of Christ,* in his passing from the tabernacle of the transitory to the presence and sight of God.[9] (emphasis added)

Thus Christ's sacrifice has been drawn into eternity, and yet since the key interior act comes from time, "time can again and again be brought into it." It is thus a "once for all" (*semel*) action that is "everlasting" (*aiōnios*); it is being made contemporary and participating in the passage to the Father. This

---

[9] Ibid., 56-57.

means not just making "present" a past event, but also an anticipation of what is to come.

This now explains the third level of the liturgy of fulfillment: how it applies to us. This liturgy is not about a replacement but about re-presentation, vicarious sacrifice. The liturgy is not about the sacrificing of animals, of a "something" that is ultimately alien to me.

But it is founded on the Passion endured by a man, who is the Son of God, and who with His "I" reaches into the mystery of the living God Himself. So it can never be a mere liturgical action (*actio liturgica*). Its origin also bears within it its future in the sense of that representation, *vicarious* sacrifice, *takes up into itself those whom it represents*; it is not external to them, but a shaping influence on them. That is, it is also an anthropological reality, not just a rite or a liturgical "game."

His self-giving to the Father on Calvary is meant to become mine, so that *I become contemporary with the Pasch of Christ and assimilated unto God*. That is why in the early Church martyrdom was regarded as a real Eucharistic celebration, the most extreme actualization of the Christian's being a contemporary with Christ, of being united with Him. The aim of the liturgy, as St. Paul says in the text referred to, is that "our bodies" (that is, our bodily existence on earth) become "a living sacrifice," united to the sacrifice of Christ. The *semel* ("once for all") wants to attain its *semper* ("always").[10]

C. Third Stage of Triad is Complete Only with Conformation to Christ's Pasch

Cardinal Ratzinger links the two distinct triads of salvation history and liturgy so that we can finally put together what may have appeared disparate. The foundation of the liturgy, its source and support, is the historical Pasch of Jesus— His cross and Resurrection, which once-for-all event has become the ever-abiding form of the liturgy:

> In the first stage the eternal is embodied in what is once-for-all [Paschal mystery]. The second stage is the entry of the eternal into our present

---

[10] Ibid.

moment in the liturgical action. And the third stage is the desire of the eternal to take hold of the worshipper's life and ultimately of all historical reality. The immediate event— the liturgy— makes sense and has a meaning for our lives only because it contains the other two dimensions. Past, present, and future interpenetrate and touch upon eternity.[11]

In this middle age of salvation history, the time of the Church, we have the newness only mediated by the "signs" (corresponding to "image" of salvation history) of salvation; we need mediation, namely, the liturgy, as we do not yet see the Lord "as He is." Now superimposing the two triads of historical developments, it becomes clear that the liturgy gives precise expression to this middle historical situation, the "between time":

> It [liturgy] expresses the "between-ness" of the time of images, in which we find ourselves. The theology of the liturgy is in a special way "symbolic theology," a theology of symbols, which connects us to what is present but hidden…. After the tearing of the Temple curtain and the opening up of the heart of God in the pierced heart of the Crucified, do we still need sacred space, sacred time, mediating symbols? Yes, we do need them precisely so that, through the "image," through the sign, we learn the openness of heaven. We need them to give us the capacity to know the mystery of God in the pierced heart of the Crucified. Christian liturgy is no longer replacement worship but the coming of the representative Redeemer to us, an entry into his representation that is an entry into reality itself….
>
> In liturgical celebration there is a kind of turning around of *exitus* to *reditus*, of departure to return, of God's descent to our ascent. The liturgy is the means by which earthly time is inserted into the time of Jesus Christ and into its present. It is the turning point in the process of redemption. The Shepherd takes the lost sheep onto his shoulders and carries it home.[12]

The first triad of salvation history illuminates the second triad of the liturgy. In the "between time" of Christ's coming in salvation history, the human act of Christ's sacrifice on Calvary is taken up into the interior act of the divine Person and thus taken up into eternity; but in the liturgy it can re-enter time because it came from time and because it is now eternal. It is only because

---

[11] Ibid., 60.
[12] Ibid., 60-61.

Christ has risen and has been taken up into eternity that this once-for-all sacrifice becomes eternal. Because this one sacrifice was done vicariously for us, the liturgy too has this vicarious character of taking us into the Passover. In the second triad of liturgy, there are three steps: (i) the sacrifice of Christ has ascended into heaven; (ii) the sacrifice descends in the "between time" of the liturgy; (iii) so as to take us up in grace and finally into eternity. But the re-presentation of Christ's mysteries in the liturgy (ii) have their completion in our sacrifice, our being taken up into His sacrifice and thereby into eternity (iii): "The liturgy is the means by which earthly time is inserted into the time of Jesus Christ and into its present." It is not complete without the spiritual sacrifice of each baptized, living the life of love that flows from conformation to Christ crucified, the living sacrifice "for" others.

Cardinal Ratzinger emphasizes that Christ's sacrifice is only complete when the world has become the place of *love*, as St. Augustine saw in his *City of God*. Only then is worship perfected and what happened on Golgotha is completed. We should avoid a certain trap. It is tempting to say that this third dimension of the liturgy expresses its moral demands, but it goes far beyond mere moralism. Here are certain elements: the Lord has gone before us and opened a way, and He Himself has become the bridge. The challenge for us now is to allow ourselves to be taken up into His *"being for"* mankind. He, the Holy One, *hallows us with the holiness that none of us could ever give ourselves*; and we are incorporated into the great historical trajectory by which the world moves toward the fulfillment of God being "all in all." In this sense, what at first seems like the moral dimension is at the same time the eschatological dynamism of the liturgy: the fullness of Christ becomes a reality, and only thus is the Paschal event completed throughout history; the "today" of Christ lasts right to the end (cf. Heb 4:7ff.). The Church has suffered from the perception of the Mass as just a means of obtaining grace, and not with the vision that the liturgy seizes and envelops us into Christ's sacrifice for the world and into His deep love for the Father in eternity. The liturgy will end one day, but this fulfillment is to last to eternity.

II. The Eucharist Propels the New Evangelization (Charles Arminjon)

After the Second Vatican Council, "liturgy" became a vague, sophisticated buzz word. Let us attempt to restore the true and full meaning of the liturgy.

First, we have seen in Cardinal Ratzinger that the liturgy is cosmic: the "once-for-all" sacrifice of Christ has entered into eternity and descends into the world again through the liturgy, so as to transform us into love and lift us up into eternity. Second, we note that it is the sacraments that constitute the primary liturgies, and all the sacraments find their fulfillment in the Eucharist. Thus, we wish to center upon the greatest of the liturgies— the Eucharistic sacrifice of the Mass. For this, we turn to an inspiring meditation on the Eucharist in Fr. Charles Arminjon's *The End of the Present World and the Mysteries of the Future Life.*

A. The Eucharist is the Apex of "Preaching the Gospel"

We tend to forget that the Eucharist is the primary force for evangelization. Let us establish a critical point: it was not Christ's preaching that saved us, but His culminating work on the cross, the Paschal mystery, which is now "re-presented" mystically in the Eucharistic sacrifice. And this "source and summit," the Eucharist, is what principally propels evangelization. It is true that the Church teaches that the primary task of the priest and bishop, as it was for Paul, is to preach the Gospel (Mk 16: 14; cf. 1 Cor 9:16; 2 Cor 5:14-17). But preaching the Gospel finds its larger context in evangelization, such that preaching leads one to seek Baptism, but which finds the greatest power of transformation into a new Christ through Eucharist. There is a perennial temptation for the priest to focus principally on his homiletic preaching, where the Eucharist is actually the dominant means for accomplishing the work of evangelization. But this temptation may also plague all laity involved in evangelization, for example, to focus on methods or programs.

Here are two examples. First, in a homily to seminarians, the late Aloysius Cardinal Ambrozic, former archbishop of Toronto, recognized this inclination in himself. In this homily, he shared how his principal thought at Mass would be on giving a good homily, when upon deeper reflection, he realized that the liturgy of the Word, the first table, finds its fulfillment and apex in the second table, the liturgy of the Eucharist. Second, even more striking is the witness of Scott Hahn, a convert from Presbyterianism, where preaching is the focus, to the Catholic faith, who revealed how it was especially his clandestine reconnoitring of the Catholic Mass and the subsequent desire to receive Christ that led him to join the Church:

Then the Liturgy of the Eucharist began. I watched and listened as the priest pronounced the words of consecration and elevated the host. And I confess, the last drop of doubt drained away at that moment. I looked and said, "My Lord and my God." As the people began going forward to receive communion, I literally began to drool, "Lord, I want you. I want communion more fully with you. You've come into my heart. You're my personal Savior and Lord, but now I think You want to come onto my tongue and into my stomach, and into my body as well as my soul until this communion is complete."

… But the next day I was back, and the next, and the next. I couldn't tell a soul. I couldn't tell my wife. But in two or three weeks I was hooked. I was head over heels in love with Christ and His Real Presence in the Blessed Sacrament. It became the source and the summit and the climax of each day, and I still couldn't tell anybody.[13]

The Power of the Eucharist in the Face of Today's Secular Culture

Fr. Arminjon notes two objections to the Eucharist: that the Eucharist is holding up the "tide of industry" or that it is not efficacious. St. John Chrysostom reminds us of its power Eucharist, which has the presence of Christ and the heavenly hosts, pouring forth graces into the world:

St. John Chrysostom tells us that our Lord Jesus Christ shows Himself at the altar as on the throne of His clemency, His hands full of bounty and grace. He is surrounded by a multitude of angels, standing in an attitude of deep respect; and, through the medium of these celestial spirits, He bestows upon men all that promotes the good of soul and body. Who would dare, then, to affirm that this divine blood, shed every day upon our altars, had less power and efficacy than the sweat of man, rainfall, and dew from the sky to fructify our meadows and increase our industry? Where do we find prosperous families and strong, developed races, except amongst those who go up to the altar and help to ensure the abundance of those fruits, by the fervor of their invocations and the power of their collaboration?[14]

---

[13] *Newman Catholic Apologetics Resources*, "The Scott Hahn Conversion Story: Protestant Minister Becomes Catholic," Catholic Adult Education Program, accessed August 28, 2018, http://zuserver2.star.ucl.ac.uk/~vgg/rc/aplgtc/hahn/m1/sctcnv.html.
[14] Charles Arminjon, *The End of the Present World and the Mysteries of the Future Life* (Manchester, NH: Sophia Institute Press, 2008), 264.

A bishop, whose wrote his doctoral thesis on the liturgy, used to say, "If a priest has celebrated Mass, he has fulfilled his priesthood."

B. Facing Opposition with Faith and the Sacraments

Fr. Arminjon enumerates a number of examples of the immense power of the Eucharist.[15] In our difficult times, we tend to forget the power of the Eucharist and the sacraments. Fr. Arminjon presents a vision of overwhelming opposition to God and the Church in our times:

> Modern society to-day, in the face of Heaven and earth, has proclaimed the most audacious boast ever conceived by human pride; it declares that it will exclude God from laws and institutions, creating a social order and felicity completely independent of Him; and, confronted with this Satanic design, it is our duty to protest loudly, saying, with the archangel, "Quis ut Deus?" [Who is like God?][16]

The words of Fr. Arminjon remind us once again of the power of the Christian faith and the sacramental life, and new Christs facing overwhelming opposition in evangelization might be consoled by this description of its universal power to reach hearts, as we find at the death of Napoleon:

> You, then, feeble and faint-hearted souls, who feel your faith faltering and weakening, shaken by the effrontery and arrogant clamour of the wicked, turn your eyes for a moment upon the Christian world where, in spite of ingenious, mendacious conspiracies, Jesus Christ continues to be loved and adored. See those crowds who fill our churches at the times of the major solemnities, kneeling humbly and invoking Jesus Christ with the unshakable conviction that their prayer will reach heaven. See the dying, as they press His blessed picture to their lips so as to fortify themselves against the anguish and the fears of their final agony. See those sorrowful countenances, bowing down at the steps of His lonely altars and straightening up again, beaming with an indescribable joy. See those sinners, stricken with remorse, beating their breasts and departing, trusting that they have regained pardon.

---

[15] Ibid., 264-267.
[16] Ibid., 268.

Such is the infallible voice of mankind; the striking testimony of popular faith; the profound cry of public conscience, which can be diminished for a day but which all the threats of the mighty and the artifices of atheistic science will never succeed in stifling.

Napoleon, on the rock of his exile, said to one of his comrades in arms, "I understand men, and I tell you that Jesus Christ was not a man." He openly confessed the presence of Jesus Christ in His sacramental life, himself asking to receive the last Viaticum of the dying; and when, by this noble act, he had solemnly professed the faith of his childhood, he added to the same comrade in arms, "I am happy, general, to have fulfilled my duty, and I wish you the same fortune when you die."[17]

C. The Sublimity of the Eucharist and the Dignity of the Priest's Office

Let us pause here to consider the vital role of priests and to provide them encouragement in their task: by perceiving the sublimity of the Eucharist through an understanding of the dignity of the priest and the sacrifice he offers. It is clear that we must affirm unequivocally that Christ is the one High Priest and possesses the only priesthood; yet, at the same time, we also affirm that the ordained priest, only a humble instrument participating in Christ's priesthood, has inexpressible dignity. Fr. Arminjon himself exalts the office of the priest, which has to do with the *sublimity of the sacrifice that is offered.* Where Abel offered only first fruits and the Patriarchs offered lambs and heifers, in the words of St. Andrew, "I sacrifice the Immaculate Lamb on the altar each day."[18] St. John Chrysostom brings to light the priest's dignity:

Priests of the Lord... the greatest things among men seem to me shorn of all glory, when I consider that which you have received. Your ministry, it is true, is performed among men; but it ranks among the celestial hierarchies, for the Paraclete is the Author of the mysteries which you accomplish; you are greater than the prophet Elijah; you bear in your hands, not fire, but the Holy Ghost, beseeching Him to pour forth His graces upon all the faithful.

Priests of the Lord, there can be no doubt but that you are greater than kings. The king commands subjects; you command God. The judgments of

17 Ibid., 269.
18 Ibid., 248.

239

the king affect only the things of time; your pronouncements will stand
through all eternity. You have no need of the bounty and riches of the king,
but the king needs your blessings and prayers…. There is no doubt but that,
in a sense, you are greater than the Virgin Mary herself…. That *fiat* she
pronounced only once; you pronounce it every day.[19]

Fr. Arminjon explains the sublime dignity of each celebration of the Mass as
a renewal of the one sacrifice by linking the priest's actions to the sacred
actions of Christ the High Priest led to Calvary. The sacredness of the
mystery that the priest enters is evident:

At Mass, we come out of the sacristy wearing on our shoulders that
mysterious chasuble, the image of the Cross that our Lord Jesus Christ bore
upon His own shoulders. The alb that covers us represents the white robe
in which the Son of God was mocked at the court of Herod, but which His
innocence transformed into a garment of dazzling brightness. We carry,
hanging from our arms, that maniple of tears, intended to wipe away the
sweat from our foreheads and restore us from our failings.

After bowing, we ascend the steps of the altar, as our Lord Jesus Christ
climbed the steps of Golgotha. We raise our hands, when we say Oremus
("let us pray"), as Jesus Christ prayed, with His hands raised toward His
Father. At the Canon, we speak in a low voice, like Jesus Christ, who, in the
Garden of Olives, moved a stone's throw away from His disciples, in order
to enter into the silence of recollection and prayer. At the Elevation, we
take the Host in our hands, just as Jesus Christ, at the Last Supper, took the
bread and wine into His holy and venerable hands. Then our words cease,
our personality disappears, and the voice of Jesus Christ replaces that of
His minister. It is no longer we who speak, no longer we who live: the body
of the priest has become the very body of God.[20]

Fr. Arminjon offers some clarity to the manner of perpetuation or
representation of the sacrifice of Calvary. Like others, he reaffirmed that it is
the same Priest, Victim, and God to whom the sacrifice is offered, while
clarifying it for us by making the distinction between the cross and the altar:

---

[19] Ibid., 250-251.
[20] Ibid., 249.

> On the Cross and at the altar, Jesus Christ offers His Father the same death. On the Cross, He offers His present death, at the altar His past and consummated death. On the Cross, He offers Himself as a sacrifice of redemption; at the altar, as a sacrifice deriving from that infinite source of grace which He once poured out on Calvary— on the Cross, in the state of a suffering man; at the altar, in the state of a supernatural, mystical man.[21]

This clarifies for us that the perpetuation of the sacrifice is not a physical but a mystical and sacramental re-presentation of the one sacrifice of Calvary at the Eucharist, as pointed out by Odo Casel.

He points out that, while politics, philosophy, and science have tried, they have not been able to create a priest. The appointed priest set up by the French Revolution who would offer some flowers at an altar was held in ridicule. Fr. Arminjon also pointed out that "It is a noteworthy fact that wherever the Eucharistic sacrifice disappears there is no priest," a fact that Protestants have discovered.[22] Then he points to a fact that is critical for our time:

> The sure means of suppressing Jesus Christ as far as possible, and of utterly destroying His reign here below, is to get rid of the priest, or at the very least empty his heart of faith, innocence, and the Christian virtues. Lately, speaking of the priest, one of the leaders of contemporary impiety said, "Let us not put him to death— he would acquire new strength in blood; martyrdom would be for him the seed of a new fecundity and a superhuman strength. Let us suffocate him in filth."[23]

This "filth" is the danger that priests must avoid. Yet, Fr. Arminjon affirms that "the priest cannot be vanquished,"[24] for, in the face of opposition, the faithful priest brings down the two words of life and eternity: "a word of eternity that, each day, brings the Living Word of God down upon the altar; a word of eternity that makes Him come down into souls, where He dwells, together with justice and the supernatural works of life."[25]

---

[21] Ibid., 258.
[22] Ibid., 251.
[23] Ibid., 252.
[24] Ibid.
[25] Ibid.

III. Liturgical Renewals to Advance the New Evangelization

Since the sin of Adam and Eve, the world has awaited the Messiah ("child" prophesied in Gen 3) and the Church Fathers see the entire Old Testament economy being fulfilled in the New Testament, especially the Messiah and His sacrifice on the cross: "When I am lifted up, I shall draw all to myself." This recapitulation is symbolized powerfully in Cecil de Mille's movie, *Ben Hur*, where the blood of Christ flowing from His wounds onto the earth symbolized a renewal of the entire universe. There is a new dawn, not directly within the external affairs of the world, but in the hearts that open to Christ, especially in three figures in the movie.

First, we see a conversion in the mother of Ben Hur, Miriam. When Ben Hur's love interest, Esther, apologized for the failure to obtain a healing for Miriam's leprosy through the encounter with Christ, Miriam replied with a heart full of wonder that Jesus looked "as though he were carrying on that cross the pain of the world". It was her heart that was healed; her body's health soon followed. Second, her words in the movie mirrored those of one of the three wise men, Balthazar, who said in awe at the sight of Calvary: "He has taken the world of our sins onto Himself." Third, Ben Hur, who previously sought vengeance on the Romans for the havoc wreaked upon his family, after seeing the crucifixion, confided to Esther: "I felt him [Christ] take the sword from my hand." This is the power of the Pasch of Calvary, which has mystically and sacramentally become the Mass. And from the small circle of apostles and disciples, armed with the Holy Spirit, especially in the Eucharist, the world would come to know Christ.

Now we come to a conundrum in our times. Given the power of the liturgy, especially the Eucharist, why does it seem that the Church is failing in our times to capture hearts, especially those of the youth, and to transform society? And given the richness of the liturgical renewal of the Second Vatican Council, how is it that we are not now experiencing a revival in the faith of Catholics, but instead find that many have abandoned the Sunday Eucharist, and those present often find themselves distracted? The inescapable fact is that most Catholics seem to be unaware of the sacrificial dimension (focusing on the meal): that the sacrifice of Calvary and of the Mass are one and the same sacrifice and are more focused on the acquisition of grace, and the priest on the rubrics or on the community. We now examine three causes: obliviousness of the presence of Christ's mysteries in the liturgy; lack of adoration; and lack of conformation to the crucified Christ; and the two deviations of celebrating self and being rooted in the past.

Cardinal Sarah captures incisively the heart of the difficulty in a Conference address at a colloquium, "The Source of the Future," in 2017. He describes a loss of mystery or adoration through a horizontalizing of faith, a loss of the sacrificial perpetuation of Calvary for a "convivial meal," that prevents a face to face encounter with God that unveils our interior life:

> They forgot that the liturgical act is not just a PRAYER, but also and above all a MYSTERY in which something is accomplished for us that we cannot fully understand but that we must accept and receive in faith, love, obedience and adoring silence. And this is the real meaning of active participation of the faithful. It is not about exclusively external activity, the distribution of roles or functions in the liturgy, but rather about an intensely active receptivity: The reception is, in Christ and with Christ, the humble offering of one-self in silent prayer and a thoroughly contemplative attitude. The serious crisis of faith, not only at the level of the Christian faithful but also and especially among many priests and bishops, *has made us incapable of understanding the Eucharistic liturgy as a sacrifice, as identical to the act performed once and for all by Jesus Christ, making present the Sacrifice of the Cross in a non-bloody manner, throughout the Church, through different ages, places, peoples and nations.* There is often a sacrilegious tendency to reduce the Holy Mass to a simple convivial meal, the celebration of a profane feast, the community's celebration of itself, or even worse, diversion from the anguish of a life that no longer has meaning or from the fear of meeting God face to face, because His glance unveils and obliges us to look truly and unflinchingly at the ugliness of our interior life.[26] (emphasis added)

A. Cosmic Liturgy Leads to Adoration

1. The Second Vatican Council has not Attained its Liturgical Reform

Odo Casel has pointed to the liturgical weaknesses of the nineteenth century, one that has continued in our times. Now we wish to identify the specific

---

[26] Robert Cardinal Sarah, "The Liturgy 'Plunges us into the Inner Life of the Trinity," 31.

false developments of the liturgy after the Second Vatican Council that have blunted and impeded evangelization in our times. In his biography, *Milestones* (146-149), Cardinal Ratzinger identifies the crisis in the Church as primarily caused by the disintegration of the liturgy, and called for a liturgical renewal: "I am convinced that the crisis in the Church that we are experiencing today is, to a large extent, due to the disintegration of the liturgy... This is why we need a new Liturgical Movement, which will call to life the real heritage of the Second Vatican Council."[27]

Archbishop Malcolm Ranjith, the former Secretary of the Congregation for Divine Worship and the Discipline of the Sacraments, wrote about this crisis.[28] He notes first Pope John XXIII's hopes for the Council, his outline of the many crises the world faced, including a state of spiritual poverty:

> Today the Church is witnessing a crisis under way within society. While humanity is on the edge of a new era, tasks of immense gravity and amplitude await the Church, as in the most tragic periods of its history. It is a question in fact of bringing the modern world into contact with the vivifying and perennial energies of the gospel, a world which exalts itself with its conquests in the technical and scientific fields, but which brings also the consequences of a temporal order which some have wished to reorganize excluding God. This is why modern society is earmarked by a great material progress to which there is not a corresponding advance in the moral field.[29]

Against the background of this dire state of the world in excluding God, Pope John XXIII then outlined the mission and hope of the Council through the vivifying power of the Church and the Gospel:

> The forthcoming Council will meet therefore and at a moment in which the Church finds very alive the desire to fortify its faith, and to contemplate itself in its own awe-inspiring unity. In the same way, it feels more urgent the duty to give greater efficiency to its sound vitality and to promote the

---

[27] Joseph Ratzinger, *Milestones*, 148-149.

[28] Archbishop Malcolm Ranjith, "True Development of the Liturgy," *First Things* 193 (May 2009): 15-17.

[29] Pope John XXIII, *Humanae Saluti*, apostolic constitution 25 December 1961, by which he convoked the Second Vatican Council, quoted in Archbishop Malcolm Ranjith, "True Development of the Liturgy," 15.

sanctification of its members, the diffusion of revealed truth, the consolidation of its agencies. This will be a demonstration of the Church, always living and always young, which feels the rhythm of the times and which in every century beautifies herself with new splendor, radiates new light, achieves new conquests, while remaining identical in herself, faithful to the divine image impressed on her countenance by her Spouse, who loves her and protects her, Christ Jesus.[30]

Pope John XXIII prophesied that the Church "which in every century beautifies herself with new splendor, radiates new light, achieves new conquests," but what he hoped for and what the Second Vatican Council intended was not attained. Archbishop Ranjith then cites Cardinal Ratzinger's diagnosis, a "false spirit" or "anti-spirit" of the Council:

> Already during its sessions and then increasingly in the subsequent period, [the authentic teaching of the Council, expressed in the documents of Vatican II] was opposed by a self-styled "spirit of the Council," which in reality is a true "anti-spirit"... According to this pernicious anti-spirit... everything that is "new" (or presumed such...) is always and in every case better than what has been or what is.[31]

Cardinal Ratzinger pointed out that "Vatican II surely did not want 'to change' the faith, but to represent it in a more effective way." And he pointed to the failure to conform to the hopes of Pope John: "The council did not take the turn that John XXIII had expected"; "it must also be admitted that, in respect to the whole Church, the prayer of Pope John that the council signify a new leap forward for the Church, to renewed life and unity, has not— at least not yet— been granted."[32] Archbishop Ranjith identified the sources of the postconciliar problems:

> An exaggerated sense of antiquarianism, anthropologism, confusion of roles between the ordained and the nonordained, a limitless provision of space for experimentation—and, indeed, the tendency to look down on some aspects of the development of the liturgy in the second millennium— were increasingly visible among certain liturgical schools. Liturgists had also

---

[30] Ibid.
[31] Joseph Ratzinger, *The Ratzinger Report* (San Francisco: Ignatius Press, 1985), 34-35.
[32] Ibid, 42.

tended to pick and choose sections of *Sacrosanctum Concilium* that seemed to be more accommodating to change or novelty, while ignoring others. Besides, there was a great sense of hurry to effect and legalize changes. Much space tended to be provided for a rather horizontalist way of looking at the liturgy. Norms of the council that tended to restrict such creativity or that were favorable to the traditional way seemed to be ignored.[33]

2. Two Pitfalls

We reiterate here what Cardinal Ratzinger wrote: "I am convinced that the crisis in the Church that we are experiencing today is to a large extent due to the disintegration of the liturgy."[34] Hans Urs von Balthasar's article, "The Grandeur of the Liturgy," identifies specifically the two primary and opposing deviations that hinder our entering the grandeur of the liturgy and encountering the living God: the extreme of celebrating self and failing to adore God; and the opposite tendency of being rooted in the past.[35]

(i) The Temptation of the Community to Celebrate Itself

Von Balthasar begins with the necessary foundational disposition: worship should be approached with "fear and trembling." He finds the context for liturgy in the Book of Revelation: "No liturgy designed by men could be 'worthy' of the subject of their homage, of God at whose throne the heavenly choirs prostrate themselves with covered faces, having cast off their crowns and ornaments before offering adoration." The awareness of one's sinfulness and unworthiness brings us to our knees. He warns us that any turn to self, whether self-development or putting self next to the Lord, is to naively deceive ourselves.[36]

Where we already find awe in the mosque or the Jewish synagogue, the Trinitarian religion brings an immense gap, where the Lamb of God Himself descends and becomes our food. He shows us the absurdity of bringing our own sacrifices in place of this majestic liturgy in this deviation:

---

[33] Ibid.
[34] Joseph Ratzinger, *Milestones: Memoirs: 1927-1977* (San Francisco: Ignatius Press, 1998), 148.
[35] Hans Urs von Balthasar, "The Grandeur of the Liturgy," *Communio* 5.4 (1978).
[36] Ibid., 344.

God's glory, the sublimity of his glory, bestows these invaluable gifts on us who must praise the glory of his grace (Eph. i.6). It is this that gives the norms and standards for the form of our worship. It would be ridiculous and blasphemous if we were to respond to the grace of God's glory with a counterglory contrived from our created endowments, trying to compete with the heavenly liturgies which Revelation describes as being completely overpowered and transfused by the glory of God. Whatever the form of our liturgical answer may be, it should strive to express only the pure and selfless reception of the divine majesty of grace....

We can bring examples of ambiguities, such as when the praise of glory that should be reserved solely for God refracts on the one who gives praise and who then appropriates part of the glory to himself. This happens often today because the danger is greater that a liturgical community measures the success of celebration by its own inspiration, by how they "feel" or how they "share," rather than being simply open to God and his gifts. There are communities which— perhaps subconsciously— celebrate themselves more than they celebrate God. This may happen in traditional as well as in progressive forms of celebration... This means that the criterion of "aliveness" of a service has become ambivalent: is it to create an openness and conversion to the Lord or a satisfied awareness of one's own aliveness?[37]

Along with the celebration of self comes many impoverishing consequences: "joviality, a certain chumminess between the celebrant and the community," seeking personal contact instead of concentrating on the Lord. Von Balthasar notes that this happens when faith in the event weakens, when the community turns towards itself:

If a somewhat immature congregation gathers to wait for the Lord and to be filled by him, but at the same time considers itself existent and substantial, having assets to which nothing essential can be added, then the eucharistic celebration degenerates into mere symbolism. The community will celebrate merely its own happy pious feelings which were there already and which become strengthened through the meeting. Pharisaism is near.[38]

---

[37] Ibid., 346-347.
[38] Ibid., 348.

(ii) Temptation to Excessive Attachment to Past Culture and Older Liturgical Rites

The second deviation is the opposite extreme, the temptation to look to the past, and von Balthasar captures the weakness with much insight:

> There are forms of liturgical prayer which are objectively noble, formulated obviously in times that possessed a truly Christian subjective attitude in prayer... which through centuries of praying gained something like added weight in dignity.

> Some people think that they can *rely on these forms*, prayed throughout the centuries by many others; they feel that this will guarantee them the desired subjective attitude. They deceive themselves. The dignity of the *form— a marvelously aged aesthetic dignity— has gained predominance in their minds over the ever-renewed, always new grandeur of the divine event, never derived from externals.*

> ... But these works can only be used in contemporary liturgy only if their beauty not only stimulates the celebrating congregation but if the listeners will reach out to that glory of God to which the creators of these works meant to guide them [e.g., Gregorian Chant, Palestrina].... When these or similar works are *prayed* by the singers, they can fill people not merely with beauty but with a sense of the holy; they can transmit a glimmer of the divine glory that was their original inspiration. The person who hears only the beauty [externals] has an "ersatz" experience... The real meaning of that which they heard eludes them.... Even beauty must die and mummifying does not become it.[39] (emphasis added)

There is a temptation to find the Church's glory in the liturgy of the past and have one's center of gravity there. A seminary priest spiritual director, counselling a seminarian who clearly manifested a one-sided attachment to the older rites, rubrics, and classics of the faith, suggested he look to the model and example of Pope John Paul II. The Pope exhibited deep contemplation at Mass and great devotional piety, but was saintly in turning outward to the presence of the Holy Spirit working powerfully in our times (e.g., Vatican II, new lay charisms, impulse towards unity) and finding Christ in the suffering, oppressed, and poor. The path of excessive attachment to the past can lead to a self-reliance on one's orthodoxy and piety but with only

---

[39] Ibid., 348-350.

an external obedience, while being led by self. The path of the saints is rooted deeply in profound self-knowledge of one's weakness and docility to the Holy Spirit.

B. The Presence of Christ's Saving Act in the Sacraments (Odo Casel)

For enlightenment, we turn to the liturgical pioneer, Dom Odo Casel, who pointed to the cause of the crisis in the nineteenth century that could very well apply to our times: "In a time when rattled, bewildered Christians were questioning the very heart and center of their faith, Dom Casel was an example of how to respond to the crisis of faith with an answer as simple as it was striking: 'the most important element in the life of the Christian is *anamnesis*, the remembrance of the Lord.'"[40]

Arno Schilson synthesized Dom Casel's contribution thus: "Casel sought ever anew to emphasize the presence of the saving act itself within the sacraments and their liturgical enactment."[41] Odo Casel's work anticipated and prepared for the renewed understanding at Vatican II of the various presences of Christ (e.g., Mystical Body, Scripture, ministers, indwelling in soul). To address our present crisis, we return to Dom Casel's great insight to bring in this renewed understanding of the presence of the mysteries of Christ in the liturgy. Cardinal Ratzinger held it in high regard, calling it "perhaps the most fruitful theological idea of the twentieth century"[42]:

> ... the cultic mystery [liturgy] is the objective and necessary exhibition and making present of Christ's saving work... In the cultic mystery, the mystery of Christ becomes visible and effective; it is thus a prolongation and further unfolding of the *oikonomia* [salvation history or, better, the acts of salvation] of Christ, which, without the cultic mystery, could not transmit itself to all the generations of the community of the faithful spread throughout space and time.[43]

---

[40] Arno Schilson, "Liturgy as the Presence of the Mysteries of the Life of Jesus According to Odo Casel," *Communio* 29.1 (2002): 44.

[41] Ibid., 39.

[42] Joseph Ratzinger, *Aus meinem Leben. Erinnerungen (1927-1977)* (Stuttgart, 1998), 61.

[43] Odo Casel, "Glaube, Gnosis und Mysterium," *Jahrbuch für Liturgiewissenschaft* 15 (1941): 194, quoted in Arno Schilson, "Liturgy as the Presence of the Mysteries," 45.

Arno Schilson explains that "Casel's proposal was thus completely different from what the conventional understanding and theological interpretation of the sacraments had to offer," which appeared to be primarily concerned with the acquisition of grace.[44] Casel's vision was much more profound— all the salvific mysteries of Christ become present in the sacraments:

> Rather, Casel sought ever anew to emphasize the presence of the saving act itself within the sacraments and their liturgical enactment. For him the sacraments were essentially and truly "mysteries," holy acts, participation in which could really become participation in the saving act of Jesus himself that was re-presented in them. Casel understood the event of salvation taking place in Christ very concretely; by no means was his an abstract conception. For him, Christ's presence was so comprehensive in the liturgy of the Church that not even the most minute moment of the life of Jesus was excluded from this liturgical re-presentation.[45]

It is our insertion into the mysteries of Christ that is precisely the preeminent means by which incorporation to Christ is accomplished:

> If, with Casel, and in accord with the New Testament, the Fathers, and best systematic theology, we define the identity of the Christian as "being in Christ," then the liturgical-sacramental action must be considered the unique foundation of Christian existence. Surpassing all other means of encountering Christ, it is the life- and strength-giving locus of an efficacious recollection and re-presentation of the mysteries of the life of Jesus, a locus where these mysteries become present.[46]

The absolutely necessary participation the Council desired, "active participation" goes beyond the distorted sense of participation in ministries to an active self-gift (spiritual sacrifice) for which it calls.

Arno Schilson explains how Dom Casel's understanding escapes the confines of the narrow post-Tridentine sacramental theology with the idea of a "holy drama," whereby the participants cannot be passive:

---

[44] Arno Schilson, "Liturgy as the Presence of the Mysteries," 43.
[45] Ibid.
[46] Ibid., 44.

With the help of this category, Casel succeeded in escaping the narrow confines of a post-Tridentine sacramental theology restricted to the efficaciousness of the sacraments and their ritually correct execution. In the context of his theology of the mysteries, Casel develops the idea that the *basic form of the liturgy is a holy drama*... All the participants of the liturgy appear as actors in the cultically presented drama of their God; indeed they even function as *"co-actors with God,"* and so as fellow protagonists. A passive presence in a sort of mute abstraction or mystical ecstasy is out of place here. The "mystery character" of the Christian liturgy requires a befitting "active participation." This is reflected by Vatican II's call for an *"actuosa participatio"* by all the faithful in the sacred drama that God himself established in Christ. In this drama each and every individual *should join with the saving act of Christ, the paschal mystery of crossing from death to life, as a reality in the present.*[47] (emphasis added)

Dom Casel diagnoses our present mistaken preoccupation: "a post-Tridentine sacramental theology restricted to the efficaciousness of the sacraments and their ritually correct execution." The true understanding of the mystery of Christ's sacrifice calls for "co-actors with God" in this "holy drama."

Dom Casel concludes that the efficaciousness of this re-presentation of Christianity's mysteries is a function of the "co-enactment" of the liturgical form, i.e., the "active participation" and conforming to this mystery by the participants. In the Mass, it entails *self-gift at the Offertory and a conformation to the crucified Christ who becomes present:* "They suffer with him, rise with him, are transfigured with him, and enter into his heavenly existence."[48] Dom Casel thus explains Joseph Ratzinger's third element of the liturgy triad.

Thus, we have a *three-fold failure today*: the post-conciliar temptation to celebrate the community, to turn toward self instead of outwardly in adoration; an incomplete understanding of the liturgy (e.g., focusing on Christ's "real presence" in the consecrated species); and the failure of the participant to make the personal sacrifice of a conformation to the Paschal mystery that becomes present in the liturgy.

---

[47] Ibid., 45-46.
[48] Ibid., 46.

C. Eucharist Completed in Adoration and Conformation to Christ's Sacrifice

Pope Benedict XVI viewed his pontificate as a wider cosmic liturgy that was driven primarily by the Eucharist: "It is always a cosmic liturgy... an entry into the liturgy of heaven."[49] Hence, for the liturgy to unleash (vs. bottling it up) its inherent power, we have to re-establish *adoration* within the framework of the liturgy, as was the goal of the young Ratzinger: "I was not interested in the specific problems of liturgical study, but in the anchoring of the liturgy in the fundamental act of our faith, and therefore also its place in our entire human existence."[50]

Thus, like the Israelites punished for their worship of Baal, we too turn away from deviations that essentially involve self-worship, and, in true adoration, one casts oneself into God's arms in abandonment and is conformed to the mystery celebrated, the Paschal mystery, the crucified Christ. We can find in the example of St. Elizabeth of the Trinity a concrete synthesis of the call for adoration by Ratzinger and von Balthasar in liturgy. Dom Vandeur's description captures this rare adoration and oblation in St. Elizabeth:

> Very few souls, it seems to me, have had such a sense of this adoration in spirit and in truth in the temple of their heart as had your spiritual daughter. To call Sister Elizabeth the perfect adorer of her God would be to describe her adequately. I will explain myself.
>
> What is adoration, adoration in spirit and in truth? Adoration is the essential, absolute homage rendered by the creature to the divine Pre-Eminence, to God Who draws us out of nothing, impresses upon us the seal of the Holy Trinity, and becomes the Divine Guest of the soul transformed by the grace of Holy Baptism. Adoration is a solemn and profound silence into which the adoring soul sinks, acknowledging that God is all and the creature nothing. Adoration is the proper and immediate act of religion, the first of the moral virtues. It gives the whole man, soul and body, to the Lord. Adoration is born and developed in the secret depths

---

[49] Joseph Ratzinger, *The Spirit of the Liturgy*, 70.
[50] Joseph Ratzinger, *Teologia della Liturgia*, Preface, vol. 1, *Opera Omnia* (Rome: Libreria Editrice Vaticana, 2008).

of his soul; the body reveals it outwardly, making it exterior by the requisite worship which completes and vivifies the sacrifice, the outward expression of the inward adoration.... This adoration leads to another kind more perfect still, one which is the crown of all religion [referring to her conformation to Christ crucified].[51]

St. Elizabeth of the Trinity died at the tender age of twenty-six in a spirit of adoration that culminated in the acceptance of the sacrifice of her life with the painful Addison's disease (her "crown"). Her conformation to Christ crucified is the test of deepest adoration. The liturgy, especially the Eucharist, makes this possible: "If we receive the Eucharist worthily, we become what we receive" (Augustine, *Easter Sermon*, 227). And through the power of the risen Christ, we become conformed to Christ in His immolated state precisely through the liturgy— Christ walks again on earth continuing His oblation and mission in us.

---

[51] Letter from Dom Eugène Vandeur, O.S.B., of the Abbaye de la Reine du Ciel, au Mont-César, Louvain, to the Superior of Carmelite Monastery in Dijon, France, dated February 15, 1910, quoted in Elizabeth of the Trinity, *The Praise of Glory: Reminiscences of Sister Elizabeth of the Trinity, a Carmelite Nun of Dijon, 1901-1906,* ed. Stanbrook Abbey, 2nd English ed. (London: R. & T. Washbourne, 1914), xxix.

CHAPTER 10

PREACHING CHRIST IN THE WORD

> This fact [Apostles receiving Holy Spirit to preach Gospel] implies and reveals a basic law of salvation history: *it is impossible to evangelize or prophesy,* or indeed to speak of the Lord and in the Lord's name, *without the grace and power of the Holy Spirit*.... As the fourth Gospel stresses, the mission of Jesus, "he whom God has sent" and who "utters the words of God," is the fruit of the gift of the Spirit, whom he has received and gives "not by measure" (cf. Jn 3:34).... The Church's life unfolds beneath that breath. *"The Holy Spirit is indeed the principal agent of the whole of the Church's mission"* (*Redemptoris missio*, n. 21, emphasis added)[1]

At the outset of writing this work, there was no plan for incorporating a chapter on liturgical preaching. But participating in a few preaching conferences, especially one delivered by Fr. Peter Cameron, O.P., led the author to adopt a few key changes to his preaching method (including preaching from the Word and less catechesis, more exegesis, focus on reaching the heart). As a result of the experience of this fruitfulness, it was felt that perhaps summary notes taken from these conferences could also be of some help to those in preaching ministry who have not had the opportunity to attend such conferences, which have the benefit of the speakers synthesizing their overall points and their main emphases. Some of these principles can also assist the laity in the new evangelization.

Two decisions on the direction for this chapter had to be made at this point. First, rather than summarize the methods of several master preachers, this chapter synthesizes one main preacher for the two reasons of (i) consistency and (ii) for the benefit of delving more deeply into one method than superficially in several. Second, Fr. Peter Cameron was chosen from a roster with highly qualified credentials because he brings the following background: he is a member of the Dominican order, dedicated to preaching; he was a homiletics professor and had years of experience as editor of *Magnificat*; he brings his playwright background into homiletics; and he has been influenced by the rich insights of the *Communion and Liberation* charism. From his travels

---

[1] Pope John Paul II, General Audience, Catechesis on the Holy Spirit: "Evangelizing in the Power, Newness, and Unity of the Holy Spirit" (Rome, July 1, 1998).

in the United States, Fr. Cameron is also convinced that preaching needs a massive renewal, and he offers effective instruction for renewing preaching within the Church.[2]

Part I of this chapter offers this synthesis of Fr. Cameron's method so that it may encourage the reader to pick up and read his book, *Why Preach?*, and that it may serve as a summary of salient points for the preacher. To complement Fr. Cameron's preaching method, this chapter also offers a few central emphases from preaching experts who bring out the richness of their different spiritual charisms: Charismatic, Dominican, and Redemptorist (Part II).

Call for Renewal in Preaching by the Church and Homiletic Experts

The goal of this chapter, in introducing master preachers, is to encourage the preacher to read the fine works of the homiletic experts or attend their conferences; it is but an appetizer to the main course. This chapter may be of help because the principal work of the priest and deacon is to preach the Gospel, especially given the call of the Church and popes to renew our preaching (e.g., *Verbum Domini* (VD) *Evangelii gaudium* (EG), and the *Homiletic Directory* (HD)). As Pope Francis wrote, "The homily is the touchstone for judging a pastor's closeness and ability to communicate with his people" (EG 135). If the Church is to bear fruit in a new evangelization, then renewal in preaching has to be a cornerstone.

The call for renewal in preaching has been made by many homiletic experts in books and conferences. Fr. James Heft, S.M. (Institute for Advanced Catholic Studies at the University of Southern California), who has spent most of his forty-one years of ministry at the university, teaching and doing campus ministry and spiritual direction, offers a brief survey of the state of Catholic preaching. He notes first that, where Scripture teaches us to preach from Scripture (e.g., 1 Pet 4:11, "Whoever preaches, let it be from the word

---

[2] Fr. Cameron was the chairman of the department of homiletics at St. Joseph's Seminary, Dunwoodie, New York, served two terms as the Director of Preaching for his Dominican Province, and was also the editor in chief of Magnificat magazine, and is a professional playwright and the artistic director of Blackfriars Repertory Theatre in New York City. He granted permission on June 27, 2016 to employ insights gained from his two-day Preaching Conference, given at St. Augustine's Seminary on June 27-28, 2016, for this book.

of God"), many have failed to do so. He offers several examples. Already in the early Church, Jerome noted that many priests did not know Scripture. Martin Luther in the Middle Ages criticized the Catholic priest for not using Scripture: "The priest takes us to fairy land... another about boon docks... In short no one speaks of the text..." Regarding the state of preaching in general, a certain archbishop of Paris in the early twentieth-century wrote: "Every Sunday there are 30,000 sermons in France; and people still believe."[3]

Fr. Heft points to insights of Charles Taylor, one of the foremost thinkers of our time, about today's typical homilies that don't demonstrate an understanding of the condition of the troubled souls of our times. The preacher offers maps or road atlases (homilies) that talk about generalities (e.g., condemning secularism), but doesn't understand the troubled condition of the hearts of the faithful; he does not preach from their situation and context:

> Both of these sorts of maps [today's homilies] are blunt instruments.... These road atlases [homilies] of belief versus disbelief, religion versus secularism, faith versus reason, provide maps that are much neater and tidier than the spaces in which we find ourselves.... [Such a map, the homily] *has room to acknowledge those hauntings of transcendence* that sometimes sneak up on us in our otherwise mundane disenchantment. At the same time, such a contoured existential cartograph should also help us feel the suffocating immanence that characterizes late modern existence, even for "believers."[4] (emphasis added)

Dr. Charles Taylor points to the more fundamental problem today: many people don't even ask the question about God, many of them are not haunted by God, many have built a road that has no reference to God— they are not asking the God question, suffering "the suffocating immanence that

---

[3] Notes are drawn from Fr. James Heft's presentation at St. Augustine's Seminary's "How to Make Catholic Preaching Better: A Conference in Homiletics" (July 7-10, 2014).

[4] Charles Taylor is described on one website as "one of the foremost thinkers of the last 50 years, recipient of the John W. Kluge Prize (the 'Nobel Prize' of the humanities and social sciences), the Templeton Prize, and the Kyoto Prize, and numerous prestigious awards and honours" and that "his magnum opus, A Secular Age (2007), [was] hailed by the New York Times as 'a work of stupendous breadth and erudition.'" Institute of Social Justice, https://isj.acu.edu.au/2016/04/15/professor-charles-taylor-to-launch-the-institute-for-social-justice/.

characterizes late modern existence, even for 'believers.'" The preacher has to begin with this context, and he has to learn to employ Scripture to speak to the hearts of our people. Fr. Cameron addresses this issue very earnestly.

I. The Method of Fr. Peter Cameron, O.P.

A. Overview of Fr. Cameron's Method

Fr. Cameron draws from Pope Francis' exhortation, *Evangelii gaudium*, and first notes that Pope Francis himself makes a general call for improving homilies. Fr. Cameron's general outline finds much convergence with the program in Pope Benedict XVI's post-synodal apostolic exhortation, *Verbum Domini* and the following quotation summarizes many key points emphasized in this chapter:

> In the Apostolic Exhortation *Sacramentum Caritatis*, I pointed out that "given the importance of the word of God, the quality of homilies needs to be improved..." ... Generic and abstract homilies which obscure the directness of God's word should be avoided, as well as useless digressions which risk drawing greater attention to the preacher than to the heart of the Gospel message. The faithful should be able to perceive clearly that the preacher has a *compelling desire to present Christ, who must stand at the centre of every homily*. For this reason preachers need to be in *close and constant contact with the sacred text*; they should prepare for the homily by *meditation and prayer*, so as to preach with *conviction and passion*. The synodal assembly asked that the following questions be kept in mind: "*What are the Scriptures being proclaimed saying? What do they say to me personally? What should I say to the community in the light of its concrete situation?*" (Pope Benedict, *Verbum Domini* 59, emphasis added)

Fr. Cameron's Goals and Overall Approach

Fr. Cameron employs a very structured approach, especially drawing from his playwriting background. Fr. Cameron's method differs from the approaches commonly used by priests and deacons in at least four main ways:

1. He follows the preaching model of Jesus;
2. His main goal is to touch the deepest chords within the hearts of the listeners;

258

3. Enabling an encounter requires that the preacher first be a witness, and;

4. His method emphasizes specifically framing a proposal, a lived idea that reaches the heart (while also watching transitional phrases, endings, and delivery). He digs deeply into the Scripture text and draws his proposals from the text itself.

The review of these four goals and overall approach will enable the reader to more fully understand Fr. Cameron's three-step structure of idea, image, and proposal that is more fully developed in Section B.

1. Jesus' Preaching Model: Encounter with Samaritan Woman at Well

Fr. Cameron's favourite Gospel pericope for preaching, the Samaritan woman at the well, provides a paradigm for preaching. Jesus reaches her, not by first correcting her sins or by revealing that He is the Messiah, but by referring to the water for which she came. Step by step, he draws her from the human need of water to the infinite need of her heart, finally touching the deepest desires of her heart in offering her "living water." Though her heart had been wounded by sin and attached to worldly pleasures, the Exceptional Presence of Jesus corresponded to the infinite need of her heart, and enabled her to be in touch with her *I*. In confronting herself and her weakness, she is able to open up to the One who revealed that He was the Messiah.

His method bears fruit: being transformed, it is she who becomes the missionary who leads the people to Him; and He also brings her back to the community (for she came to the well at midday to be alone). Jesus calls her "daughter," meaning He has not only helped her, He has also generated her (we arrive at this conclusion when we see the instances when Jesus uses "daughter," e.g., Jairus' daughter, Mk 5:41, "παιδίου").

2. His goal is to Reach the Listener's Heart through an Encounter with Christ

This section, it appears, constitutes the heart of Fr. Cameron's preaching method, as was illustrated in Jesus' encounter with the Samaritan woman at the well. It is based on the foundational insight of Msgr. Luigi Giussani, which can be simplistically summarized thus: our modern society has not come to Christ because we are not in touch with the deepest part of ourselves, our heart, and thus we are not aware of, and do not attach ourselves to, the "Exceptional Presence" that is Jesus Christ. Fr. Cameron synthesizes the thought of Msgr. Luigi Giussani with remarkable clarity in *Why Preach?* (pp. 17-38, with the subtitle, "Beginning from Human Experience"). With the background of Msgr. Giussani's insights, Fr. Cameron then summarizes the preacher's task in light of the fundamental human need in 7 points:

> ➤ reactivating the religious sense of the hearers;
> ➤ educating the religious sense by revealing the truths of their own *I*;
> ➤ enticing them to trust the elementary experience of their hearts;
> ➤ teaching them not to give in to life's troubles through following the infallible yearning of their heart;
> ➤ offering a *proposal* that is a response to a *lived question*;
> ➤ finding the *correspondence* in Scripture to what the human heart desires;
> ➤ realizing that people expect to recognize in the homily and the homilist an Exceptional Presence that corresponds to their hearts (pp. 38-42).

Our People Need a Defibrillator to Awaken Their Hearts

Fr. Cameron has the keen insight that people don't know how to reach their hearts, don't know what it is that they need. In a talk given during his visit to Canada, Cardinal Ratzinger defined preaching without even referring to God: "The aim of preaching is to tell a man who he is and what he must do to be himself. Its intention is to disclose to him the truth about himself, that is, what he can base his life on and what he can die for."[5] He is saying that it is true that people don't know the teachings about God; but their greatest problem is that they don't know how to be human, they don't pay attention to happiness, they don't trust their heart, and that they don't follow it, for it will lead to something that they can't attain. So when the demands of the heart keep calling, we capitulate to and compromise with four key attractions: pleasure, possessions, power, or prestige.

---

[5] Joseph Cardinal Ratzinger, *The Nature and Mission of Theology*, trans. Adrian Walker (San Francisco: Ignatius Press, 1995), 62, 63.

Therefore, preaching has to be an act that leads them to be human, to be themselves, and not give in to self, to the four attractions, which lead to the abyss and darkness. We have to lead them to their hearts, rather than preach at them. Why, someone might ask, does the Church not use emails, tweets, or bring down screens for preaching?— because these latter forms are communication by analogy; they are derivative. The most productive mode of communication, by contrast, is speaking from a pulpit: person-to-person. When real communication happens, there is communication between self and another self. We see person-to-person communication in receiving the Eucharist that leads to communion. The Eucharist is important for us because it reaches the heart. People may be of different cultural backgrounds, but they all have the *same human heart*. Every preacher needs to pick up spiritual defibrillator pads and put them on the listeners and say "clear!" People need to get back their hearts. For Fr. Cameron, there are two possible results when we try to expunge desire from our hearts: we either give ourselves totally to pleasure or we become zombies.

Preach as a Mother Addressing Children's Needs to Touch Their Hearts

A parish priest, especially in hearing Confessions, encounters many woes in people's hearts: woundedness, fear, anxiety, guilty feelings, deep loneliness, etc. Where we need to reach them is the heart: it is the place of encounter, of decisions, etc. Consequently, we return to the cardinal rule for preaching: *Preach unto others as you would have them preach to you*. When people are lonely, wounded, etc., the last thing they need is a discourse or a speech; we should preach "in the same way that a mother speaks to her child" (Pope Francis):

> It reminds us that the Church is a mother, and that she preaches in the same way that a mother speaks to her child, knowing that the child trusts that what she is teaching is for his or her benefit, for children know that they are loved. Moreover, a good mother can recognize everything that God is bringing about in her children, she listens to their concerns and learns from them. (EG 139)

In addition, the United States Conference of Catholic Bishops (USCCB) teaches that the preacher must preach to the needs of the people and not preach what they don't need: "Homilies are inspirational when they touch the deepest levels of the human heart and address the real questions of human experience" (p. 15); "Only when the homilist, in a spirit of faith and love, is conscious of his own deepest experience and those of his people can he preach persuasively to them" (p. 34); "the homilist must have empathy for human experience, observe it closely and sympathetically, and incorporate it into his preaching" (p. 29). So we can ask ourselves, what homilies have we heard that have most touched us?

3. Enabling a Personal Encounter with Jesus Requires "Witnesses"

For Fr. Cameron, preaching should lead to a personal encounter with Jesus, and as such, it needs witnesses. As Romano Guardini taught, the essence of Christianity is not an idea but a Person; and our hearts long for Christ for whom we are made. And the event of this encounter is mediated through others, especially the preacher (see *Why Preach?*, 51-56). Fr. Cameron notes that, for this reason, the smartest men are not necessarily the best preachers. The test of the preacher's fruitfulness is if people ask him, "How can you be that way?"; for when we see a witness, we see the true person behind that witness. There is, however, a common temptation, as noted by *The Homiletics Directory* 6: "Finally, the time for the homily should not be taken up with the preacher's personal story. There is no question that people can be deeply moved by personal stories, but the homily should express the faith of the Church, and not simply the preacher's own story." While the Church warns the preacher to avoid preaching himself, he still needs to be a witness to Christ: "Furthermore, the preacher needs to speak in such a way that his hearers can sense his belief in the power of God" (HD 7). So this archaic one-man preaching is to give people the sense that the preacher himself has had an encounter with Christ and is excited. It is irresistible when we hear someone preach with that conviction:

> Whoever wants to preach must be the first to let the word of God move him deeply and become incarnate in his daily life…. For all these reasons, before preparing what we will actually say when preaching, we need to let ourselves be penetrated by that word which will also penetrate others, for it is a living and active word, like a sword… This has great pastoral importance. Today too, people prefer to listen to witnesses: they "thirst for authenticity" and "call for evangelizers to speak of a God whom they themselves know and are familiar with, as if they were seeing him." (EG 150)

Fr. Cameron says that the people know when we preach superficially from our heads. Pope Francis teaches that the preacher has to first give God a new yes in his life each day (daily conversion), and only then does his homily become a manifestation of the yes he makes. Preaching is quasi-sacramental, the visible sign of an invisible grace, a "heart to heart communication which takes place in the homily and possesses a quasi-sacramental character, because faith comes from what is heard" (HD 6; cf. EG 142). It touches the listener, not because the preacher is persuasive, but because *the preacher's life manifests a sacramental reality of what he is preaching*. It manifests itself in the passion and ardour, and sincerity and certainty, with which he preaches and it moves people.

For example, when Fr. Cameron meets someone who has the deep quality of being unflappable, he is moved. The people are hungry for this sacramental witness, through whom they touch Christ.

4. To Awaken the Heart, Begin with the "Lived Question" (the Idea)

Fr. Cameron proposes three steps for preaching: *an idea, an image, and a proposal or application.* Here we examine the first, the "idea" or "lived question." For Fr. Cameron, the main problem with preaching today is that we preach to the head and not to the heart.

To use an example, one can talk about the merits of taking Castor oil, but to get your child to take it, especially because of its bad taste, you have to convince him to take it— you have *address his will or his desire.* During the Reformation, Catholic scholars presented their arguments and the Reformers fired back their response. It never came to anything, in part because they did not sit down and dialogue, but also in part because it was all at the level of intellect. The intellect by itself does not convince; we need to get to the "*lived question.*"

Finding the "lived question" is to preach to their hearts, to their true deepest needs. Fr. Cameron used an example to show how we fail to go to our deepest experience. When he asked attendees at a preaching conference what their deepest experiences were, one priest complained that his deepest experience is that he is made for holiness but could not attain it. But that was not his deepest experience; it was rather his unsuccessful search for *happiness* that is his greatest need.

How can we discern the lived question? We do so by answering this question: *This gospel is meaningful for my life because*: _____. Every lived question asks Jesus' first question in the Gospels: **"What are you looking for"** (question addressed to John when He saw John following Him).

The homily must touch the deepest experiences of love, beauty, justice, etc. It is something that is good, or something that delights me. But very often it starts from a simple concern— recall the Samaritan woman's need for water at the well. And what is at the core of the needs of the human heart? What our hearts need is a presence and, above all, for what Luigi Giussani calls an "Exceptional Presence" (Jesus). Fr. Cameron draws this out beautifully in *Why Preach?* (pp. 47-51).

Fr. Cameron takes an approach that differs profoundly from some common approaches that either provide catechesis, move the feelings, or entertain. The goal for him is to engage the parishioners at the deepest levels of their hearts, and if we help move them towards Christ ever so little, we have been "successful."

As such, he finds that his ideal length for a homily is eight minutes, but states that eight to ten minutes would be reasonable. He points to the wisdom of Pope Francis, who counsels brief homilies, because he sets it within the larger framework of the liturgy, e.g., the Sunday Mass, and what time we can reasonably give to the homily given the time needed for the other elements:

> The liturgical proclamation of the Word of God… is not so much a time for meditation and catechesis as a dialogue between God and his people. (EG 137) The homily should be brief and avoid taking the semblance of a speech or lecture…. If the homily goes on too long, it will affect the two characteristic elements of the liturgical celebration: it's balance and its rhythm. (EG 138)

B. A Concrete Three-Step Process: Idea, Image, Proposal

Background Needed for "Actualizing Sacred Scripture" (Idea)

We begin with four prefatory points to actualizing the text.

(a) Presupposition: Digging Deeply and Drawing Paradigms from the Scripture Text.

> Certainly, to understand properly the meaning of the central message of a text we need *to relate it to the teaching of the entire Bible* as handed on by the Church. This is an important principle of biblical interpretation which recognizes that the Holy Spirit has inspired not just a part of the Bible, but the Bible as a whole, and that in some areas people have grown in their understanding of God's will on the basis of their personal experience.
>
> It also prevents erroneous or partial interpretations which would contradict other teachings of the same Scriptures. *But it does not mean that we can weaken the distinct and specific emphasis of a text* which we are called to preach. One of the defects of a tedious and ineffectual preaching is precisely *its inability to transmit the intrinsic power of the text* which has been proclaimed. (EG 148 emphasis added)

(b) Homily is for Enabling a Confrontation with Christ, the Word

Fr. Cameron describes in *Why Preach?* that Scripture, the Word of God, is given so that we have an encounter with the Word (the Son of the Father). For this Bible text is the Word Himself, illustrating this with a beautiful quote from Maurice Zundel. If you open the missal's texts of Scripture,

> your silent soul will soon experience the feeling of an ineffable encounter, and you will understand that the Bible is more than a book: it is a presence, a *person*. It is the eternal Word which greets you in every one of its words, the Word of the Father in whom is every Truth and who is Truth itself.[6]

Scripture is formulated, especially with stories, not primarily for presenting teaching or ethics, but precisely for confrontation that provokes an encounter with God. He quotes Amos N. Wilder about this dynamic:

---

[6] Maurice Zundel, *The Gospel Within* (Sherbrooke: Editions Paulines, 1993), 68.

> What makes such stories and such dialogue so formidable is that in each one God, as it were, forces us to give him a face-to-face answer.... The personal dramatic character of the Gospel itself necessarily involves confrontation, not instruction in the ordinary sense but the living encounter of heart and heart, voice and voice, and that this has inevitably registered itself in the ongoing story of the Christ and in the style of the New Testament. As we have observed, it is as though God says to men one by one: "Look me in the eye."[7]

It is the role of the preacher to enable this confrontation. He does this by "actualizing" the text: making the text relevant, linking it to the life of the listener so as to awaken him. This chapter examines the task of actualizing the text, as the preacher often finds the task of consulting various sources daunting, and may not even have the requisite reference books.

A very helpful resource that Fr. Cameron uses and recommends is the Verbum Bible software. It enables the preacher to quickly pull together on one computer screen many resources (lectionary, translations of Scripture, concordances, commentaries, Gospel parallels, and many other resources, e.g., Church Fathers, Aquinas' *Summa*), and synchronizes all the resources on the Scripture text being examined in one screen. With such a "library," the preacher can access and compare resources with a series of clicks of tabs.

(c) Beyond the Literal Sense, the Spiritual Senses are Employed to Discern the Meaning

We run into the problem in the contemporary exegesis of texts of focusing almost exclusively on the historical-critical method (one method within the literal or historical sense). The Church's Tradition has long understood that, beyond the literal sense, there are three spiritual senses.

The *Catechism of the Catholic Church* affirms this (nn. 115-119), e.g., quoting a medieval couplet: "The Letter speaks of deeds; Allegory to faith; the Moral how to act; Anagogy our destiny." While we must, of course, take it into account, as Fr. Cameron points out, the literal sense on its own, which though indispensable, is not adequate: the historical-critical method gives valuable

---

[7] Amos N. Wilder, *Early Christian Rhetoric: The Language of the Gospel* (Cambridge, MA: Harvard University Press, 1971), 68, 57, 60, 48, 54, quoted in Peter Cameron, *Why Preach?: Encountering Christ in God's Word* (San Francisco: Ignatius Press, 2009), 69.

technical information about the text, but it does not yet arrive at the sense or meaning.

Fr. Cameron supports this by drawing from various authorities (Lineamenta for the Synod on Word of God, Joseph Ratzinger, Hans Urs von Balthasar, Alonzo Schökel, Francis Martin). Raniero Cantalamessa compares the exclusive use of the historical-critical method on Scripture to seeking to understand a consecrated host through chemical analysis: "Historical-critical analysis, even when carried to the heights of perfection, only represents the first step in knowledge of the Bible, the step concerning the letter."[8]

Verbum Domini (VD) teaches the need to include the second level of spiritual exegesis that incorporates three elements of interpretation: unity of the whole Bible; through the living Tradition; and the analogy of faith:

> As a consequence of the absence of the second methodological level, a profound gulf is opened up between scientific exegesis and lectio divina. This can give rise to a lack of clarity in the preparation of homilies. (VD 35)

> Access to a proper understanding of biblical texts is only granted to the person who has an affinity with what the text is saying on the basis of life experience. (VD 30)

Furthermore, the historical-critical method, giving objective information, does not ask what the text means. Hence Fr. Cameron seeks to "actualize" the text by looking generally for three overarching aspects: (i) what the text reveals of the significance (meaning) applied to my life; (ii) how it applies to contemporary circumstances; and (iii) the use of appropriate language— here we are speaking of a *proposal*. Scripture speaks to our hearts, so preaching Scripture is preaching to our hearts by making a proposal. The goal is to ensure that the will of the listener is also involved, so as to challenge their freedom. So we hear the homily in order to be able to respond "yea" or "nay" to a proposal.

---

[8] Raniero Cantalamessa, *The Mystery of God's Word* (Collegeville, MN: The Liturgical Press, 1994), 83.

(d) Three Overall Dynamics with the Text

In *Why Preach?*, Fr. Cameron breaks down the actualization of the text into three specific dynamics: (i) objective (the fact and details provided by the Evangelist, e.g., see earlier exegesis of Samaritan woman); (ii) personal (characters, actions, and dialogues); and (iii) response. The USCCB's *Fulfilled in Your Hearing: The Homily in the Sunday Assembly* teaches: "The homily is not so much *on* the Scriptures as *from* and *through* them." It entails examining syntax, a concordance, questions, images-motifs, parallelisms, implied subtext, how it makes you feel, context, relationship to Bible, purpose and strategy of author, etc.[9] Fr. Cameron's instructions also give us a clue to the purpose of examining these three dynamics— the *intentionality*: "Once you have identified all the 'evidence' and 'clues' in the text, ask: *Why* are they here? What literary and therefore theological purpose do they serve? Why is the story told the way it is?"[10] Greater clarity can be attained by examining more fully the specifics of the process of Fr. Cameron's method.

Three-Part Structure of the Homily

Fr. Cameron believes that lack of structure could be the principal reason for a poor homily. Many, if not most, priests and deacons diligently go about preparing homilies with some basic approach: perhaps reading or praying over the text, consulting resources, finding a suitable point, giving a real-life example, and offering some exhortation. But such a basic approach, while good, does not possess the very directed structure that Fr. Cameron proposes: *an idea, an image, and a proposal or application.* Fr. Cameron observes that homilies can fail from four main causes: (i) a lack of a theological approach; (ii) but also a lack of a proposal, a lack of a judgment to be made by the listeners (yes or no); (iii) using a scatter gun approach but with nothing for the parishioners to sink their teeth into; and (iv) a lack of structure (Pope Francis' counsel), which can comprise simply four or five concrete things that we can look at.

---

[9] Peter Cameron, *Why Preach?*, 88-95.
[10] Ibid., 93-94.

We recommend that the reader look at Fr. Cameron's *Why Preach?* for more details on the specifics of writing an effective proposal which, for the sake of brevity, is not developed in this chapter.[11]

1. The Idea (Lived Question): Actualizing or Unleashing the Text

(i) Context: Immediate and Overall Levels

Fr. Cameron teaches us that the first step of looking for clues is the *context*, such as when an event happens, and what comes before or after the text. For example, we note that the parable of the Good Samaritan is followed by Jesus' visit to Mary and Martha: both are about hospitality. Another example is that of one Gospel placing an event at the beginning of Jesus' life, while another placed the same event at the end— this has theological import for what the sacred writer is emphasizing. For the larger context, Fr. Cameron suggests in *Why Preach?* looking for the *subtext*, "what is implied but not explicitly stated? What can you read between the lines? What does the writer leave unsaid..."; and *the relationship of this passage within the biblical book, but also to the entire Bible.*[12] As a spiritual exercise for entering more deeply into the biblical text, he suggests using the Gospel of the year in the 3-year Sunday cycle for one's daily meditation.

(ii) Literary Considerations: Parables are about Jesus

Second, Fr. Cameron offers a key interpretative insight. Parables are not mainly about Jesus' teaching or His rules, but about *His Person*. Yet, preachers are inclined to reduce parables to some kind of teaching or moral. Yet, during a storm, we don't need a bracelet with a teaching like, "Jesus saves," but we have an existential question, such as "where are you now in this storm, Jesus?" Even more, the preacher is inclined to make the Prodigal Son parable a moral about forgiveness; yet, though it was available to him, Luke stayed away from the word "forgiveness." We must go more deeply and encounter the sublime revelation, namely, the abyss of the Father's mercy, and get our hands dirty in all its implications. So Fr. Cameron counsels us to look at Scripture as you would look at a person you are going to love. With someone

[11] Ibid., 40-42, 142-143, 174-175, 177.
[12] Ibid., 93.

we love, we will always find something new that is beautiful; and as we enter the Scripture text more and more each year, it becomes bigger.

(iii) *Dramatis Personae*: Examine the Characters and Dialogue

The third step is to make *a list of the characters and see what is significant about them as it illuminates the text* (e.g., in the parable of the man being robbed on way to Jericho, examine who the inn owner is by consulting authorities like St. Augustine, using concordances, Interlinear Greek-English, *Catena Aurea*, etc.). In making a list of players, we must remember that sometimes not all of the players appear on the stage.

We note first that the fullest telling event of the healing of Jairus' daughter is in Mark 5:22-42. Second, we note that Mark's Gospel is a Passion narrative, everything that precedes is preparation for the cross. Third, Mark is using a literary device, an inter-collation or sandwich: the insertion of the woman is the "meat," the key for interpreting the story. That is, the request for healing and the actual healing of the child (two pieces of bread of the sandwich) is interrupted by healing of the Samaritan woman's blood, which gives us the confidence (faith) when the message was received to not disturb Jesus because the child had died.

Now why does this woman go to such an exorbitant action? Perhaps this woman acted thus with faith because she had heard of His miracles; yet this woman being unnamed could be anybody. She is the most important person there because of her Christian witness, yet that person can be anyone of "us." The only person who gets named is Jairus, as Mark also intentionally leaves out the girl's name, even though she is the one who gets raised to life.

Thus, the story is really about Jairus, indicated by the inclusion of his name. We can get distracted by the miracle, but what Jesus does for the faith in Jairus is a much greater miracle (otherwise, Jesus is just a miracle worker). We cannot understand Jesus apart from the cross. Mark helps us to read the text without getting lost, for we read between the lines.

(iv) Dialogues Reveal Details

In all dialogues found in the text, we note carefully: what is actually spoken, what is not said, who speaks; and we pay special attention to any questions Jesus asks— they are meant for us.

(v) Verbs are a Powerhouse of Theology

Fr. Cameron counsels us to always scrutinize the verbs, which are a "powerhouse" of theology. In the parable of the talents, rather than make the homily about tenderness to an unfortunate person (man with one talent thrown into the darkness), we find a key in the verb that the sacred author uses, "entrust" or "hand over" when he had other possibilities: "For it will be like a man going on a journey, who called his servants and entrusted to them his property." To "hand over" is not a financial word, but an exquisite word, *"paredoken"* (παϱεδωϰεν), to hand over his property. The only time this word is used in the Gospels (look up through a concordance) is when various figures are handing Jesus over to his death: Judas, Pilate, Jesus, crowd, or Father of Jesus. The insight here is that Jesus becomes the ultimate talent that is handed-over or entrusted. Once the parable is read with the awareness of just this one word, we see what the author is intending.

We can see the power of verbs in another parable, that of the Good Samaritan. For example, the Good Samaritan being "moved with compassion" is an expression we should look up in the Greek original in an inter-linear Greek-English Bible (or simply Google-search it). Looking to see where else this expression appears in the Gospel of Luke (concordance), we find that it appears in the *Benedictus* of the Nativity narrative, "In the tender compassion of our God," as well as in the compassion of the Father for the Prodigal Son. Now we have three very strong texts, and we go to prayer and ask God for help with these. A second word we can look up in this parable is the Samaritan's "hoisting" the wounded man on his feet. It could be hoisting by a donkey, and this leads us to Jesus on a donkey going to Jerusalem. Our experience is that what seems like daunting research is made very accessible by the Verbum Bible software.

(vi) **Note Vocabulary Specific to Sacred Writer's Style**

We use the concordance to see if any words are particular to the author's style. In the parable of the landowner, it would seem that the owner of the vineyard was unjust in paying the same salary to those who worked longer; but once we see the details, we see that it is equitable. We note first that Jesus did not avoid this controversy by having the first ones paid first; He deliberately has them paid last. If we think of Jesus using parables to explain the kingdom of God ("the kingdom is like…"), then looking more deeply, we see that this parable is really about answering who the subject is: "The kingdom of God is like a landowner." So if we are not happy with this landowner (Jesus), we are not going to be happy in heaven. What is it that Jesus is trying to get them to see, what is the ultimate issue? Here we want to stay with the Scripture text, as it is written in a very concrete way and in order to provoke. One word Jesus uses is important: "Are you *envious*…" We find this word used also in the Sermon on the Mount, and envy there is having an evil eye. That is, I am looking at something I should not be looking at, which causes me to be angry. They would not have been angry if they had not seen the last workers paid first. Their problem was envy. We see here the importance of examining the words, the vocabulary.

(vii) **Specifics: Images, Repetitions, Symbols, Parallelisms, Themes, Motifs**

Fr. Cameron counsels us to note *the literary devices and forms* the author uses: "*What images, repetitions, symbols, parallelisms, themes, or motifs are in the passage?* Be very attentive to the *sacred writer's style and 'voice'* as an author."[13] Continuing the parable of the landowner, we look to see if there is any special information provided by the sacred author: time, place, setting, circumstances, order of events, names, and biographical facts. For example, in terms of time, we discover that the event of giving the parable happens at the end of Jesus' life. What is the motivation for the crowd to bring Jesus to Pilate? The envy mentioned earlier has to be crucified in them. They have to get rid of the evil eye, so they must stop looking at what they should not be looking at—which is a form of pornography. The workers who are angry can go through all the

---

[13] Ibid., 92.

arguments, one by one, with the landowner, but it does not help them. For them, the landowner is a bad man. Now we go deeper and look at other details. The landowner goes out five times, noting also when he goes out. Why on earth would an owner, and not the manager, be going out five times?

The conclusion appears to be clear: it seems to be much more about the landowner's being concerned about the poor workers. So all of this anger directed towards this man seems unfounded. If they knew this man is concerned about people, how should they respond to him? It should be with *gratitude*. So instead of grumbling at this man, if your wife is sick and you have no money to buy medicine, then you should approach the landowner to ask the man for mercy too, to ask as a beggar since the landowner is *moved by mercy*. And you expect the landowner to respond, "Of course, how much do you need?" Jesus did not change the order precisely to make us angry. Instead of looking at this with an evil eye, look instead with the *landowner's eyes*, then we will see it differently. He pays them not because they are good, but because He is good. Fr. Cameron cites an author who gave an ironical scene of entering heaven at the end time: the sinners dancing with joy, rejoicing in God's mercy, lead the way, while the people who thought they were good "with their virtue burned out of them," coming at the back.

(viii) **Personal Impact: How does the passage strike you?**

Once we have taken of all these steps, we have to confront this text personally, as mentioned in both *Verbum Domini* and *Evangelii gaudium*. How does this passage strike me? We follow where Christ is leading us, and we always read between the lines. And when you have done that, we should work with *one sheet of paper*; if it goes beyond one page, our homily is too long. The big temptation is to think that, since I have done all this research, I have to put it all in. But St. Thomas says that things are received according to the mode of the receiver. *How does the Holy Spirit resonate in your soul so that you experience more deeply the embrace from the Lord.*

Yet the lived question must come from the *text* (not from outside, e.g., from our own ideas). This approach can cause the congregation, after they have seen the riches of the Bible and its different levels of meaning, to turn to the Bible. *To unleash what it means*, one of things we can do is look at when the event is happening (means something different at the beginning of Jesus' life; it is weightier at end of His life).

2. Image

In the previous section, we looked at finding a principal *idea, a "lived question,"* that addresses the listener's heart. Now, this structured approach entails finding an image for the lived question as the second step. We should not give more ideas but we want the message to sink in more, to see it more in the flesh:

> One of the most important things is to learn how to use images in preaching, how to appeal to imagery. Sometimes examples are used to clarify a certain point, but these examples usually appeal only to the mind. Images, on the other hand, help people better to appreciate and accept the message we wish to communicate. An attractive image makes the message seem familiar, close to home, practical and related to everyday life. A successful image can make people savour the message, awaken a desire and move the will towards the Gospel. A good homily, an old teacher once told me, should have "an idea, a sentiment, an image." (EG 157)

For Fr. Cameron, this image is the *heart of preaching.* So we must start early in the week to prepare the homily. We get the theology for the homily from the Scripture text in order to find the image that pierces the listener's heart today (not what pierced him a few years ago). Here we have to pray and beg, or look at films or the internet. You are making a parable (image) of a parable. Take something you know, smash it against the text, and then come up with a new idea. Thus, having found the lived question, we are well along (e.g., "Who is my neighbour" in the Good Samaritan parable, such as the colleagues at work or family members); but the second step now is to find the image.

3. Proposal

Then the third step is to offer something in terms of an application (proposal). *Lack of a proposal or application* is one of the main reasons why preaching fails: there is either *inadequate means of actualizing the text,* or *insufficient means to unleash the text.*

Structure: Begin with the Audience, "How will they Feel?"

Most of us don't know what structure is (apart from beginning, middle, and end of a play or paper). Action movies give an external structure, but the internal elements that undergird them is what you must have. Otherwise the satisfaction is lacking, the structure that should be there for you to enjoy is missing. A lot of this can be summarized by the word "structure," which includes the feeling engendered.

Here, Fr. Cameron turns to his experience of playwriting. In a course given by Donna Cooper (*Writing Great Screenplays for Film and TV*), Fr. Cameron first learned what structure truly means. It does not begin with how to put this together— it begins with the audience. In creating a structure, the first question I have to ask is *what can my audience take*. If I give something that exceeds their capacity, then it is not only unfruitful but also frustrating. Our people feel as they as if they can't take it all in and become almost nauseous. So I want to exploit what I know of what they can take in, so that I can use it in the most strategic way. Our people's attention span is about three minutes, largely due to television. She says that structure is an *emotional response*, is the unfolding of my homily so that it is moving towards a climax. So you always start at the *end*, the climax is how you want the people to feel— as Pope Francis says, a message is also the *effect*. You may want them to feel courageous, zealous, remorseful, on fire to pray, but don't mix them. This will determine what you will include in your homily. Thus a structure is directing the homily towards a goal, the effect, Fr. Cameron constantly asks, "How will they *feel*?"

Skeleton of Homily to Enable the Desired Result

In major movies, movie directors know that they must insert at the twenty-seventh minute some crisis or major event around which the whole movie revolves, which will spur us on to watch the rest of the movie. Pope Francis says that our homilies have to be brief, how it fits proportionally within a Mass. Fr. Cameron thinks that a homily should be 8 minutes long (not less, but notes that some cultures are offended if they don't get 20 minutes). For an 8 minute homily, the 2 minute-mark should be the moment when there is an explosion, so that the people are with you, that will keep them engaged.

But after two or three more minutes, they will be distracted again, so you have to get them again: "You have made this claim, but I am not going to believe you because you say so, you need to verify it." We note the efficacy of Peter's preaching by simply telling the people the great actions of God, which lead the people to ask him, "What should we do." That is, this story is too good to be true; if Jesus forgave Peter, then we want that forgiveness as well. Had Peter begun by telling them what they "should" do without the grace of seeing God's goodness first, they would have reacted negatively.

A helpful structural exercise is to make a minute by minute composition. Take a piece of paper and set up the eight minutes of your homily thus:

- Minute 1: has to break down the wall of resistance.

- Minute 2: the big explosion from *your proposal* should come in minute 2. Then you use your transitional phrase. Now you can't make the mistake of jam-packing it like a meatball: if there is too much meat without breadcrumbs, the meatball will not hold. If the listeners are struck by something so that they say "wow," then you have to give some fill so that they can allow it to sink in. You have to know the congregation, how much they can take. Perhaps knowing the congregation means that I can't preach a three point homily but only one point and reiterate it in different ways. So give enough time so that it can register and move from the intellect to the will.

- Minute 3: an image might be good (but not another concept), to reconsider in light of the *story*, which could take 3 or 4 minutes. This also helps with verification.

- Minute 6-7: Now we have the application. "What do we have to do with our lives, what is the first thing we ought to do" (words of crowd to Peter). People suffer because preachers don't listen to them— they talk at them, and not to them. So we should be very down-to-earth, speaking in a colloquial way. And again, you don't have to give everything; just offer one thing they can do.

A final helpful exercise is *to practice introducing our endings*. We have to memorize the ending, to come with a climatic, synthesizing ending. The best endings are the ones that turn to the beginning of the story or opening remark, but give it a Christic twist. It may never have occurred to them before but you have brought light into this text. He cautions us to avoid two common mistakes: we don't want the pilot to land and take off again repeatedly; and to add new information at the end ("Oh, I forgot this"). At the end, we should just synthesize.

Synthesis: Three Emphases in Brief

Fr. Cameron's overall method can be summarized briefly in three emphases.

1. *Overall Approach to Reach Hearts*: Fr. Cameron is primarily interested in facilitating an encounter with Christ through Scripture that is the Logos incarnated. To this end, he underscores the need to reach the depths of each soul that longs for beauty, truth, love, community, etc., pointing out their present state of fear, loneliness, guilty feelings, worry, etc. In this, he has been influenced by the powerful vision of Msgr. Luigi Giussani. Fr. Cameron sees the role of the preacher as to enable the people to reach down to this fundamental level, that the preacher needs a defibrillator to awaken their hearts. He emphasizes the importance of the preacher as witness: that the lived example of the preacher makes the message irresistible.

Fr. Cameron, in *Why Preach?*, takes this more deeply. What the preacher is called to is not to give doctrine or to persuade, but **to mediate** (preacher as mediator) **an encounter with Jesus, the One who is the answer to all their hearts' longings**. It involves an opening of the listener's *I* to encounter the preacher's *I*, who has encountered the living Christ and expresses his *I* (self) that has been touched by that encounter (sublimity). The preacher imitates Christ's method with the Samaritan woman, with His thirst (for souls, love) encountering the woman's thirst, through which a communication and a transformation took place[14]: "For what the preacher brings about is not just 'persuasion' but 'transport,'" an awakening.[15]

---

[14] Ibid., 96-117.
[15] Ibid., 117.

2. *Find the Lived Question*: Fr. Cameron digs deeply into the Scripture text to find the "lived question" and seeks to draw the listener's heart through the context of the Scripture text. He emphasizes that each sacred writer (e.g., Luke) has his own "theology," that is expressed in the text. Thus the preacher must be sensitive to keys that flow from the sacred writer's slant: e.g., when his usual vocabulary is not used, especially *verbs*; to other instances where he has used a key word (concordance); the meaning in the original Greek, etc.

Not only is Fr. Cameron sensitive to the theology of the sacred writer, he also seeks to draw the listener into the deeper levels and to live out of this theology. t this conference, Bishop Robert Barron reinforced this, recalling Vatican II's dream of a revival in the reading of the Bible and conviction that the preacher ought to draw the listeners into the biblical world, especially through making links from the Old Testament to the newness of Christ.[16]

3. *Listener and Structure*: Drawing from his playwright background, two elements come to the fore. First, Fr. Cameron begins with "structure" in the sense of beginning with the listener, with his needs and context, such that it is the listener's needs that determine the structure.

Second, the structure of the homily is given much direction from playwriting like that of a movie: when to insert the "explosion" that will engage the listener's attention; how to phrase the proposal to draw a "yea" or "nay" from the listener; how to use several key transitional phrases to develop overall flow; how to use endings as a climax and synthesis.

It might be helpful to highlight Fr. Jude Siciliano's caution against bypassing the *Pre-critical stage*, turning immediately to commentaries or personal interpretations. Imitating God's two steps of keeping silence before He created and then breaking the silence to create, the preacher's all-important first step is silence: it is a *listening, lectio*, or *scrutatio*. To use an image, instead of our catching the rabbit, *this allows the rabbit to catch us*. Many preachers cut this stage short, where the rabbit [God] catches the preacher.

---

[16] Bishop Robert Barron, "Preaching the Transformative Word" (conference presented at St. Augustine's Seminary, Conference on Catholic Preaching, St. Augustine's Seminary, Toronto, ON, August 7, 2018).

Fr. Siciliano also notes the benefit of presenting first what God has done, synthesized by the saying, "the indicative precedes the imperative": Peter at Pentecost first reveals the magnificent things God has done in Christ, leading people, "cut to the heart," to ask, "Brethren, what shall we do?" (Acts 2:37)[17]

II. Key Spiritual Points from Three Master Preachers

(Charismatic Renewal, Dominican, Redemptorist)[18]

A. Bishop Sam Jacobs: Charismatic Charism

Preaching in the Power of the Holy Spirit

Bishop Sam Jacobs gave a one-day preaching seminar that emphasized above all preaching in the power of the Holy Spirit. As personal testimony, he shared how as a young and popular associate pastor, he felt that there was something missing in his life and ministry, and he cried to God for light. He discerned later that the help came through his first contact with the Charismatic Renewal in 1969. The language he uses is common to the Renewal but derives from Scripture. He heard a priest talking about the importance of establishing the kingship of Christ in ourselves and making God the Lord of our life. Fr. Jacobs came to realize that he was making himself the lord of his life and doing things under his own power in his ministry (e.g., preaching). He was doing the things at the natural level but not in the Spirit. So he invited the Holy Spirit to come into his life and to anoint him. The inner peace that flooded his heart from doing this confirmed for him that God had answered the prayer of his heart. Now he seeks only to preach in Jesus' name and in the power of the Holy Spirit. The one key for Bishop Jacobs is being in deep relationship with the Lord in prayer.

---

[17] Jude Siciliano, "Preaching Master Conference" (conference presented at St. Augustine's Seminary, Toronto, ON, June 29-30, 2015).

[18] These notes of James Heft (mentioned earlier in the chapter), James Sullivan, and James Wallace are drawn from their presentations at the Preaching Conference held to mark St. Augustine's Seminary's Centenary, "How To Make Catholic Preaching Better: A Conference in Homiletics" (presented at St. Augustine's Seminary, Toronto, July 7-10, 2014). The one exception is Bishop Sam Jacobs' preaching seminar, which was given at St. Augustine's Seminary on June 26, 2017.

Preaching with the Efficacy of Christ

Bishop Jacobs drew several examples of the call to improve preaching, including from Pope Benedict XVI and Pope Francis. He noted that the USSCB wrote that year after year the people of God in the pews have called for a renewal in preaching in the Church, they were getting homilies that left them tepid and inclined to leave the Church. He summarized two aspects to Jesus' preaching: Jesus spoke with authority, such that people flocked to listen to him, for He was preaching with the anointing of the Spirit; as Jesus did many deeds and wonders and signs, when we preach like Jesus did, we should see signs and wonders after our preaching. He made several suggestions in this regard: believe in the anointing power of the Holy Spirit; pray that the gifts of the Holy Spirit be continually stirred in us; pray for the Holy Spirit's power during homily preparation; admit that we are powerless before the Holy Spirit; and ask before praying the Collect that the Holy Spirit anoint the preacher and the listeners.

B. Fr. James Sullivan, O.P.: Dominican Charism

Obligation to Study: People Seek Truth

Fr. James Sullivan's insights reflect strongly his Dominican charism. There is an imperative that we must not only be on fire, but be enlightened by the fullness of Revelation and the path travelled by God's word in the Church and people's hearts (EV 144). As fire and fervor can quickly dissipate, we also need to be enlightened. What precedes both fire and enlightenment is *study*, a serious matter. Dominican spirituality teaches: "Before all else, our study should aim principally and ardently at this that we might be able to be useful to the souls of our neighbours" (*Primitive Constitutions of the Order of Preachers,* prologue). If we don't study, we end up thinking our own thoughts all the time. The Dominican Constitutions also teach: "It is all the more fitting that they should devote themselves to study, because from the tradition of the Order they are more specially called to cultivate mankind's inclination toward truth." Fr. Sullivan has great confidence that, when people hear the truth (or good or beauty), they want it. The preacher should be excited about what he is preaching. And he should not be reading the text: he does not need notes, for he should speak from the heart.

Love of God and Prayer: Example of St. Thomas

Finally, Fr. Sullivan turns to prayer and love. Regarding the importance of prayer for preaching, he looks to the example of St. Thomas Aquinas. Fr. Jean Pierre Torrell writes in his work, *St. Thomas Aquinas: The Person and His Work*: "Every time St. Thomas Aquinas wished to study, to teach, etc., he first withdrew into secret, and prayed, pouring out tears that God may reveal His mysteries." Another biographer of St. Thomas wrote: "Life is less a confession of faith but an arduous search for this truth, a life inseparable from study and prayer."

Regarding desire for God and love, he looks to St. Thomas, who used to pray intensely before and after Mass. After Mass one day in Naples, a sacristan reported this event, in which the Lord said to Thomas, "Thomas, you have written well of me, what would you like?" His reply was, "*Non, nisi Te, Domine*" ("Only You, Lord"). In our contemplation, we are in pursuit of God: we never settle for the little that we now have, which would mean that we are dead; *we must want God, seek Him, pursue Him*, who is the goal of our preaching.

C. Fr. James A. Wallace, C.Ss.R.: Redemptorist Charism

Preaching Begins with Staying with Jesus ("Come and see")

Fr. James Wallace identifies deeply with the method and ardour of the founder of the Redemptorists, St. Alphonsus Liguori. The preaching of St. Alphonsus brought about a great renewal in his times, making even a brief examination of his method very worthwhile.[19] We should note first that, for Fr. Wallace, the basic text for preachers is Mark 3: 13-14: "And he went up on the mountain, and called to him those whom he desired; and they came to him. And he appointed twelve, *to be with him*, and to be sent out to preach." We have been called by Jesus, but first of all *to be with Him*— this is the all-important point of departure.

---

[19] Fr. James Wallace joined the Washington Theological Union faculty in 1987. He is a former president of the Catholic Association of Teachers of Homiletics and of the Religious Speech Communication Association. Among his books are *Preaching to the Hungers of the Heart* (Liturgical Press, 2002); *Witnessing the Holy Land with Artist Ellouise Schoettler* (Paulist Press, 1999); and *Imaginal Preaching* (Paulist Press, 1995).

New Ardour: Love of God and Desire for Salvation of Souls

Fr. Wallace highlights above all passion or ardour. What is new in preaching is not the content, for it is all about Christ. The last two popes taught that there are three new things needed for preaching: *new expressions, new methods of getting the message across, and new ardour.* St. Alphonsus himself was a man of great ardour, who founded a congregation that has always kept in touch with preaching, including parish missions. But the vision of Alphonsus for evangelization called for a new ardour.

While he did not write much about preaching, we find in his work, *The Dignity and Duties of a Priest*, about eight pages on preaching. There we find seven *"brush-strokes"* for preaching: (i) learning and studying are necessary; (ii) live an exemplary life as witness; (iii) foster affection for mental prayer; (iv) speak from the heart; (v) have the right intention; (vi) address all who are present; and (vii) have concern for rules, structure, and right words.

Of these seven, great harm can be done if a preacher is not a man of prayer and study. These seven constitute a verbal portrait of St. Alphonsus, and as we read his method, we can ask what helps us stir up the fires of love (ardour)? What appears to be the golden thread in these seven brush-strokes is precisely this ardour, namely, *this love of God and burning desire for the salvation of the world.* To make this method come alive, it is recommended that the preacher sees it enlivened by the attractive and inspiring figure and life of St. Alphonsus Liguori.

CHAPTER 11

MARY, MORNING STAR OF THE NEW EVANGELIZATION

This maternity of Mary in the order of grace began with the consent which she gave in faith at the Annunciation and which she sustained without wavering beneath the cross, and lasts until the eternal fulfillment of all the elect. Taken up to heaven *she did not lay aside this salvific duty, but by her constant intercession continued to bring us the gifts of eternal salvation. By her maternal charity, she cares for the brethren of her Son,* who still journey on earth surrounded by dangers and cultics, until they are led into the happiness of their true home. Therefore the Blessed Virgin is invoked by the Church under the titles of *Advocate, Auxiliatrix, Adjutrix, and Mediatrix.* (LG nn. 61-62, emphasis added)

Pope John Paul II Sets Mary's Place in the Plan of Salvation: Morning Star

We engage in the new evangelization with great confidence because Christ Himself sends us out and because He also bestowed the beloved Holy Spirit upon the Church to accompany her in her mission. What may be less evident is that the plan of the Blessed Trinity also includes the accompaniment and powerful intercession of Mary, the spouse of the Holy Spirit and the Mother of the Church (see *Lumen gentium* quotation above). Pope John Paul II, in *Redemptoris Mater* in preparation for the Third Millennium, has set the program for us for the Third Millennium, presenting Mary's role with salvation history as the "Morning Star": "… it becomes fully comprehensible that in this present period we wish to turn in a special way to her, the one who in the 'night' of the Advent expectation began to shine like a true 'Morning Star' (Stella Matutina)."

In fact, even though it is not possible to establish an exact chronological point for identifying the date of Mary's birth, the Church has constantly been aware that Mary appeared on the horizon of salvation history before Christ. It is a fact that when "the fullness of time" was definitively drawing near— the saving advent of Emmanuel— she who was from eternity destined to be his Mother already existed on earth. The fact that she "preceded" the coming of Christ is reflected every year in the liturgy of Advent. Therefore, if to that ancient historical expectation of the Savior we compare these years which are bringing us closer to the end of the second Millennium after Christ and to the beginning of the third, it becomes fully comprehensible that in this present period we wish to turn in a special way to her, the one who in the "night" of the Advent expectation began to shine like a true "Morning Star" (Stella Matutina). For just as this star, together with the "dawn," precedes the rising of the sun, so Mary from the time of her Immaculate Conception preceded the coming of the Savior, the rising of the "Sun of Justice" in the history of the human race. (RM 3)

Commenting on *Lumen gentium's* teaching, John Paul II more fully gave a sense of universal significance of Mary as mother. He explained that Mary as "a mother to us in the order of grace" is of universal scope and therefore "does not allow any limitation of her motherly love": "Indeed, with these words the Crucified One established an intimate relationship between Mary and his beloved disciple, a typological figure of universal scope, intending to offer his Mother as Mother to all mankind."[1] He gives clarity to the uniqueness of her work as an extension of Christ's: "He [God] wanted to unite to the Redeemer's intercession as a priest that of the Blessed Virgin as a mother."[2] Thus, in the Father's plan, Christ's intercession as priest is joined to Mary's intercession as mother. This is captured by a saying that St. Louis de Montfort and St. Maximilian Kolbe would fully support: "Why do more people not come to Christ? It is because they don't go through Mary." The Church as a whole, as they did in the beginnings of the Church, in her present task of re-evangelization, should look once more to Mary as their Morning Star.

As John Paul II teaches, what is deeply consoling is that Mary is especially present to those in danger and suffering, but above all to those whose salvation is in danger:

Christians call upon Mary as "Helper," recognizing her motherly love which sees her children's needs and is ready to come to their aid, especially when their eternal salvation is at stake. The conviction that Mary is close to those

---

[1] Pope John Paul II, General Audience, "Mary has Universal Spiritual Motherhood," September 24, 1997, n. 2, vatican.va, accessed August 18, 2018, https://w2.vatican.va/content/john-paul-ii/en/audiences/1997/documents/hf_jp-ii_aud_24091997.html
[2] Ibid., n. 4.

who are suffering or in situations of serious danger has prompted the faithful to invoke her as "Benefactress."[3]

As "maternal mediatrix," she both presents our desires and petitions and transmits God's divine gifts to us, "interceding continually on our behalf."[4] This is truly a remarkable vision of a loving heavenly mother who dotes on us and accompanies us each step of our life.

I. The Marian Principle: Mary Mirrors Christ's Trajectory

A. Introducing the Marian principle

Adrienne von Speyr will introduce us to the incredible revelation of Mary's comprehensive role in the Church as the idea of the Church, perpetually generating her, such that she lives in Mary. Hans Urs von Balthasar now reveals the foundation of such an economy, how this became possible. He teaches that Mary fundamentally mirrors the Son: as the Son is the beloved of the Father and is the extension of the Father's being and love in creation, so Mary too is beloved of the Trinity and her life is an overflow of the Trinity in the world and is also a mirror of the Incarnate Son, including His Passion. Since von Balthasar has written more than most read in their lifetime, it is necessary to find a guide into his rich and voluminous works. We find a very fine synthesis of von Balthasar's Marian principle in Bishop Brendan Leahy's published work, *The Marian principle: In the Ecclesiology of Hans Urs von Balthasar.*[5] The following is but a summary of Bishop Leahy's work (often using his own words or paraphrasing them).

The Marian principle "Summarizes the Deepest Contents of Conciliar Renewal"

It was Pope John Paul II himself, in a Wednesday general audience, who made a remarkable statement, acknowledging the incredible emerging importance of the "Marian profile": "At the dawn of the new millennium, we

---

[3] Ibid., n. 5.

[4] Ibid.

[5] Brendan Leahy, *The Marian principle: In the Ecclesiology of Hans Urs von Balthasar* (New York: New City Press, 2000). The book is a modified version of his doctoral thesis, *The Marian principle in the Church in the Ecclesiology of Hans Urs von Balthasar* (Berlin: Peter Lang, 1996), with the Marian principle covered in Chapter 5 (pp. 153-224). In 2013, Leahy was appointed and consecrated bishop of Limerick, Ireland.

notice with joy the emergence of the 'Marian profile' of the Church that summarizes the deepest contents of conciliar renewal."[6] His reference to the "Marian profile" points to the significant contribution of the great theologian, Hans Urs von Balthasar, for our times. The Marian profile or principle has been received positively by both Pope John Paul II and Cardinal Ratzinger. We can add to Brendan Leahy's elaboration by giving the setting the following parallel: Son–Mary-Church. That is, the Marian profile presents the Son in relation to the Father, and Mary, as the archetype of this very relation of the Son to the Father, in turn lives this relation to the Son but to Peter, who in the Church represents the Son. The Church, as a consequence, is Marian in her very essence. Thus Mary mirrors the Son in the Trinity and lives Jesus' expropriation and surrender, which constitutes the true heart of Christian life.

Petrine and Marian principles

Hans Urs Von Balthasar employs a key distinction between masculine and feminine action applied to the Father and Son respectively that helps illuminate their relationship. The Father is theologically masculine (in initiating and giving), the Son's part is theologically feminine (in being led and receiving). These two dimensions are extended to the Church in the Petrine and Marian principles: Peter (hierarchy, institution) represents Christ, who is masculine to the Church; and Mary (baptized) is feminine in relation to Christ as God, and thus to Peter, who represents Christ.

Applying the masculine and feminine dimensions found in the Father and Son respectively to the Church helps us to identify what is at the heart of Christian life. Von Balthasar begins by first noting that there was a constellation of figures or people around Jesus, that he calls "principles" or "profiles," that continue dimensions of Christ in salvation history. He then identifies four primary principles: Peter, Paul (e.g., missionary), John (e.g., contemplative), and James, a basic four-fold structure in the early developing Church and that continues in the Church.[7] But von Balthasar sees that all principles in the Church can be summed up in two fundamental figures or

---

[6] John Paul II, Wednesday audience, 23 November 1998. *"L'Osservatore Romano"* [English Edition], 2 December 1998, p. 19.

[7] Brendan Leahy, *The Marian principle*, 64-66.

principles: Petrine and Marian. The Petrine principle, the masculine dimension, symbolizes the hierarchy or institution, or more simply all those who hold ministerial positions in the Church (pope, bishops, priests). Now Peter's role of authority and dispensing the sacraments are indispensable, for without the sacraments, for example, the Church would die spiritually.

Nevertheless, Peter can only give the holy things, and the giving of the holy things does not make one holy, which is the goal of Christian life. And this is precisely what the Marian receiving principle represents, all the baptized, whose vocation is to holiness. While Peter's masculine role of governance and administering the sacraments sustains and guides the Church, the core of the Church is the feminine dimension, receiving grace to live as a child to the Father— holiness— which is what Mary represents. It is the difference between doing and being, work and sanctification, or being a worker for God and a child of God. Peter gives the "holy things," but he too has to "receive" them to become holy.[8]

The Christian is called to receptivity, mirroring Jesus' receptivity to the Father. And Mary is the fundamental point of internal unity of the Church and personalizes the Church in two ways: the whole countenance of the Church has a Marian transparency; and as both Mother of the Word and His Bride who co-operates in redemption, Mary is the all-embracing principle of the Church, where all other profiles find their fundamental point of internal unity. The interplay between the Marian and Petrine profiles reflects the unity between Christ and His Bride.

That is, if Peter is the point of external unity (hierarchy), the missionary communion of the Church finds her more fundamental internal point of unity in her Marian archetype and personal center, which is *holiness and fruitfulness*.[9] If the baptized person understood this centrality of Marian feminine "receptivity" of holiness and is not fixated on the masculine "doing" in ministry, the Church would be reformed.

---

[8] Ibid., 66-67.
[9] Ibid., 66.

The value of this Marian principle is evident from Hans Urs von Balthasar's vision that the spirituality of Mary is the "spirituality of all spiritualities," of all charisms, and of all lay movements. This is a tremendous insight, as we typically view Mary merely as a devotion. This insight was confirmed in a milestone decision when Vatican II Council Fathers voted and ratified the decision to insert a document on Mary as a chapter in *Lumen gentium*, the Dogmatic Constitution on the Church. What is even more remarkable is that the Council Fathers ratified the decision to put her in the last chapter of *Lumen gentium*, its apex. This means that Mary is not only an object of devotion but has to do with the very life of the Church radiating Christ to the world— the Church is Marian in her essence. For it is the charism of holiness (Baptism) that makes the Church grow and be fruitful— and Mary is the archetypal Church.[10]

For Hans Urs von Balthasar, the concrete signs of the Marian principle are found today especially in the new lay movements, looking to where the Church is a breathtaking adventure (think of the flowering of holiness through the mendicant orders with the appearance of St. Francis of Assisi and St. Dominic). The true "spiritual energies of holiness," the "regenerative energies in the Church," or "bombs" of the presence of the Holy Spirit are to be found in the subjective Marian dimension (not the institutional) of the Church. As such, the Marian principle is necessary for ecumenical dialogue and for building a Christian culture.[11] All this may seem rather academic or abstract. Let us allow von Balthasar to show us the depths of the richness of Mary's role in the Marian principle, previously introduced in *New Christ: Divine Filiation* (Ch. 7). This vision should turn our world upside down.

B. Background to the Marian principle

1. The Communion within the Trinity Extended to Man

Theodramatic Framework: Spousal Relationship between God and Man

For Hans Urs von Balthasar, the Trinitarian communion of Persons is mirrored in the theo-dramatic (drama between God and man) framework of

---

[10] Ibid., 164-165.
[11] Ibid., 170-173.

human life. Communion, founded on Trinitarian communion, is a central feature of von Balthasar's ecclesiology. He considers the logic of communion to be one which shapes all of God's dealings with mankind. To begin, the entire plan of creation and redemption was itself decided upon in a Trinitarian fashion (by the three Persons in communion). *The atmosphere in which God decides to create and redeem us is Trinitarian (mutual love among the divine Persons) and it is this Trinitarian reciprocity which God wants to impress upon creation*— here is another ineffable and profound insight— *human life mirrors Trinitarian life*.

Not only does God want to work for us, He also wants to work with us as within the Trinity in mutual love. Simply put, a theo-dramatic structure (God-man dialogue) follows from God desiring a partner or spouse, inviting us to an unheard-of divine elevation. Thus there is a theo-dramatic framework, where redemption is viewed in terms of a "marriage" drama involving God and humanity as the main actors, as it were, God as "Romeo" inviting man as "Juliet" to divine espousals.[12] The following was already briefly introduced in Chapter 6 (Love of Christ's Church and Mission).

The Centrality of the Son's Feminine Dimension before the Father and in History

The original drama between Father and Son, as Hans Urs von Balthasar noted, with a male-female polarity is already present within the Trinity. As described earlier, there is an overall structure described theologically as "masculine" and theologically "feminine," a suprasexual spousal framework within the Trinity between Father and Son. Let us briefly explain the Trinitarian background: Father and Son are eternally pouring themselves out in the Holy Spirit in this infinite ecstasy of love to each other. This infinite, ecstatic expropriation of outpouring of Self that is the essence of the Trinity is transplanted into creation to bear tremendous fruitfulness. This extending is mirrored in the two greatest human loves, spousal (marriage) and filial, the source and prototype of which are derived from the Trinity.

Within this "theo-dramatic" perspective, Christ is both totally turned toward the Father (guided by the Holy Spirit) and toward humanity, as God chooses

---

12 Ibid., 50-51.

to need a human partner (spouse). Man created in the image of Christ also has the Son's feminine or receiving dimension before the Father. Taking his lead from Scripture, von Balthasar notes some features of the conjugal relationship between man and woman, which explains why it is the "highest parable" for expressing God's encounter with humanity: two distinct persons that are involved; a union which makes one flesh and is fruitful; the opposition of sexes makes union possible. The male's role is employed as an analogy for *God's initiating role* in the divine-human encounter.[13] Depicting woman as the paradigm of creation's feminine *responsiveness* to God is based on a number of reasons: her fruitfulness appears more active and explicit in that she is the principle of common fruitfulness. The language of man-woman relationship conveys the unity in distinction between Christ and His Bride and Body. It helps here to define von Balthasar's terminology: "expropriating" (divesting, emptying) oneself, gives rise to "self-surrender," so that in receiving ("receptivity" or "reciprocity"), gives rise to divine "fruitfulness" (giving birth to children of God). Thus, within the theo-drama, God seeks a marriage relationship, in which the bride (mankind) expropriates herself (allows herself to be taken up), thus giving birth to children of God.

Von Balthasar notes the man-woman polarity running through the events of creation and redemption.[14] To confirm this insight, von Balthasar identifies a feminine principle operative throughout the history of salvation that can be traced from the very first pages of Genesis onward. The more humanity (as spouse of God) hears and responds to God's call, the more it takes on this feminine countenance, personified by Israel, Mary, and the Church. Noting that the apocalyptic visionary (John) saw Woman-Sion-Mary-Church-Holy City as a unity, von Balthasar writes of a corporate individual personality-Synagogue-Mary-Church, with which he wants to convey the whole continuum of the feminine principle in the history of salvation. His thoughts on the feminine principle are clearly influenced by various writers (Dante, Scheeben, Bouyer, de Chardin, Russian sophiology).[15]

---

[13] Hans Urs von Balthasar is aware of the limitations of this analogy: such as the fact that Adam is never to be identified with God; God needs no partner; the male's function in procreation is marginal and incidental in comparison to God's action.

[14] Ibid., 52-54.

[15] Ibid., 54-60.

In sum, there is an infinitely rich spousal dynamic existing within the Trinity between the Father and the Son that is fruitful of the Holy Spirit and then of creation, that is now transplanted within creation, with Mary, our Mother and model, mirroring the Son's key feminine (spousal) mediating role, with its expropriation, receptivity, and fruitfulness.

2. The Trinitarian Dynamic of Expropriation in Mary— Immolation

Expropriation for a Theodramatic Framework in Human Life

Now we apply the Son's role and fruitfulness to Mary. The Marian principle finds its value in that Mary reflects perfectly her Son— *by expropriating herself.* The man-woman polarity in marriage's unconditional self-gift by the two spouses is a symbol of the totality of a divine self-gift in expropriation. Mary is the explanation or paradigm of our encounter with the mystery of God disclosed in Jesus Christ. This requires elaboration. In her encounter with God, she does not eliminate her own history, but fulfills and surpasses her dreams, precisely by *delivering herself totally over to God* (expropriating herself, as Jesus did). She lives outside herself, not making any plans.

The depth of this abandonment can be illuminated by a profound experience given to von Balthasar himself at the age of 18. So momentous was that event that he felt as if he had been struck by lightning. He himself had gone through a period of growing emptiness, when he found that the modern "masculine" attitude placed the artist ahead of his work. In that decisive moment of conversion during a thirty-day retreat in the Black Forest, he mystically felt called to simply wait and let himself be taken up by God instead of making his own plans. He described experiencing this "expropriation" of himself as a participation of Christ's death and Resurrection, in which God shatters us and also heals us in doing so. Von Balthasar finds this expropriation at the heart of Jesus, expressing His total abandonment to the Father in a similar vein: "he [Jesus] renounces sovereignty over his own existence…. That existence is to become a monument to the Father in the world. His life must speak of the Father and not of himself."[16] Herein lies the key to von Balthasar's thought. Christ's disciple must also learn this total self-surrender,

---

16 Hans Urs von Balthasar, *Theology of History*, 51.

making no plans, but allowing God to use him as He wills (the new Christ may find Jean-Pierre de Caussade's *Abandonment to Divine Providence* most helpful here). To be in God has the characteristics of a new event: in Jesus Christ we are projected, as the Son that He is, toward the Father whose word is always love.[17]

Culmination of Expropriation: Mary is Forsaken with the Forsaken One

Von Balthasar's mystical insight of total abandonment, not making any plans and allowing God to take him into service, finds its apex among humanity lived in Mary. Mary, mirroring the Son's self-surrender to the Father, had to be initiated into this entirely new way or path, that was Jesus Himself, and above all, its apex at the cross. Jesus' few rebuffs of Mary serve a purpose, to teach the disciples what they have to transcend (being human) in order to enter into the novelty of the family that the Son came to establish. It is not physical descent but doing the will of the Father that is the entrance ticket into this new family. *Mary's first "yes" at the Annunciation is so pure, unlimited, and definitive* that it includes all the destiny of the Son, which includes the cross. The sword never ceases to pierce her.

There is a second "yes" required at the cross, a second overshadowing that is the most fruitful one. The Passion of Jesus is the most decisive deed, in which an eternal dialogue of love is opened. Mary is set into this event, *disappearing into the crowd and the last place.* Christ's highest point of abandonment embraces all the humanity's nostalgia for God, all our questions searching for an answer. Her "yes" is significant in the drama, echoing His forsakenness. She both facilitates and embodies the goal of redemption. She is the sign of redeemed humanity, yet appears as the most distant from Him in her purity and in His forsakenness. Mary experiences abandonment in her consent to the total abandonment of and by her Son. In this anguish of her Son's God-forsakenness, she sees the whole truth about the fallen world. *There is a mutual forsakenness; Mary's is a non-bloody martyrdom.* Calvary is the apex of her self-surrender in love. From Good Friday to Easter Sunday, Mary is deprived of the center of her soul— her Son.[18]

---

[17] Brendan Leahy, *The Marian principle*, 40-49.
[18] Ibid., 88-92.

3. Mary's Receiving and Pouring out Summum of Love— Fruitfulness

Holy Spirit so Fills Mary that He is "Quasi-Incarnate" in her

Mary's spousal "yes" is analogous to Jesus' obedience to the Father and allows the Holy Spirit to be "touched" by the Incarnation. St. Maximilian Kolbe phrases this point more concretely as Mary becoming totally open so that the Holy Spirit becomes "quasi-incarnate" in Mary.[19] The Annunciation begins a uniquely new journey in history, with Christ coming from the bosom of the eternal Father to the womb of the temporal mother. Her "yes" of communion echoes Jesus' obedience to the Father. It is a yes of maximum activity, an all-embracing vow within which occurs the miracle of motherhood.

It would be difficult to exaggerate the centrality of the Annunciation theme in von Balthasar's overall framework. In overshadowing Mary, the Father's great love has entered the world and Mary has become a living tabernacle. There are two major points of the scene of the Annunciation. (1) It is the first explicit revelation of God's Triune life (the angel announced both the Incarnation as well as the entire mystery of the Trinity). There is also a Trinitarian inversion of the inner-divine relationship between the Holy Spirit and the Son, who now empties Himself and allows the Spirit to take the lead. (2) It tells us about Mary's link with the Holy Spirit (e.g., as the vessel of the Holy Spirit). At the Annunciation, the Holy Spirit Himself is touched in a way analogous to the Incarnation of the Son and gains a particular contact with humanity, now exploring the furthest depths of human liberty (Holy Spirit as "quasi-incarnate" in the world in Mary).[20]

Mary is the Bride who Fulfills the Love Contract with God in the Name of Humanity

So great and pivotal was Mary's "yes" (as Mother and Bride of God) that it was given in the name of humanity in advance, reversing Eve's disobedience. Mary's location in the mystery means that the unique design God has for

---

[19] Ibid., 80-83. Von Balthasar does not accept Mary as having made a private vow of virginity, for he sees her as simply seeking God's unique will for her. Her childlike abandonment can in some way be seen as an inner virginity. She does not reflect upon herself but rests in her Lord (Lk 1:48) and gives herself over to Him.
[20] Ibid., 81-82.

Mary originates within the Trinitarian dialogue of love that decided upon creation and redemption. That is, God included Mary's "yes" as an indispensable part of His plan to unite all things under Christ. She was "chosen before the foundation of the world" both as the Saviour's mother and also to correspond to the Son and *be presented by Him to Himself as that "bride" who would conclude in advance for all, and in all, the love contract between God and the world.* Thus, von Balthasar, having followed both exegetical studies and the Tradition since the Early Church Fathers, traces the woman in Genesis 3:15 to Mary. God did not condemn man to despair in banishing him from paradise. She is the promised one who would turn Eve's curse into a blessing.[21]

Revolution of Love is Poured into the World through Mary, Creating a Family

Mary's "yes" (especially at the Incarnation and the cross) launches her into a journey that is communitarian (joined to both the Trinity and mankind). In abandoning herself totally, being totally guided by the "two hands" of God (the Son and Holy Spirit), the relationship of love between the divine Persons is seen constantly in her. At the same time, the movement of God at the Annunciation is directed toward everyone, a movement of enfleshment (incarnating) of the Word in our world and history, and drawing both into the unity of God.

Mary was aware of the dimensions of what had happened, of a "revolution of love," implied in her Magnificat. Love has poured itself down upon the earth, and it is Mary's lowliness that lies at the heart of this divine revolution beginning among us: *the summum of love is poured into her, so as to flow from her into the world.* It is a revolution of great social and historical implications. Mary is drawn into the inward communion of destiny with all generations. Mary is liberation theology in person (Mary bringing all grace is liberation, anticipating ultimate salvation/liberation).[22]

Jesus is generating a new family at the cross, and the motherhood of Mary is transferred to a new "son"— first to the Twelve, and ultimately, to all of us. In the novelty of this new relationship, we see Christ in one another. The

---

[21] Ibid., 71-75.
[22] Ibid., 83-85.

world now takes the place of Jesus in this relationship to Mary, and God is to be found in our brothers and sisters.

Mary Prefigured in the Old Testament

Since Jesus as key to salvation history was prefigured in the Old Testament, given Mary's central role, as the "helper" of the second Adam, she likewise is already prefigured in the Old Testament. In this plan prepared in eternity, history was prepared for Jesus in Mary, who would welcome and nurture him from within the world (i.e., not only through the Father's nurturing from above). In God the Father's plan, the welcoming history is summarized in Mary: the Old Testament in Gen 3 not only prefigured the "child" but also the "woman" (Mary). Von Balthasar makes additional Old Testament links. Following René Laurentin's exegetical analysis of Luke's Infancy Narratives with their mosaic of Old Testament references, von Balthasar applies to Mary the "Daughter of Sion" motif (Zeph 3:14), the holy remnant (Israel from exile) expecting God's promises of salvation. Pope Gregory I regarded Mary as the personification of the Synagogue, the people who have come together in expectation of the Messiah. Von Balthasar stretched this theme of expectancy and, together with the early Church writers and Rupert of Deutz, views Mary as the prophetess of the Old Testament (e.g., like Anna). Thus, like Jesus, Mary too is prefigured throughout the Old Testament (e.g., Luke's vision of the ark of the covenant fulfilled in Mary). The Holy Spirit has prepared the terrain in history in Mary, and *"it is in Mary that all roads meet."* She is the ultimate woman and spouse of God.[23]

II. Mary and the Church (Adrienne Von Speyr)

A. The Church in Mary: Mould of Christ

Rare is it to find such profound insights into the immense role of Mary as in Adrienne von Speyr, whose writings are reminiscent of those of the Church Fathers. Her mystical depths fittingly complement the systematic theology of her collaborator, Hans Urs von Balthasar. Her article, "Mary in the Church," can serve as an introduction to the vast dimensions of Mary's role in the

---

[23] Ibid., 78-80

Church, especially in regard to the holy Mass.[24] Von Speyr pulls aside the veil to reveal lofty mysteries that will likely be revolutionary to many.

The basic background of her vision is that, because Mary has so opened herself to Christ and accompanied Him, both exteriorly and interiorly, Christ has chosen to include her in all His mysteries of His plan, not only earthly, but also in grace and redemption, such that mankind will live through both Christ's and Mary's mysteries. We see an analogous, though more limited, incorporation by Christ of His apostles: because they had shared in His trials, He has made them the perpetual foundation of the Church and judges of mankind.

Mary's Expropriation: The Church is Called to Live through Mary's Obedience

As noted in von Balthasar, von Speyr sets Mary within the Trinitarian relationships, and especially with the Son, which Trinitarian background constitutes the deepest reality of life (a Trinitarian dynamic that each Christian must also enter). She points out that, while it is Christ who forms the inner spirit or disposition of the Church, He employs Mary as the source of the disposition of "feeling with the Church" (commonly called *sentire cum Ecclesia*): "For Mary 'feeling with the Church' means letting the Son form her so completely into the Church that she desires to be nothing more than the idea, the prototype of this Church— a prototype which the Son made from her." Von Speyr is presenting the core insight that Mary as opening herself completely to allow Christ to configure her such that she becomes the very form of the Church. To understand how she has become the form of the Church, we have to understand first her total "expropriation" (total emptying) of herself, so that the subjective personal and private feelings have become objectified, so to speak, in the Church.

More concretely, this expropriation involves a total giving up of one's own plans and leaving oneself totally available to God (recall von Balthasar's experience at age of 18). It is saying a "yes" of total surrender in advance. In emptying herself, she makes room for God, and in her the action is all God. Christ Himself asks her to express the essence of the Church in herself, by

---

[24] Adrienne von Speyr, "Mary in the Church," *Communio* 20 (1993): 451-456.

remaining "who you are, but be so for everyone," which is the objective idea (plan) the Father had for the Church eternally. Just as Saul attained the highest freedom in being taken into service, so too Mary is led to the "highest obedience from a limited to the highest possible freedom…. it is to be ready for everything."[25] Blessed Dina Bélanger explained that her fallen ego had to be mystically annihilated by Christ so that He could act in her.

What should surprise us is that Mary's relationship to Christ already circumscribes all human relationship to Him. It is specifically Mary's total receptivity, mirroring that of Jesus to the Father, that is the core of all Christian life. The passivity (receptivity) of her readiness is already active in its core. *All in the Church are called to live from the Mother's obedience, for the Church's obedience and the Mother's obedience are inseparable.* This concretely signifies that in the infinity of the mutual relations between Son and Mother, "there are contained in advance all situations which the Church and the man of the Church can encounter…. The relationship of the Mother to the Son is the standard by which man can measure himself and his spirit."[26] In her quality as expecting Bride, she unites all those who wait on the Son. The Lord uses her, not only as the starting point and model, but also so that *she moves toward Him with the Church.*

What we are seeing Adrienne von Speyr do is setting up an entirely new complementary structure: not only does the disciple go to the Father in the Son, *he also goes to the Father in Mary as well.* And this is in part because the Church is Marian and lives from "the Mother's obedience." The Church thus has a second foundation in Mary (within the first foundation that is Christ).

B. Mary is the Idea of and Perpetually Generates the Church

And what should astound us further is the next insight, which develops more fully the outline of Mary's role in von Speyr's *Handmaid of the Lord.* She first provides the helpful background as to how this immense role developed. Mary was not simply assigned her role as mother of the Church in a legal fashion (e.g., which Pope Paul VI explicitly proclaimed at Vatican II).

---

[25] Ibid., 451-452.
[26] Ibid., 452.

For Adrienne von Speyr, Mary's overarching role was developed by a methodical preparation by the Lord in three existential life-stages: the first overshadowing of the Holy Spirit that brought about the Incarnation of the Son; the preparation by the Incarnate Son to incorporate Mary into His larger mission (expanding her); and the second overshadowing at Pentecost by which Mary generates the Mystical Body as she had given birth to Christ, its Head, both forming one birth:

> When the Holy Spirit overshadowed her the first time, he made the incarnate Son come into being as a concrete individual human being in the womb of her body. The Spirit in her created the physical Son. Then came a second period; the Son within her recreated her in the Spirit, from being physical mother to becoming Bride and Church as well. It [her life with Christ] was a period of expansion, of transformation of the earthly into the Christian, the catholic, the universal. And so the third period matures: the Son, having returned to the Father, *sends the Holy Spirit down upon her again [at Pentecost] so that the whole concreteness of the Church's body may come into being now in this second overshadowing....* Only through the actual descent of the Spirit does her potential ecclesial fruitfulness become actual.[27] (emphasis added)

Mary Perpetually Generates the Church as "the Norm, the Idea, the Prototype"

The next insight has profound and unexpected implications: at Pentecost, Mary is given the fruitfulness to *perpetually generate the Church*. Thus the body of Christ is born from Mary twice: "as head and as members" (first, Christ's physical body; then Christ's Mystical Body). As a result, Mary has become "the norm, the idea, the prototype of the Church." In Mary, the Church finds her origin, identity, and her goal:

> On account of this the Mother now becomes the norm, the idea, the prototype of the Church. In her alone the Church is exactly as it should be: the Bride without blemish or wrinkle. From her it receives the capacity to correspond in all things to the Bridegroom.... Thus, in and from the Mother the body of Christ is born twice— as head and as members. But it is one single body and therefore one single birth.[28]

---

[27] Adrienne von Speyr, *Handmaid of the Lord*, 140.
[28] Ibid., 140-141.

Thus, having participated in Christ's trajectory and Christ's mission during her earthly life by His very will and plan, Mary now participates in giving birth to the Church. To become the Church, we have to become Marian: Mary not only generates the Church in Christ, she is also the idea and form of the Church— this is a profound revelation. To become the Church or to be conformed to Christ, one has to live all three levels of devotion to Mary (prayer to Mary, imitation of Mary, and living Mary), to arrive at the third level of living Mary.

C. The Church Lives from the Mysteries of Mary

But that is not all. Not only does Mary perpetually generate the Church in Christ, not only is she the idea and prototype of the Church, the Church also lives from the mysteries of Mary, especially from the relationships between the Mother and the Son. So complete is her "yes" and so rich are their relations that they circumscribe all our relations with God:

> Thus when the Church suffers on earth and goes through persecutions and hard times, it takes part in the mysteries of the Mother, who went through them in her earthly life. It is the Mother herself who initiates the Church into her mysteries…. And in the Mother's life with her Son, in the infinity of their mutual relationships, there are contained in advance all situations which the Church and the man of the Church can encounter…. Our obedience to the Church, at its most positive, lives from the Mother's obedience to the Lord; for that is ecclesial obedience, and the Church, when she obeys, is not separable from Mary's obedience, insofar as she herself is the Bride of Christ.[29]

Adrienne von Speyr makes a startling conclusion: Mary has been "given the right of co-redemption" as a gift (not surprising, given the revelation just unveiled), by initiating the Church into the mysteries of suffering, that is, the mysteries of redemption:

> Into this, his work of the Cross, the Son initiates his Mother…. In Mary, this *second, spiritual motherhood* becomes perfect actuality. But Mary's fruitfulness, although she is unique and especially chosen, opens a new way for everyone. As Mary is included in the work of salvation, *so she includes all*

---

[29] Ibid., 150.

and lets an eternal cycle of love between herself and her divine Son become living for everyone.... From the Son she receives the right of co-redemption, but, because this is a gift of the Son, it does not exhaust itself in her but goes beyond her and is given further by her.... The pregnancy is imposed upon her but even here she is co-operating, so that the first fruit of her co-operation is the Son himself; and the second is the Son's work, the redemption. In this way also she becomes the *co-redeemer*.[30] (emphasis added)

To sum up, in God's plan, the Church would live from rich relationships between Jesus and the Mother: "... she includes all and lets an eternal cycle of love between herself and her divine Son become living for everyone." As the Mother is involved with the first step of the Incarnation, the Son introduces her to its purpose (the cross), and accomplishes a second birth (the Church), and as the second Eve, she collaborates with the second Adam.

Mary's Unlimited Power is Established after her Assumption

While Mary was prepared by Christ during His lifetime and while power was already given her at Pentecost, Mary's present unlimited power was fully established only after her Assumption. Adrienne von Speyr makes a parallel: as Mary received the Son of God at the Incarnation, so He receives her at her Assumption; as she gave her assent, now the Son gives His assent; where her reception is finite as that of a creature, His reception of her is limitless. Now her power becomes *unlimited because it is united to Christ's unlimited power.*

This assent is divine and immeasurable and gives the Mother's assent its whole heavenly limitlessness. As long as the Mother was in the world, she was as limited as any human being... From the moment of the Assumption on, she receives the power to be able to do what the Son wills, without limits. She knows no more boundaries except those that we on earth set against her work. Only our No can hold back her eternal Yes.[31]

As Christ's Resurrection was already the conclusion of his earthly mission and preparation to ascend to His Father, so her Assumption has become her Easter. Those days between Easter and His Ascension were already a beginning to her earthly mission. As the Son who surveyed the fruits of the

---

[30] Ibid., 38.
[31] Ibid., 146.

mystery of His Easter, so to the Mother is now revealed how much she formed part of the work of redemption, and how much of it stems from her.[32] Like Jesus explaining to the two disciples on the way to Emmaus how all of Scripture spoke of Him, so the Mother now sees how the whole plan worked, and what significant part she played:

> And now she sees everything that she has believed until now: she beholds the divinity of her Son, which she certainly always worshipped, but only as the veiled mystery existing in him and before her. She looks into the abyss that is the Father and sees the Holy Spirit, who once overshadowed her and has been with her ever since. She perceives the coherence of the whole salvation history, the fulfillment of the prophecies, and she sees her own place within it. *She understands how necessary she was in this saving event and how much God counted on her.* She sees the first promises when man was driven out of Paradise and sees that all generations had waited for her assent in order to find their path to paradise again.
>
> But she also sees that God did not have to worry for a moment whether she would speak this assent, *since he had hidden her in himself from all eternity— to such an extent that her whole freedom could consist of nothing other than assent to the service of her God. So completely did he destine her from all eternity to be queen that her only course was to be his handmaid eternally.*[33] (emphasis added)

God's confidence derives from the fact that "he had hidden her in himself from all eternity— to such an extent that her whole freedom could consist of nothing other than assent to the service of her God," fulfilling God's plan to be Mother and Queen.

D. Living the Mass in Mary

To see how deeply Mary's role is intertwined with the entire Christian life of her children, her role in the Mass is an astonishing revelation of how we do everything in her. In establishing the Mother as bringing the Church toward Jesus, Mary also receives a share in the Church's service of God, above all, in the Mass.[34] As Vatican II's *Sacrosanctum concilium* has noted, the liturgy, and,

---

[32] Ibid., 146-147.
[33] Ibid., 147-148.
[34] Adrienne von Speyr, "Mary in the Church," *Communio* 20 (1993): 452-453.

above all the Eucharist, is the source and summit of Christian life (SC 10, 41), dedicating an entire chapter to the Eucharist (Ch. II).[35]

But Mary is not just present in the way the heavenly hosts are present at the liturgy, nor is she just an intercessor there. For the liturgy is a renewal of the drama of the mysteries of Christ's earthly life, and Mary was very much part of that drama.

Thus, Mary is an active protagonist in the drama of the liturgy, which itself is the primary instrument in evangelization. Now we can proceed to Adrienne von Speyr's further insight. Von Speyr divides the work of Mary at the Holy Mass in our participation of her work in the four parts of the Mass: Beginning (as her pregnancy, gathering all towards communion with the Lord); Offertory (her total assent); Consecration (assists in giving Christ to the world); and Communion (we participate in her perfect receptivity). Now we begin to see the depths of how the Church lives in Mary.

(i) The Beginning of the Mass is the time of *pregnancy*, of expectation, as the Old Testament waited for Christ's coming: "In the end it is she who gathers everything that has gone before and focuses it on the Lord; it is she who gives the Church the spirit and the capacity to guide every prayer and proclamation toward unity in the Lord, which is coming at the consecration."[36]

(ii) At the Offertory, everything is offered to the Lord, *but within Mary's lowly but total assent*: "And when the Church… presents the bread and the wine, she is already offering the Son to the Father, in hidden fashion. And as the Mother becomes handmaid through her assent, the priest and the whole community become servants of the Lord through the Offertory."[37]

(iii) The Consecration corresponds to the descent of the Son into the womb of Mary and Mary immediately gives Him to the world. At the Mass, it is the Lord who descends into His Church to give Himself to the world. It is the Holy Spirit who is the agent of the entire work and works to the degree of

---

[35] The Lineamenta of the 2004 XI Ordinary General Assembly of the Synod of Bishops was entitled: "The Eucharist: Source and Summit of the Life and Mission of the Church."
[36] Adrienne von Speyr, "Mary in the Church," 453.
[37] Ibid.

the readiness in faith of the Church. Mary, as the Lord's bride and helpmate, is the "*assistant*" at the liturgy

> ... which she performs at the consecration as she did at the time of the miracles. She had been expressly present at the miracle in Cana and herself cooperated in it because she occasioned it. And so she must necessarily be present at the sacramental transformation, of which that miracle was the foreshadowing. But her action here is wholly merged with Christ's.[38]

> Her surrender at the Incarnation becomes a *lasting fruitfulness*. The Lord's human nature originates anew in her. Her surrender is contained within His surrender at the Consecration, and "*it is she who teaches the Church to surrender herself to the Lord according to his example.*"[39] (emphasis added)

(iv) Mary is the perfect receiver (holy Communion), and everyone participates in her receiving. Where many are anxious or troubled by their lack of worthiness or preparation,

> [T]hrough a grace of the Mother this reception is robbed of every difficulty: it may now take place in joy, trust and an almost soaring lightheartedness. *She surrounds the communicant and unites her reception of the Son with his*, by collecting and preserving for him the graces that he lets fall out of impotence of heedlessness, and she puts them at his disposal as a reserve at the precise time when he needs them.[40] (emphasis added)

She simplifies the entire reception, and the communicant enters into her "yes," no longer concerned about his preparation and worthiness: "Just as the Son brings the sinner to the Father in Confession, by filling out his deficiencies and reforming him into a child of God, the Mother supplements the Christian at Communion for the reception of the Son."[41] Thus Mary's is a hidden but indispensable presence at Holy Mass and at every ecclesial prayer:

> The Mother's presence in every ecclesial prayer, celebration and action becomes understandable. She is as if made visible within the whole space

---

[38] Ibid., 454.
[39] Ibid.
[40] Ibid., 454-455.
[41] Ibid., 455.

of the Church... it is she who sums up the meaning of the multiplicity of pictures, altars, chapels, decorations and the many devotions in their unity that converges on the Lord. She gathers the faithful into both interior and exterior recollection on the Son by forming the bridge from the multiplicity... to the unity of her divine head."[42]

When the encounter with the Lord is overwhelming, Mary receives them and teaches them the power of a simple act of thanksgiving. As it is not abstract, the space at Mass and in the church is all Marian, for she

> sees to it that the visible and spiritual space of the church form a liveable dwelling, a lovable homeland for the faithful... one tended by a Mother in which provision is made for all the longings and necessities of man; for his needs for spiritual peace and clarification, for teaching, for nourishment and for recreation.[43]

Thus Mary and the Church are not separable: "The spirit and reality of Mary lives in the Church, and the less apparently she does her work, the more omnipresent she is."[44] It is known that she overcomes all heresies, as she always maintains the right relationship of distance and nearness, but also because she subordinates herself to Peter and John as willed by Christ: "While the Lord, in masculine form, reveals and interprets the Father to us, the Mother's feminine nature reveals to us many qualities of grace and of the heavenly and divine world."[45]

Adrienne von Speyr presents us with a profound vision of Mary's overarching role within Christ's work in leading us to the Father within the Church.

Synthesis

Brendan Leahy points to a key insight for Mary's role in the new evangelization: "von Balthasar linked a proper understanding of Mary with the Church's new evangelization."[46] Brendan Leahy's doctoral thesis

---

[42] Ibid.
[43] Ibid., 455-456.
[44] Ibid., 456.
[45] Ibid.
[46] Ibid., 19.

describes von Balthasar viewing a renewal in the Church taking place from within— through Mary:

> Already before the Second Vatican Council... von Balthasar contended that a renewed Mariology was preparing the way for a future theology of the Church. He felt that new bases were being provided for a modern ecclesial consciousness, and this especially for the laity. In short, he wrote of a new *sentire Ecclesiae* which was emerging, and it was Marian. And so he could write that Mary as model, ideal, an essence of the Church is assuming a particular importance in today's ecclesial era.[47]

Mary was more than a model or type of the Church; she is a principle: the form of the Church and the womb from which the Church lives. This is captured somewhat generally in the cover image of von Balthasar's doctoral thesis, that depicts a figure of Mary, with a mantle open over her outstretched arms in which all humanity is embraced. Mary in the Eucharist is still the only one capable of receiving Jesus today:

> In the poverty of her "expropriated" womb, Mary stands behind everyone, and with all the poor and sinful, and within them, as the only one capable of receiving in her womb the seed of God which is thousands of times eucharistically multiplied... Mary represents a true matrix of the Church to be generated.[48]

For von Balthasar, there is an "inseparability of Trinity, Christology, and ecclesiology" (Mary as form and generator of the Church, flowing from Christ and the Trinity), from which emerge three key elements in his theodramatic framework centered on Mary: "mystery-communion-mission."[49] These are the three points of reference in the "Theo-drama," the drama of love between God and each person, that mirrors the love between the Father and Son in heaven and on earth.

---

[47] Brendan Leahy, *The Marian principle in the Church in the Ecclesiology of Hans Urs von Balthasar*, 16-17.
[48] Ibid., 174.
[49] Ibid., 26.

The Fallout from Isolating Mariology

Given Mary's central role in theology, the Church, the liturgy, and evangelization, we can readily understand the crisis caused by the decline of Mariology before and after Vatican II (the publication of Pope Paul's *Marialis Cultus* changed this). Von Balthasar points out that there has been a theological isolation to the sidelines of Mariology, which should be restored to the Tradition, for Mariology is an indispensable part of the objective Christian doctrine of salvation, as we can see from Irenaeus via Augustine to Anselm and Bernard.

We have just had a glimpse of her vital role through Adrienne von Speyr and Hans Urs von Balthasar. But we can already see the important role of Mariology to Christian Tradition and life by looking at the four Marian dogmas: Theotokos (Mother of God) as the rightful setting for Christology in the early Church; her Immaculate Conception as a statement whose setting is the doctrine of grace and redemption; her ever-virginity as requisite for becoming Mother of God, a reflection of the theology of the Covenant and consequently for the doctrine of the people of God; and her Assumption as part of the universal doctrine of the Last Things.[50]

Von Balthasar warns that isolating Mariology will lead to the isolation of holding to Jesus merely as concrete proof of the love of the Father (e.g., Jesus as brother, Eucharist as food, etc., bringing everything down to a merely human level), and not rooted in the doctrine of the Trinity.[51]

In sum, what a vast chasm we discern between the customary vision of Mary as merely an optional devotion and the vision presented by Adrienne von Speyr and Hans Urs von Balthasar. Now we understand more fully why Adrienne von Speyr teaches that Mary is the archetype of the Church, generates the Church, and that the Church lives in Mary and her mysteries. Von Balthasar provides, in particular, the background: a vast plan of God in which Mary would mirror the Son and be that second intrinsic foundation (a foundation within Christ, the ultimate Foundation). What depths she has lived: living the intimacy with the Trinity even on earth; reliving the Son's

---

[50] Hans Urs von Balthasar, "The Marian principle in the Church," *Elucidations*, 101-113.
[51] Ibid.

expropriation; living the spousal relationship with the Holy Spirit, such that He has become "quasi-incarnate" in her; making the love contract-covenant with God in the name of humanity; receiving the "summum of love," which the world was unable to receive, and allowing it to be poured into the world; generating each baptized, who lives from her mysteries; her self-surrender pointing to the core of Christian holiness; and being "forsaken with the Forsaken One." Mirroring the Son, the key is the totality of self-gift or expropriation of a *Bride* who thereby becomes a *Mother*. It is this woman who is the "morning star of the new evangelization." We have not yet plumbed the depths of Mary's role.

CONCLUSION

Final Note: Going Forward in the New Evangelization

It is fitting that, as the "trilogy" of three manuscripts by this author began with the Trinity as love, the conclusion of this third book ends with trinitarian love. We do this by giving a trinitarian context to the new evangelization from an insight of the papal nuncio to Canada, Archbishop Luigi Bonazzi. Speaking to seminarians during a weekend retreat,[1] he unfolded the significance of the mystery of the Trinity for us by asking, "What is my house (home)?" He began with the Christian foundation, that the central mystery of our faith is the one and triune God, whose essence is love. He noted that it is because God is not a monad but a Trinity that He can create outside Himself. The essence of his meditation was that each Person of the Trinity (not only the Son) lives kenotically, giving Himself totally to the others. Thus the Father gives Himself to the Son in a total expropriation without holding anything back, the Son receives and in turn gives Himself totally, and the fruit of this self-giving is the Holy Spirit, who is love-communion.

Thus the essence of the Trinity is this total self-giving that is love; only love exists— reality is love. This means that the primary goal of Christian life is not to love God but to allow God to love us— to first receive His love. In receiving His love, in experiencing His love, we are now able to give love. Archbishop Bonazzi then answered his original question: he desires to live in the house of "being," for being is love, which entails the gift of myself with expropriation, with a renunciation of myself. To give a concrete example, to a wife who complained of the difficulties she had with the weaknesses of her husband, Archbishop Bonazzi suggested that she try to love him, for only love brings life and at the end only love will change her husband. Thus the new evangelization is ultimately about first receiving the love of the three Persons and then, in response, seeking to share the treasure of this trinitarian love with others. The new disciple of Christ must be a person of communion.

---

[1] Archbishop Luigi Bonazzi, weekend retreat at St. Augustine's Seminary, Toronto, February 29, 2020.

The lay person, priest, or consecrated soul, as new Christs through Baptism, are all called to engage in the new evangelization, to share in the trinitarian love. They should know the same consolation that the apostles and first disciples of Christ experienced. For these latter understood that they were sent by Christ ("Go out into the whole world") and in the power of the Holy Spirit, notwithstanding the universal opposition and persecution they encountered: by the Jewish authorities, by the Roman Emperors, and by practically every new civilization they approached: "The blood of martyrs become the seed of faith." The Acts of the Apostles reveals how the Holy Spirit, like a general, spurred Christ's disciples outwards.

As mentioned by one historian, without wealth, education, and influence, the first disciples of Jesus fanned out in mission or from fleeing persecution, and brought the faith to whole world. They were able to do this because Christ not only sent them, He was one with them, as Saul (apostle Paul) would come to discover: "'Saul, Saul, why do you persecute me?'... 'I am Jesus, whom you are persecuting'" (Acts 9:4-5). Christ has become one with His Mystical Body, the Church. But to accomplish this, He "gave up His spirit," meaning, He released to the Church the Holy Spirit, the Love between the Father and the Son, the Gift that brings all other gift.

In the inspired vision of Pope John Paul II, the Lord wills a new evangelization, advent, and Pentecost for the third millennium, mirroring that of the first evangelization at the beginning of the Church. For this, God has provided the Second Vatican Council and is sending anew the Holy Spirit. We look at this eschatologically. The new Christs are not alone, because they are held by the two hands of the Father— the Son and the Holy Spirit; that is, they are held in the embrace of the holy Trinity. In this battle, they are led by the Queen of heaven, St. Michael and the hosts of angels, and the entire heavenly court.

Only at the eschaton will we understand the massive scale of God's plan and the battle involved. The opposition is overwhelming, but Christ says to us as He did to the first disciples, "In the world you face persecution. But take courage; I have conquered the world!" (Jn 16:33, NRSV). We do not look at the enemy, but keep our eyes on Christ, who on the cross has vanquished Satan and "conquered the world."

A Note of Consolation

Nevertheless, for those engaging in the difficult work of the new evangelization, there can be discouragement with the manifold difficulties faced but also from the experience of personal weakness. Pope St. John XXIII captured something of the task and crisis we face (quoted earlier):

> Today the Church is witnessing a crisis underway within society. While humanity is at the threshold of a new age, immensely serious and broad tasks await the Church, as in the most tragic periods of her history. It is a question in fact of bringing the perennial life-giving energies of the Gospel to the modern world, a world that boasts of its technical and scientific conquests but also bears the effects of a temporal order that some have wanted to reorganize by excluding God. This is why modern society is characterized by great material progress but without a corresponding advance in the moral sphere. Thence a weakening in aspirations towards the values of the spirit; thence the tendency to seek only the earthly pleasures that technological progress brings so easily within the reach of all; thence also a quite new and disturbing fact: the existence of a militant atheism operating all over the world. (*Humanae salutis*, n. 2)

In light of this crisis, let us point to three texts that may console the new apostle in the new evangelization. First, as is manifest in the Acts of the Apostles, it is the Holy Spirit who is the Protagonist of the new evangelization. St. Thérèse understood that, to the degree we are united to Him, to that degree the Holy Spirit will touch those whom we meet so that they will be drawn to the Beloved, Christ:

> Ah! Divine Jesus, you know I love you. The Spirit of Love sets me aflame with his fire. In loving you I attract the Father.

> My weak heart holds him forever. I ask Jesus to draw me into the flames of His love, to unite me so closely to Him that He live and act in me. I feel that the more the fire of love burns within my heart, the more I shall say: "Draw me," the more also the souls who will approach me (poor little piece of iron, useless if I withdraw from the divine furnace), the more these souls will run swiftly in the odor of the ointments of their Beloved, for a soul that is burning with love cannot remain inactive.[2]

---

[2] St. Thérèse of Lisieux, *Manuscript*, C 36r.

The new Christ who is led by the Holy Spirit finds Him in each present moment. Like Cardinal van Thuan, he decides, "I am not going to wait. I will live each present moment, filling it to the brim with love":

> Once Mother Teresa of Calcutta wrote me: "What is important is not how many actions we perform, but the intensity of love that we put into each action."

> How does one achieve this intensity of love in the present moment? I simply think that I must live each day, each minute as the last one of my life. To leave aside everything accidental, to concentrate only on the essential. Each word, each gesture, each telephone call, each decision is the most beautiful of my life; I keep my love for everyone, my smile; I am afraid of wasting even one second by living it without meaning...[3]

The second text has to do with the cross and evangelization. Jean-Pierre de Caussade points out how when the Holy Spirit takes over in a soul, it feels as if God is destroying the soul but these trials in fact bring troves of grace through them to the world and through which Christ finds His victory in each new Calvary. The Holy Spirit is writing a beautiful story: "we, if we are holy, are the paper; our sufferings and actions are the ink,"[4] and only in heaven will we see the glory of this sublime story He Himself is writing that is perfect in each abandoned new Christ:

> The soul knows nothing of God's operations, yet it receives from them all the efficacy through countless events which it believes will destroy it. There is nothing we can do about this ignorance. We must just put up with it. But it is within this ignorance that God gives himself and all other things.... He [soul] often thinks it will kill him....

> We should try always to carry ourselves with the air of a child blessed by God's grace and his good will. What on earth have we to fear if we follow him? As his children, led and upheld by him, our whole attitude should be one of fearlessness. The terrors we meet on our journey are really nothing. They are sent only so that our lives may be made more splendid by our overcoming them. God involves us in every kind of trouble, and ordinary

---

[3] F.X. Nguyen van Thuan, *Five Loaves and Two Fish* (The Community of our Lady of Lavang, 2000), 9, 13-14.
[4] Jean-Pierre de Caussade, *Abandonment to Divine Providence*, 45 (see also 46).

human common sense, seeing no way out of it, realizes all its weakness and shortcomings and feels completely baffled. It is at this moment that God appears in all his glory to those who belong to him and disentangles them from all their troubles... Every step we take under his command is a victory. God has his pen and an open book before him, and in this book he writes a blessed story which will end only when the world ends, for it is an account of God's dealings with men and women.[5]

Third, we leave the final word to our Lady, her message of consolation to St. Juan Diego in Mexico. We present again these words, so that each of us, new apostles of the new evangelization, can hear them as if she were addressing them to each of us personally as Mother Teresa heard them:

Mother Teresa allowed our Lady to prepare and arrange all within and around her, and she entrusted her entire future to her care. This is why, though she faced trials and problems of every kind, Mother Teresa never worried. All was left to our Lady, the one who had said so tenderly to Juan Diego:

"Listen and keep in your heart, my littlest one: there is nothing for you to fear, let nothing afflict you. Let not your face or your heart be worried. Do not fear this sickness or any other illness. Let nothing worry or afflict you. Am I not here, I who am your mother? Are you not in my shadow, under my protection? Am I not the fountain of your joy? Are you not in the folds of my mantle, in my crossed arms? Is there anything else you need? Don't let anything afflict you or perturb you."[6]

---

[5] Ibid., 111-112.

[6] Fr. Joseph Langford, *Mother Teresa: In the Shadow of Our Lady* (Huntington, IN: Our Sunday Visitor, 2016), 37. 158

Made in the USA
Columbia, SC
26 September 2021